Kubernetes – An Ent Guide

Second Edition

Effectively containerize applications, integrate enterprise systems, and scale applications in your enterprise

Marc Boorshtein

Scott Surovich

BIRMINGHAM—MUMBAI

Kubernetes – An Enterprise Guide
Second Edition

Producer: Suman Sen
Acquisition Editor – Peer Reviews: Saby Dsilva
Project Editor: Amisha Vathare
Content Development Editor: Alex Patterson
Copy Editor: Safis Editing
Technical Editor: Aniket Shetty
Proofreader: Safis Editing
Indexer: Manju Arasan
Presentation Designer: Ganesh Bhadwalkar

First published: November 2020
Second edition: December 2021

Production reference: 3170522

Published by Packt Publishing Ltd.
Livery Place
35 Livery Street
Birmingham
B3 2PB, UK.

ISBN 978-1-80323-003-0

www.packt.com

Contributors

About the authors

Marc Boorshtein has been a software engineer and consultant for twenty years and is currently the CTO of Tremolo Security, Inc. Marc has spent most of his career building identity management solutions for large enterprises, U.S. Government civilian agencies, and local government public safety systems. Marc has recently focused on applying identity to DevOps and Kubernetes, building open source tools for automating the security of infrastructure. Marc is a CKAD, and can often be found in the Kubernetes Slack channels answering questions about authentication and authorization.

To my wife, for supporting me building Tremolo Security and giving up a full time salary to build to do so. To my sons for keeping me on my toes, my mom for raising me and giving me my persistence, and in memory of my dad who pushed me to be my own boss and start my own company.

Scott Surovich has been in information technology for over 20 years and currently works at a Global Tier 1 bank as the Global Container Engineering lead and is the product owner for hybrid cloud Kubernetes deployments. Throughout his career he has worked on multiple Engineering teams in large enterprises and government agencies. He is an active in the community as a co-lead of the CNCF Financial Services Working Group and contributor to multiple open-source projects.

Scott has authored and reviewed other Kubernetes books, and has written and curated multiple chapters for Google's book, Anthos in Action. He holds the CKA, CKAD, and Mirantis Kubernetes certifications, and he was one of the first people to receive Google's premier certification as a Google Certified Hybrid Multi-Cloud Fellow.

I would like to thank my wife, Kim, for always being supportive and understanding of my technology addiction. To my mother, Adele, and in memory of my father, Gene, for teaching me to never give up, and that I can do anything that I set my mind to. To my brother, Chris, for the friendly competitions that always kept me striving to be better. Finally, a special thank you to my colleagues for not only supporting the book, but my role and the platform offering in the bank.

About the reviewer

Sergei Bulavintsev is a cloud solutions architect at Altoros. He is passionate about open source, cloud-native infrastructure, and tools that increase developers' productivity. He has successfully migrated multiple customers to the cloud and Kubernetes, advocating and implementing the GitOps approach. Sergei is an active member of his local cloud-native community and holds industry certifications such as CKA, CKAD, CKS, and RHCA lvl 2.

I would like to thank my wife, Elena, and our two children, Maria and Maxim, for their support and patience. I also thank my family, friends, and colleagues, who have helped me become who I am today.

Join our book's Discord space

Join the book's Discord workspace for a monthly *Ask me Anything* session with the authors: https://packt.link/K8EntGuide

Table of Contents

Preface

Kubernetes has taken the world by storm, becoming the standard infrastructure for DevOps teams to develop, test, and run applications. Most enterprises are either running it already, or are planning to run it in the next year. A look at job postings on any of the major job sites shows that just about every big-name company has Kubernetes positions open. The fast rate of adoption has lead to Kubernetes-related positions growing by over 2,000% in the last 4 years.

One common problem that companies are struggling to address is the lack of enterprise Kubernetes knowledge. Since the technology is relatively new, and even newer for production workloads, companies have had issues trying to build teams to run clusters reliably. Finding people with basic Kubernetes skills is becoming easier, but finding people with knowledge on topics that are required for enterprise clusters is still a challenge.

Who this book is for

We created this book to help DevOps teams to expand their skills beyond the basics of Kubernetes. It was created from the years of experience we have working with clusters in multiple enterprise environments.

There are many books available that introduce Kubernetes and the basics of installing clusters, creating deployments, and using Kubernetes objects. Our plan was to create a book that would go beyond a basic cluster, and to keep the book a reasonable length, we will not re-hash the basics of Kubernetes. Readers should have some experience with Kubernetes before reading this book.

While the primary focus of the book is to extend clusters with enterprise features, the first section of the book will provide a refresher of key Docker topics, and Kubernetes objects. It is important that you have a solid understanding of Kubernetes objects in order to get the most out of the more advanced chapters.

What this book covers

Chapter 1, Docker and Container Essentials, covers the problems Docker and Kubernetes address for developers. You will be introduced to Docker, including the Docker daemon, data, installation, and using the Docker CLI.

Chapter 2, Deploying Kubernetes Using KinD, covers KinD, a powerful tool that allows you to create a Kubernetes cluster ranging from a single node cluster to a full multi-node cluster. The chapter goes beyond a basic KinD cluster, explaining how to use a load-balancer running HAProxy to load-balance worker nodes. By the end of this chapter, you will understand how KinD works and how to create a custom multi-node cluster, which will be used for the exercises in the chapters.

Chapter 3, Kubernetes Bootcamp, provides a refresher on Kubernetes, and if you are new to Kubernetes, this chapter will cover most of the objects that a cluster includes. It will explain each object with a description of what each object does and its function in a cluster. It is meant to be a refresher, or a "pocket guide" to objects. It does not contain exhaustive details for each object (that would require a second book).

Chapter 4, Services, Load Balancing, ExternalDNS, and Global Balancing, explains how to expose a Kubernetes deployment using services. Each service type will be explained with examples, and you will learn how to expose them using both a layer 7 and layer 4 load balancer. In this chapter, you will go beyond the basics of a simple Ingress controller, installing MetalLB, to provide layer 4 access to services. You will also learn about two add-ons that benefit Enterprise clusters by install an incubator project called external-dns to provide dynamic name resolution for the services exposed by MetalLB and K8GB, which provides native Kubernetes Global Load Balancing.

Chapter 5, Integrating Authentication into Your Cluster, answers the question "once your cluster is built, how will users access it?" In this chapter we'll detail how OpenID Connect works and why you should use it to access your cluster. You'll also learn how to authenticate your pipelines, and finally we'll also cover several anti-patterns that should be avoided and explain why they should be avoided.

Chapter 6, RBAC Policies and Auditing, explains that once users have access to a cluster, you need to know how to limit their access. Whether you are providing an entire cluster to your users or just a namespace, you'll need to know how Kubernetes authorizes access via its **role-based access control (RBAC)** system. In this chapter, we'll detail how to design RBAC policies, how to debug them, and different strategies for multi-tenancy.

Chapter 7, Deploying a Secured Kubernetes Dashboard, covers the Kubernetes Dashboard, which is often the first thing users try to launch once a cluster is up and running. There's quite a bit of mythology around the security (or lack thereof).

Your cluster will be made of other web applications too, such as network dashboards, logging systems, and monitoring dashboards. This chapter looks at how the dashboard is architected, how to properly secure it, and examples of how not to deploy it with details as to why.

Chapter 8, Extending Security Using Open Policy Agent, provides you the guidance you need to deploy the OpenPolicyAgent and GateKeeper to enable policies that can't be implemented using RBAC. We'll cover how to deploy GateKeeper, how to write policies in Rego, and how to test your policies using OPA's built-in testing framework.

Chapter 9, Node Security with GateKeeper, deals with the security of the nodes that run your Pods. We will discuss how to securely design your containers so they are harder to abuse and how build policies using GateKeeper that constrain your containers from accessing resources they don't need.

Chapter 10, Auditing Using Falco, DevOps AI, and ECK, explains that Kubernetes includes event logging for API access, but it doesn't have the ability to capture container runtime events. To address this limitation, we will install a project that was donated to the CNCF by Sysdig called Falco. Using Falco, you will learn how to trigger actions based on events captured by Falco using Kubeless functions, and how to present the data that is captured by Falco using FalcoSideKick to forward events to the FalcoSidekick-UI and the **ECK** stack (**Elastic Cloud on Kubernetes**).

Chapter 11, Backing Up Workloads, explains how to create a backup of your cluster workloads for disaster recovery, or cluster migrations, using Velero. You will go hands-on to create an S3-compatible storage location using MinIO to create a backup of example workloads and restore the backup to a brand new cluster to simulate a cluster migration.

Chapter 12, An Introduction to Istio, explains that many enterprises use a service mesh to provide advanced features such as security, traffic routing, authentication, tracing, and observability to a cluster. This chapter will introduce you to Istio, a popular open-source mesh, and its architecture, along with the most commonly used resources provided it provides. You will deploy Istio to your KinD cluster with an example application and learn how to observe the behavior of an application using an observability tool called Kiali.

Chapter 13, Building and Deploying Applications on Istio, acknowledges that once you've deployed Istio, you'll want to develop and deploy applications that use it! This chapter starts with a walk-through of the differences between monoliths and micro-services and how they're deployed. Next, we'll step through building a micro-service to run in Istio and get into advanced topics like authentication, authorization, and service-to-service authentication for your services. You will also learn how to secure Kiali access by leveraging existing roles in Kubernetes using an OIDC provider and JSON Web Tokens.

Chapter 14, Provisioning a Platform, discusses how to build a platform for automating a multi-tenant cluster with GitLab, Tekton, ArgoCD, GateKeeper, and OpenUnison. We'll explore how to build pipelines and how to automate their creation. We'll explore how the objects that are used to drive pipelines are related to each other, how to build relationships between systems, and finally, how to create a self-service workflow for automating the deployment of pipelines.

To get the most out of this book

You should have a basic understanding of the Linux, basic commands, tools like Git and a text editor like vi.

The book chapters contain both theory and hands-on exercises. We feel that the exercises help to reinforce the theory, but they are not required to understand each topic. If you want to do the exercises in the book, you will need to meet the requirement in the table below.

Requirements for the chapter exercises.	Version
Ubuntu Server	20.04 or higher

All exercises use Ubuntu, but most of them will work on other Linux installations. *Chapter 10, Auditing using Falco, DevOps AI, and ECK* has steps that are specific to Ubuntu and the exercise will likely fail to deploy correctly on other Linux installations.

Download the example code files

The code bundle for the book is hosted on GitHub at `https://github.com/PacktPublishing/Kubernetes---An-Enterprise-Guide-2E`. We also have other code bundles from our rich catalog of books and videos available at `https://github.com/PacktPublishing/`. Check them out!

Download the color images

We also provide a PDF file that has color images of the screenshots/diagrams used in this book. You can download it here: `https://static.packt-cdn.com/downloads/9781803230030_ColorImages.pdf`.

Supplementary content

Here's a link to the YouTube channel (created and managed by the authors Marc Boorshtein and Scott Surovich) that contains videos of the labs from this book, so you can see them in action even before you start on your own: `https://packt.link/N5qjd`.

Conventions used

There are a number of text conventions used throughout this book.

`CodeInText`: Indicates code words in text, database table names, folder names, filenames, file extensions, pathnames, dummy URLs, user input, and Twitter handles. For example; "The `--name` option will set the name of the cluster to `cluster01`, and `--config` tells the installer to use the `cluster01-kind.yaml` config file."

A block of code is set as follows:

```
apiVersion: apps/v1
kind: Deployment
metadata:
  labels:
    app: grafana
  name: grafana
  namespace: monitoring
```

When we wish to draw your attention to a particular part of a code block, the relevant lines or items are set in bold:

```
apiVersion: apps/v1
kind: Deployment
metadata:
  labels:
    app: grafana
  name: grafana
  namespace: monitoring
```

Any command-line input or output is written as follows:

```
PS C:\Users\mlb> kubectl create ns not-going-to-work
namespace/not-going-to-work created
```

Bold: Indicates a new term, an important word, or words that you see on the screen, for example, in menus or dialog boxes, also appear in the text like this. For example: "Hit the **Finish Login** button at the bottom of the screen."

 Warnings or important notes appear like this.

 Tips and tricks appear like this.

Get in touch

Feedback from our readers is always welcome.

General feedback: Email `feedback@packtpub.com`, and mention the book's title in the subject of your message. If you have questions about any aspect of this book, please email us at `questions@packtpub.com`.

Errata: Although we have taken every care to ensure the accuracy of our content, mistakes do happen. If you have found a mistake in this book we would be grateful if you would report this to us. Please visit, `http://www.packtpub.com/submit-errata`, selecting your book, clicking on the Errata Submission Form link, and entering the details.

Piracy: If you come across any illegal copies of our works in any form on the Internet, we would be grateful if you would provide us with the location address or website name. Please contact us at `copyright@packtpub.com` with a link to the material.

If you are interested in becoming an author: If there is a topic that you have expertise in and you are interested in either writing or contributing to a book, please visit `http://authors.packtpub.com`.

Share your thoughts

Once you've read *Kubernetes – An Enterprise Guide, Second Edition,* we'd love to hear your thoughts! Scan the QR code below to go straight to the Amazon review page for this book and share your feedback.

https://packt.link/r/1803230037

Your review is important to us and the tech community and will help us make sure we're delivering excellent quality content.

1

Docker and Container Essentials

Containers are one of the most transformational technologies that we have seen in years. Technology companies, corporations, and end users have all adopted them to handle everyday workloads. Increasingly, **commercial off-the-shelf (COTS)** applications are transforming from traditional installations into fully containerized deployments. With such a large technology shift, it is essential for anyone in the information technology realm to learn about containers.

In this chapter, we will introduce the problems that containers address. After an introduction to why containers are important, we will introduce the runtime that launched the modern container frenzy, Docker, and explain its relationship to Kubernetes. We'll also cover how Kubernetes' recent deprecation of support for Docker as a runtime impacts the use of Docker and why you should still be familiar with how to use it. By the end of this chapter, you will understand how to install Docker and how to use the most common Docker CLI commands.

In this chapter, we will cover the following topics:

- Understanding the need for containerization
- Kubernetes deprecating Docker
- Understanding Docker
- Installing Docker
- Using the Docker CLI

Before we begin, you may have read that Kubernetes will be deprecating Docker as a compatible runtime in an upcoming release. This change will affect many businesses that work with containerization and Kubernetes. We will dig into it in the *Understanding why Kubernetes is depreciating Docker* section but rest assured that Docker is still the best way to introduce you to containers and the advantages that they deliver. It will still be used on many systems that run containers locally, rather than with an orchestration platform like Kubernetes.

Technical requirements

This chapter has the following technical requirement:

- An Ubuntu 20.04+ server with a minimum of 4 GB of RAM, though 8 GB is suggested.
- You can access the code for this chapter by going to this book's GitHub repository: `https://github.com/PacktPublishing/Kubernetes---An-Enterprise-Guide-2E/tree/main/chapter1`.

Understanding the need for containerization

You may have experienced a conversation like this at your office or school:

> **Developer**: *"Here's the new application. It went through weeks of testing and you are the first to get the new release."*
>
> *….. A little while later …..*
>
> **User**: *"It's not working. When I click the submit button, it shows an error about a missing dependency."*
>
> **Developer**: *"That's weird; it's working fine on my machine."*

This is one of the most frustrating things a developer can encounter when delivering an application. Often, the issues that creep up are related to a library that the developer had on their machine, but it wasn't included in the distribution of the package. It may seem like an easy fix for this would be to include all the libraries alongside the release, but what if this release contains a newer library that overwrites the older version, which may be required for a different application?

Developers need to consider their new releases, as well as any potential conflicts with any existing software on users' workstations. This often becomes a careful balancing act that requires larger deployment teams to test the application on different system configurations. It can also lead to additional rework for the developer or, in some extreme cases, full incompatibility with an existing application.

There have been various attempts to make application delivery easier over the years. First, there are solutions such as **VMware**'s **ThinApp**, which virtualizes an application (not to be confused with virtualizing an operating system). It allows you to package the application and its dependencies into a single executable package. This packaging eliminates the issues of an application's dependencies conflicting with another application's dependencies since the application is in a self-contained package. This provided application isolation not only eliminates dependency issues but also provides an enhanced level of security and eases the burden of operating system migrations.

You may or may not have heard of application packaging, or the term application-on-a-stick, before reading this book. It sounds like a great solution to the "it worked on my machine" issue. There are many reasons it hasn't taken off as expected, though. For starters, most offerings are paid solutions that require a substantial investment. Besides licensing, they require a "clean PC," which means that for every application you want to virtualize, you need to start with a base system. The package you want to create uses the differences between the base installation and anything that was added after the initial system snapshot. The differences are then packaged into your distribution file, which can be executed on any workstation.

We've mentioned application virtualization to highlight that application issues such as "it works on my machine" have had different solutions over the years. Products such as **ThinApp** are just one attempt at solving the problem. Other attempts include running the application on a server using **Citrix**, **Remote Desktop**, **Linux containers**, chroot jails, and even **virtual machines**.

Understanding why Kubernetes is deprecating Docker

In December 2020, Kubernetes announced the deprecation of Docker as a supported container runtime. We thought it would be important to explain how the announcement affects any reason for using, or not using, Docker.

The announcement is only related to using Docker as the container runtime in a cluster – it is important to note that this is the only impact that removing Docker will have. You can still create new containers using Docker and they will run on any runtime that supports the **Open Container Initiative** (**OCI**) specification.

When you create a container using Docker, you are creating a container that is OCI compliant, so it will still run on Kubernetes clusters that are running any Kubernetes-compatible container runtime.

To fully explain the impact and the alternatives that will be supported, we need to understand what a container runtime is. A high-level definition would be that a container runtime is the software layer that runs and manages containers. Like many components that make up a Kubernetes cluster, the runtime is not included as part of Kubernetes – it is a pluggable module that needs to be supplied by a vendor, or by you, to create a functioning cluster.

There are many technical reasons that led up to the decision to deprecate Docker, but at a high level, the main concerns were:

- Docker contains multiple pieces inside of the Docker executable to support its own remote API and **user experience** (**UX**). Kubernetes only requires one component in the executable, dockerd, which is the runtime process that manages containers. All other pieces of the executable contribute nothing to using Docker in a Kubernetes cluster. These extra components made the binary bloated, and could lead to additional bugs, security, or performance issues.

- Docker does not conform to the **Container Runtime Interface** (**CRI**) standard, which was introduced to create a set of standards to easily integrate container runtimes in Kubernetes. Since it doesn't comply, the Kubernetes team has had extra work that only caters to supporting Docker.

When it comes to local container testing and development, you can still use Docker on your workstation or server. Building on the previous statement, if you build a container on Docker and the container successfully runs on your Docker runtime system, it will run on a Kubernetes cluster that is not using Docker as the runtime.

Removing Docker will have very little impact on most users of Kubernetes in new clusters. Containers will still run using any standard method, as they would with Docker as the container runtime. If you happen to manage a cluster, you may need to learn new commands when you troubleshoot a Kubernetes node – you will not have a Docker command on the node to look at running containers, or to clean up volumes, etc...

At the time of writing this chapter, Kubernetes supports the following runtimes in place of Docker:

- `containerd`
- `Rocket (rkt)`
- `CRI-O`

- Frakti
- cri-containerdL: https://github.com/containerd/cri
- singularity-cri: https://github.com/sylabs/singularity-cri

This list will evolve; you can always view the latest supported runtimes on the Kubernetes Git at https://github.com/kubernetes/community/blob/master/contributors/devel/sig-node/container-runtime-interface.md.

Since we are focusing on general containers and we will be using Docker as our runtime to create KinD clusters, we will not go into too many details on the alternative runtimes. They are only being mentioned here to explain the alternatives that can be used on a cluster.

For more details on the impact of deprecating Docker, refer to the article called *Don't Panic: Kubernetes and Docker* on the Kubernetes.io site at https://kubernetes.io/blog/2020/12/02/dont-panic-kubernetes-and-docker/.

Now, let's introduce Docker and how you can use it to create and manage containers.

Introducing Docker

The industry and even end users needed something that was easier and cheaper – enter Docker containers. Containers are not a new technology; they have been used in various forms for years. What Docker did was make them accessible to the average developer.

Docker brought an abstraction layer to the masses. It was easy to use and didn't require a clean PC for every application before creating a package, thus offering a solution for dependency issues, but most attractive of all, it was *free*. Docker became a standard for many projects on GitHub, where teams would often create a Docker container and distribute the Docker image or **Dockerfile** to team members, providing a standard testing or development environment. This adoption by end users is what eventually brought Docker to the enterprise and, ultimately, what made it the standard it has become today.

While there are many books on Docker, this book focuses on the base topics of Docker that are used to interact with containers. This book will be focusing on what you will need to know when trying to use a local Kubernetes environment. There is a long and interesting history of Docker and how it evolved into the standard container image format that we use today. We encourage you to read about the company and how they ushered in the container world we know today.

While our focus is not to teach Docker inside out, we felt that those of you who are new to Docker would benefit from a quick primer on general container concepts.

If you have some Docker experience and understand terminology such as ephemeral and stateless, feel free to continue to the *Installing Docker* section.

Understanding Docker

This book was created with the assumption that you have some basic knowledge of Docker and container concepts. We realize that not everyone may have played with Docker or containers in the past, so we wanted to present a crash course on container concepts and using Docker.

 If you are new to containers, we suggest reading the documentation that can be found on Docker's website for additional information: `https://docs.docker.com/`.

Containers are ephemeral

The first thing to understand is that container images are ephemeral.

For those of you who are new to Docker, the term "ephemeral" means short-lived. By design, a container can be destroyed at any time and brought back up with no interaction from a user. In the following example, someone interactively adds files to a web server. These added files are only temporary since the base image does not have these files included in it.

This means that once a container is created and running, any changes that are made to the image *will not* be saved once the container is removed, or destroyed, from the Docker host. Let's look at an example:

1. You start a container running a web server using **NGINX** on your host without any base **HTML** pages.

2. Using a Docker command, you execute a copy command to copy some web files into the container's filesystem.

3. To test that the copy was successful, you browse to the website and confirm that it is serving the correct web pages.

4. Happy with the results, you stop the container and remove it from the host. Later that day, you want to show a co-worker the website and you start your NGINX container. You browse to the website again, but when the site opens, you receive a 404 error (page not found error).

What happened to the files you uploaded before you stopped and removed the container from the host?

The reason your web pages cannot be found after the container was restarted is that all containers are **ephemeral**.

Whatever is in the base container image is all that will be included each time the container is initially started. Any changes that you make inside a container are short-lived.

If you need to add permanent files to an existing image, you need to rebuild the image with the files included or, as we will explain in the *Persistent data* section later in this chapter, you could mount a Docker volume in your container. At this point, the main concept to understand is that containers are ephemeral.

But wait! You may be wondering, "*If containers are ephemeral, how did I add web pages to the server?*". Ephemeral just means that changes will not be saved; it doesn't stop you from making changes to a running container.

Any changes made to a running container will be written to a temporary layer, called the **container layer**, which is a directory on the local host filesystem. The Docker storage driver is in charge of handling requests that use the container layer. This location will store any changes in the container's filesystem so that when you add the HTML pages to the container, they will be stored on the local host. The container layer is tied to the container ID of the running image and it will remain on the host system until the container is removed from Docker, either by using the CLI or by running a Docker prune job.

If a container is ephemeral and the image cannot be written to, how can you modify data in the container? Docker uses image layering to create multiple linked layers that appear as a single filesystem.

Docker images

At a high level, a Docker image is a collection of image layers, each with a JSON file that contains metadata for the layer. These are all combined to create the running application that you interact with when a container image is started.

You can read more about the contents of an image on Docker's GitHub at `https://github.com/moby/moby/blob/master/image/spec/v1.md`.

Image layers

As we mentioned in the previous section, a running container uses a container layer that is "on top" of the base image layer, as shown in the following diagram:

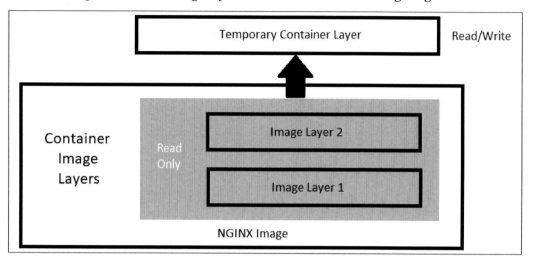

Figure 1.1: Docker image layers

The image layers cannot be written to since they are in a read-only state, but the temporary container layer is in a writeable state. Any data that you add to the container is stored in this layer and will be retained as long as the container is running.

To deal with multiple layers efficiently, Docker implements copy-on-write, which means that if a file already exists, it will not be created. However, if a file is required that does not exist in the current image, it will be written. In the container world, if a file exists in a lower layer, the layers above it do not need to include it. For example, if layer 1 had a file called /opt/nginx/index.html in it, layer 2 does not need the same file in its layer.

This explains how the system handles files that either exist or do not exist, but what about a file that has been modified? There will be times where you'll need to "replace" a file that is in a lower layer. You may need to do this when you are building an image or as a temporary fix to a running container issue. The copy-on-write system knows how to deal with these issues. Since images read from the top down, the container uses only the highest layer file. If your system had a /opt/nginx/index.html file in layer 1 and you modified and saved the file, the running container would store the new file in the container layer. Since the container layer is the topmost layer, the new copy of index.html would always be read before the older version in the image layer.

Persistent data

Being limited to ephemeral-only containers would severely limit the use cases for Docker. It is very likely that you will have some use cases that will require persistent storage, or data that will remain if you stop a container.

This may seem like we are contradicting our earlier statement that containers are ephemeral, but that is still true. When you store data in the container image layer, the base image does not change. When the container is removed from the host, the container layer is also removed. If the same image is used to start a new container, a new container image layer is also created. So, the container is ephemeral, but by adding a Docker volume to the container, you can store data outside of the container, thus gaining data persistency.

Accessing services running in containers

Unlike a physical machine or a virtual machine, containers do not connect to a network directly. When a container needs to send or receive traffic, it goes through the Docker host system using a bridged **NAT network** connection. This means that when you run a container and you want to receive incoming traffic requests, you need to expose the ports for each of the containers that you wish to receive traffic on. On a Linux-based system, `iptables` has rules to forward traffic to the Docker daemon, which will service the assigned ports for each container.

That completes the introduction to base containers and Docker. In the next section, we will explain how to install Docker on a host.

Installing Docker

The hands-on exercises in this book will require that you have a working Docker host. You can follow the steps in this book, or you can execute the script located in this book's GitHub repository, in the `chapter1` directory, called `install-docker.sh`.

Today, you can install Docker on just about every hardware platform out there. Each version of Docker acts and looks the same on each platform, making development and using Docker easy for people who need to develop cross-platform applications. By making the functions and commands the same between different platforms, developers do not need to learn a different container runtime to run images.

The following is a table of Docker's available platforms. As you can see, there are installations for multiple operating systems, as well as multiple CPU architectures:

Platform	X86_64	ARM	ARM64/AARCH64	s390x	ARM64 (Apple Chip)
Docker Desktop Windows	✓				
Docker Desktop macOS	✓				✓
CentOS	✓		✓		
Debian	✓	✓	✓		
Fedora	✓		✓		
Raspbian		✓			
RHEL				✓	
SLES				✓	
Ubuntu	✓	✓	✓	✓	

Figure 1.2: Available Docker platforms

 Images that are created using one architecture cannot run on a different architecture. This means that you cannot create an image based on x86 hardware and expect that same image to run on your Raspberry Pi running an ARM processor. It's also important to note that while you can run a Linux container on a Windows machine, you cannot run a Windows container on a Linux machine.

The installation procedures that are used to install Docker vary between platforms. Luckily, Docker has documented many of the installation procedures on their website: `https://docs.docker.com/install/`.

In this chapter, we will install Docker on an Ubuntu 18.04 system. If you do not have an Ubuntu machine to install on, you can still read about the installation steps, as each step will be explained and does not require that you have a running system to understand the process. If you have a different Linux installation, you can use the installation procedures outlined on Docker's site at `https://docs.docker.com/`. Steps are provided for CentOS, Debian, Fedora, and Ubuntu, and there are generic steps for other Linux distributions.

Preparing to install Docker

Before we start the installation, we need to consider what storage driver to use. The storage driver is what provides the union filesystem, which manages the layers of the container and how the writeable layer of the container is accessed.

In most installations, you won't need to change the default storage driver since a default option will be selected. If you are running a Linux kernel that is at least version 4.0 or above, your Docker installation will use the `overlay2` storage driver; earlier kernels will install the AUFS storage driver.

For reference, along with the `overlay2` and `AUFS` drivers, Docker supports the `btrfs` storage driver. However, these are rarely used in new systems and are only mentioned here as a reference.

If you would like to learn about each storage driver, take a look at the following Docker web page, which details each driver and its use cases: `https://docs.docker.com/storage/storagedriver/select-storage-driver/`.

Now that you understand the storage driver requirements, the next step is to select an installation method. You can install Docker using one of three methods:

- Add the Docker repositories to your host system
- Install the package manually
- Use a supplied installation script from Docker

The first option is considered the best option since it allows for easy installation and making updates to the Docker engine. The second option is useful for enterprises that do not have internet access to servers, also known as **air-gapped servers**. The third option is used to install edge and testing versions of Docker and is not suggested for production use.

Since the preferred method is to add Docker's repository to our host, we will use that option and explain the process we should use to add the repository and install Docker.

Installing Docker on Ubuntu

Now that we have finished preparing everything, let's install Docker. (If you ran the install script from the book repo, you do not need to execute any of the installation steps)

1. The first step is to update the package index by executing `apt-get update`:

```
sudo apt-get update
```

2. Next, we need to add any packages that may be missing on the host system to allow HTTPS apt access:

```
sudo apt-get install -y apt-transport-https ca-certificates curl
gnupg lsb-release
```

3. To pull packages from Docker's repository, we need to add their keys. You can add keys by using the following command, which will download the `gpg` key and add it to your system:

```
curl -fsSL https://download.docker.com/linux/ubuntu/gpg | sudo
gpg --dearmor -o /usr/share/keyrings/docker-archive-keyring.gpg
```

Now, add Docker's repository to your host system:

```
echo "deb [arch=amd64 signed-by=/usr/share/keyrings/docker-
archive-keyring.gpg] https://download.docker.com/linux/ubuntu
$(lsb_release -cs) stable" | sudo tee /etc/apt/sources.list.d/
docker.list > /dev/null
```

With all the prerequisites completed, you can install Docker on your server:

```
sudo apt-get update && sudo apt-get install -y  docker-ce
docker-ce-cli containerd.io
```

4. Docker is now installed on your host, but like most new services, Docker is
    not currently running and has not been configured to start with the system.
    To start Docker and enable it on startup, use the following command:

```
sudo systemctl enable docker && systemctl start docker
```

Now that we have Docker installed, let's get some configuration out of the way. First,
we'll grant permissions to Docker.

Granting Docker permissions

In a default installation, Docker requires root access, so you will need to run all
Docker commands as root. Rather than using sudo with every Docker command, you
can add your user account to a new group on the server that provides Docker access
without requiring sudo for every command.

If you are logged on as a standard user and try to run a Docker command, you will
receive an error:

```
Got permission denied while trying to connect to the
Docker daemon socket at unix:///var/run/docker.sock: Get
http://%2Fvar%2Frun%2Fdocker.sock/v1.40/images/json: dial unix /var/
run/docker.sock: connect: permission denied
```

To allow your user, or any other user you may want to add, to execute Docker
commands, you need to add the users to a new group called docker that was created
during the installation of Docker. The following is an example command you can use
to add the currently logged-on user to the group:

```
sudo usermod -aG docker $USER
```

To add the new members to your account, you can either log off and log back into the Docker host, or activate the group changes using the `newgrp` command:

```
newgrp docker
```

Finally, you can test that it works by running the standard hello-world image (note that we do not require `sudo` to run the Docker command):

```
docker run hello-world
```

You should see the output shown below, which verifies that your user has access to Docker:

```
Unable to find image 'hello-world:latest' locally
latest: Pulling from library/hello-world
2db29710123e: Pull complete
Digest: sha256:37a0b92b08d4919615c3ee023f7ddb068d12b8387475d64c622ac30f
45c29c51
Status: Downloaded newer image for hello-world:latest

Hello from Docker!
```

This message shows that your installation appears to be working correctly.

To generate this message, Docker took the following steps:

1. The Docker client contacted the Docker daemon
2. The Docker daemon pulled the hello-world image from Docker Hub (amd64)
3. The Docker daemon created a new container from that image that runs the executable that produces the output you are currently reading
4. The Docker daemon streamed that output to the Docker client, which sent it to your terminal

To try something more ambitious, you can run an Ubuntu container with:

```
$ docker run -it ubuntu bash
```

Share images, automate workflows, and more with a free Docker ID: `https://hub.docker.com/`

For more examples and ideas, visit `https://docs.docker.com/get-started/`

Now that we've granted Docker permission to run without `sudo`, we can start unlocking the commands at our disposal by learning how to use the Docker CLI.

Using the Docker CLI

You used the Docker CLI when you ran the `hello-world` container to test your installation. The Docker command is what you will use to interact with the Docker daemon. Using this single executable, you can do the following, and more:

- Start and stop containers
- Pull and push images
- Run a shell in an active container
- Look at container logs
- Create Docker volumes
- Create Docker networks
- Prune old images and volumes

This chapter is not meant to include an exhaustive explanation of every Docker command; instead, we will explain some of the common commands that you will need to use to interact with the Docker daemon and containers. Since we consider volumes and networking to be very important topics to understand for this book, we will go into additional details on those topics.

You can break down Docker commands into two categories: general Docker commands and Docker management commands. The standard Docker commands allow you to manage containers, while management commands allow you to manage Docker options such as managing volumes and networking.

docker help

It's common to forget an option or the syntax for a command, and Docker realizes this. Whenever you get stuck trying to remember a command, you can always use the `docker help` command to refresh your memory.

docker run

To run a container, use the `docker run` command with the provided image name. Before executing a `docker run` command, you should understand the options you can supply when starting a container.

In its simplest form, an example command you can use to run an NGINX web server would be `docker run bitnami/nginx:latest`. While this will start a container running NGINX, it will run in the foreground, showing logs of the application running in the container. Press *Ctrl* + *C* to stop running the container:

```
nginx 22:52:27.42
nginx 22:52:27.42 Welcome to the Bitnami nginx container
nginx 22:52:27.43 Subscribe to project updates by watching https://
github.com/bitnami/bitnami-docker-nginx
nginx 22:52:27.43 Submit issues and feature requests at https://github.
com/bitnami/bitnami-docker-nginx/issues
nginx 22:52:27.44
nginx 22:52:27.44 INFO  ==> ** Starting NGINX setup **
nginx 22:52:27.49 INFO  ==> Validating settings in NGINX_* env vars
nginx 22:52:27.50 INFO  ==> Initializing NGINX
nginx 22:52:27.53 INFO  ==> ** NGINX setup finished! **

nginx 22:52:27.57 INFO  ==> ** Starting NGINX **
```

To run a container as a background process, you need to add the `-d` option to your Docker command, which will run your container in detached mode. Now, when you run a detached container, you will only see the container ID, instead of the interactive, or attached, screen:

```
[root@localhost ~]# docker run -d bitnami/nginx:latest
5283811f91f02ecc2d0adf5ed74ea001b5136b6991e4ff815ee03a0691a05735
```

Figure 1.3: Container ID displayed

```
[root@localhost ~]# docker run -d bitnami/nginx:latest
13bdde13d0027e366a81d9a19a56c736c28feb6d8354b363ee738d2399023f80
[root@localhost ~]#
```

By default, containers will be given a random name once they are started. In our previous detached example, the container has been given the name `silly_keldysh`:

```
CONTAINER ID       IMAGE                          NAMES
13bdde13d002       bitnami/nginx:latest           silly_keldysh
```

If you do not assign a name to your container, it can quickly get confusing as you start to run multiple containers on a single host. To make management easier, you should always start your container with a name that will make it easier to manage. Docker provides another option with the `run` command: the `--name` option. Building on our previous example, we will name our container `nginx-test`. Our new `docker run` command will be as follows:

```
docker run --name nginx-test -d bitnami/nginx:latest
```

Just like running any detached image, this will return the container ID, but not the name you provided. In order to verify the container ran with the name `nginx-test`, we can list the containers using the `docker ps` command.

docker ps

Every day, you will need to retrieve a list of running containers or a list of containers that have been stopped. The Docker CLI has an option called `ps` that will list all running containers, or if you add an extra option to the `ps` command, all containers that are running and have been stopped. The output will list the containers, including their container ID, image tag, entry command, the creation date, status, ports, and the container name. The following is an example of containers that are currently running:

CONTAINER ID	IMAGE	COMMAND	CREATED
72212346d765	nginx	"nginx -g 'daemon of…"	6 seconds ago
7967c50b260f	rancher/rancher:latest	"entrypoint.sh"	3 days ago

Figure 1.4: Currently running containers

CONTAINER ID	IMAGE	COMMAND	CREATED
13bdde13d002	bitnami/nginx:latest	"/opt/bitnami/script…"	Up 4 hours
3302f2728133	registry:2	"/entrypoint.sh /etc…"	Up 3 hours

This is helpful if the container you are looking for is currently running. What if the container was stopped, or even worse, what if you started the container and it failed to start and then stopped? You can view the status of all containers, including previously run containers, by adding the -a option to the `docker ps` command. When you execute `docker ps -a`, you will see the same output from a standard `ps` command, but you will notice that the list may include additional containers.

How can you tell what containers are running versus which ones have stopped? If you look at the STATUS field of the list, the running containers will show a running time; for example, Up xx hours, or Up xx days. However, if the container has been stopped for any reason, the status will show when it stopped; for example, Exited (0) 10 minutes ago.

IMAGE	COMMAND	CREATED	STATUS
bitnami/nginx:latest minutes	"/opt/bitnami/script…"	10 minutes ago	Up 10
bitnami/nginx:latest (0) 10 minutes ago	"/opt/bitnami/script…"	12 minutes ago	Exited

A stopped container does not mean there was an issue running the image. There are containers that may execute a single task and, once completed, the container may stop gracefully. One way to determine whether an exit was graceful or whether it was due to a failed startup is to check the logs of the container.

docker start and stop

To stop a running container, use the `docker stop` option with the name of the container you want to stop. You may wish to stop a container due to the resources on the host since you may have limited resources and can only run a few containers simultaneously.

If you need to start that container at a future time for additional testing or development, execute `docker start container name`, which will start the container with all of the options that it was originally started with, including any networks or volumes that were assigned.

docker attach

You may need to access a container interactively to troubleshoot an issue or to look at a log file. One method to connect to a running container is to use the `docker attach container name` command. When you attach to a running container, you will connect to the running container's process, so if you attach to a container running a process, you are not likely to just see a command prompt of any kind. In fact, you may see nothing but a blank screen for some time until the container outputs some data to the screen.

You must be careful once you attach to the container – you may accidentally stop the running process and, in turn, stop the container. Let's use an example of attaching to a web server running NGINX. First, we need to verify that the container is running using `docker ps`:

```
CONTAINER ID    IMAGE                 COMMAND                  STATUS
4a77c14a236a    nginx                 "/docker-entrypoint.…"   Up 33
seconds
3302f2728133    registry:2            "/entrypoint.sh /etc…"   Up 8
minutes
13bdde13d002    bitnami/nginx:latest  "/opt/bitnami/script…"   Up 14
minutes
```

Using the `attach` command, we execute `docker attach 4a77c14a236a`.

Once you attach to the running container process, it may appear that nothing is happening. When you attach to a process, you will only be able to interact with the process, and the only output you will see is data being sent to standard output. In the case of the NGINX container, the `attach` command has attached to the NGINX process. To show this, we will leave the attachment and curl to the web server from another session. Once we curl to the container port, you will see logs outputted to the attached console:

```
[root@astra-master manifests]# docker attach 4a77c14a236a
172.17.0.1 - - [15/Oct/2021:23:28:31 +0000] "GET / HTTP/1.1" 200 615
"-" "curl/7.61.1" "-"
172.17.0.1 - - [15/Oct/2021:23:28:33 +0000] "GET / HTTP/1.1" 200 615
"-" "curl/7.61.1" "-"
172.17.0.1 - - [15/Oct/2021:23:28:34 +0000] "GET / HTTP/1.1" 200 615
"-" "curl/7.61.1" "-"
172.17.0.1 - - [15/Oct/2021:23:28:35 +0000] "GET / HTTP/1.1" 200 615
"-" "curl/7.61.1" "-"
172.17.0.1 - - [15/Oct/2021:23:28:36 +0000] "GET / HTTP/1.1" 200 615
"-" "curl/7.61.1" "-"
```

Attaching to a running container has varying benefits, depending on what is running in the container.

We mentioned that you need to be careful once you attach to the container. Those who are new to Docker may attach to the NGINX image and assume that nothing is happening on the server or the attach failed. Since they think that there may be an issue, since it's just sitting there, they may decide to break out of the container using the standard *Ctrl + C* keyboard command. This will send them back to a bash prompt, where they may run `docker ps` to look at the running containers:

```
root@localhost:~# docker ps
CONTAINER ID      IMAGE   COMMAND      CREATED      STATUS
root@localhost:~#
```

Where is the NGINX container? We didn't execute a `docker stop` command, and the container was running until we attached to the container. Why did the container stop after the attachment?

When an attachment is made to a container, you are attached to the running process. All keyboard commands will act in the same way as if you were at a physical server that was running NGINX in an interactive shell. This means that when the user used *Ctrl + C* to return to a prompt, they stopped the running NGINX process.

If a container's running process stops, the container will also stop, and that's why the docker ps command does not show a running container.

Rather than use *Ctrl + C* to return to a prompt, the user should have used *Ctrl + P*, followed by *Ctrl + Q*.

There is an alternative to the attach command: the docker exec command. The exec command differs from an attach command since you supply the process to execute on the container.

docker exec

A better option when it comes to interacting with a running container is the exec command. Rather than attach to the container, you can use the docker exec command to execute a process in the container. You need to supply the container name and the process you want to execute in the image. Of course, the process must be included in the running image – if you do not have the bash executable in the image, you will receive an error when trying to execute bash in the container.

We will use an NGINX container as an example again. We will verify that NGINX is running using docker ps and then, using the container ID or the name, we execute into the container. The command syntax is docker exec <options> <container name> <command>:

```
root@localhost:~# docker exec -it nginx-test bash
I have no name!@a7c916e7411:/app$
```

The option we included is -it, which tells exec to run in an interactive TTY session. Here, the process we want to execute is bash. Notice how the name changed from the original user and hostname. The hostname is localhost, while the container name is @a7c916e7411. You may also have noticed that the current working directory changed from ~ to /app and that the prompt is not running as a root user, as shown by the $ prompt.

You can use this session the same way you would a standard SSH connection; you are running bash in the container.

Since we are not attached to the container, *Ctrl + C* will not stop any process from running. To exit an interactive session, you only need to type in exit, followed by *Enter*, which will exit the container. If you then run docker ps, you will notice that the container is still in a running state.

Next, let's see what we can learn about Docker log files.

docker logs

The docker logs command allows you to retrieve logs from a container using the container name or container ID that you retrieved using the docker ps command. You can view the logs from any container that was listed in your ps command; it doesn't matter if it's currently running or stopped.

Log files are often the only way to troubleshoot why a container may not be starting up, or why a container is in an exited state. For example, if you attempted to run an image and the image starts and suddenly stops, you may find the answer by looking at the logs for that container.

To look at the logs for a container, you can use the docker logs <container ID or name> command.

To view the logs for a container with a container ID of 7967c50b260f, you would use the following command:

```
docker logs 7967c50b260f
```

This will output the logs from the container to your screen, which may be very long and verbose. Since many logs may contain a lot of information, you can limit the output by supplying the logs command with additional options. The following table lists the options available for viewing logs:

Logs Options	Description
-f	Follow the log output (can also use --follow).
--tail xx	Show log output starting from the end of the file and retrieve xx lines.
--until xxx	Show log output before the xxx timestamp. xxx can be a timestamp; for example, 2020-02-23T18:35:13. xxx can be a relative time; for example, 60m.
--since xxx	Show log output after the xxx timestamp. xxx can be a timestamp; for example, 2020-02-23T18:35:13. xxx can be a relative time; for example, 60m.

Table 1.1: Logs options

Checking log files is a process you will find yourself doing often, and since they can be very lengthy, knowing options like tail, until, and since will help you to find the information in a log quicker.

docker rm

Once you name a container, the assigned name cannot be used to start a different container unless you remove it using the `docker rm` command. If you had a container running called `nginx-test` that was stopped and you attempted to start another container with the name `nginx-test`, the Docker daemon would return an error, stating that the name is in use:

```
Conflict.  The container name "/nginx-test" is already in use
```

This container is not running, but the daemon knows that the container name was used previously and that it's still in the list of previously run containers.

If you want to reuse the same name, you need to remove the container before starting another container with that name. This is a common scenario when you are testing container images. You may start a container only to discover an issue with the application or image. You stop the container, fix the image/application issue, and want to redeploy using the same name. Since the name was in use previously and is still part of the Docker history, you will need to remove the container before reusing the name.

To remove the nginx-test container, simply execute `docker rm nginx-test`:

```
root@localhost ~:# docker rm nginx-test
nginx-test
root@localhost ~:#
```

Assuming the container name is correct and it's not running, the only output you will see is the name of the image that you have removed.

We haven't discussed Docker volumes, but when removing a container that has a volume, or volumes, attached, it's a good practice to add the -v option to your remove command. Adding the -v option to the `docker rm` command will remove any volumes that were attached to the container.

Summary

In this chapter, you learned how Docker can be used to solve common development issues, including the dreaded "it works on my machine" problem. We also presented an introduction to the most commonly used Docker CLI commands that you will use on a daily basis. We closed out this chapter by looking at how to handle persistent data for a container and customizing container networking.

In the next chapter, we will start our Kubernetes journey with an introduction to KinD, a utility that provides an easy way to run multi-node Kubernetes test servers on a single workstation.

Questions

1. A single Docker image can be used on any Docker host, regardless of the architecture used.

   a. True

   b. False

2. What does Docker use to merge multiple image layers into a single filesystem?

   a. Merged filesystem

   b. NTFS filesystem

   c. EXT4 filesystem

   d. Union filesystem

3. Kubernetes is only compatible with the Docker runtime engine.

   a. True

   b. False

4. When you edit a container's filesystem interactively, what layer are the changes written to?

   a. Operating system layer

   b. Bottom-most layer

   c. Container layer

   d. Ephemeral layer

5. Assuming the image contains the required binaries, what Docker command allows you to gain access to a container's bash prompt?

   a. `docker shell -it <container> /bin/bash`

   b. `docker run -it <container> /bin/bash`

   c. `docker exec -it <container> /bin/bash`

   d. `docker spawn -it <container> /bin/bash`

6. When a container is stopped, the Docker daemon will delete all traces of the container.

    a. True

    b. False

7. What command will show you a list of all containers, including any stopped containers?

    a. `docker ps -all`

    b. `docker ps -a`

    c. `docker ps -list`

    d. `docker list all`

Join our book's Discord space

Join the book's Discord workspace for a monthly *Ask me Anything* session with the authors: `https://packt.link/K8EntGuide`

2
Deploying Kubernetes Using KinD

One of the largest obstacles to learning Kubernetes is having enough resources to create a cluster for testing or development. Like most IT professionals, we like to have a Kubernetes cluster on our laptops for demonstrations and for testing products in general.

Often, you may have a need to run a multiple node cluster, or multiple clusters for a complex demonstration or testing, such as a multi-cluster service mesh. These scenarios would require multiple servers to create the necessary clusters, which, in turn, would require a lot of RAM and a hypervisor.

To do full testing on a multiple cluster scenario, you would need to create multiple nodes for each cluster. If you created the clusters using virtual machines, you would need to have enough resources to run the virtual machines. Each of the machines would have an overhead including disk space, memory, and CPU utilization.

But what if you could create a cluster using just containers? Using containers, rather than full virtual machines, will give you the ability to run additional nodes due to the reduced system requirements, create and delete clusters in minutes with a single command, use script cluster creation, and allow you to run multiple clusters on a single host.

Using containers to run a Kubernetes cluster provides you with an environment that would be difficult for most people to deploy using virtual machines or physical hardware due to resource constraints. To explain how to run a cluster using only containers locally, we will use **Kubernetes in Docker (KinD)** to create a Kubernetes cluster on your Docker host.

We will deploy a multi-node cluster that you will use in future chapters to test and deploy components such as Ingress controllers, authentication, RBAC, security policies, and more.

In this chapter, we will cover the following topics:

- Introducing Kubernetes components and objects
- Using development clusters
- Installing KinD
- Creating a KinD cluster
- Reviewing your KinD cluster
- Adding a custom load balancer for Ingress

Let's get started!

Technical requirements

This chapter has the following technical requirements:

- A Docker host installed using the steps from *Chapter 1, Docker and Container Essentials*
- Installation scripts from this book's GitHub repository

You can access the code for this chapter by going to this book's GitHub repository: `https://github.com/PacktPublishing/Kubernetes---An-Enterprise-Guide-2E/tree/main/chapter2`.

We thought it was important to point out that this chapter will reference multiple Kubernetes objects, some without a lot of context. *Chapter 3, Kubernetes Bootcamp*, goes over Kubernetes objects in detail, many with commands you can use to understand them, so we thought having a cluster to use while reading about this would be useful.

Most of the base Kubernetes topics covered in this chapter will be discussed in future chapters, so if some topics may be a bit foggy after you've read this chapter, don't fear! They will be discussed in detail in later chapters.

Introducing Kubernetes components and objects

Since this chapter will refer to common Kubernetes objects and components, we wanted to provide a short table of terms that you will see and a brief definition of each to provide context.

In *Chapter 3, Kubernetes Bootcamp*, we will go over the components of Kubernetes and the base set of objects that are included in a cluster. We will also discuss how to interact with a cluster using the kubectl executable:

Component	Description
Control Plane	API-Server: Frontend of the control plane that accepts requests from clients.
	`kube-scheduler`: Assigns workloads to nodes.
	`etcd`: Database that contains all cluster data.
	`kube-controller-manager`: Watches for node health, pod replicas, endpoints, service accounts, and tokens.
Node	`kubelet`: The agent that runs a pod based on instructions from the control plane.
	`kube-proxy`: Creates and deletes network rules for pod communication.
	Container runtime: Component responsible for running a container.

Object	Description
Container	A single immutable image that contains everything needed to run an application.
Pod	The smallest object that Kubernetes can control. A pod holds a container, or multiple containers. All containers in a pod are scheduled on the same server in a shared context (that is, each container in a pod can address other pods using 127.0.0.1).
Deployment	Used to deploy an application to a cluster based on a desired state, including the number of pods and rolling update configuration.
Storage Class	Defines storage providers and presents them to the cluster.
Persistent Volume (PV)	Provides a storage target that can be claimed by a Persistent Volume Request.
Persistent Volume Claim (PVC)	Connects (claims) a Persistent Volume so that it can be used inside a pod.
Container Network Interface (CNI)	Provides the network connection for pods. Common CNI examples include Flannel and Calico.
Container Storage Interface (CSI)	Provides the connection between pods and storage systems.

Table 2.1: Kubernetes components and objects

While these are only a few of the objects that are available in a Kubernetes cluster, they are the main objects we will mention in this chapter. Knowing what each resource is and having basic knowledge of their functionality will help you understand this chapter and deploy a KinD cluster.

Interacting with a cluster

To test our KinD installation, we will interact with the cluster using the kubectl executable. We will go over kubectl in *Chapter 3, Kubernetes Bootcamp*, but since we will be using a few commands in this chapter, we wanted to provide the commands we will use in a table with an explanation of what the options provide:

Kubectl command	Description
`kubectl get <object>`	Retrieves a list of the requested object. Example: `kubectl get nodes`.
`kubectl create -f <manifest-name>`	Creates the objects in the `include` manifest that is provided. `create` can only create the initial objects; it cannot update the objects.
`kubectl apply -f <manifest-name>`	Deploys the objects in the `include` manifest that is provided. Unlike the `create` option, the `apply` command can update objects, as well as create objects.
`kubectl patch <object-type> <object-name> -p {patching options}`	Patches the supplied `object-type` with the options provided.

Table 2.2: Basic kubectl commands

In this chapter, you will use these basic commands to deploy parts of the cluster that we will use throughout this book.

Next, we will introduce the concept of development clusters and then focus on one of the most popular tools used to create development clusters: KinD.

Using development clusters

Over the years, various tools have been created to install development Kubernetes clusters, allowing admins and developers to perform testing on a local system. Many of these tools worked for basic Kubernetes tests, but they often had limitations that made them less than ideal for quick, advanced scenarios.

Some of the most common solutions available are as follows:

- Docker Desktop
- Rancher Desktop
- minikube
- kubeadm
- K3s

Each solution has benefits, limitations, and use cases. Some solutions limit you to a single node that runs both the control plane and worker nodes. Others offer multi-node support but require additional resources to create multiple virtual machines. Depending on your development or testing requirements, these solutions may not meet your needs completely.

It seems that a new solution is coming out every few weeks, and one of the newest options for creating development clusters is a project from a KinD Kubernetes **Special Interest Group (SIG)**.

Using a single host, KinD allows you to create multiple clusters, and each cluster can have multiple control plane and worker nodes. The ability to run multiple nodes allows advanced testing that would have required more resources using another solution. KinD has been very well received by the community and has an active Git community at `https://github.com/kubernetes-sigs/kind`, as well as a Slack channel (*#kind*).

 Do not use KinD as a production cluster or expose a KinD cluster to the internet. While KinD clusters offer most of the same features you would want in a production cluster, it has **not** been designed for production environments.

Why did we select KinD for this book?

When we started this book, we wanted to include theory, as well as hands-on experience. KinD allows us to provide scripts to spin up and spin down clusters, and while other solutions can do something similar, KinD can create a new multi-node cluster in minutes. We wanted to separate the control plane and worker nodes to provide a more "realistic" cluster. In order to limit the hardware requirements and to make Ingress easier to configure, we will only create a two-node cluster for the exercises in this book.

A multi-node cluster can be created in a few minutes and once testing has been completed, clusters can be torn down in a few seconds. The ability to spin up and spin down clusters makes KinD the perfect platform for our exercises. KinD's requirements are simple: you only need a running Docker daemon to create a cluster. This means that it is compatible with most operating systems, including the following:

- Linux
- macOS running Docker Desktop
- Windows running Docker Desktop
- Windows running WSL2

 At the time of writing, KinD does not offer support for Chrome OS.

While KinD supports most operating systems, we have selected Ubuntu 20.04 as our host system. Some of the exercises in this book require files to be in specific directories and selecting a single Linux version helps us make sure the exercises work as designed. If you do not have access to an Ubuntu server at home, you can create a compute instance in a cloud provider such as **Google Cloud Platform (GCP)**. Google offers $300 in credit, which is more than enough to run a single Ubuntu server for a few weeks. You can view GCP's free options at `https://cloud.google.com/free/`.

Now, let's explain how KinD works and what a base KinD Kubernetes cluster looks like, before we move on to creating our first cluster.

Working with a base KinD Kubernetes cluster

At a high level, you can think of a KinD cluster as consisting of a **single** Docker container that runs a control plane node and a worker node to create a Kubernetes cluster. To make the deployment easy and robust, KinD bundles every Kubernetes object into a single image, known as a node image. This node image contains all the required Kubernetes components to create a single-node or multi-node cluster.

Once a KinD cluster is running, you can use Docker to exec into a control plane node container and look at the process list. In the process list, you will see the standard Kubernetes components for the control plane nodes running:

```
     TIME CMD
00:00:00 /sbin/init
00:00:00 /lib/systemd/systemd-journald
00:00:17 /usr/local/bin/containerd
00:00:00 /usr/local/bin/containerd-shim-runc-v2 -namespace k8s.io -id 2079ca3d203
00:00:00 /usr/local/bin/containerd-shim-runc-v2 -namespace k8s.io -id 9ee0fe46c62
00:00:00 /pause
00:00:00 /pause
00:00:00 /usr/local/bin/containerd-shim-runc-v2 -namespace k8s.io -id 476635887b0
00:00:00 /usr/local/bin/containerd-shim-runc-v2 -namespace k8s.io -id 483ff964102
00:00:00 /pause
00:00:00 /pause
00:00:21 kube-apiserver --advertise-address=172.18.0.4 --allow-privileged=true --
00:00:06 kube-controller-manager --allocate-node-cidrs=true --authentication-kube
00:00:06 etcd --advertise-client-urls=https://172.18.0.4:2379 --cert-file=/etc/ku
00:00:03 kube-scheduler --authentication-kubeconfig=/etc/kubernetes/scheduler con
00:00:03 /usr/bin/kubelet --bootstrap-kubeconfig=/etc/kubernetes/bootstrap-kubele
00:00:00 /usr/local/bin/containerd-shim-runc-v2 -namespace k8s.io -id f2d236f617b
00:00:00 /usr/local/bin/containerd-shim-runc-v2 -namespace k8s.io -id e15d3f05f78
00:00:00 /pause
00:00:00 /usr/local/bin/kube-proxy --config=/var/lib/kube-proxy/config.conf --hos
00:00:00 /bin/kindnetd
00:00:00 bash
00:00:00 ps -ef
```

Figure 2.1: Host process list showing control plane components

If you were to exec into a worker node to check the components, you would see all the standard worker node components:

```
     TIME CMD
00:00:00 /sbin/init
00:00:00 /lib/systemd/systemd-journald
00:00:08 /usr/local/bin/containerd
00:00:12 /usr/bin/kubelet --bootstrap-kubeconfig=/etc/kubernetes/bootstrap-kub
00:00:00 /usr/local/bin/containerd-shim-runc-v2 -namespace k8s.io -id 0b4d6d0c
00:00:00 /usr/local/bin/containerd-shim-runc-v2 -namespace k8s.io -id 48699dfc
00:00:00 /pause
00:00:00 /pause
00:00:00 /usr/local/bin/kube-proxy --config=/var/lib/kube-proxy/config.conf --
00:00:00 /bin/kindnetd
00:00:00 bash
00:00:00 ps -ef
```

Figure 2.2: Host process list showing worker components

We will cover the standard Kubernetes components in *Chapter 3, Kubernetes Bootcamp,* including kube-apiserver, kubelets, kube-proxy, kube-scheduler, and kube-controller-manager.

In addition to standard Kubernetes components, both KinD nodes have an additional component that is not part of most standard installations: Kindnet. Kindnet is a **Container Network Interface (CNI)** solution that provides networking to a Kubernetes cluster.

The Kubernetes CNI is a specification that allows Kubernetes to utilize a large list of CNI-based software solutions including Calico, Flannel, Cilium, Kindnet, and more.

In the case of KinD clusters, Kindnet is the included, default CNI when you install a base KinD cluster. While Kindnet is the default CNI, you have the option to disable it and use an alternative, such as Calico, which we will use for our KinD cluster.

Now that you have seen each node and the Kubernetes components, let's take a look at what's included with a base KinD cluster. To show the complete cluster and all the components that are running, we can run the `kubectl get pods --all-namespaces` command. This will list all the running components on the cluster, including the base components we will discuss in *Chapter 3, Kubernetes Bootcamp*. In addition to the base cluster components, you may notice a running pod in a namespace called `local-path-storage`, along with a pod named `local-path-provisioner`. This pod is running one of the add-ons included in KinD, providing the cluster with the ability to auto-provision `PersistentVolumeClaims`:

```
NAMESPACE            NAME                                          READY   STATUS
kube-system          coredns-558bd4d5db-qbfgl                      1/1     Running
kube-system          coredns-558bd4d5db-tdl7g                      1/1     Running
kube-system          etcd-temp-control-plane                       1/1     Running
kube-system          kindnet-hjjr6                                 1/1     Running
kube-system          kindnet-jc4p8                                 1/1     Running
kube-system          kube-apiserver-temp-control-plane             1/1     Running
kube-system          kube-controller-manager-temp-control-plane    1/1     Running
kube-system          kube-proxy-4hf6n                              1/1     Running
kube-system          kube-proxy-x7lp7                              1/1     Running
kube-system          kube-scheduler-temp-control-plane             1/1     Running
local-path-storage   local-path-provisioner-547f784dff-wthkp       1/1     Running
```

Figure 2.3: kubectl get pods showing local-path-provisioner

Most development cluster offerings provide similar, common functions that people need to test deployments on Kubernetes. They all provide a Kubernetes control plane and worker nodes, and most include a default CNI for networking. Few offerings go beyond this base functionality, and as Kubernetes workloads mature, you may find the need for additional plugins such as `local-path-provisioner`. We will leverage this component heavily in some of the exercises in this book because without it, we would have a tougher time deploying many of the examples we use in the exercises.

Why should you care about persistent volumes in your development cluster? It's all about learning – as Kubernetes has matured, more organizations have moved stateful workloads to containers, with many of these deployments requiring persistent storage for their data. Having the ability to work with storage resources on your KinD cluster is a great way to learn about working with storage, all without needing any extra requirements.

Most production clusters running Kubernetes will provide persistent storage to developers. Usually, the storage will be backed by storage systems based on block storage, S3, or NFS.

Aside from NFS, most home labs rarely have the resources to run a full-featured storage system. `local-path-provisioner` removes this limitation from users by providing all the functions to your KinD cluster that an expensive storage solution would provide.

In *Chapter 3, Kubernetes Bootcamp*, we will discuss a few API objects that are part of Kubernetes storage. We will discuss the `CSIdrivers`, `CSInodes`, and `StorageClass` objects. These objects are used by the cluster to provide access to the backend storage system. Once installed and configured, pods consume the storage using the `PersistentVolumes` and `PersistentVolumeClaims` objects. Storage objects are important to understand, but when they were first released, they were difficult for most people to test since they aren't included in most Kubernetes development offerings.

KinD recognized this limitation and chose to bundle a project from Rancher called `local-path-provisioner`, which is based on the Kubernetes local persistent volumes that were introduced in Kubernetes 1.10.

You may be wondering why anyone would need an add-on since Kubernetes has native support for local host persistent volumes. While support may have been added for local persistent storage, Kubernetes has not added auto-provisioning capabilities. CNCF does offer an auto-provisioner, but it must be installed and configured as a separate Kubernetes component. KinD makes it easy to auto-provision since the provisioner is included in all base installations.

Rancher's project provides the following to KinD:

- Auto-creation of `PersistentVolumes` when a `PersistentVolumeClaim` request is created
- A default `StorageClass` named `standard`

When the auto-provisioner sees a `PersistentVolumeClaim` (**PVC**) request hit the API server, a `PersistentVolume` will be created and the pod's PVC will be bound to the newly created `PersistentVolume`. The PVC can then be used by a pod that requires persistent storage.

The `local-path-provisioner` adds a feature to KinD clusters that greatly expands the potential test scenarios that you can run. Without the ability to auto-provision persistent disks, it would be a challenge to test many pre-built deployments that require persistent disks.

With the help of Rancher, KinD provides you with a solution so that you can experiment with dynamic volumes, storage classes, and other storage tests that would otherwise be impossible to run outside of an expensive home lab or a data center.

We will use the provisioner in multiple chapters to provide volumes to different deployments. We will point these out to reinforce the advantages of using auto-provisioning.

Understanding the node image

The node image is what provides KinD the magic to run Kubernetes inside a Docker container. This is an impressive accomplishment since Docker relies on a `systemd` running system and other components that are not included in most container images.

KinD starts off with a base image, which is an image the team has developed that contains everything required for Docker, Kubernetes, and `systemd`. Since the base image is based on an Ubuntu image, the team removes services that are not required and configures `systemd` for Docker. Finally, the node image is created using the base image.

 If you want to know the details of how the base image is created, you can look at the Dockerfile in the KinD team's GitHub repository at `https://github.com/kubernetes-sigs/kind/blob/main/images/base/Dockerfile`.

KinD and Docker networking

Since KinD uses Docker as the container engine to run the cluster nodes, all clusters are limited to the same network constraints that a standard Docker container is limited to. These limitations do not limit testing your KinD Kubernetes cluster from the local host, but they can lead to issues when you want to test containers from other machines on your network.

When you install KinD, a new Docker bridge network will be created, called kind. This network configuration was introduced in KinD v0.8.0, which resolved multiple issues from previous versions that used the default Docker bridge network. Most users will not notice this change, but it's important to know this, as you start to create more advanced KinD clusters with additional containers that you may need to run on the same network with KinD. If you have the requirement to run additional containers on the KinD network, you will need to add `--net=kind` to your `docker run` command.

Along with the Docker networking considerations, we must consider the Kubernetes CNI as well. Officially, the KinD team has limited the networking options to only two CNIs: Kindnet and Calico. Kindnet is the only CNI they will support but you do have the option to disable the default Kindnet installation, which will create a cluster without a CNI installed. After the cluster has been deployed, you can deploy a CNI manifest such as Calico.

Many Kubernetes installations for both small development clusters and enterprise clusters use Tigera's Calico for the CNI and as such, we have elected to use Calico as our CNI for the exercises in this book.

Keeping track of the nesting dolls

Running a solution such as KinD can get confusing due to the container-in-a-container deployment. We compare this to Russian nesting dolls, where one doll fits into another, then another, and so on. As you start to play with KinD for your own cluster, you may lose track of the communication paths between your host, Docker, and the Kubernetes nodes. To keep your sanity, you should have a solid understanding of where each component is running and how you can interact with each one.

The following diagram shows the three layers that must be running to form a KinD cluster. It's important to note that each layer can only interact with the layer directly above it. This means that the KinD container in layer 3 can only see the Docker image running in layer 2, and the Docker image can see the Linux host running in layer 1. If you wanted to communicate directly from the host to a container running in your KinD cluster, you would need to go through the Docker layer, and then to the Kubernetes container in layer 3.

This is important to understand so that you can use KinD effectively as a testing environment:

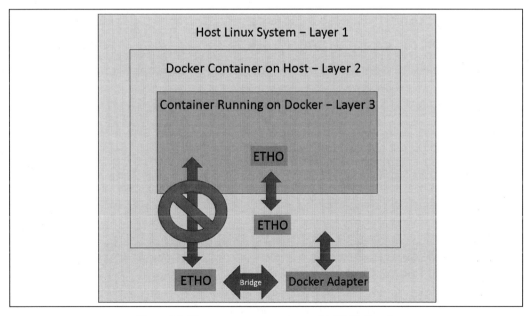

Figure 2.4: Host cannot communicate with KinD directly

As an example, consider that you want to deploy a web server to your Kubernetes cluster. You deploy an Ingress controller in the KinD cluster and you want to test the site using Chrome on your Docker host or a different workstation on the network. You attempt to target the host on port 80 and receive a failure in the browser. Why would this fail?

The pod running the web server is in layer 3 and cannot receive direct traffic from the host or machines on the network. In order to access the web server from your host, you will need to forward the traffic from the Docker layer to the KinD layer. In our case, we need port 80 and port 443. When a container is started with a port, the Docker daemon will forward the incoming traffic from the host to the running Docker container:

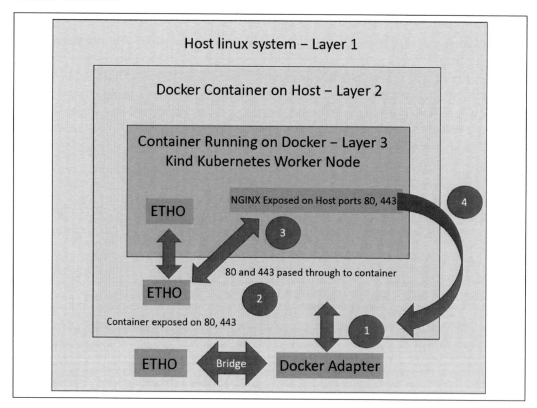

Figure 2.5: Host communicates with KinD via an Ingress controller

With ports 80 and 443 exposed on the Docker container, the Docker daemon will now accept incoming requests for 80 and 443 and the NGINX Ingress controller will receive the traffic. This works because we have exposed ports 80 and 443 in two places on the Docker layer. We have exposed it in the Kubernetes layer by running our NGINX container using host ports 80 and 443.

This installation process will be explained later in this chapter, but for now, you just need to understand the basic flow.

On the host, you make a request for a web server that has an Ingress rule in your Kubernetes cluster:

1. The request looks at the IP address that was requested (in this case, the local IP address).
2. The Ingress on the Docker container running our Kubernetes node is listening on the IP address for ports 80 and 443, so the request is accepted and sent to the running container.
3. The NGINX pod in your Kubernetes cluster has been configured to use the host ports 80 and 443, so the traffic is forwarded to the pod.
4. The user receives the requested web page from the web server via the NGINX Ingress controller.

This is a little confusing, but the more you use KinD and interact with it, the easier this becomes.

To use a KinD cluster for your development requirements, you need to understand how KinD works. So far, you have learned about the node image and how the image is used to create a cluster. You've also learned how KinD network traffic flows between the Docker host and the containers running the cluster. With this base knowledge, we will move on to creating a Kubernetes cluster using KinD.

Installing KinD

The files for this chapter are located in the KinD directory. You can use the provided files, or you can create your own files from this chapter's content. We will explain each step of the installation process in this section.

 At the time of writing, the current version of KinD is 0.11.0, supporting Kubernetes clusters up to 1.21.1

Installing KinD – prerequisites

KinD can be installed using a few different methods, but the easiest and quickest way to start building KinD clusters is to download the KinD binary and the standard Kubernetes kubectl executable to interact with the cluster.

Installing kubectl

Since KinD is a single executable, it does not install `kubectl`. If you do not have `kubectl` installed and you are using an Ubuntu 20.04 system, you can install it by running `snap install`, or you may download it from Google directly.

To install `kubectl` using `snap`, you only need to run a single command:

```
sudo snap install kubectl --classic
```

To install `kubectl` from Google, you need to download the binary, give it the execute permission, and move it to a location in your system's path variable. This can be completed using the steps outlined below:

```
curl -LO https://storage.googleapis.com/kubernetes-release/
release/`curl -s https://storage.googleapis.com/kubernetes-release/
release/stable.txt`/bin/linux/amd64/kubectl
chmod +x ./kubectl
sudo mv ./kubectl /usr/local/bin/kubectl
```

Now that you have `kubectl`, we can move on to downloading the KinD executable.

Installing the KinD binary

Installing KinD is an easy process; it can be done with a single command. You can install KinD by running the included script in this book's repository, located at `/chapter2/install-kind.sh`. Alternatively, you can use the steps below to install it manually:

```
curl -Lo ./kind https://kind.sigs.k8s.io/dl/v0.11.1/kind-linux-amd64
chmod +x ./kind
sudo mv ./kind /usr/bin
```

Once installed, you can verify that KinD has been installed correctly by typing `kind version` into the prompt:

```
kind version
```

This will return the installed version:

```
kind v0.11.1 go1.16.4 linux/amd64
```

The KinD executable provides every option you will need to maintain a cluster's life cycle. Of course, the KinD executable can create and delete clusters, but it also provides the following capabilities:

- Can create custom build base and node images
- Can export `kubeconfig` or log files
- Can retrieve clusters, nodes, or `kubeconfig` files
- Can load images into nodes

Now that you have installed the KinD utility, you are almost ready to create your KinD cluster. Before we execute a few `create cluster` commands, we will explain some of the creation options that KinD provides.

Creating a KinD cluster

Now that you have met all the requirements, you can create your first cluster using the KinD executable. The KinD utility can create a single-node cluster, as well as a complex cluster that's running multiple nodes for the control plane with multiple worker nodes. In this section, we will discuss the KinD executable options. By the end of the chapter, you will have a two-node cluster running – a single control plane node and a single worker node.

 For the exercises in this book, we will install a multi-node cluster. The simple cluster configuration is an example and should not be used for our exercises.

Creating a simple cluster

To create a simple cluster that runs the control plane and a worker node in a single container, you only need to execute the KinD executable with the `create cluster` option.

Let's create a quick single-node cluster to see how quickly KinD creates a fast development cluster. On your host, create a cluster using the following command:

```
kind create cluster
```

This will quickly create a cluster with all the Kubernetes components in a single Docker container by using a cluster name of `kind`. It will also assign the Docker container a name of `kind-control-plane`. If you want to assign a cluster name, rather than the default name, you need to add the `--name <cluster name>` option to the `create cluster` command:

```
Creating cluster "kind" ...
 ✓ Ensuring node image (kindest/node:v1.21.1) 🖼
 ✓ Preparing nodes 📜
 ✓ Writing configuration 📄
 ✓ Starting control-plane 🕹
 ✓ Installing CNI 🔌
 ✓ Installing StorageClass 💾
Set kubectl context to "kind-kind"
You can now use your cluster with:

kubectl cluster-info --context kind-kind
Not sure what to do next? 😊 Check out https://kind.sigs.k8s.io/docs/
user/quick-start/
```

The `create` command will create the cluster/modify the kubectl `config` file. KinD will add the new cluster to your current kubectl `config` file, and it will set the new cluster as the default context. The context is the configuration that will be used to access a cluster and namespace with a set of credentials. We can verify that the cluster was created successfully by listing the nodes using the kubectl utility:

```
kubectl get nodes
```

This will return the running nodes, which, for a basic cluster, are single nodes:

```
NAME                 STATUS    ROLES                     AGE   VERSION
kind-control-plane   Ready     control-plane,master      32m   v1.21.1
```

The main point of deploying this single-node cluster was to show you how quickly KinD can create a cluster that you can use for testing. For our exercises, we want to split up the control plane and worker node so that we can delete this cluster using the steps in the next section.

Deleting a cluster

When you have finished testing, you can delete the cluster using the `delete` command:

```
kind delete cluster --name <cluster name>
```

The `delete` command will quickly delete the cluster, including any entries related to the KinD cluster in your `kubeconfig` file.

A quick single-node cluster is useful for many use cases, but you may want to create a multi-node cluster for various testing scenarios. Creating a more complex cluster requires that you create a config file.

Creating a cluster config file

When creating a multi-node cluster, such as a two-node cluster with custom options, we need to create a cluster config file. The config file is a YAML file and the format should look familiar. Setting values in this file allows you to customize the KinD cluster, including the number of nodes, API options, and more. The config file we'll use to create the cluster for the book is shown here – it is included in this book's repository at `/chapter2/cluster01-kind.yaml`:

```
kind: Cluster
apiVersion: kind.x-k8s.io/v1alpha4
networking:
  apiServerAddress: "0.0.0.0"
  disableDefaultCNI: true
  apiServerPort: 6443
kubeadmConfigPatches:
- |
  apiVersion: kubeadm.k8s.io/v1beta2
  kind: ClusterConfiguration
  metadata:
    name: config
  networking:
    serviceSubnet: "10.96.0.1/12"
    podSubnet: "10.240.0.0/16"
nodes:
- role: control-plane
  extraPortMappings:
  - containerPort: 2379
    hostPort: 2379
  extraMounts:
  - hostPath: /dev
    containerPath: /dev
  - hostPath: /var/run/docker.sock
    containerPath: /var/run/docker.sock
- role: worker
```

```
  extraPortMappings:
  - containerPort: 80
    hostPort: 80
  - containerPort: 443
    hostPort: 443
  - containerPort: 2222
    hostPort: 2222
  extraMounts:
  - hostPath: /dev
    containerPath: /dev
  - hostPath: /var/run/docker.sock
    containerPath: /var/run/docker.sock
```

Details about each of the custom options in the file are provided in the following table:

Config Options	Option Details
apiServerAddress	This configuration option tells the installation what IP address the API server will listen on. By default it will use 127.0.0.1, but since we plan to use the cluster from other networked machines, we have selected to listen on all IP addresses.
disableDefaultCNI	This setting is used to enable or disable the Kindnet installation. The default value is false, but since we want to use Calico as our CNI, we need to set it to true.
kubeadmConfigPatches	This section allows you to set values for other cluster options during the installation. For our configuration, we are setting the CIDR ranges for the ServiceSubnet and the podSubnet.
nodes	This section is where you define the nodes for the cluster. For our cluster, we will create a single control plane node, and a single worker node.
- role: control-plane	The role section allows you to set options for nodes. The first role section is for the control-plane. We have added options to map the localhosts /dev and /var/run/docker.sock, which will be used in the Falco chapter, later in the book.
- role: worker	This is the second node section, which allows you to configure options that the worker nodes will use. For our cluster, we have added the same local mounts that will be used for Falco, and we have also added additional ports to expose for our Ingress controller.

extraPortMappings	To expose ports to your KinD nodes, you need to add them to the extraPortMappings section of the configuration. Each mapping has two values, the container port, and the host port. The host port is the port you would use to target the cluster, while the container port is the port that the container is listening on.
extraMounts	The extraMounts section allows you to add extra mount points to the containers. This comes in handy to expose mounts like /dev and /var/run/docker.sock that we will need for the Falco chapter.

Table 2.3: KinD configuration options

If you plan to create a cluster that goes beyond a single-node cluster without using advanced options, you will need to create a configuration file. Understanding the options available to you will allow you to create a Kubernetes cluster that has advanced components such as Ingress controllers or multiple nodes to test failure and recovery procedures for deployments.

Now that you know how to create a simple all-in-one container for running a cluster and how to create a multi-node cluster using a config file, let's discuss a more complex cluster example.

Multi-node cluster configuration

If you only wanted a multi-node cluster without any extra options, you could create a simple configuration file that lists the number and node types you want in the cluster. The following config file will create a cluster with three control plane nodes and three worker nodes:

```
kind: Cluster
apiVersion: kind.x-k8s.io/v1alpha4
nodes:
- role: control-plane
- role: control-plane
- role: control-plane
- role: worker
- role: worker
- role: worker
```

Using multiple control plane servers introduces additional complexity since we can only target a single host or IP in our configuration files. To make this configuration usable, we need to deploy a load balancer in front of our cluster.

KinD has considered this, and if you do deploy multiple control plane nodes, the installation will create an additional container running a HAProxy load balancer. During the creation of a multi-node cluster, you will see a few additional lines regarding configuring an extra load balancer, joining additional control-plane nodes and joining extra worker nodes – as shown below:

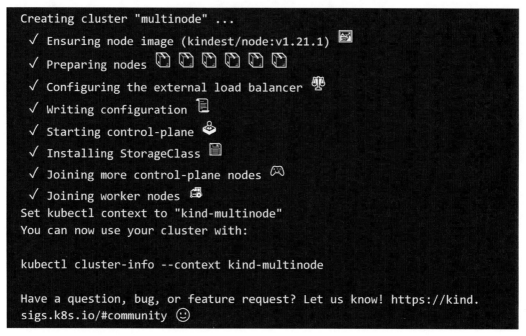

```
Creating cluster "multinode" ...
 ✓ Ensuring node image (kindest/node:v1.21.1) 🖼
 ✓ Preparing nodes 📄 📄 📄 📄 📄 📄
 ✓ Configuring the external load balancer ⚖
 ✓ Writing configuration 📜
 ✓ Starting control-plane 🕹
 ✓ Installing StorageClass 💾
 ✓ Joining more control-plane nodes 🎮
 ✓ Joining worker nodes 🖥
Set kubectl context to "kind-multinode"
You can now use your cluster with:

kubectl cluster-info --context kind-multinode

Have a question, bug, or feature request? Let us know! https://kind.
sigs.k8s.io/#community ☺
```

If we look at the running containers from a multi-node config, we will see six node containers running and a HAProxy container:

Container ID	Image	Port	Names
d9107c31eedb	kindest/ haproxy:v20200708-548e36db	0.0.0.0:6443	multinode-external-load-balancer
03a113144845	kindest/node:v1.21.1	127.0.0.1:44445->6443/tcp	multinode-control-plane3
9b078ecd69b7	kindest/node:v1.21.1		multinode-worker2
b779fa15206a	kindest/node:v1.21.1		multinode-worker
8171baafac56	kindest/node:v1.21.1	127.0.0.1:42673->6443/tcp	multinode-control-plane

3ede5e163eb0	kindest/node:v1.21.1	127.0.0.1:43547->6443/tcp	multinode-control-plane2
6a85afc27cfe	kindest/node:v1.21.1		multinode-worker3

Table 2.4: KinD configuration options

Since we have a single host, each control plane node and the HAProxy container are running on unique ports. Each container needs to be exposed to the host so that they can receive incoming requests. In this example, the important one to note is the port assigned to HAProxy, since that's the target port for the cluster. If you were to look at the Kubernetes config file, you would see that it is targeting `https://127.0.0.1:42673`, which is the port that's been assigned to the HAProxy container.

When a command is executed using `kubectl`, it is sent directly to the HAProxy server. Using a configuration file that was created by KinD during the cluster's creation, the HAProxy container knows how to route traffic between the three control plane nodes. In the HAProxy container, we can verify the configuration by viewing the config file, found at `/usr/local/etc/haproxy/haproxy.cfg`:

```
# generated by kind
global
  log /dev/log local0
  log /dev/log local1 notice
  daemon

resolvers docker
  nameserver dns 127.0.0.11:53

defaults
  log global
  mode tcp
  option dontlognull
  # TODO: tune these
  timeout connect 5000
  timeout client 50000
  timeout server 50000
  # allow to boot despite dns don't resolve backends
  default-server init-addr none

frontend control-plane
```

```
  bind *:6443

  default_backend kube-apiservers

backend kube-apiservers
  option httpchk GET /healthz
  # TODO: we should be verifying (!)
  server multinode-control-plane multinode-control-plane:6443 check
check-ssl verify none resolvers docker resolve-prefer ipv4
  server multinode-control-plane2 multinode-control-plane2:6443 check
check-ssl verify none resolvers docker resolve-prefer ipv4
  server multinode-control-plane3 multinode-control-plane3:6443 check
check-ssl verify none resolvers docker resolve-prefer ipv4
```

As shown in the preceding configuration file, there is a backend section called `kube-apiservers` that contains the three control plane containers. Each entry contains the Docker IP address of a control plane node with a port assignment of `6443`, targeting the API server running in the container. When you request `https://127.0.0.1:32791`, that request will hit the HAProxy container, then, using the rules in the HAProxy configuration file, the request will be routed to one of the three nodes in the list.

Since our cluster is now fronted by a load balancer, we have a highly available control plane for testing.

The included HAProxy image is not configurable. It is only provided to handle the control plane and to load balance the API servers. Due to this limitation, if you needed to use a load balancer for the worker nodes, you will need to provide your own.

An example use case for this would be if you wanted to use an Ingress controller on multiple worker nodes. You would need a load balancer in front of the worker nodes to accept incoming `80` and `443` requests that would forward the traffic to each node running NGINX. At the end of this chapter, we have provided an example configuration that includes a custom HAProxy configuration for load balancing traffic to the worker nodes.

Customizing the control plane and Kubelet options

You may want to go further than this to test features such as OIDC integration or Kubernetes feature gates. KinD uses the same configuration that you would use for a kubeadm installation. As an example, if you wanted to integrate a cluster with an OIDC provider, you could add the required options to the configuration patch section:

```
kind: Cluster
apiVersion: kind.x-k8s.io/v1alpha4
kubeadmConfigPatches:
- |
  kind: ClusterConfiguration
  metadata:
    name: config
  apiServer:
    extraArgs:
      oidc-issuer-url: "https://oidc.testdomain.com/auth/idp/k8sIdp"
      oidc-client-id: "kubernetes"
      oidc-username-claim: sub
      oidc-client-id: kubernetes
      oidc-ca-file: /etc/oidc/ca.crt
nodes:
- role: control-plane
- role: control-plane
- role: control-plane
- role: worker
- role: worker
- role: worker
```

For a list of available configuration options, take a look at the *Customizing control plane configuration with kubeadm* page on the Kubernetes site at `https://kubernetes.io/docs/setup/production-environment/tools/kubeadm/control-plane-flags/`.

Now that you have created the cluster file, you can create your KinD cluster.

Creating a custom KinD cluster

Finally! Now that you are familiar with KinD, we can move forward and create our cluster.

We need to create a controlled, known environment, so we will give the cluster a name and provide the config file that we discussed in the previous section.

Make sure that you are in your cloned repository under the chapter2 directory. If you want to create the entire cluster using our supplied script, you can simply execute the create-cluster.sh script in the chapter2 directory.

If you want to create a KinD cluster interactively, with our required options, you need to run the KinD installer with the following config file, which is found in the chapter2 directory:

```
kind create cluster --name cluster01 --config cluster01-kind.yaml
```

The --name option will set the name of the cluster to cluster01, and --config tells the installer to use the cluster01-kind.yaml config file.

When you execute the installer on your host, KinD will start the installation and tell you each step that is being performed. The entire cluster creation process should take less than 2 minutes:

```
Creating cluster "cluster01" ...
 ✓ Ensuring node image (kindest/node:v1.21.1) 🖼
 ✓ Preparing nodes 📦 📦 📦 📦 📦 📦
 ✓ Writing configuration 📜
 ✓ Starting control-plane 🕹
 ✓ Installing StorageClass 💾
 ✓ Joining worker nodes 🚜
Set kubectl context to "kind-cluster01"
You can now use your cluster with:
kubectl cluster-info --context kind-cluster01
Have a question, bug, or feature request? Let us know! https://kind.
sigs.k8s.io/#community 😊
```

The final step in the deployment creates or edits an existing Kubernetes config file. In either case, the installer creates a new context with the name kind-<cluster name> and sets it as the default context.

While it may appear that the cluster installation procedure has completed its tasks, the cluster **is not** ready yet.

Some of the tasks take a few minutes to fully initialize and since we disabled the default CNI to use Calico, we still need to deploy Calico to provide cluster networking.

Installing Calico

To provide networking to the pods in the cluster, we need to install a CNI. We have elected to install Calico as our CNI and since KinD only includes the Kindnet CNI, we need to install Calico manually.

If you were to pause after the creation step and look at the cluster, you would notice that some pods are in a pending state:

```
coredns-6955765f44-86l77    0/1  Pending  0  10m
coredns-6955765f44-bznjl    0/1  Pending  0  10m
local-path-provisioner-7    0/1  Pending  0  11m 745554f7f-jgmxv
```

The pods listed here require a working CNI to start. This puts the pods into a pending state, where they are waiting for a network. Since we did not deploy the default CNI, our cluster does not have networking support. To get these pods from pending to running, we need to install a CNI – and for our cluster, that will be Calico.

To install Calico, we will use the standard Calico operator deployment, requiring only two manifests. To deploy the Calico operator, use the following commands:

```
kubectl create -f https://docs.projectcalico.org/manifests/tigera-operator.yaml
```

Then deploy the custom resources. Since we are setting the CIDR range to a custom range, we have included a custom resource manifest in the repository, in the chapter2 directory:

```
kubectl create -f calico.yaml
```

As it deploys, you will see that a number of Kubernetes objects are created.

The installation process will take about a minute and you can check on its status using kubectl get pods -n kube-system. You will see that three Calico pods were created. Two are calico-node pods, while the other is the calico-kube-controller pod:

```
NAME                                        READY STATUS  RESTARTS AGE
calico-kube-controllers -5b644bc49c-nm5wn   1/1   Running  0       64s
calico-node-4dqnv                           1/1   Running  0       64s
calico-node-vwbpf                           1/1   Running  0       64s
```

If you check the two CoreDNS pods in the `kube-system` namespace again, you will notice that they have changed from the pending state, from before we installed Calico, to being in a running state:

```
coredns-6955765f44-86177   1/1   Running   0   18m
coredns-6955765f44-bznjl   1/1   Running   0   18m
```

Now that the cluster has a working CNI installed, any pods that were dependent on networking will be in a running state.

Installing an Ingress controller

We have a chapter dedicated to Ingress to explain all the technical details. Since we are deploying a cluster and we require Ingress for future chapters, we need to deploy an Ingress controller to show a complete cluster build. All these details will be explained in more detail in *Chapter 4, Services, Load Balancing, ExternalDNS, and Global Balancing*.

Installing the NGINX Ingress controller requires only two manifests, which we will pull from the internet to make the installation easy. To install the controller, execute the following command:

```
kubectl apply -f https://raw.githubusercontent.com/kubernetes/ingress-
nginx/master/deploy/static/provider/kind/deploy.yaml
```

The deployment will create a few Kubernetes objects that are required for Ingress in a namespace called `ingress-nginx`:

```
namespace/ingress-nginx created
serviceaccount/ingress-nginx created
configmap/ingress-nginx-controller created
clusterrole.rbac.authorization.k8s.io/ingress-nginx created
clusterrolebinding.rbac.authorization.k8s.io/ingress-nginx created
role.rbac.authorization.k8s.io/ingress-nginx created
rolebinding.rbac.authorization.k8s.io/ingress-nginx created
service/ingress-nginx-controller-admission created
service/ingress-nginx-controller created
deployment.apps/ingress-nginx-controller created
validatingwebhookconfiguration.admissionregistration.k8s.io/ingress-
nginx-admission created
serviceaccount/ingress-nginx-admission created
clusterrole.rbac.authorization.k8s.io/ingress-nginx-admission created
clusterrolebinding.rbac.authorization.k8s.io/ingress-nginx-admission
created
```

```
role.rbac.authorization.k8s.io/ingress-nginx-admission created
rolebinding.rbac.authorization.k8s.io/ingress-nginx-admission created
job.batch/ingress-nginx-admission-create created
job.batch/ingress-nginx-admission-patch created
```

Since this manifest has been created for KinD, you do not need to edit or patch the deployment for any reason, it comes preconfigured to integrate with KinD by default.

Congratulations! You now have a fully functioning, two-node Kubernetes cluster running Calico with an Ingress controller.

Reviewing your KinD cluster

With a Kubernetes cluster now available, we have the ability to look at Kubernetes objects first-hand. This will help you understand the next chapter, *Kubernetes Bootcamp*, where we will cover many of the base objects included in a Kubernetes cluster. While we will explain most objects in the next chapter, we need to introduce the objects that Kubernetes uses to provide storage. In the next section we introduce the objects included with KinD that provide persistent storage to your workloads. In particular, we will discuss the storage objects that are included with your KinD cluster.

KinD storage objects

Remember that KinD includes Rancher's auto-provisioner to provide automated persistent disk management for the cluster. Kubernetes has a number of storage objects, there is one object that the auto-provisioner does not require since it uses a base Kubernetes feature: it does not require a `CSIdriver`. Since the ability to use local host paths as PVCs is part of Kubernetes, we will not see any `CSIdriver` objects in our KinD cluster.

The first objects in our KinD cluster we will discuss are our `CSInodes`. Any node that can run a workload will have a `CSInode` object. On our KinD clusters, both nodes have a `CSInode` object, which you can verify by executing `kubectl get csinodes`:

```
NAME                       DRIVERS   AGE
cluster01-control-plane    0         20m
cluster01-worker           0         20m
```

If we were to describe one of the nodes using `kubectl describe csinodes <node name>`, you would see the details of the object:

```
Name:           cluster01-worker
Labels:         <none>
```

```
Annotations:              storage.alpha.kubernetes.io/migrated-plugins:
kubernetes.io/cinder
CreationTimestamp:    Sun, 27 Jun 2021 00:12:03 +0000
Spec:
Events:  <none>
```

The main thing to point out is the Spec section of the output. This lists the details of any drivers that may be installed to support backend storage systems. Since we do not have a backend storage system, we do not require an additional driver on our cluster.

Storage drivers

As we already mentioned, your KinD cluster does not have any additional storage drivers installed. If you execute kubectl get csidrivers, the API will not list any resources.

KinD storage classes

To attach to any cluster-provided storage, the cluster requires a StorageClass object. Rancher's provider creates a default storage class called standard. It also sets the class as the default StorageClass, so you do not need to provide a StorageClass name in your PVC requests. If a default StorageClass is not set, every PVC request will require a StorageClass name in the request. If a default class is not enabled and a PVC request fails to set a StorageClass name, the PVC allocation will fail since the API server won't be able to link the request to a StorageClass.

> On a production cluster, it is considered a good practice to omit assigning a default StorageClass. Depending on your users, you may have deployments that forget to set a class, and the default storage system may not fit the deployment needs. This issue may not occur until it becomes a production issue, and that may impact business revenue or the company's reputation. If you don't assign a default class, the developer will encounter a failed PVC request, and the issue will be discovered before any harm comes to the business. It also forces developers to provide a StorageClass that matches desired performance, letting them use cheaper storage for non-critical systems, or high-speed storage for critical workloads.

To list the storage classes on the cluster, execute kubectl get storageclasses, or use the shortened version with sc instead of storageclasses:

```
NAME   PROVISIONER  RECLAIMPOLICY      VOLUMEBINDINGMODE
ALLOWVOLUMEEXPANSION
standard (default)   rancher.io/local-path   Delete
WaitForFirstConsumer  false
```

Next, let's learn how to use the provisioner.

Using KinD's storage provisioner

Using the included provisioner is very simple. Since it can auto-provision the storage and is set as the default class, any PVC requests that are coming in are seen by the provisioning pod, which then creates `PersistentVolume` and `PersistentVolumeClaim`.

To show this process, let's go through the necessary steps. The following is the output of running `kubectl get pv` and `kubectl get pvc` on a base KinD cluster:

```
kubectl get pv
No resources found
```

Remember that `PersistentVolume` is not a namespaced object, so we don't need to add a namespace option to the command. PVCs are namespaced objects, so I told Kubernetes to show me the PVCs that are available in all the namespaces. Since this is a new cluster and none of the default workloads require persistent disk, there are no PV or PVC objects.

Without an auto-provisioner, we would need to create a PV before a PVC could claim the volume. Since we have the Rancher provisioner running in our cluster, we can test the creation process by deploying a pod with a PVC request like the one listed here, which we will name `pvctest.yaml`:

```
kind: PersistentVolumeClaim
apiVersion: v1
metadata:
  name: test-claim
spec:
  accessModes:
    - ReadWriteOnce
  resources:
    requests:
      storage: 1Mi
---
kind: Pod
apiVersion: v1
```

```
metadata:
  name: test-pvc-claim
spec:
  containers:
  - name: test-pod
    image: busybox
    command:
      - "/bin/sh"
    args:
      - "-c"
      - "touch /mnt/test && exit 0 || exit 1"
    volumeMounts:
      - name: test-pvc
        mountPath: "/mnt"
  restartPolicy: "Never"
  volumes:
    - name: test-pvc
      persistentVolumeClaim:
        claimName: test-claim
```

This PVC request will be named `test-claim` in the default namespace and it requests a 1 MB volume. We do need to include the `StorageClass` option since KinD has set a default `StorageClass` for the cluster.

To create the PVC, we can execute a `create` command using kubectl, such as `kubectl create -f pvctest.yaml` – Kubernetes will return, stating that the PVC has been created, but it's important to note that this does not mean that the PVC is fully working. The PVC object has been created, but if any dependencies are missing in the PVC request, it will still create the object, though it will fail to fully create the PVC request.

After creating a PVC, you can check the real status using one of two options. The first is a simple `get` command; that is, `kubectl get pvc`. Since my request is in the default namespace, I don't need to include a namespace value in the `get` command (note that we had to shorten the volume's name so that it fits the page):

NAME	STATUS	VOLUME	CAPACITY	ACCESS MODES	STORAGECLASS
AGE					
test-claim	Bound	pvc-b6ecf50…	1Mi	RWO	standard
15s					

We know that we created a PVC request in the manifest, but we did not create a PV request. If we look at the PVs now, we will see that a single PV was created from our PVC request. Again, we shortened the PV name in order to fit the output on a single line:

NAME	CAPACITY	ACCESS MODES	RECLAIM POLICY	STATUS	CLAIM
pvc-b6ecf…	1Mi	RWO	Delete	Bound	default/test-
claim					

With so many workloads requiring persistent disks, it is very important to understand how Kubernetes workloads integrate with storage systems. In this section, you learned how KinD adds the auto-provisioner to the cluster. We will reinforce our knowledge of these Kubernetes storage objects in the next chapter, *Chapter 3, Kubernetes Bootcamp*.

Adding a custom load balancer for Ingress

 This section is a complex topic that covers adding a custom HAProxy container that you can use to load balance worker nodes in a KinD cluster. *You should not deploy these steps on the KinD cluster that we will use for the remaining chapters.*

We added this section for anybody that may want to know more about how to load balance between multiple worker nodes.

KinD does not include a load balancer for worker nodes. The included HAProxy container only creates a configuration file for the API server; the team does not officially support any modifications to the default image or configuration. Since you will interact with load balancers in your everyday work, we wanted to add a section on how to configure your own HAProxy container in order to load balance between three KinD nodes.

First, we will not use this configuration for any of chapters in this book. We want to make the exercises available to everyone, so to limit the required resources, we will always use the two-node cluster that we created earlier in this chapter. If you want to test KinD nodes with a load balancer, we suggest using a different Docker host or waiting until you have finished this book and deleting your KinD cluster.

Installation prerequisites

We assume that you have a KinD cluster based on the following configuration:

- Any number of control plane nodes
- Three worker nodes
- Cluster name is `cluster01`
- A working version of **Kindnet or Calico** as the **CNI**
- NGINX Ingress controller installed

Creating the KinD cluster configuration

Since you will use an HAProxy container exposed on ports `80` and `443` on your Docker host, you do not need to expose any ports in your cluster `config` file.

To make a test deployment easier, you can use the example cluster config shown here, which will create a simple six-node cluster with Kindnet disabled:

```
kind: Cluster
apiVersion: kind.x-k8s.io/v1alpha4
networking:
  apiServerAddress: "0.0.0.0"
  disableDefaultCNI: true
kubeadmConfigPatches:
- |
  apiVersion: kubeadm.k8s.io/v1beta2
  kind: ClusterConfiguration
  metadata:
    name: config
  networking:
    serviceSubnet: "10.96.0.1/12"
    podSubnet: "192.168.0.0/16"
nodes:
- role: control-plane
- role: control-plane
- role: control-plane
- role: worker
- role: worker
- role: worker
```

You need to install Calico using the same manifest that we used earlier in this chapter. After installing Calico, you need to install the NGINX Ingress controller using the steps provided earlier in this chapter.

Once you've deployed Calico and NGINX, you should have a working base cluster. Now, you can move on to deploying a custom HAProxy container.

Deploying a custom HAProxy container

HAProxy offers a container on Docker Hub that is easy to deploy, requiring only a config file to start the container.

To create the configuration file, you will need to know the IP addresses of each worker node in the cluster. In this book's GitHub repository, we have included a script file that will find this information for you, create the config file, and start the HAProxy container. It is located under the HAProxy directory and is called HAProxy-ingress.sh.

To help you better understand this script, we will break out sections of the script and detail what each section is executing. Firstly, the following code block gets the IP addresses of each worker node in our cluster and saves the results in a variable. We will need this information for the backend server list:

```bash
#!/bin/bash
worker1=$(docker inspect --format '{{ .NetworkSettings.IPAddress }}' cluster01-worker)
worker2=$(docker inspect --format '{{ .NetworkSettings.IPAddress }}' cluster01-worker2)
worker3=$(docker inspect --format '{{ .NetworkSettings.IPAddress }}' cluster01-worker3)
```

Next, since we will use a bind mount when we start the container, we need to have the configuration file in a known location. We elected to store it in the current user's home folder, under a directory called HAProxy:

```bash
# Create an HAProxy directory in the current users home folder
mkdir ~/HAProxy
```

Next, the following part of the script will create the HAProxy directory:

```bash
# Create the HAProxy.cfg file for the worker nodes
tee ~/HAProxy/HAProxy.cfg <<EOF
```

The global section of the configuration sets process-wide security and performance settings:

```
global
  log /dev/log local0
  log /dev/log local1 notice
  daemon
```

The `defaults` section is used to configure values that will apply to all frontend and backend sections in the configuration value:

```
defaults
  log global
  mode tcp
  timeout connect 5000
  timeout client 50000
  timeout server 50000
frontend workers_https
  bind *:443
  mode tcp
  use_backend ingress_https
backend ingress_https
  option httpchk GET /healthz
  mode tcp
  server worker $worker1:443 check port 80
  server worker2 $worker2:443 check port 80
  server worker3 $worker3:443 check port 80
```

This tells HAProxy to create a frontend called `workers_https` and the IP addresses and ports to bind for incoming requests, to use TCP mode, and to use a backend named `ingress_https`.

The `ingress_https` backend includes the three worker nodes that are using port 443 as a destination. The check port is a health check that will test port 80. If a server replies on port 80, it will be added as a target for requests. While this is an HTTPS port 443 rule, we are only using port 80 to check for a network reply from the NGINX pod:

```
frontend workers_http
  bind *:80
  use_backend ingress_http
backend ingress_http
  mode http
  option httpchk GET /healthz
  server worker $worker1:80 check port 80
  server worker2 $worker2:80 check port 80
  server worker3 $worker3:80 check port 80
```

This `frontend` section creates a frontend that accepts incoming HTTP traffic on port 80. It then uses the list of servers in the backend, named `ingress_http`, for endpoints.

Just like in the HTTPS section, we are using port **80** to check for any nodes that are running a service on port **80**. Any endpoint that replies to the check will be added as a destination for HTTP traffic, and any nodes that do not have NGINX running on them will not reply, which means they won't be added as destinations:

```
EOF
```

This ends the creation of our file. The final file will be created in the `HAProxy` directory:

```
# Start the HAProxy Container for the Worker Nodes
docker run --name HAProxy-workers-lb -d -p 80:80 -p 443:443 -v ~/
HAProxy:/usr/local/etc/HAProxy:ro HAProxy -f /usr/local/etc/HAProxy/
HAProxy.cfg
```

The final step is to start a Docker container running HAProxy with our created configuration file containing the three worker nodes, exposed on the Docker host on ports **80** and **443**.

Now that you have learned how to install a custom HAProxy load balancer for your worker nodes, let's look at how the configuration works.

Understanding HAProxy traffic flow

The cluster will have a total of eight containers running. Six of these containers will be the standard Kubernetes components; that is, three control plane servers and three worker nodes. The other two containers are KinD's HAProxy server, and your own custom HAProxy container:

```
IMAGE                       PORTS                                        NAMES
haproxy                     0.0.0.0:80->80/tcp, 0.0.0.0:443->443/tcp     haproxy-workers-lb
kindest/haproxy:2.1.1-alpine  0.0.0.0:32776->6443/tcp                    cluster01-external-load-balance

kindest/node:v1.17.0                                                     cluster01-worker
kindest/node:v1.17.0        127.0.0.1:32801->6443/tcp                    cluster01-control-plane
kindest/node:v1.17.0        127.0.0.1:32799->6443/tcp                    cluster01-control-plane3
kindest/node:v1.17.0                                                     cluster01-worker2
kindest/node:v1.17.0        127.0.0.1:32800->6443/tcp                    cluster01-control-plane2
kindest/node:v1.17.0                                                     cluster01-worker3
```

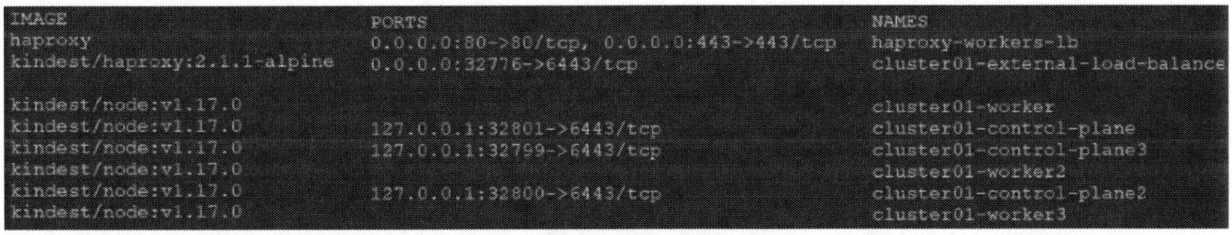

Figure 2.6: Custom HAProxy container running

There are a few differences between this cluster output versus our two-node cluster for the exercises. Notice that the worker nodes are not exposed on any host ports. The worker nodes do not need any mappings since we have our new HAProxy server running. If you look at the HAProxy container we created, it is exposed on host ports **80** and **443**. This means that any incoming requests to the host on port **80** or **443** will be directed to the custom HAProxy container.

The default NGINX deployment only has a single replica, which means that the Ingress controller is running on a single node. If we look at the logs for the HAProxy container, we will see something interesting:

```
[NOTICE] 093/191701 (1) : New worker #1 (6) forked
[WARNING] 093/191701 (6) : Server ingress_https/worker is DOWN, reason:
Layer4 connection problem, info: "SSL handshake failure (Connection
refused)", check duration: 0ms. 2 active and 0 backup servers left. 0
sessions active, 0 requeued, 0 remaining in queue.
[WARNING] 093/191702 (6) : Server ingress_https/worker3 is DOWN,
reason: Layer4 connection problem, info: "SSL handshake failure
(Connection refused)", check duration: 0ms. 1 active and 0 backup
servers left. 0 sessions active, 0 requeued, 0 remaining in queue.
[WARNING] 093/191702 (6) : Server ingress_http/worker is DOWN, reason:
Layer4 connection problem, info: "Connection refused", check duration:
0ms. 2 active and 0 backup servers left. 0 sessions active, 0 requeued,
0 remaining in queue.
[WARNING] 093/191703 (6) : Server ingress_http/worker3 is DOWN, reason:
Layer4 connection problem, info: "Connection refused", check duration:
0ms. 1 active and 0 backup servers left. 0 sessions active, 0 requeued,
0 remaining in queue.
```

You may have noticed a few errors in the log, such as SSL handshake failure and Connection refused. While these do look like errors, they are actually failed checked events on the worker nodes. Remember that NGINX is only running in a single pod, and since we have all three nodes in our HAProxy backend configuration, it will check for the ports on each node. Any nodes that fail to reply will not be used to load balance traffic. In our current config, this does load balance, since we only have NGINX on one node. It does, however, provide high availability to the Ingress controller.

If you look carefully at the log output, you will see how many servers are active on the defined backend; for example:

```
check duration: 0ms. 1 active and 0 backup servers left.
```

Each server pool in the log output shows 1 active endpoint, so we know that the HAProxy has successfully found an NGINX controller on both port 80 and 443.

To find out which worker the HAProxy server has connected to, we can use the failed connections recorded in the log. Each backend will list the failed connections.

For example, we know that the node that is working is `cluster01-worker2` based on the logs that show the other two worker nodes as `DOWN`:

```
Server ingress_https/worker is DOWN Server ingress_https/worker3 is
DOWN
```

Let's simulate a node failure to prove that HAProxy is providing high availability to NGINX.

Simulating a kubelet failure

Remember that KinD nodes are ephemeral and that stopping any container may cause it to fail on restart. So, how can we simulate a worker node failure since we can't simply stop the container?

To simulate a failure, we can stop the kubelet service on a node, which will alert `kube-apisever` so that it doesn't schedule any additional pods on the node. In our example, we want to prove that HAProxy is providing HA support for NGINX. We know that the running container is on `worker2`, so that's the node we want to "take down."

The easiest way to stop `kubelet` is to send a `docker exec` command to the container:

```
docker exec cluster01-worker2 systemctl stop kubelet
```

You will not see any output from this command, but if you wait a few minutes for the cluster to receive the updated node status, you can verify the node is down by looking at a list of nodes:

```
kubectl get nodes
```

You will receive the following output:

```
NAME                        STATUS      ROLES       AGE
cluster01-control-plane     Ready       master      45m
cluster01-control-plane2    Ready       master      45m
cluster01-control-plane3    Ready       master      43m
cluster01-worker            Ready       <none>      43m
cluster01-worker2           NotReady    <none>      43m
cluster01-worker3           Ready       <none>      43m
```

Figure 2.7: worker2 is in a NotReady state

This verifies that we just simulated a kubelet failure and that `worker2` is in a `NotReady` status.

Any pods that were running before the kubelet "failure" will continue to run, but `kube-scheduler` will not schedule any workloads on the node until the kubelet issue is resolved. Since we know the pod will not restart on the node, we can delete the pod so that it can be rescheduled on a different node.

You need to get the pod name and then delete it to force a restart:

```
kubectl get pods -n ingress-nginx
```

This will return the pods in the namespace, for example:

```
nginx-ingress-controller-7d6bf88c86-r7ztq
```

Delete the ingress controller pod using kubectl:

```
kubectl delete pod nginx-ingress-controller-7d6bf88c86-r7ztq -n
ingress-nginx
```

This will force the scheduler to start the container on another worker node. It will also cause the HAProxy container to update the backend list, since the NGINX controller has moved to another worker node.

If you look at the HAProxy logs again, you will see that HAProxy has updated the backends to include `cluster01-worker3` and that it has removed `cluster01-worker2` from the active servers list:

```
[WARNING] 093/194006 (6) : Server ingress_https/worker3 is UP, reason:
Layer7 check passed, code: 200, info: "OK", check duration: 4ms. 2
active and 0 backup servers online. 0 sessions requeued, 0 total in
queue.
[WARNING] 093/194008 (6) : Server ingress_http/worker3 is UP, reason:
Layer7 check passed, code: 200, info: "OK", check duration: 0ms. 2
active and 0 backup servers online. 0 sessions requeued, 0 total in
queue.
[WARNING] 093/195130 (6) : Server ingress_http/worker2 is DOWN, reason:
Layer4 timeout, check duration: 2000ms. 1 active and 0 backup servers
left. 0 sessions active, 0 requeued, 0 remaining in queue.
[WARNING] 093/195131 (6) : Server ingress_https/worker2 is DOWN,
reason: Layer4 timeout, check duration: 2001ms. 1 active and 0 backup
servers left. 0 sessions active, 0 requeued, 0 remaining in queue.
```

If you plan to use this HA cluster for additional tests, you will want to restart the kubelet on `cluster01-worker2`.

If you plan to delete the HA cluster, you can just run a KinD cluster delete and all the nodes will be deleted.

Summary

In this chapter, you learned about the Kubernetes SIG project called KinD. We went into details on how to install optional components in a KinD cluster, including Calico as the CNI and NGINX as the Ingress controller. Finally, we covered the details of the Kubernetes storage objects that are included with a KinD cluster.

Hopefully, with the help of this chapter, you now understand the power that using KinD can bring to you and your organization. It offers an easy-to-deploy, fully configurable Kubernetes cluster. The number of running clusters on a single host is theoretically limited only by the host resources.

In the next chapter, we will dive into Kubernetes objects. We've called the next chapter *Kubernetes Bootcamp* since it will cover the majority of the base Kubernetes objects and what each one is used for. The next chapter can be considered a "Kubernetes pocket guide." It contains a quick reference to Kubernetes objects and what they do, as well as when to use them.

It's a packed chapter and is designed to be a refresher for those of you who have experience with Kubernetes, or as a crash course for those of you who are new to Kubernetes. Our intention with this book is to go beyond the base Kubernetes objects since there are many books on the market today that cover the basics of Kubernetes very well.

Questions

1. What object must be created before you can create a `PersistentVolumeClaim`?

    a. PVC

    b. Disk

    c. `PersistentVolume`

    d. `VirtualDisk`

2. KinD includes a dynamic disk provisioner. Which company created the provisioner?

    a. Microsoft

    b. CNCF

    c. VMware

    d. Rancher

3. If you created a KinD cluster with multiple worker nodes, what would you install to direct traffic to each node?

   a. Load balancer

   b. Proxy server

   c. Nothing

   d. Network load balancer

4. True or false: A Kubernetes cluster can only have one CSIdriver installed.

   a. True

   b. False

Join our book's Discord space

Join the book's Discord workspace for a monthly *Ask me Anything* session with the authors: `https://packt.link/K8EntGuide`

3

Kubernetes Bootcamp

We are sure that many of you have used Kubernetes in some capacity — you may have clusters running in production or you may have kicked the tires using kubeadm, Minikube, or Docker Desktop. Our goal for this book is to go beyond the basics of Kubernetes and, as such, we didn't want to rehash all the basics of Kubernetes. Instead, we added this chapter as a bootcamp for anyone that may be new to Kubernetes or might have only played around with it a bit.

Since this is a bootcamp chapter, we will not go in depth into every topic, but by the end, you should know enough about the basics of Kubernetes to understand the remaining chapters. If you have a strong Kubernetes background, you may still find this chapter useful as a refresher, and we will get into more complex topics starting in *Chapter 4, Services, Load Balancing, ExternalDNS, and Global Balancing*.

In this chapter, we will cover the components of a running Kubernetes cluster, which include the control plane and the worker node(s). We will detail each Kubernetes resource and its use cases. If you have used Kubernetes in the past and are comfortable using kubectl and fully understand Kubernetes resources (such as **DaemonSets**, **StatefulSets**, and **ReplicaSets**), this chapter may be a good review before moving on to *Chapter 4, Services, Load Balancing, ExternalDNS, and Global Balancing*, and K8GB. In this chapter, we will cover the following topics:

- An overview of Kubernetes components
- Exploring the control plane
- Understanding the worker node components
- Interacting with the API server
- Introducing Kubernetes resources

By the end of this chapter, you will have a solid understanding of the most commonly used cluster resources. Understanding Kubernetes resources is important for both cluster operators and cluster administrators.

Technical requirements

This chapter has no technical requirements.

If you want to execute commands while learning about the resources, you can use the KinD cluster that was deployed in the previous chapter.

An overview of Kubernetes components

In any infrastructure, it is always a good idea to understand how the systems work together to provide services. With so many installer options out there today, many Kubernetes users have not had the need to understand how Kubernetes components integrate.

A few short years ago, if you wanted to run a Kubernetes cluster, you needed to install and configure each component manually. It was a steep learning curve to install a functioning cluster, which often led to frustration, causing many people and companies to say "*Kubernetes is just too difficult.*" The advantage of installing manually was that you truly understood how each component interacted, and if your cluster ran into issues after installation, you knew what to look for.

Nowadays, most people will click a button on a cloud provider and have a fully functioning Kubernetes cluster in minutes. On-premises installations have become just as easy, with options from Google, Red Hat, Rancher, and more removing the complexities of installing a Kubernetes cluster. The issues we see occur when you run into a problem or have questions after the installation. Since you didn't configure the Kubernetes components, you may not be able to explain to a developer how a Pod is scheduled on a worker node. Lastly, since you are running an installer provided by a third party, they may enable or disable features that you are not aware of, leading to an installation that may be against your company's security standards.

To understand how Kubernetes components work together, you must first understand the different components of a Kubernetes cluster.

The following diagram is from the `Kubernetes.io` site and shows a high-level overview of a Kubernetes cluster component:

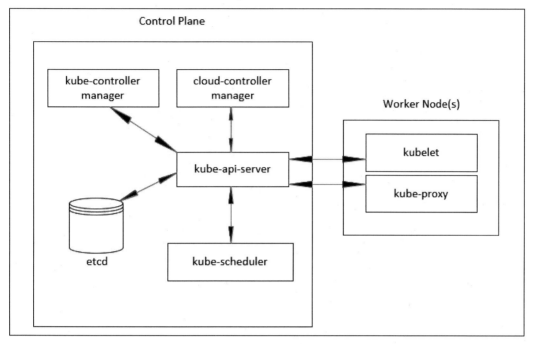

Figure 3.1: Kubernetes cluster components

As you can see, the Kubernetes cluster is made up of several components. As we progress through the chapter, we'll discuss these components and the role they play in a Kubernetes cluster.

Exploring the control plane

As its name suggests, the control plane controls every aspect of a cluster. If your control plane goes down, you can probably imagine that your cluster will encounter issues. Without a control plane, a cluster will not have any scheduling abilities, which means that workloads that are running will remain running unless they are stopped and restarted. Since the control plane is extremely important, it is always suggested that you have at least three master nodes. Many production installations run more than three master nodes, but the number of installed nodes should always be an odd number. Let's look at why the control plane and its components are so vital to a running cluster by examining each one.

The Kubernetes API server

The first component to understand in a cluster is the kube-apiserver component. Since Kubernetes is **application programming interface (API)**-driven, every request that comes into a cluster goes through the API server. Let's look at a simple get nodes request using an API endpoint, as follows:

```
https://10.240.100.100:6443/api/v1/nodes?limit=500
```

One common method users of Kubernetes deploy to interact with the API server is the kubectl utility. Every command that is issued using kubectl calls an API endpoint behind the scenes. In the preceding example, we executed a kubectl get nodes command, which sent an API request to the kube-apiserver process on 10.240.100.100 on port 6443. The API call requested the /api/vi/nodes endpoint, which returned a list of the nodes in the cluster:

NAME VERSION	STATUS	ROLES	AGE
home-k8s-control-plane v1.21.1	Ready	control-plane,master	45d
home-k8s-control-plane2 v1.21.1	Ready	control-plane,master	45d
home-k8s-control-plane3 v1.21.1	Ready	control-plane,master	45d
home-k8s-worker v1.21.1	Ready	worker	45d
home-k8s-worker2 v1.21.1	Ready	worker	45d
home-k8s-worker3 v1.21.1	Ready	worker	45d

Without a running API server, all requests to your cluster will fail. So, as you can see, it is very important to have a kube-apiserver component always running. By running three or more master nodes, we can limit any impact of losing a master node.

 When running more than one master node, you need to have a load balancer in front of the cluster. The Kubernetes API server can be fronted by most standard solutions, including F5, HAProxy, and Seesaw.

The Etcd database

It's not a stretch to say that Etcd simply is your Kubernetes cluster. Etcd is a fast and highly available distributed key-value database that Kubernetes uses to store all cluster data. Each resource in a cluster has a key in the database. If you logged in to the node—or Pod—running Etcd, you could use the etcdctl executable to look at all of the keys in the database. The following code snippet shows an example from a cluster running KinD:

```
EtcdCTL_API=3 etcdctl --endpoints=https://127.0.0.1:2379 --cacert=/etc/
kubernetes/pki/etcd/ca.crt --key=/etc/kubernetes/pki/etcd/server.key
--cert=/etc/kubernetes/pki/etcd/server.crt get / --prefix --keys-only
```

The output from the preceding command contains too much data to list it all in this chapter. A base KinD cluster will return approximately 317 entries. All keys start with /registry/<resource>. For example, one of the keys that was returned is the ClusterRole for the cluster-admin key, as follows: /registry/clusterrolebindings/cluster-admin.

We can use the key name to retrieve the value using the etcdctl utility by slightly modifying our previous command, as follows:

```
EtcdCTL_API=3 etcdctl --endpoints=https://127.0.0.1:2379 --cacert=/
etc/kubernetes/pki/etcd/ca.crt --key=/etc/kubernetes/pki/etcd/
server.key --cert=/etc/kubernetes/pki/etcd/server.crt get /registry/
clusterrolebindings/cluster-admin
```

The output will contain characters that cannot be interpreted by your shell, but you will get an idea of the data stored in Etcd. For the cluster-admin key, the output shows us the following:

```
/registry/clusterrolebindings/cluster-admin
k8s
2
rbac.authorization.k8s.io/v1ClusterRoleBinding
cluster-admin"*$96d9796d-528d-417f-9117-a47b0bb219542        Z,
rbac-defaultsb3otstrapping
+rbac.authorization.kubernetes.io/autoupdatetruez4
Grouprbac.authorization.k8s.iosystem:masters"7
rbac.authorization.k8s.io
cluster-admin"            ClusterRole
```

Figure 3.2: etcdctl ClusterRoleBinding output

The reason we explain the entries in etcd is to provide a background on how Kubernetes uses it to run a cluster. You have seen the output for the `cluster-admin` key directly from the database, but in everyday life you would query the API server using `kubectl get clusterrolebinding cluster-admin -o yaml`, which would return the following:

```
apiVersion: rbac.authorization.k8s.io/v1
kind: ClusterRoleBinding
metadata:
  annotations:
    rbac.authorization.kubernetes.io/autoupdate: "true"
  creationTimestamp: "2020-03-22T18:50:48Z"
  labels:
    kubernetes.io/bootstrapping: rbac-defaults
  name: cluster-admin
  resourceVersion: "95"
  selfLink: /apis/rbac.authorization.k8s.io/v1/clusterrolebindings/cluster-admin
  uid: 96d9796d-528d-417f-9117-a47b0bb21954
roleRef:
  apiGroup: rbac.authorization.k8s.io
  kind: ClusterRole
  name: cluster-admin
subjects:
- apiGroup: rbac.authorization.k8s.io
  kind: Group
  name: system:masters
```

Figure 3.3: kubectl ClusterRoleBinding output

If you look at the output from the `kubectl` command and compare it with the output from the `etcdctl` query, you will see matching information. When you execute `kubectl` commands, the request goes to the API server, which then queries the etcd database for the resource's information.

kube-scheduler

As the name suggests, the `kube-scheduler` component oversees the scheduling of pods on nodes. The scheduler watches for pods that have not been assigned a node, deciding the pods' placement based on the resource requirements of the pod. Using the pod requirements, the scheduler will use a set of criteria, including available node resources, constraints, selectors, and affinity/anti-affinity rules. Nodes that meet the requirements are called feasible nodes and from the final node list, the pod will be scheduled on one of the nodes.

kube-controller-manager

The `kube-controller-manager` component is a collection of multiple controllers that are included in a single binary.

Including the four controllers in a single executable reduces complexity by running all four in a single process. The four controllers included in the kube-controller-manager component are the node, replication, endpoints, and service account and token controller (serviceaccounts).

Each controller provides a unique function to a cluster, and each controller and its function is listed here:

Controller	Description
Node	Monitors each node's availability. If a node goes offline, the node controller will update the status so that the scheduler does not attempt to start a workload on a failed node.
Replication	Monitors the number of replicas for pods, and will add or remove replicas based on the defined desired state.
Endpoints	Responsible for creating endpoints to pods that are included with a service.
Serviceaccounts	Monitors all service accounts.
Namespace	Monitors all namespaces.

Table 3.1: Controllers and their functions

Each controller runs a non-terminating (never-ending) control loop. These control loops monitor the state of each resource, making any changes required to normalize the state of the resource. For example, if you needed to scale a deployment from one to three nodes, the replication controller would notice that the current state has one Pod running, and the desired state is to have three Pods running. To move the current state to the desired state, two additional Pods will be requested by the replication controller.

cloud-controller-manager

This is one component that you may not have run into, depending on how your clusters are configured. Similar to the kube-controller-manager component, this controller contains four controllers in a single binary. The included controllers are the node, route, service, and volume controllers—each controller is responsible for interacting with their respective cloud service provider offering.

Understanding the worker node components

Worker nodes, as the name implies, are responsible for running workloads. When we discussed the `kube-scheduler` component of the control plane, we mentioned that when a new Pod is scheduled, the `kube-scheduler` component will decide which node to run the Pod on. It does this using information that has been sent to it from the worker nodes. This information is constantly updated to help spread Pods around a cluster to utilize resources efficiently.

Each worker node has two main components, kubelet and kube-proxy:

kubelet

You may hear a worker node referred to as a `kubelet`. The `kubelet` is an agent that runs on all worker nodes, and it is responsible for running the actual containers.

kube-proxy

Contrary to the name, `kube-proxy` is not a proxy server at all. `kube-proxy` is actually responsible for routing network communication between a Pod and the network.

Container runtime

Each node also needs a container runtime. A container runtime is responsible for running the containers. The first thing you might think of is Docker. While Docker is a container runtime, it is not the only runtime option available. Over the last year, other options have become available and are quickly replacing Docker as the preferred container runtime. The two most prominent Docker replacements are CRI-O and containerd.

For the book exercises, we will create a Kubernetes cluster using KinD. At the time of writing, KinD only offers official support for Docker as the container runtime, with limited support for Podman.

Interacting with the API server

As we mentioned earlier, you interact with the API server using either direct API requests or the `kubectl` utility. We will focus on using `kubectl` for the majority of our interaction in this book, but we will call out using direct API calls where applicable.

Using the Kubernetes kubectl utility

kubectl is a single executable file that allows you to interact with the Kubernetes API using a **command-line interface (CLI)**. It is available for most major operating systems and architectures, including Linux, Windows, and Mac.

Installation instructions for most operating systems are located on the Kubernetes site at `https://kubernetes.io/docs/tasks/tools/install-kubectl/`. Since we are using Linux as our operating system for the exercises in the book, we will cover installing kubectl on a Linux machine. Follow these steps:

1. To download the latest version of kubectl, you can run a curl command that will download it, as follows:

```
curl -LO https://storage.googleapis.com/kubernetes-release/
release/`curl -s https://storage.googleapis.com/kubernetes-
release/release/stable.txt`/bin/linux/amd64/kubectl
```

2. After downloading, you need to make the file executable by running the following command:

```
chmod +x ./kubectl
```

3. Finally, we will move the executable to our path, as follows:

```
sudo mv ./kubectl /usr/local/bin/kubectl
```

You now have the latest kubectl utility on your system and can execute kubectl commands from any working directory.

Kubernetes is updated every 4 months. This includes upgrades to the base Kubernetes cluster components and the kubectl utility. You may run into a version mismatch between a cluster and your kubectl command, requiring you to either upgrade or download your kubectl executable. You can always check the version of both by running a kubectl version command, which will output the version of both the API server and the kubectl client. The output from a version check is shown in the following code snippet:

```
Client Version: version.Info{Major:"1", Minor:"21",
GitVersion:"v1.21.1", GitCommit:"8b5a19147530eaac9476b0ab82980b408
8bbc1b2", GitTreeState:"clean", BuildDate:"2021-09-15T21:38:50Z",
GoVersion:"go1.16.8", Compiler:"gc", Platform:"linux/amd64"}
Server Version: version.Info{Major:"1", Minor:"22",
GitVersion:"v1.22.1", GitCommit:"5e58841cce77d4bc13713ad2b91fa0d96
1e69192", GitTreeState:"clean", BuildDate:"2021-05-21T23:01:33Z",
GoVersion:"go1.16.4", Compiler:"gc", Platform:"linux/amd64"}
```

As you can see from the output, the kubectl client is running version 1.22.1 and the cluster is running 1.22.1. A minor version difference in the two will not cause any issues. In fact, the official supported version difference is within one major version release. So, if your client is running version 1.21 and the cluster is running 1.22, you would be within the supported version difference. While this may be supported, it doesn't mean that you won't run into issues if you are trying to use any new commands or resources included in the higher version. In general, you should try to keep your cluster and client version in sync to avoid any issues.

Through the remainder of this chapter, we will discuss Kubernetes resources and how you interact with the API server to manage each one. But before diving into the different resources, we wanted to mention one commonly overlooked option of the kubectl utility: the verbose option.

Understanding the verbose option

When you execute a kubectl command, the only outputs you will see by default are any direct responses to your command. If you were to look at all Pods in the kube-system namespace, you would receive a list of all Pods. In most cases this is the desired output, but what if you issued a get Pods request and received an error from the API server? How could you get more information about what might be causing the error?

By adding the verbose option to your kubectl command, you can get additional details about the API call itself and any replies from the API server. Often, the replies from the API server will contain additional information that may be useful to find the root cause of the issue.

The verbose option has multiple levels ranging from 0 to 9; the higher the number, the more output you will receive.

The following screenshot has been taken from the Kubernetes site, detailing each level and what the output will include:

Verbosity	Description
--v=0	Generally useful for this to *always* be visible to a cluster operator.
--v=1	A reasonable default log level if you don't want verbosity.
--v=2	Useful steady state information about the service and important log messages that may correlate to significant changes in the system. This is the recommended default log level for most systems.
--v=3	Extended information about changes.
--v=4	Debug level verbosity.
--v=6	Display requested resources.
--v=7	Display HTTP request headers.
--v=8	Display HTTP request contents.
--v=9	Display HTTP request contents without truncation of contents.

Figure 3.4: Verbosity description

You can experiment with the levels by adding the -v or --v option to any `kubectl` command.

General kubectl commands

The CLI allows you to interact with Kubernetes in an imperative and declarative manner. Using an imperative command involves you telling Kubernetes what to do—for example, `kubectl run nginx --image nginx`. This tells the API server to create a new deployment called `nginx` that runs an image called `nginx`. While imperative commands are useful for development and quick fixes or testing, you will use declarative commands more often in a production environment. In a declarative command, you tell Kubernetes what you want. To use declarative commands, you send a manifest to the API server, written in either **JavaScript Object Notation (JSON)** or **YAML Ain't Markup Language (YAML)**, which declares what you want Kubernetes to create.

`kubectl` includes commands and options that can provide general cluster information or information about a resource. The table below contains a cheatsheet of commands and what they are used for. We will use many of these commands in future chapters, so you will see them in action throughout the book:

Cluster Commands	
`api-resources`	Lists supported API resources.
`api-versions`	Lists supported API versions.
`cluster-info`	Lists cluster information, including the API server and other cluster endpoints.
`cluster-info dump`	Gets detailed cluster information to troubleshoot issues.
Object Commands – Can be executed against most objects.	
`get <object>`	Retrieves a list or a single object.
`describe <object>`	Provides details on an object.
`logs <pod name>`	Retrieves the logs for a pod.
`edit <object>`	Edits an object interactively.
`delete <object>`	Deletes an object.
`label <object>`	Creates or deletes a label for an object.
`annotate <object>`	Creates or deletes an annotation for an object.
`run`	Creates a deployment, pod, or job depending on the `--restart` option provided in the command line. The default action is to create a deployment.

Table 3.2: Cluster and Object commands

With an understanding of each Kubernetes component and how to interact with the API server using imperative commands, we can now move on to Kubernetes resources and how we use `kubectl` to manage them.

Introducing Kubernetes resources

This section will contain a lot of information and, since this is a bootcamp, we will not go into deep details on each resource. As you can imagine, each resource could have its own chapter, or multiple chapters, in a book. Since there are many books on Kubernetes that go into detail on the base resources, we will only cover the required details of each to have an understanding of each one. In the following chapters, we will include additional details for resources as we build out our cluster using the book exercises.

Before we go on to understand what Kubernetes resources really are, let's first explain Kubernetes manifests.

Kubernetes manifests

The files that we will use to create Kubernetes resources are referred to as manifests. A manifest can be created using YAML or JSON—most manifests use YAML, and that is the format we will use throughout the book.

The content of a manifest will vary depending on the resource, or resources, that will be created. At a minimum, all manifests require a base configuration that includes the apiVersion, resource KinD, and metadata fields, as can be seen here:

```
apiVersion: apps/v1
kind: Deployment
metadata:
  labels:
    app: grafana
  name: grafana
  namespace: monitoring
```

The preceding manifest alone is not complete; we are only showing the beginning of a full deployment manifest. As you can see in the file, we start with the three required fields that all manifests are required to have: the apiVersion, kind, and metadata fields.

You may also notice that there are spaces in the file. YAML is very format-specific, and if the format of any line is off by even a single space, you will receive an error when you try to deploy the manifest. This takes time to get used to, and even after creating manifests for a long time, formatting issues will still pop up from time to time.

What are Kubernetes resources?

When you want to add or delete something from a cluster, you are interacting with Kubernetes resources. This interaction is how you declare your desired state for the resource, which may be to create, delete, or scale a resource. Based on the desired state, the API server will make sure that the current state equals the desired state. For example, if you have a deployment that starts with a single replica, you can change the deployment resource from 1 to 3 replicas. When the API server sees that the current state is 1, it will scale the deployment out to 3 replicas by creating the additional 2 pods.

To retrieve a list of resources a cluster supports, you can use the kubectl api-resources command. The API server will reply with a list of all resources, including any valid short name, namespace support, and supported API group.

There are approximately 58 base resources included with a base cluster, but an abbreviated list of the most common resources is shown below:

NAME	SHORTNAMES	APIGROUP	NAMESPACED
configmaps	cm		TRUE
endpoints	ep		TRUE
events	ev		TRUE
namespaces	ns		FALSE
nodes	no		FALSE
persistentvolumeclaims	pvc		TRUE
persistentvolumes	pv		FALSE
pods	po		TRUE
replicationcontrollers	rc		TRUE
resourcequotas	quota		TRUE
secrets			TRUE
serviceaccounts	sa		TRUE
services	svc		TRUE
customresourcedefinitions	crd,crds	apiextensions.k8s.io	FALSE
daemonsets	ds	apps	TRUE
deployments	deploy	apps	TRUE
replicasets	rs	apps	TRUE
statefulsets	sts	apps	TRUE
horizontalpodautoscalers	hpa	autoscaling	TRUE
cronjobs	cj	batch	TRUE
jobs	batch		TRUE
events	ev	events.k8s.io	TRUE
ingresses	ing	extensions	TRUE
ingresses	ing	networking.k8s.io	TRUE
networkpolicies	netpol	networking.k8s.io	TRUE
podsecuritypolicies	psp	policy	FALSE
clusterrolebindings		rbac.authorization.k8s.io	FALSE
clusterroles		rbac.authorization.k8s.io	FALSE
rolebindings		rbac.authorization.k8s.io	TRUE
roles		rbac.authorization.k8s.io	TRUE
csidrivers		storage.k8s.io	FALSE
csinodes		storage.k8s.io	FALSE
storageclasses	sc	storage.k8s.io	FALSE

Table 3.3: Kubernetes API resources

Since this chapter is a bootcamp, we will offer a brief review of many of the resources in the list. In order to ensure that you can follow the remaining chapters, we will provide an overview of each resource and how to interact with it.

Some resources will also be explained in greater detail in future chapters, including `Ingress`, `RoleBindings`, `ClusterRoles`, `StorageClasses`, and more.

Reviewing Kubernetes resources

To make this section easier to follow, we will present each resource in the order it is provided by the `kubectl api-services` command.

Depending on which version of Kubernetes you're running, you may not see a `metadata.selfLink` attribute. This attribute was removed in version 1.20 and has broken many controllers that rely on that link. The example below will assume that the `selfLink` attribute is not available.

Most resources in a cluster are run in a namespace, and to create/edit/read them, you should supply the `-n <namespace>` option to any `kubectl` command. To find a list of resources that accept a namespace option, you can reference the output from our previous `get api-server` command. If a resource can be referenced by a namespace, the namespaced column will show `true`. If the resource is only referenced by the cluster level, the namespaced column will show `false`.

ConfigMaps

A ConfigMap stores data in key-value pairs, providing a way to keep your configuration separate from your application. ConfigMaps may contain data from a literal value, files, or directories.

Here is an imperative example:

```
kubectl create configmap <name> <data>
```

The `<data>` option will vary based on the source of the ConfigMap. To use a file or a directory, you supply the `--from-file` option and either the path to a file or an entire directory, as shown here:

```
kubectl create configmap config-test --from-file=/apps/nginx-config/
nginx.conf
```

This would create a new ConfigMap named `config-test`, with the `nginx.conf` key containing the content of the `nginx.conf` file as the value.

If you need to have more than one key added in a single ConfigMap, you could put each file into a directory and create the ConfigMap using all of the files in the directory. As an example, you have three files in a directory located at `~/config/myapp`.

These three files each contain data, and are called `config1`, `config2`, and `config3`. To create a ConfigMap that would add each file into a key, you need to supply the `--from-file` option and point to the directory, as follows:

```
kubectl create configmap config-test --from-file=/apps/config/myapp
```

This would create a new `ConfigMap` with three key values called `config1`, `config2`, and `config3`. Each key will contain a value equal to the content of each file in the directory.

To quickly show a `ConfigMap`, using the example to create a `ConfigMap` from a directory, we can retrieve the `ConfigMap` using the `get` command, `kubectl get configmaps config-test`, resulting in the following output:

```
NAME             DATA    AGE
config-test      3       7s
```

We can see that the ConfigMap contains three keys, shown as a 3 under the DATA column. To look in greater detail, we can use the same `get` command and output the value of each key as YAML by adding the `-o yaml` option to the `kubectl get configmaps config-test` command, resulting in the following output:

```
apiVersion: v1
data:
  config1: |
    First Configmap Value
  config2: |
    Yet Another Value from File2
  config3: |
    The last file - Config 3
kind: ConfigMap
metadata:
  creationTimestamp: "2021-10-10T01:38:51Z"
  name: config-test
  namespace: default
  resourceVersion: "6712"
  uid: a744d772-3845-4631-930c-e5661d476717
```

Looking at the preceding output, you can see that each key matches the filenames, and the value for each key contains the data in each respective file.

One limitation of ConfigMaps that you should keep in mind is that the data is easily accessible to anyone with permissions to the resource. As you can see from the preceding output, a simple `get` command shows the data in cleartext.

Due to this design, you should never store sensitive information such as a password in a ConfigMap. Later in this section, we will cover a resource that was designed to store sensitive information, called a Secret.

Endpoints

An endpoint maps a service to a Pod or Pods. This will make more sense when we explain the `Service` resource. For now, you only need to know that you can use the CLI to retrieve endpoints by using the `kubectl get endpoints` command. In a new KinD cluster, you will see a value for the Kubernetes API server in the default namespace, as illustrated in the following code snippet:

```
NAMESPACE    NAME        ENDPOINTS         AGE
default      Kubernetes  172.17.0.2:6443   22h
```

The output shows that the cluster has a service called `kubernetes` that has an endpoint at the **Internet Protocol (IP)** address `172.17.0.2` on port `6443`. The IP that is returned in our example is the address that our Docker control plane container has been assigned.

Later, you will see how looking at endpoints can be used to troubleshoot service and ingress issues.

Events

The `Events` resource will display any events for a namespace. To get a list of events for the `kube-system` namespace, you would use the `kubectl get events -n kube-system` command.

Namespaces

A namespace is a resource to divide a cluster into logical units. Each namespace allows granular management of resources, including permissions, quotas, and reporting.

The `namespace` resource is used for namespace tasks, which are cluster-level operations. Using the `namespace` resource, you can execute commands including `create`, `delete`, `edit`, and `get`.

The syntax for the command is `kubectl <verb> ns <namespace name>`.

For example, to describe the `kube-system` namespace, we would execute a `kubectl describe namespaces kube-system` command.

This will return information for the namespace, including any labels, annotations, and assigned quotas, as illustrated in the following code snippet:

```
Name: kube-system
Labels: <none>
Annotations: <none>
Status: Active
No resource quota.
No LimitRange resource.
```

In the preceding output, you can see that this namespace does not have any labels, annotations, or resource quotas assigned.

This section is only meant to introduce the concept of namespaces as a management unit in multi-tenant clusters. If you plan to run clusters with multiple tenants, you need to understand how namespaces can be used to secure a cluster.

Nodes

The `nodes` resource is a cluster-level resource that is used to interact with the cluster's nodes. This resource can be used with various actions including `get`, `describe`, `label`, and `annotate`.

To retrieve a list of all of the nodes in a cluster using `kubectl`, you need to execute a `kubectl get nodes` command. On a new KinD cluster running a simple one-node cluster, this would display as follows:

```
NAME                STATUS   ROLES    AGE   VERSION
kind-control-plane  Ready    master   22h   v1.17.0
```

You can also use the nodes resource to get details of a single node using the `describe` command. To get a description of the KinD node listed previously, we can execute `kubectl describe node kind-control-plane`, which would return details on the node, including consumed resources, running Pods, IP **classless inter-domain routing (CIDR)** ranges, and more.

Persistent Volume Claims

We will describe **Persistent Volume Claims (PVCs)** in more depth in a later chapter, but for now you just need to know that a PVC is used by a Pod to consume persistent storage. A PVC uses a **persistent volume (PV)** to map the storage resource. As with most resources we have discussed, you can issue `get`, `describe`, and `delete` commands on a PVC resource. Since these are used by Pods, they are a `namespaced` resource, and must be created in the same namespace as the Pod(s) that will use the PVC.

PVs

PVs are used by PVCs to create a link between the PVC and the underlying storage system. Manually maintaining PVs is a messy task and it should be avoided, since Kubernetes includes the ability to manage most common storage systems using the **Container Storage Interface** (**CSI**). As mentioned in the **PVC** resource section, we will discuss in a later chapter how Kubernetes can automatically create the PVs that will be linked to PVCs.

Pods

The Pod resource is used to interact with the Pods that are running your container(s). Using the `kubectl` utility, you can use commands such as `get`, `delete`, and `describe`. For example, if you wanted to get a list of all Pods in the `kube-system` namespace, you would execute a `kubectl get Pods -n kube-system` command that would return all Pods in the namespace, as follows:

```
NAME                                                  READY   STATUS    RESTARTS
AGE
calico-kube-controllers-c6c8dc655-vnrt7               1/1     Running   0
15m
calico-node-4d9px                                     1/1     Running   0
15m
calico-node-r4zsj                                     1/1     Running   0
15m
coredns-558bd4d5db-8mxzp                              1/1     Running   0
15m
coredns-558bd4d5db-fxnkt                              1/1     Running   0
15m
etcd-cluster01-control-plane                          1/1     Running   0
15m
kube-apiserver-cluster01-control-plane                1/1     Running   0
15m
kube-controller-manager-cluster01-control-plane       1/1     Running   0
15m
kube-proxy-npxqd                                      1/1     Running   0
15m
kube-proxy-twn7s                                      1/1     Running   0
15m
kube-scheduler-cluster01-control-plane                1/1     Running   0
15m
```

While you can create a Pod directly, you should avoid doing so unless you are using a Pod for quick troubleshooting. Pods that are created directly cannot use many of the features provided by Kubernetes, including scaling, automatic restarts, or rolling upgrades.

Instead of creating a Pod directly, you should use a Deployment, a StatefulSet, or, in some rare cases, a `ReplicaSet` resource or replication controller.

Replication controllers

Replication controllers will manage the number of running Pods, keeping the desired replicas specified running at all times. If you create a replication controller and set the replica count to 5, the controller will always keep five Pods of the application running.

Replication controllers have been replaced by the `ReplicaSet` resource, which we will discuss in its own section. While you can still use replication controllers, you should consider using a Deployment or a `ReplicaSet`.

ResourceQuotas

It is becoming very common to share a Kubernetes cluster between multiple teams, referred to as a multi-tenant cluster. Since you will have multiple teams working in a single cluster, you should consider creating quotas to limit the potential of a single tenant consuming all the resources in a cluster or on a node.

Limits can be set on most cluster resources, including the following:

- Central processing unit (CPU)
- Memory
- PVCs
- ConfigMaps
- Deployments
- Pods, and more

Setting a limit will stop any additional resources from being created once the limit is hit. If you set a limit of 10 Pods for a namespace and a user creates a new Deployment that attempts to start 11 Pods, the eleventh Pod will fail to start up and the user will receive an error.

A basic manifest file to create a quota for memory and CPU would look like this:

```
apiVersion: v1
kind: ResourceQuota
metadata:
```

```
  name: base-memory-cpu
spec:
  hard:
    requests.cpu: "2"
    requests.memory: 8Gi
    limits.cpu: "4"
    limits.memory: 16Gi
```

This will set a limit on the total amount of resources the namespace can use for CPU and memory requests and limits.

Many of the options you can set in a quota are self-explanatory, like pods, PVCs, services, etc... When you set a limit, it means that the set limit is the maximum allowed for that resource in the namespace. For example, if you set a limit on a pod to 5, when an attempt is made to create a sixth pod in that namespace, it will be denied.

Some quotas have more than one option that can be set, specifically, CPU and memory. In our example, both resources have set a request and a limit. Both values are very important to understand to ensure efficient use of your resources and to limit the potential availability of the application.

A request is essentially a reservation of that specific resource. When a pod is deployed, you should always set a request on your CPU and memory, and the value should be the minimum required to start your application. This value will be used by the scheduler to find a node that meets the request that has been set. If there are no nodes with the requested resource available, the pod will fail to be scheduled.

Now, since a request will reserve the resource, that means once all nodes in the cluster have 100% of requests assigned, any additional pod creations will be denied since the requests are at 100%. Even if your actual cluster CPU or memory utilization is at 10%, pods will fail to be scheduled since the request, or **reservation**, is at 100%. If requests are not carefully thought out, it will lead to wasted resources and that will lead to an increased cost to run the platform.

Limits on CPU and memory set the maximum value that the pod will be able to utilize. This is different from a request since limits are not a reservation of the resource. However, limits still need to be carefully planned out from an application side. If you set the CPU limit too low, the application may experience performance issues, and if you set the memory limit too low, the pod will be terminated, impacting availability while it is restarted.

Once a quota has been created, you can view the usage using the `kubectl describe` command. In our example, we named the `ResourceQuota` as `base-memory-cpu`.

To view the usage, we will execute the `kubectl get resourcequotas base-memory-cpu` command, resulting in the following output:

```
Name: base-memory-cpu
Namespace: default
Resource Used Hard
-------- ---- ----
limits.cpu 0 4
limits.memory 0 16Gi
requests.cpu 0 2
requests.memory 0 8Gi
```

`ResourceQuotas` are used to control a cluster's resources. By allocating the resources to a namespace, you can guarantee that a single tenant will have the required CPU and memory to run their application, while limiting the impact that a poorly written application can have on other applications.

Secrets

Earlier, we described how to use a `ConfigMap` resource to store configuration information. We mentioned that `ConfigMap` should never be used to store any type of sensitive data. This is the job of a Secret.

Secrets are stored as Base64-encoded strings, which aren't a form of encryption. So, why separate Secrets from `ConfigMap`? Providing a separate resource type offers an easier way to maintain access controls and the ability to inject sensitive information using an external secret management system

Secrets can be created using a file, directory, or from a literal string. As an example, we have a MySQL image we want to execute, and we would like to pass the password to the Pod using a Secret. On our workstation, we have a file called `dbpwd` in our current working directory that has our password in it. Using the `kubectl` command, we can create a Secret by executing `kubectl create secret generic mysql-admin --from-file=./dbpwd`.

This would create a new a Secret called `mysql-admin` in the current namespace, with the content of the `dbpwd` file. Using `kubectl`, we can get the output of the Secret by running the `kubectl get secret mysql-admin -o yaml` command, which would output the following:

```
apiVersion: v1
data:
  dbpwd: c3VwZXJzZWNyZXQtcGFzc3dvcmQK
kind: Secret
```

```
metadata:
  creationTimestamp: "2020-03-24T18:39:31Z"
  name: mysql-admin
  namespace: default
  resourceVersion: "464059"
  uid: 69220ebd-c9fe-4688-829b-242ffc9e94fc
type: Opaque
```

Looking at the preceding output, you can see that the `data` section contains the name of our file and then a Base64-encoded value, which was created from the content of the file.

If we copy the Base64 value from the Secret and pipe it out to the `base64` utility, we can easily decode the password, as follows:

```
echo c3VwZXJzZWNyZXQtcGFzc3dvcmQK | base64 -d
supersecret-password
```

 When using the `echo` command to Base64-encode strings, add the `-n` flag to avoid adding an additional \n. Instead of `echo 'test' | base64`, use `echo -n 'test' | base64`.

Everything is stored in Etcd, but we are concerned that someone may be able to hack into the master server and steal a copy of the Etcd database. Once someone has a copy of the database, they could easily use the `etcdctl` utility to look through the content to retrieve all of our Base64-encoded Secrets. Luckily, Kubernetes added a feature to encrypt Secrets when they are written to a database.

Enabling this feature can be fairly complex for many users, and while it sounds like a good idea, it does present some potential issues that you should consider before implementing it. If you would like to read the steps on encrypting your Secrets at rest, you can view these on the Kubernetes site at `https://kubernetes.io/docs/tasks/administer-cluster/encrypt-data/`.

Another option to secure Secrets is to use a third-party secrets management tool such as HashiCorp's Vault or CyberArk's Conjur.

Service accounts

Kubernetes uses service accounts to enable access controls for workloads. When you create a Deployment, you may need to access other services or Kubernetes resources.

Since Kubernetes is a secure system, each resource or service your application tries to access will evaluate **role-based access control (RBAC)** rules to accept or deny the request.

Creating a service account using a manifest is a straightforward process, requiring only a few lines in the manifest. The following code snippet shows a service account manifest to create a service account for a Grafana Deployment:

```
apiVersion: v1
kind: ServiceAccount
metadata:
  name: grafana
  namespace: monitoring
```

You combine the service account with role bindings and Roles to allow access to the required services or objects.

When you create a `ServiceAccount`, a secret will also be created that stores a static token, the CA certificate for the cluster, and the name of the `Namespace` the `Secret` is in. This token does not have an expiration and should not be used outside of the cluster.

Services

When you create a pod, it will receive an IP address from the CIDR range that was assigned when the cluster was created. In most clusters, the assigned IPs are only addressable within the cluster itself, referred to as "island mode." Since pods are ephemeral, the assigned IP address will likely change during an application's life cycle, which becomes problematic when any service or application needs to connect to the pod. To address this, we can create a Kubernetes service, which will also receive an IP address, but since services aren't deleted during an application's life cycle, the address will remain the same.

A service will dynamically maintain a list of pods to target based on labels that match the service selector, creating a list of endpoints for the service.

A service stores information about how to expose the application, including which Pods are running the application and the network ports to reach them.

Each service has a network type that is assigned when they are created, and they include the following:

- `ClusterIP`: A network type that is only accessible inside the cluster itself. This type can still be used for external requests using an Ingress controller, which will be discussed in a later chapter. The ClusterIP type is the default type that will be used if no type is specified when you create a service.

- **NodePort**: A network type that exposes the service to a random port between ports `30000` and `32767`. This port becomes accessible by targeting any worker node in a cluster on the assigned `NodePort`. Once created, each node in the cluster will receive the port information and incoming requests will be routed via `kube-proxy`.

- **LoadBalancer**: This type requires an add-on to use inside a cluster. If you are running Kubernetes on a public cloud provider, this type will create an external load balancer that will assign an IP address to your service. Most on-premises Kubernetes installations do not include support for the `LoadBalancer` type, but some offerings such as Google's Anthos do offer support for it. In a later chapter, we will explain how to add an open source project called `MetalLB` to a Kubernetes cluster to provide support for the `LoadBalancer` type.

- **ExternalName**: This type is different from the other three. Unlike the other three options, this type will not assign an IP address to the service. Instead, this is used to map the internal Kubernetes **Domain Name System (DNS)** name to an external service.

As an example, we have deployed a Pod running Nginx on port `80`. We want to create a service that will allow this Pod to receive incoming requests on port `80` from within the cluster. The code for this can be seen in the following snippet:

```
apiVersion: v1
kind: Service
metadata:
  labels:
    app: nginx-web-frontend
  name: nginx-web
spec:
  ports:
  - name: http
    port: 80
    targetPort: 80
  selector:
    app: nginx-web
```

In our manifest, we create a label with a value of `app` and assign a value of `nginx-web-frontend`. We have called the service itself `nginx-web` and we exposed the service on port `80`, targeting the Pod port of `80`. The last two lines of the manifest are used to assign the Pods that the service will forward to, also known as Endpoints. In this manifest, any Pod that has the label of `app` with a value of `nginx-web` in the namespace will be added as an endpoint to the service. Finally, you may have noticed that we didn't specify a service type in our manifest. Since we didn't specify the type, it will be created as the default service type of ClusterIP.

CustomResourceDefinitions

CustomResourceDefinitions (CRDs) allow anyone to extend Kubernetes by integrating their application into a cluster as a standard resource. Once a CRD is created, you can reference it using an API endpoint, and it can be interacted with using standard `kubectl` commands.

DaemonSets

A `DaemonSet` allows you to deploy a Pod on every node in a cluster, or a subset of nodes. A common use for a `DaemonSet` is to deploy a log forwarding Pod such as Fluentd to every node in a cluster. Once deployed, the `DaemonSet` will create a Fluentd Pod on all existing nodes. Since a `DaemonSet` deploys to all nodes, any additional nodes that are added to a cluster will have a Fluentd Pod started once the node has joined the cluster.

Deployments

We mentioned earlier that you should never deploy a Pod directly. One reason for this is that you cannot scale a pod or perform a rolling upgrade when a pod is created in this way. Deployments offer you many advantages, including a way to manage your upgrades declaratively and the ability to roll back to previous revisions. Creating a Deployment is actually a three-step process that is executed by the API server: a Deployment is created, which creates a ReplicaSet, which then creates the Pod(s) for the application.

Even if you don't plan to scale or perform rolling upgrades to the application, you should still use Deployments by default so that you can leverage the features at a future date.

ReplicaSets

ReplicaSets can be used to create a Pod or a set of Pods (replicas). Similar to the `ReplicationController` resource, a `ReplicaSet` will maintain the set number of Pods defined in the replica count. If there are too few Pods, Kubernetes will make up the difference and create the missing Pods. If there are too many Pods for a ReplicaSet, Kubernetes will delete Pods until the number is equal to the replica count set.

In general, you should avoid creating ReplicaSets directly. Instead, you should create a Deployment, which will create and manage a ReplicaSet.

StatefulSets

StatefulSets offer some unique features when creating Pods. They provide features that none of the other Pod creation methods offer, including the following:

- Known Pod names
- Ordered Deployment and scaling
- Ordered updates
- Persistent storage creation

The best way to understand the advantages of a `StatefulSet` is to review an example manifest from the Kubernetes site, shown in the following screenshot:

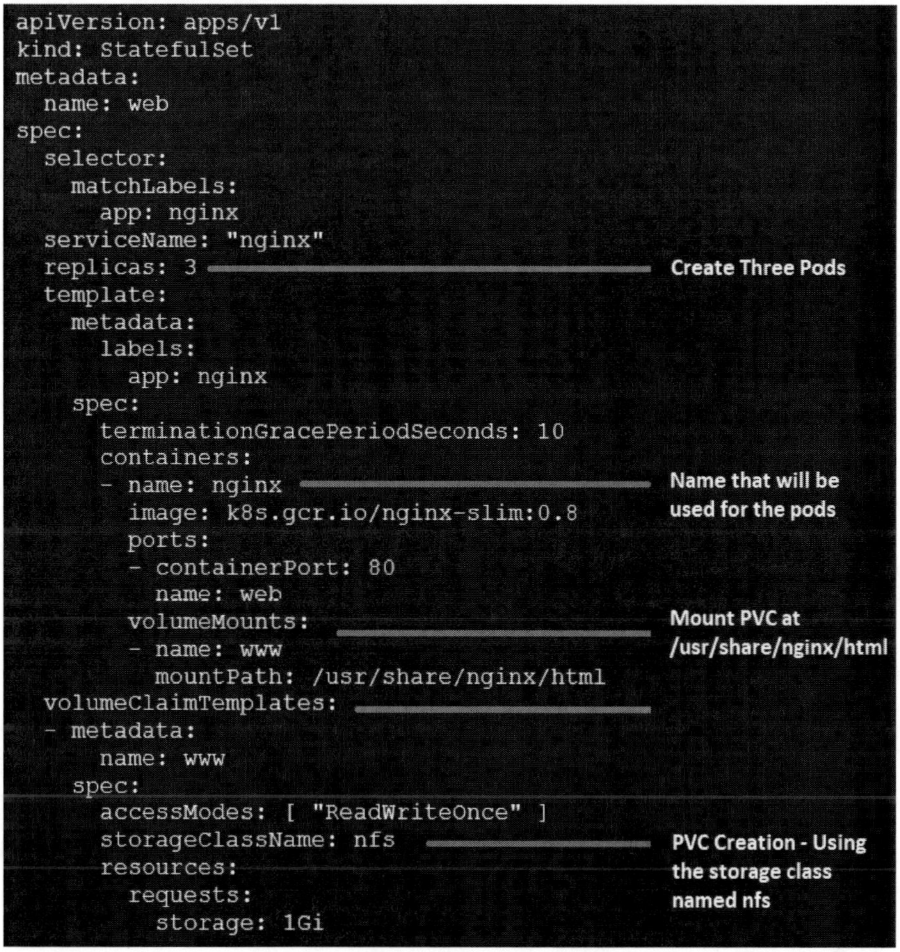

```
apiVersion: apps/v1
kind: StatefulSet
metadata:
  name: web
spec:
  selector:
    matchLabels:
      app: nginx
  serviceName: "nginx"
  replicas: 3 ━━━━━━━━━━━━━━━━━━━━━━━━━━━━  Create Three Pods
  template:
    metadata:
      labels:
        app: nginx
    spec:
      terminationGracePeriodSeconds: 10
      containers:
      - name: nginx ━━━━━━━━━━━━━━━━━━━━  Name that will be
        image: k8s.gcr.io/nginx-slim:0.8   used for the pods
        ports:
        - containerPort: 80
          name: web
        volumeMounts:
        - name: www ━━━━━━━━━━━━━━━━━━━━  Mount PVC at
          mountPath: /usr/share/nginx/html  /usr/share/nginx/html
  volumeClaimTemplates: ━━━━━━━━━━━━━━━━
  - metadata:
      name: www
    spec:
      accessModes: [ "ReadWriteOnce" ]
      storageClassName: nfs ━━━━━━━━━━━  PVC Creation - Using
      resources:                          the storage class
        requests:                         named nfs
          storage: 1Gi
```

Figure 3.5: StatefulSet manifest example

Now, we can look at the resources that the `StatefulSet` created.

The manifest specifies that there should be three replicas of a Pod named `nginx`. When we get a list of Pods, you will see that three Pods were created using the `nginx` name, with an additional dash and an incrementing number. This is what we meant in the overview when we mentioned that Pods will be created with known names, as illustrated in the following code snippet:

```
NAME    READY   STATUS    RESTARTS   AGE
web-0   1/1     Running   0          4m6s
web-1   1/1     Running   0          4m2s
web-2   1/1     Running   0          3m52s
```

The Pods are also created in order—`web-0` must be fully deployed before `web-1` is created, and then finally `web-2`.

Finally, for this example, we also added a PVC to each Pod using the `VolumeClaimTemplate` in the manifest. If you look at the output of the `kubectl get pvc` command, you will see that three PVCs were created with names we expected (note that we removed the `VOLUME` column due to space), as illustrated in the following code snippet:

```
NAME        STATUS   CAPACITY   ACCESS MODES   STORAGECLASS AGE
www-web-0   Bound    1Gi        RWO            nfs 13m
www-web-1   Bound    1Gi        RWO            nfs 13m
www-web-2   Bound    1Gi        RWO            nfs 12m
```

In the `VolumeClaimTemplate` section of the manifest, you will see that we assigned the name `www` to the PVC claim. When you assign a volume in a StatefulSet, the PVC name will combine the name used in the claim template, combined with the name of the Pod. Using this naming, you can see why Kubernetes assigned the PVC names `www-web-0`, `www-web-1`, and `www-web-2`.

HorizontalPodAutoscalers

One of the biggest advantages of running a workload on a Kubernetes cluster is the ability to easily scale your Pods. While you can scale using the `kubectl` command or by editing a manifest's replica count, these are not automated and require manual intervention.

Horizontal Pod Autoscalers (HPAs) provide the ability to scale an application based on a set of criteria. Using metrics such as CPU and memory usage, or your own custom metrics, you can set a rule to scale your Pods up when you need more Pods to maintain your service level.

After a cooldown period, Kubernetes will scale the application back to the minimum number of Pods defined in the policy.

To quickly create an HPA for an `nginx` Deployment, we can execute a `kubectl` command using the `autoscale` option, as follows:

```
kubectl autoscale deployment nginx --cpu-percent=50 --min=1 --max=5
```

You can also create a Kubernetes manifest to create your HPAs. Using the same options as those we did in the CLI, our manifest would look like this:

```
apiVersion: autoscaling/v1
kind: HorizontalPodAutoscaler
metadata:
  name: nginx-deployment
spec:
  maxReplicas: 5
  minReplicas: 1
  scaleTargetRef:
    apiVersion: apps/v1
    kind: Deployment
    name: nginx-deployment
  targetCPUUtilizationPercentage: 50
```

Both options will create an HPA that will scale our `nginx-deployment nginx` Deployment up to 5 replicas when the Deployment hits a CPU utilization of 50%. Once the Deployment usage falls below 50% and the cooldown period is reached (by default, 5 minutes), the replica count will be reduced to 1.

CronJobs

If you have used Linux cronjobs in the past, then you already know what a Kubernetes `CronJob` resource is. If you don't have a Linux background, a cronjob is used to create a scheduled task. As another example, if you are a Windows person, it's similar to Windows scheduled tasks.

An example manifest that creates a `CronJob` is shown in the following code snippet:

```
apiVersion: batch/v1
kind: CronJob
metadata:
  name: hello-world
spec:
  schedule: "*/1 * * * *"
```

```
    jobTemplate:
      spec:
        template:
          spec:
            containers:
            - name: hello-world
              image: busybox
              args:
              - /bin/sh
              - -c
              - date; echo Hello World!
    restartPolicy: OnFailure
```

The `schedule` format follows the standard `cron` format. From left to right, each * represents the following:

- Minute (0–59)
- Hour (0–23)
- Day (1–31)
- Month (1–12)
- Day of the week (0–6) (Sunday = 0, Saturday = 6)

Cron jobs accept step values, which allow you to create a schedule that can execute every minute, every 2 minutes, or every hour.

Our example manifest will create a `cronjob` that runs an image called `hello-world` every minute and outputs `Hello World!` in the Pod log.

Jobs

Jobs allow you to execute a specific number of executions of a Pod or Pods. Unlike a `cronjob` resource, these Pods are not run on a set schedule, but rather they will execute once created.

Ingress

You may have noticed that the `Ingress` resource was listed twice in our `api-server` output. This will happen to resources as Kubernetes upgrades are released and resources are changed in the API server. In the case of Ingress, it was originally part of the extensions API and was moved to the `networking.k8s.io` API in version 1.16. The project will wait a few releases before deprecating the old API call, so in our example cluster running Kubernetes 1.21, using either API will work. In version 1.18, the Ingress extensions were deprecated.

While we created this book around Kubernetes 1.21, we wanted to point out that before publishing, Kubernetes 1.22 was released and the extensions/v1beta1 and networking.k8s.io/v1beta1 for Ingress have been removed from the API completely.

We will discuss Ingress in depth in the next chapter, but as a quick introduction to what an Ingress provides, it allows you to expose your application to the outside world using an assigned URL.

NetworkPolicies

NetworkPolicy resources let you define how network traffic, both ingress (incoming) and egress (outgoing), can flow through your cluster. They allow you to use Kubernetes native constructs to define which Pods can talk to other Pods. If you've ever used security groups in **Amazon Web Services (AWS)** to lock down access between two groups of systems, it's a similar concept. As an example, the following policy will allow traffic on port 443 to Pods in the myns namespace from any namespace with the app.kubernetes.io/name: ingress-nginx label on it (which is the default label for the nginx-ingress namespace):

```
apiVersion: networking.k8s.io/v1
kind: NetworkPolicy
metadata:
  name: allow-from-ingress
  namespace: myns
spec:
  PodSelector: {}
  policyTypes:
  - Ingress
  ingress:
  - from:
    - namespaceSelector:
        matchLabels:
          app.kubernetes.io/name: ingress-nginx
    ports:
    - protocol: TCP
      port: 443
```

A NetworkPolicy is another resource that you can use to secure a cluster. They should be used in all production clusters, but in a multi-tenant cluster, they should be considered a **must-have** to secure each namespace in the cluster.

PodSecurityPolicies

PodSecurityPolicies (**PSPs**) are how your cluster protects your nodes from your containers. They allow you to limit the actions that a Pod can execute in a cluster. Some examples include denying access to the HostIPC and HostPath, and running a container in a privileged mode.

Starting with Kubernetes 1.21, PSPs have been deprecated and will be removed when Kubernetes 1.25 is released. A replacement has been added as an alpha feature in version 1.22 called the PodSecurity admission controller. Since it's an alpha feature, we will still focus on the standard PSPs since use cases covered by PSPs will also be covered by the new PodSecurity admission controller.

We'll get into the details of PSPs in *Chapter 9, Node Security with GateKeeper*. The key point to remember about PSPs is that without them, your containers can do almost anything on your nodes.

ClusterRoleBindings

Once you have defined a `ClusterRole`, you bind it to a subject via a `ClusterRoleBinding`. A `ClusterRole` can be bound to a user, group, or service account.

We'll explore `ClusterRoleBinding` details in *Chapter 6, RBAC Policies and Auditing*.

ClusterRoles

A `ClusterRole` combines a set of permissions for interacting with your cluster's API. It combines a verb or action with an API group to define a permission. For instance, if you only want your **continuous integration/continuous delivery (CI/CD)** pipeline to be able to patch your Deployments so that it can update your image tag, you might use a `ClusterRole` like this:

```
apiVersion: rbac.authorization.k8s.io/v1
kind: ClusterRole
metadata:
  name: patch-deployment
  rules:
  - apiGroups: ["apps/v1"]
    resources: ["deployments"]
    verbs: ["get", "list", "patch"]
```

A `ClusterRole` can apply to APIs at both the cluster and namespace levels.

RoleBindings

The `RoleBinding` resource is how you associate a Role or `ClusterRole` with a subject and namespace. For instance, the following `RoleBinding` will allow the `aws-codebuild` user to apply the `patch-openunison` ClusterRole to the `openunison` namespace:

```
apiVersion: rbac.authorization.k8s.io/v1
kind: RoleBinding
metadata:
  name: patch-openunison
  namespace: openunison
subjects:
- kind: User
  name: aws-codebuild
  apiGroup: rbac.authorization.k8s.io
roleRef:
  kind: ClusterRole
  name: patch-deployment
  apiGroup: rbac.authorization.k8s.io
```

Even though this references a `ClusterRole`, it will only apply to the `openunison` namespace. If the `aws-codebuild` user tries to patch a Deployment in another namespace, the API server will stop it.

Roles

As with a `ClusterRole`, Roles combine API groups and actions to define a set of permissions that can be assigned to a subject. The difference between a `ClusterRole` and a `Role` is that a `Role` can only have resources defined at the namespace level and applies only within a specific namespace.

CSI drivers

Kubernetes uses the `CsiDriver` resource to connect nodes to a storage system.

You can list all CSI drivers that are available on a cluster by executing the `kubectl get csidriver` command. In one of our clusters, we are using NetApp's SolidFire for storage, so our cluster has the Trident CSI driver installed, as can be seen here:

```
NAME CREATED AT
csi.trident.netapp.io 2019-09-04T19:10:47Z
```

CSI nodes

To avoid storing storage information in the node's API resource, the `CSINode` resource was added to the API server to store information generated by the CSI drivers. The information that is stored includes mapping Kubernetes node names to CSI node names, CSI driver availability, and the volume topology.

Storage classes

Storage classes are used to define a storage endpoint. Each storage class can be assigned labels and policies, allowing a developer to select the best storage location for their persistent data. You may create a storage class for a backend system that has all **Non-Volatile Memory Express (NVMe)** drives, assigning it the name `fast`, while assigning a different class to a NetApp **Network File System (NFS)** volume running standard drives, using the name `standard`.

When a PVC is requested, the user can assign a `StorageClass` that they wish to use. When the API server receives the request, it finds the matching name and uses the `StorageClass` configuration to create the volume on the storage system using a provisioner.

At a very high level, a `StorageClass` manifest does not require a lot of information. Here is an example of a storage class using a provisioner from the Kubernetes incubator project to provide NFS auto-provisioned volumes, named `nfs`:

```
apiVersion: storage.k8s.io/v1
kind: StorageClass
metadata:
name: nfs
provisioner: nfs
```

Storage classes allow you to offer multiple storage solutions to your users. You may create a class for cheaper, slower storage while offering a second class that supports high throughput for high data requirements. By providing a different class to each offering, you allow developers to select the best choice for their application.

Summary

In this chapter, you were thrown into a Kubernetes bootcamp that presented a lot of technical material in a short amount of time. Try to remember that this will all become easier as you get into the Kubernetes world in more depth. We realize that this chapter had a lot of information on many resources. Many of the resources will be used in later chapters, and they will be explained in greater detail.

You learned about each Kubernetes component and how they interact to create a cluster. With this knowledge, you have the required skills to look at errors in a cluster and determine which component may be causing an error or issue. We covered the control plane of a cluster where the `api-server`, `kube-scheduler`, Etcd, and control managers run. The control plane is how users and services interact with a cluster; using the `api-server` and the `kube-scheduler` will decide which worker node to schedule your Pod(s) on. You also learned about Kubernetes nodes that run the `kubelet` and `kube-proxy` components, and a container runtime.

We covered the `kubectl` utility that you will use to interact with a cluster. You also learned some common commands that you will use daily, including `logs` and `describe`.

In the next chapter, we will create a development Kubernetes cluster that we will use as the base cluster for the remaining chapters. Throughout the remainder of the book, we will reference many of the resources that were presented in this chapter, helping to explain them by using them in real-world examples.

Questions

1. A Kubernetes control plane does not include which of the following components?

    a.   api-server

    b.   kube-scheduler

    c.   Etcd

    d.   Ingress controller

2. What is the name of the component that keeps all of the cluster information?

    a.   api-server

    b.   Master controller

    c.   kubelet

    d.   Etcd

3. Which component is responsible for selecting the node that will run a workload?

    a.   kubelet

    b.   api-server

    c.   kube-scheduler

    d.   Pod-scheduler

4. Which option would you add to a `kubectl` command to see additional output from a command?

    a. Verbose

    b. -v

    c. –verbose

    d. -log

5. Which service type creates a randomly generated port, allowing incoming traffic to any worker node on the assigned port to access the service?

    a. LoadBalancer

    b. ClusterIP

    c. None — it's the default for all services

    d. NodePort

6. If you need to deploy an application on a Kubernetes cluster that requires known node names and a controlled startup of each Pod, which object would you create?

    a. StatefulSet

    b. Deployment

    c. ReplicaSet

    d. ReplicationController

Join our book's Discord space

Join the book's Discord workspace for a monthly *Ask me Anything* session with the authors: `https://packt.link/K8EntGuide`

4
Services, Load Balancing, ExternalDNS, and Global Balancing

Before systems like Kubernetes were available, scaling an application often required a manual process that could involve multiple teams, and multiple processes, in many larger organizations. To scale out a common web application, you would have to add additional servers, and update the frontend load balancer to include the additional servers. We will discuss load balancers in this chapter, but for a quick introduction to anyone that may be new to the term, a load balancer provides a single point of entry to an application. The incoming request is handled by the load balancer, which routes traffic to any backend server that hosts the application. This is a very high-level explanation of a load balancer, and most offer very powerful features well beyond simply routing traffic, but for the purpose of this chapter, we are only concerned with the routing features.

When you deploy an application to a Kubernetes cluster, your pods are assigned ephemeral IP addresses. Since the assigned addresses are likely to change as pods are restarted, you should never target a service using a pod IP address; instead, you should use a service object, which will map a service IP address to backend pods based on labels. If you need to offer service access to external requests, you can deploy an Ingress controller, which will expose your service to external traffic on a per-URL basis. For more advanced workloads, you can deploy a load balancer, which provides your service with an external IP address, allowing you to expose any IP-based service to external requests.

We will explain how to implement each of these by deploying them on our KinD cluster. To help us understand how the Ingress works, we will deploy an NGINX Ingress controller to the cluster and expose a web server. Since Ingress rules are based on the incoming URL name, we need to be able to provide stable DNS names. In an enterprise environment, this would be accomplished using standard DNS. Since we are using a development environment without a DNS server, we will use a popular service from nip.io.

The chapter will end with two advanced topics. In the first, we will explain how you can dynamically register service names using an ETCD-integrated DNS zone with the Kubernetes incubator project, external-dns. The second advanced topic will explain how to set up an integrated Kubernetes global balancer to offer highly available services that can span multiple clusters, using a new CNCF project called K8GB.

As you may imagine, these topics can get very involved and to fully understand them, they require examples and detailed explanations. Due to the complexity of the subjects covered in this chapter, we have formatted the chapter into "mini chapters."

In this chapter, we will cover the following topics:

- Exposing workloads to requests
  - Understanding Kubernetes service options

- Using Kubernetes load balancers
  - Layer 7 load balancers
  - Layer 4 load balancers

- Enhancing basic load balancers for the enterprise
- Making service names available externally
- Load balancing between multiple clusters

By the end of the chapter, you will have a strong understanding of the multiple options for exposing your workloads in a single Kubernetes cluster. You will also learn how to leverage an open source global load balancer to provide access to workloads that run on multiple clusters.

Technical requirements

This chapter has the following technical requirements:

- An Ubuntu 18.03 or 20.04 server with a minimum of 4 GB of RAM.

- A KinD cluster configured using the configuration from *Chapter 2, Deploying Kubernetes Using KinD*.

You can access the code for this chapter by going to this book's GitHub repository: `https://github.com/PacktPublishing/Kubernetes---An-Enterprise-Guide-2E/tree/main/chapter4`.

Exposing workloads to requests

Over the years, we have discovered that the three most commonly misunderstood concepts in Kubernetes are services, Ingress controllers, and load balancers. In order to expose your workloads, you need to understand how each object works and the options that are available to you. Let's look at these in detail.

Understanding how services work

As we mentioned in the introduction, any pod that is running a workload is assigned an IP address at pod startup. Many events will cause a deployment to restart a pod, and when the pod is restarted, it will likely receive a new IP address. Since the addresses that are assigned to pods may change, you should never target a pod's workload directly.

One of the most powerful features that Kubernetes offers is the ability to scale your deployments. When a deployment is scaled, Kubernetes will create additional pods to handle any additional resource requirements. Each pod will have an IP address, and as you may know, most applications only target a single IP address or name. If your application were to scale from a single pod to 10 pods, how would you utilize the additional pods?

Services use Kubernetes labels to create a dynamic mapping between the service itself and the pods running the workload. The pods that are running the workload are labeled when they start up. Each pod has the same label that is defined in the deployment. For example, if we were using an NGINX web server in our deployment, we would create a deployment with the following manifest:

```
apiVersion: apps/v1
kind: Deployment
metadata:
  labels:
    run: nginx-frontend
  name: nginx-frontend
spec:
  replicas: 3
```

```
selector:
  matchLabels:
    run: nginx-frontend
template:
  metadata:
    labels:
      run: nginx-frontend
  spec:
    containers:
    - image: bitnami/nginx
      name: nginx-frontend
```

This deployment will create three NGINX servers and each pod will be labeled with `run=nginx-frontend`. We can verify whether the pods are labeled correctly by listing the pods using kubectl, and adding the `--show-labels` option, `kubectl get pods --show-labels`.

This will list each pod and any associated labels:

```
nginx-frontend-6c4dbf86d4-72cbc                    1/1       Running          0
19s      pod-template-hash=6c4dbf86d4,run=nginx-frontend
nginx-frontend-6c4dbf86d4-8zlwc                    1/1       Running          0
19s      pod-template-hash=6c4dbf86d4,run=nginx-frontend
nginx-frontend-6c4dbf86d4-xfz6m                    1/1       Running          0
19s      pod-template-hash=6c4dbf86d4,run=nginx-frontend
```

As you can see from the preceding output, each pod has a label, `run=nginx-frontend`. You will use this label when you create your service for the application, configuring the service to use the label to create the endpoints.

Creating a service

Now that you know how a service will use labels to create endpoints, let's discuss the service options we have in Kubernetes.

This section will introduce each service type and show you how to create a service object. Each type will be detailed in its own section after the general introduction.

Kubernetes services can be created using one of four types:

Service Type	Description
ClusterIP	Creates a service that is accessible from inside of the cluster.
NodePort	Creates a service that is accessible from inside or outside of the cluster using an assigned port.
LoadBalancer	Creates a service that is accessible from inside or outside of the cluster. For external access, an additional component is required to create the load-balanced object.
ExternalName	Creates a service that does not target an endpoint in the cluster. Instead, it is used to provide a service name that targets any external DNS name as an endpoint.

Table 4.1: Kubernetes service types

 There is an additional service type that can be created known as a headless service. A headless service will not allocate a cluster IP to the service, which means Kubernetes will only provide round-robin DNS load balancing, and kube-proxy will not handle any requests for the service. The most common use case for this type of service is a StatefulSet since they provide a controlled naming that is known for each pod that is created.

A headless service is created by specifying **none** for the clusterIP spec in the service definition.

To create a service, you need to create a service object that includes the `kind`, a `selector`, a `type`, and any `ports` that will be used to connect to the service. For our NGINX deployment, we want to expose the service on ports `80` and `443`. We labeled the deployment with `run=nginx-frontend`, so when we create a manifest, we will use that name as our selector:

```
apiVersion: v1
kind: Service
metadata:
  labels:
    run: nginx-frontend
  name: nginx-frontend
spec:
  selector:
    run: nginx-frontend
  ports:
```

```
  - name: http
    port: 80
    protocol: TCP
    targetPort: 80
  - name: https
    port: 443
    protocol: TCP
    targetPort: 443
  type: ClusterIP
```

If a type is not defined in a service manifest, Kubernetes will assign a default type of `ClusterIP`.

Now that a service has been created, we can verify that it was correctly defined using a few `kubectl` commands. The first check we will perform is to verify that the service object was created. To check our service, we use the `kubectl get services` command:

```
NAME              TYPE        CLUSTER-IP      EXTERNAL-IP     PORT(S)
AGE
nginx-frontend    ClusterIP   10.43.142.96    <none>       80/TCP,443/TCP
3m49s
```

After verifying that the service has been created, we can verify that the endpoints were created. Using kubectl, we can verify the endpoints by executing `kubectl get ep <service name>`:

```
NAME              ENDPOINTS
nginx-frontend    10.42.129.9:80,10.42.170.91:80,10.42.183.124:80 + 3
more...
```

We can see that the service shows three endpoints, but it also shows a `+3 more` in the endpoint list. Since the output is truncated, the output from a `get` is limited and it cannot show all of the endpoints. Since we cannot see the entire list, we can get a more detailed list if we describe the endpoints. Using kubectl, you can execute the `kubectl describe ep <service name>` command:

```
Name:         nginx-frontend
Namespace:    default
Labels:       run=nginx-frontend
Annotations:  endpoints.kubernetes.io/last-change-trigger-time:
2020-04-06T14:26:08Z
Subsets:
```

```
Addresses:              10.42.129.9,10.42.170.91,10.42.183.124
NotReadyAddresses:      <none>
Ports:
  Name        Port   Protocol
  ----        ----   --------
  http        80     TCP
  https       443    TCP
Events:   <none>
```

If you compare the output from our `get` and `describe` commands, it may appear that there is a mismatch in endpoints. The `get` command showed a total of six endpoints: it showed three IP endpoints and, because it was truncated, it also listed a +3, for a total of six endpoints. The output from the `describe` command shows only three IP addresses, and not six. Why do the two outputs appear to show different results?

The `get` command will list each endpoint and port in the list of addresses. Since our service is defined to expose two ports, each address will have two entries, one for each exposed port. The address list will always contain every socket for the service, which may list the endpoint addresses multiple times, once for each socket.

The `describe` command handles the output differently, listing the addresses on one line with all of the ports listed below the addresses. At first glance, it may look like the `describe` command is missing three addresses, but since it breaks the output into multiple sections, it will only list the addresses once. All ports are broken out below the address list; in our example, it shows ports **80** and **443**.

Both commands show the same data, but it is presented in a different format.

Now that the service is exposed to the cluster, you could use the assigned service IP address to connect to the application. While this would work, the address may change if the service object is deleted and recreated. So, rather than target an IP address, you should use the DNS that was assigned to the service when it was created.

In the next section, we will explain how to use internal DNS names to resolve services.

Using DNS to resolve services

In the world of physical machines and virtual servers, you have probably targeted a DNS record to communicate with a server. If the IP address of the server changed, then assuming you had dynamic DNS enabled, it would not have any effect on the application. This is the advantage of using names rather than IP addresses as endpoints.

When you create a service, an internal DNS record is created that can be queried by other workloads in the cluster. If all pods are in the same namespace, then we can target the services using a simple, short name like `mysql-web`; however, you may have some services that will be used by multiple namespaces, and when workloads need to communicate to a service outside of their own namespace, you must target the service using the full name. The following is an example table showing how a service may be targeted from namespaces:

Cluster name: `cluster.local` Target Service: `mysql-web` Target Service Namespace: `database`	
Pod Namespace	Valid Names to Connect to the MySQL Service
`database`	`mysql-web`
`kube-system`	`mysql-web.database.svc` `mysql-web.database.svc.cluster.local`
`production-web`	`mysql-web.database.svc` `mysql-web.database.svc.cluster.local`

Table 4.2: Internal DNS examples

As you can see from the preceding table, you can target a service that is in another namespace by using a standard naming convention, *.<namespace>.svc.<cluster name>*. In most cases, when you are accessing a service in a different namespace, you do not need to add the cluster name since it should be appended automatically.

To build on the general services concept, let's get into the details of each of the types and how we can use them to access our workloads.

Understanding different service types

When you create a service, you need to specify a service type. The service type that is assigned will configure how the service is exposed to either the cluster or external traffic.

The ClusterIP service

The most commonly used, and misunderstood, service type is ClusterIP. If you look back at our table, you can see that the description for the ClusterIP type states that the service allows connectivity to the service from within the cluster. The ClusterIP type does not allow any external traffic to the exposed service.

The idea of exposing a service to only internal cluster workloads can be a confusing concept. Why would you expose a service that can only be used by workloads in the cluster?

For a minute, let's forget about external traffic entirely. We need to concentrate on our current deployment and how each component interacts to create our application. Using the NGINX example, we will expand the deployment to include a backend database that services the web server.

Our application will have two deployments, one for the NGINX servers, and one for the database server. The NGINX deployment will create five replicas, while the database server will consist of a single replica. The NGINX servers need to connect to the database server to pull data for the web pages.

So far, this is a simple application: we have our deployments created, a service for the NGINX servers called the web frontend, and a database service called `mysql-web`. To configure the database connection from the web servers, we have decided to use a ConfigMap that will target the database service. What do we use in the ConfigMap as the destination for the database?

You may be thinking that since we are using a single database server, we could simply use the IP address. While this would initially work, any restarts to the pod would change the address and the web servers would fail to connect to the database. A service should always be used, even if you are only targeting a single pod. Since the database deployment is called `mysql-web`, our ConfigMap should use that name as the database server.

By using the service name, we will not run into issues when the pod is restarted since the service targets the labels rather than an IP address. Our web servers will simply query the Kubernetes DNS server for the service name, which will contain the endpoints of any pod that has a matching label.

The NodePort service

A NodePort service will expose your service internally to the cluster, as well as externally to the network. At first glance, this may look like the go-to service when you want to expose a service. It exposes your service to everybody, but it does this by using something called a NodePort, and using it for external service access can become difficult to maintain. It is also very confusing for users to use a NodePort or remember when they need to access a service over the network.

To create a service that uses the NodePort type, you just need to set the type to NodePort in your manifest. We can use the same manifest that we used earlier to expose an NGINX deployment from the ClusterIP example, only changing the type to `NodePort`:

```
apiVersion: v1
kind: Service
metadata:
```

```
    labels:
      run: nginx-frontend
    name: nginx-frontend
spec:
    selector:
      run: nginx-frontend
    ports:
    - name: http
      port: 80
      protocol: TCP
      targetPort: 80
    - name: https
      port: 443
      protocol: TCP
      targetPort: 443
    type: NodePort
```

We can view the endpoints in the same way that we did for a ClusterIP service, using kubectl. Running `kubectl get services` will show you the newly created service:

```
NAME                TYPE       CLUSTER-IP      EXTERNAL-IP    PORT(S)
AGE
nginx-frontend      NodePort   10.43.164.118   <none>         80:31574/
TCP,443:32432/TCP   4s
```

The output shows that the type is NodePort and that we have exposed the service IP address and the ports. If you look at the ports, you will notice that, unlike a ClusterIP service, a NodePort service shows two ports rather than one. The first port is the exposed port that the internal cluster services can target, and the second port number is the randomly generated port that is accessible from outside of the cluster.

Since we exposed both ports 80 and 443 for the service, we will have two NodePorts assigned. If someone needs to target the service from outside of the cluster, they can target any worker node with the supplied port to access the service.

Figure 4.1: NGINX service using NodePort

Each node maintains a list of the NodePorts and their assigned services. Since the list is shared with all nodes, you can target any functioning node using the port and Kubernetes will route it to a running pod.

To visualize the traffic flow, we have created a graphic showing the web request to our NGINX pod:

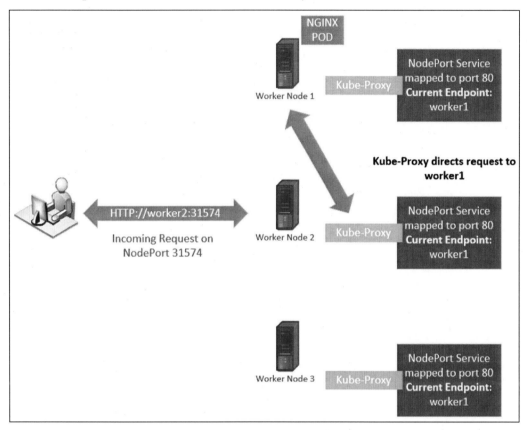

Figure 4.2: NodePort traffic flow overview

There are some issues to consider when using a NodePort to expose a service:

- If you delete and recreate the service, the assigned NodePort will change.
- If you target a node that is offline or having issues, your request will fail.
- Using NodePort for too many services may get confusing. You need to remember the port for each service and remember that there are no *external* names associated with the service. This may get confusing for users who are targeting services in the cluster.

Because of the limitations listed here, you should limit using NodePort services.

The LoadBalancer service

Many people starting out in Kubernetes read about services and discover that the LoadBalancer type will assign an external IP address to a service. Since an external IP address can be addressed directly by any machine on the network, this is an attractive option for a service, which is why many people try to use it first. Unfortunately, since many users start by using an on-premises Kubernetes cluster, they run into headaches trying to create a LoadBalancer service.

The LoadBalancer service relies on an external component that integrates with Kubernetes to create the IP address assigned to the service. Most on-premise Kubernetes installations do not include this type of service. When you try to use a LoadBalancer service without the support infrastructure, you will find that your service shows <pending> in the EXTERNAL-IP status column.

We will explain the LoadBalancer service and how to implement it later in the chapter.

The ExternalName service

The ExternalName service is a unique service type with a specific use case. When you query a service that uses an ExternalName type, the final endpoint is not a pod that is running in the cluster, but an external DNS name.

To use an example that you may be familiar with outside of Kubernetes, this is similar to using c-name to alias a host record. When you query a c-name record in DNS, it resolves to a host record rather than an IP address.

Before using this service type, you need to understand potential issues that it may cause for your application. You may run into issues if the target endpoint is using SSL certificates. Since the hostname you are querying may not be the same as the name on the destination server's certificate, your connection may not succeed because of the name mismatch. If you find yourself in this situation, you may be able to use a certificate that has **subject alternative names** (**SAN**) added to the certificate. Adding alternative names to a certificate allows you to associate multiple names with a certificate.

To explain why you may want to use an ExternalName service, let's use the following example:

FooWidgets Application Requirements

FooWidgets is running an application on their Kubernetes cluster that needs to connect to a database server running on a Windows 2019 server called `sqlserver1.foowidgets.com` (`192.168.10.200`).

The current application is deployed to a namespace called `finance`.

The SQL server will be migrated to a container in the next quarter.

You have two requirements:

- Configure the application to use the external database server using only the cluster's DNS server.

- FooWidgets cannot make any configuration changes to the applications after the SQL server is migrated.

Based on the requirements, using an ExternalName service is the perfect solution. So, how would we accomplish the requirements? (This is a theoretical exercise; you do not need to execute anything on your KinD cluster):

1. The first step is to create a manifest that will create the ExternalName service for the database server:

```
apiVersion: v1
kind: Service
metadata:
  name: sql-db
  namespace: finance
spec:
  type: ExternalName
  externalName: sqlserver1.foowidgets.com
```

2. With the service created, the next step is to configure the application to use the name of our new service. Since the service and the application are in the same namespace, you can configure the application to target the name `sql-db`.

3. Now, when the application queries for `sql-db`, it will resolve to `sqlserver1.foowidgets.com`, and, ultimately, the IP address of `192.168.10.200`.

This accomplishes the initial requirement, connecting the application to the external database server using only the Kubernetes DNS server.

You may be wondering why we didn't simply configure the application to use the database server name directly. The key is the second requirement; limiting any reconfiguration when the SQL server is migrated to a container.

Since we cannot reconfigure the application once the SQL server is migrated to the cluster, we will not be able to change the name of the SQL server in the application settings. If we configured the application to use the original name, `sqlserver1.foowidgets.com`, the application would not work after the migration. By using the ExternalName service, we can change the internal DNS service name by replacing the ExternalHost service name with a standard Kubernetes service that points to the SQL server.

To accomplish the second goal, go through the following steps:

1. Delete the `ExternalName` service.

2. Create a new service using the name `ext-sql-db` that uses `app=sql-app` as the selector. The manifest would look like the one shown here:

```
apiVersion: v1
kind: Service
metadata:
  labels:
    app: sql-db
  name: sql-db
  namespace: finance
spec:
  ports:
  - port: 1433
    protocol: TCP
    targetPort: 1433
  name: sql
  selector:
    app: sql-app
  type: ClusterIP
```

Since we are using the same service name for the new service, no changes need to be made to the application. The app will still target the name `sql-db`, which will now use the SQL server deployed in the cluster.

Now that you know about services, we can move on to load balancers, which will allow you to expose services externally using standard URL names and ports.

Introduction to load balancers

In this second section, we will discuss the basics between utilizing layer 7 and layer 4 load balancers. To understand the differences between the types of load balancers, it's important to understand the **Open Systems Interconnection (OSI)** model. Understanding the different layers of the OSI model will help you to understand how different solutions handle incoming requests.

Understanding the OSI model

When you hear about different solutions to expose an application in Kubernetes, you will often hear a reference to layer 7 or layer 4 load balancing. These designations refer to where each operates in the OSI model. Each layer offers different functionality; a component that runs at layer 7 offers different functionality to a component in layer 4.

To begin, let's look at a brief overview of the seven layers and a description of each. For this chapter, we are interested in the two highlighted sections, **layer 4** and **layer 7**:

OSI Layer	Name	Description
7	Application	Provides application traffic, including HTTP and HTTPS
6	Presentation	Forms data packets and encryption
5	Session	Controls traffic flow
4	Transport	Communication traffic between devices, including TCP and UDP
3	Network	Routing between devices, including IP
2	Data Link	Performs error checking for physical connection (MAC address)
1	Physical	Physical connection of devices

Table 4.3: OSI model layers

You don't need to be an expert in the OSI layers, but you should understand what layer 4 and layer 7 load balancers provide and how each may be used with a cluster.

Let's go deeper into the details of layers 4 and 7:

- **Layer 4**: As the description states in the chart, layer 4 is responsible for the communication of traffic between devices. Devices that run at layer 4 have access to TCP/UDP information. Load balancers that are layer-4 based provide your applications with the ability to service incoming requests for any TCP/UDP port.

- **Layer 7**: Layer 7 is responsible for providing network services to applications. When we say application traffic, we are not referring to applications such as Excel or Word; instead, we are referring to the protocols that support the applications, such as HTTP and HTTPS.

This may be very new for some people and to completely understand the layers would require multiple chapters – which would be beyond the scope of this book. The main point we want you to take away from this introduction is that applications like databases cannot be exposed externally using a layer 7 load balancer. To expose an application that does not use HTTP traffic requires the use of a layer 4 load balancer.

In the next section, we will explain each load balancer type and how to use them in a Kubernetes cluster to expose your services.

Layer 7 load balancers

Kubernetes provides layer 7 load balancers in the form of an Ingress controller. There are a number of solutions when it comes to providing Ingress to your clusters, including the following:

- NGINX
- Envoy
- Traefik
- HAproxy

Typically, a layer 7 load balancer is limited in the functions it can perform. In the Kubernetes world, they are implemented as Ingress controllers that can route incoming HTTP/HTTPS requests to your exposed services. We will go into detail on implementing NGINX as a Kubernetes Ingress controller in the *Creating Ingress rules* section.

Name resolution and layer 7 load balancers

To handle layer 7 traffic in a Kubernetes cluster, you deploy an Ingress controller. Ingress controllers are dependent on incoming names to route traffic to the correct service. In a legacy server deployment model, you would create a DNS entry and map it to an IP address.

Applications that are deployed on a Kubernetes cluster are no different – the user will use a DNS name to access the application.

Oftentimes, you will create a new wildcard domain that will target the Ingress controller via an external load balancer, such as an F5, HAproxy, or SeeSaw.

Let's assume that our company is called FooWidgets and we have three Kubernetes clusters, fronted by an external load balancer with multiple Ingress controller endpoints. Our DNS server would have entries for each cluster, using a wildcard domain that points to the load balancer's virtual IP address:

Domain Name	IP Address	K8s Cluster
`*.cluster1.` `foowidgets.com`	`192.168.200.100`	Production001
`*.cluster2.` `foowidgets.com`	`192.168.200.101`	Production002
`*.cluster3.` `foowidgets.com`	`192.168.200.102`	Development001

Table 4.4: Example wildcard domain names for Ingress

The following diagram shows the entire flow of the request:

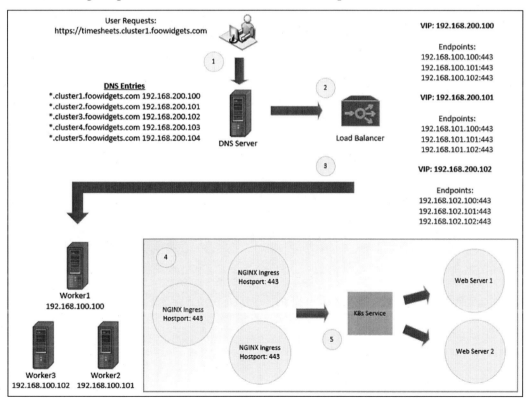

Figure 4.3: Multiple-name Ingress traffic flow

Each of the steps in *Figure 4.3* is detailed here:

1. Using a browser, the user requests the URL `https://timesheets.cluster1.foowidgets.com`.

2. The DNS query is sent to a DNS server. The DNS server looks up the zone details for `cluster1.foowidgets.com`. There is a single entry in the DNS zone that resolves to the VIP, or virtual IP address, assigned on the load balancer for the domain.

3. The load balancer's VIP for `cluster1.foowidgets.com` has three backend servers assigned, pointing to three worker nodes where we have deployed Ingress controllers.

4. Using one of the endpoints, the request is sent to the Ingress controller.

5. The Ingress controller will compare the requested URL to a list of Ingress rules. When a matching request is found, the Ingress controller will forward the request to the service that was assigned to the Ingress rule.

To help reinforce how Ingress works, it will help to create Ingress rules on a cluster to see them in action. Right now, the key takeaways are that Ingress uses the requested URL to direct traffic to the correct Kubernetes services.

Using nip.io for name resolution

Most personal development clusters, such as our KinD installation, may not have enough access to add records to a DNS server. To test Ingress rules, we need to target unique hostnames that are mapped to Kubernetes services by the Ingress controller. Without a DNS server, you need to create a localhost file with multiple names pointing to the IP address of the Ingress controller.

For example, if you deployed four web servers, you need to add all four names to your local hosts. An example of this is shown here:

```
192.168.100.100 webserver1.test.local
192.168.100.100 webserver2.test.local
192.168.100.100 webserver3.test.local
192.168.100.100 webserver4.test.local
```

This can also be represented on a single line rather than multiple lines:

```
192.168.100.100 webserver1.test.local webserver2.test.local webserver3.
test.local webserver4.test.local
```

If you use multiple machines to test your deployments, you will need to edit the host file on every machine that you plan to use for testing. Maintaining multiple files on multiple machines is an administrative nightmare and will lead to issues that will make testing a challenge.

Luckily, there are free services available that provide DNS services that we can use without configuring a complex DNS infrastructure for our KinD cluster.

Nip.io is the service that we will use for our KinD cluster name resolution requirements. Using our previous web server example, we will not need to create any DNS records. We still need to send the traffic for the different servers to the NGINX server running on `192.168.100.100` so that Ingress can route the traffic to the appropriate service. Nip.io uses a naming format that includes the IP address in the hostname to resolve the name to an IP. For example, say that we have four web servers that we want to test called `webserver1`, `webserver2`, `webserver3`, and `webserver4`, with Ingress rules on an Ingress controller running on `192.168.100.100`.

As we mentioned earlier, we do not need to create any records to accomplish this. Instead, we can use the naming convention to have nip.io resolve the name for us. Each of the web servers would use a name with the following naming standard:

```
<desired name>.<INGRESS IP>.nip.io
```

The names for all four web servers are listed in the following table:

Web Server Name	Nip.io DNS Name
webserver1	webserver1.192.168.100.100.nip.io
webserver2	webserver2.192.168.100.100.nip.io
webserver3	webserver3.192.168.100.100.nip.io
webserver4	webserver4.192.168.100.100.nip.io

Table 4.5: Nip.io example domain names

When you use any of the preceding names, nip.io will resolve them to `192.168.100.100`. You can see an example ping for each name in the following screenshot:

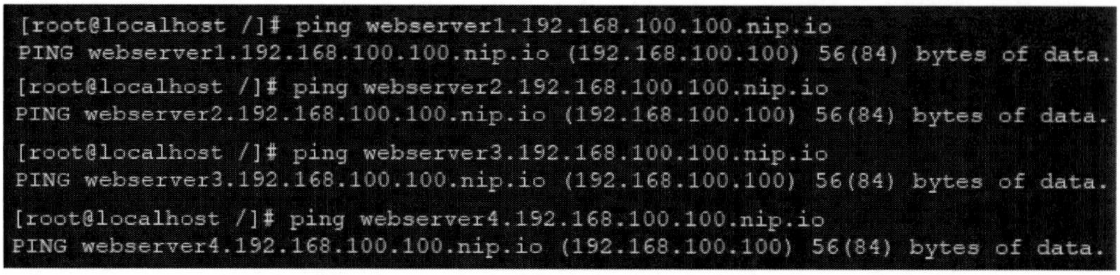

```
[root@localhost /]# ping webserver1.192.168.100.100.nip.io
PING webserver1.192.168.100.100.nip.io (192.168.100.100) 56(84) bytes of data.
[root@localhost /]# ping webserver2.192.168.100.100.nip.io
PING webserver2.192.168.100.100.nip.io (192.168.100.100) 56(84) bytes of data.
[root@localhost /]# ping webserver3.192.168.100.100.nip.io
PING webserver3.192.168.100.100.nip.io (192.168.100.100) 56(84) bytes of data.
[root@localhost /]# ping webserver4.192.168.100.100.nip.io
PING webserver4.192.168.100.100.nip.io (192.168.100.100) 56(84) bytes of data.
```

Figure 4.4: Example name resolution using nip.io

This may look like it has very little benefit since you are supplying the IP address in the name. Why would you need to bother using nip.io if you know the IP address?

Remember that the Ingress rules require a unique name to route traffic to the correct service. While the name may not be required for you to know the IP address of the server, the name is required for the Ingress rules. Each name is unique, using the first part of the full name—in our example, that is webserver1, webserver2, webserver3, and webserver4.

By providing this service, nip.io allows you to use any name for Ingress rules without the need to have a DNS server in your development cluster.

Now that you know how to use nip.io to resolve names for your cluster, let's explain how to use a nip.io name in an Ingress rule.

Creating Ingress rules

Remember, Ingress rules use names to route the incoming request to the correct service.

The following is a graphical representation of an incoming request, showing how Ingress routes the traffic:

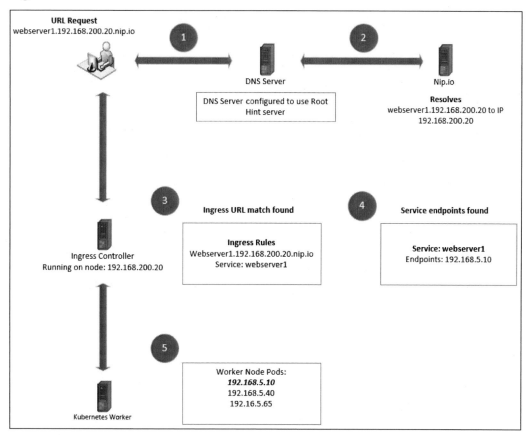

Figure 4.5: Ingress traffic flow

Figure 4.5 shows a high-level overview of how Kubernetes handles incoming Ingress requests. To help explain each step in more depth, let's go over the five steps in greater detail. Using the graphic provided in *Figure 4.5*, we will explain each numbered step in detail to show how ingress processes the request:

1. The user requests a URL in their browser named `http://webserver1.192.168.200.20.nio.io`. A DNS request is sent to the local DNS server, which is ultimately sent to the nip.io DNS server.

2. The nip.io server resolves the domain name to the IP address of `192.168.200.20`, which is returned to the client.

3. The client sends the request to the Ingress controller, which is running on `192.168.200.20`. The request contains the complete URL name, `webserver1.192.168.200.20.nio.io`.

4. The Ingress controller looks up the requested URL name in the configured rules and matches the URL name to a service.

5. The service endpoint(s) will be used to route traffic to the assigned pods.

6. The request is routed to an endpoint pod running the web server.

Using the preceding example traffic flow, let's go over the Kubernetes objects that need to be created:

1. First, we need a simple web server running in a namespace. We will simply deploy a base NGINX web server in the default namespace. Rather than create a manifest manually, we can create a deployment quickly using the following `kubectl create deployment` command:

   ```
   kubectl create deployment nginx-web --image bitnami/nginx
   ```

2. Using the `create deployment` option is a shortcut that will create a deployment called `nginx-web` in the default namespace. You may notice that the output will give you a warning that the run is being deprecated.

3. Next, we need to create a service for the deployment. Again, we will create a service using a kubectl command, `kubectl expose`. The Bitnami NGINX image runs on port `8080`, so we will use the same port to expose the service:

   ```
   kubectl expose deployment nginx-web --port 8080 --target-port
   8080
   ```

   This will create a new service called `nginx-web` for our deployment, called `nginx-web`.

4. Now that we have our deployment and service created, the last step is to create the Ingress rule. To create an Ingress rule, you create a manifest using the object type `Ingress`. The following is an example Ingress rule that assumes that the Ingress controller is running on `192.168.200.20`. If you are creating this rule on your host, you should use the **IP address of your Docker host**.

   Create a file called `nginx-ingress.yaml` with the following content:

   ```
   apiVersion: networking.k8s.io/v1
   kind: Ingress
   metadata:
   ```

```
      name: nginx-web-ingress
  spec:
    rules:
    - host: "webserver1.192.168.200.20.nip.io"
      http:
        paths:
        - path: /
          pathType: Exact
          backend:
            service:
              name: nginx-web
              port:
                number: 8080
```

5. Create the Ingress rule using `kubectl apply`:

```
kubectl apply -f nginx-ingress.yaml
```

6. You can test the deployment from any client on your internal network by browsing to the Ingress URL, `http://webserver1.192.168.200.20.nip.io`.

7. If everything has been created successfully, you should see the NGINX welcome page:

Figure 4.6: NGINX web server using nip.io for Ingress

Using the information in this section, you can create Ingress rules for multiple containers using different hostnames. Of course, you aren't limited to using a service like nip.io to resolve names; you can use any name resolution method that you have available in your environment. In a production cluster, you will have an enterprise DNS infrastructure, but in a lab environment, such as our KinD cluster, nip.io is the perfect tool for testing scenarios that require proper naming conventions.

We will use nip.io naming standards throughout the book, so it's important to understand the naming convention before moving on to the next chapter.

Layer 7 load balancers, such as NGINX Ingress, are used by many standard workloads, such as web servers. There will be deployments that will require a more complex load balancer, one that runs at a lower layer of the OSI model. As we move down the model, we gain lower-level features. In our next section, we will discuss layer 4 load balancers.

> If you deployed the NGINX example on your cluster, you should delete the service and the Ingress rules:
>
> To delete the Ingress rule, execute the following command: `kubectl delete ingress nginx-web-ingress`
>
> To delete the service, execute the following command: `kubectl delete service nginx-web`
>
> You can leave the NGINX deployment running for the next section.

Layer 4 load balancers

Layer 4 of the OSI model is responsible for protocols such as TCP and UDP. A load balancer that is running in layer 4 accepts incoming traffic based on the only IP address and port. The incoming request is accepted by the load balancer, and based on a set of rules, the traffic is sent to the destination IP address and port.

There are lower-level networking operations in the process that are beyond the scope of this book. HAproxy has a good summary of the terminology and example configurations on their website at `https://www.haproxy.com/fr/blog/loadbalancing-faq/`.

Layer 4 load balancer options

There are multiple options available to you if you want to configure a layer 4 load balancer for a Kubernetes cluster. Some of the options include the following:

- HAproxy
- NGINX Pro
- SeeSaw
- F5 Networks
- MetalLB
- And more...

Each option provides layer 4 load balancing, but for the purpose of this book, we felt that MetalLB was the best choice.

Using MetalLB as a layer 4 load balancer

Remember that in *Chapter 2, Deploying Kubernetes Using KinD*, we had a diagram showing the flow of traffic between a workstation and the KinD nodes. Because KinD was running in a nested Docker container, a layer 4 load balancer would have had certain limitations when it came to networking connectivity. Without additional network configuration on the Docker host, you will not be able to target the services that use the LoadBalancer type outside of the Docker host itself.

If you deploy MetalLB to a standard Kubernetes cluster running on a host, you will not be limited to accessing services outside of the host itself.

MetalLB is a free, easy-to-configure layer 4 load balancer. It includes powerful configuration options that give it the ability to run in a development lab or an enterprise cluster. Since it is so versatile, it has become a very popular choice for clusters requiring layer 4 load balancing.

In this section, we will focus on installing MetalLB in layer 2 mode. This is an easy installation and works for development or small Kubernetes clusters. MetalLB also offers the option to deploy using BGP mode, which allows you to establish peering partners to exchange networking routes. If you would like to read about MetalLB's BGP mode, you can read about it on MetalLB's site at `https://metallb.universe.tf/concepts/bgp/`.

Installing MetalLB

To deploy MetalLB on your KinD cluster we have included a script called `install-metallb.sh` in the `chapter4` repository directory. The script will execute the commands below, but we have included them to explain the process or to guide you if you decide to deploy it manually:

1. The following will create a new namespace called `metallb-system` with a label of `app: metallb`:

   ```
   kubectl apply -f https://raw.githubusercontent.com/metallb/
   metallb/v0.10.2/manifests/namespace.yaml
   ```

2. This will deploy MetalLB to your cluster. It will create all the Kubernetes objects required, including `PodSecurityPolicies`, `ClusterRoles`, `Bindings`, `DaemonSet`, and a `deployment`:

```
kubectl apply -f https://raw.githubusercontent.com/metallb/
metallb/v0.10.2/manifests/metallb.yaml
```

3. The last command will create a secret in the `metallb-system` namespace that has a randomly generated value. This secret is used by MetalLB to encrypt communications between speakers:

```
kubectl create secret generic -n metallb-system memberlist
--from-literal=secretkey="$(openssl rand -base64 128)"
```

Now that MetalLB has been deployed to the cluster, you need to supply a MetalLB configuration file to complete the setup.

Understanding MetalLB's configuration file

MetalLB is configured using a ConfigMap that contains the configuration. Since we will be using MetalLB in layer 2 mode, the required configuration file is fairly simple and only requires one piece of information: the IP range that you want to create for services.

To keep the configuration simple, we will use a small range from the Docker subnet in which KinD is running. If you were running MetalLB on a standard Kubernetes cluster, you could assign any range that is routable in your network, but we are limited with our KinD clusters.

To get the subnet that Docker is using, we can inspect the KinD bridge network that we are using:

```
docker network inspect kind | grep -i subnet
```

In the output, you will see the assigned subnet, similar to the following:

```
"Subnet": "172.18.0.0/16"
```

This is an entire class-B address range. We know that we will not use all of the IP addresses for running containers, so we will use a small range from the subnet in our MetalLB configuration.

Let's create a new file called `metallb-config.yaml` and add the following to the file:

```
apiVersion: v1
kind: ConfigMap
metadata:
  namespace: metallb-system
  name: config
data:
  config: |
    address-pools:
    - name: default
      protocol: layer2
      addresses:
      - 172.18.200.100-172.18.200.125
```

The manifest will create a ConfigMap in the `metallb-system` namespace called `config`. The configuration file will set MetalLB's mode to layer 2 with an IP pool called `default`, using the range of `172.18.200.100` through `172.18.200.125` for LoadBalancer services.

You can assign different addresses based on the configuration names. We will show this when we explain how to create a LoadBalancer service.

Finally, deploy the manifest using kubectl:

```
kubectl apply -f metallb-config.yaml
```

To understand how MetalLB works, you need to know the installed components and how they interact to assign IP addresses to services.

MetalLB components

The second manifest in our deployment is what installs the MetalLB components to the cluster. It deploys a DaemonSet that includes the speaker image and a DaemonSet that includes the controller image. These components communicate with each other to maintain a list of services and assigned IP addresses:

The speaker

The speaker component is what MetalLB uses to announce the LoadBalancer services on the node. It is deployed as a DaemonSet since the deployments can be on any worker node, and therefore, each worker node needs to announce the workloads that are running. As services are created using a LoadBalancer type, the speaker will announce the service.

If we look at the speaker log from a node, we can see the following announcements:

```
{"caller":"main.go:176","event":"startUpdate","msg":"start of
service update","service":"my-grafana-operator/grafana-operator-
metrics","ts":"2020-04-21T21:10:07.437231123Z"}
{"caller":"main.go:189","event":"endUpdate","msg":"end of
service update","service":"my-grafana-operator/grafana-operator-
metrics","ts":"2020-04-21T21:10:07.437516541Z"}
{"caller":"main.go:176","event":"startUpdate","msg":"start of
service update","service":"my-grafana-operator/grafana-operator-
metrics","ts":"2020-04-21T21:10:07.464140524Z"}
{"caller":"main.go:246","event":"serviceAnnounced","ip":"10.2.1.72","ms
g":"service has IP, announcing","pool":"default","protocol":"layer2","
service":"my-grafana-operator/grafana-operator-metrics","ts":"2020-04-
21T21:10:07.464311087Z"}
{"caller":"main.go:249","event":"endUpdate","msg":"end of
service update","service":"my-grafana-operator/grafana-operator-
metrics","ts":"2020-04-21T21:10:07.464470317Z"}
```

The preceding announcement is for Grafana. After the announcement, you can see that it has been assigned an IP address of `10.2.1.72`.

The controller

The controller will receive the announcements from the speaker on each worker node. Using the same service announcement shown previously, the controller log shows the announcement and the IP address that the controller assigned to the service:

```
{"caller":"main.go:49","event":"startUpdate","msg":"start of
service update","service":"my-grafana-operator/grafana-operator-
metrics","ts":"2020-04-21T21:10:07.437701161Z"}
{"caller":"service.go:98","event":"ipAllocated","ip":"10.2.1.72","msg
":"IP address assigned by controller","service":"my-grafana-operator/
grafana-operator-metrics","ts":"2020-04-21T21:10:07.438079774Z"}
{"caller":"main.go:96","event":"serviceUpdated","msg":"updated
service object","service":"my-grafana-operator/grafana-operator-
metrics","ts":"2020-04-21T21:10:07.467998702Z"}
```

In the second line of the log, you can see that the controller assigned the IP address of `10.2.1.72`.

Creating a LoadBalancer service

Now that you have installed MetalLB and understand how the components create the services, let's create our first LoadBalancer service on our KinD cluster.

In the layer 7 load balancer section, we created a deployment running NGINX that we exposed by creating a service and an Ingress rule. At the end of the section, we deleted the service and the Ingress rule, but we kept the NGINX deployment for this section. If you followed the steps in the Ingress section and have not deleted the service and Ingress rule, please do so before creating the LoadBalancer service. If you did not create the deployment at all, you will need an NGINX deployment for this section:

1. You can create a quick NGINX pod by executing the following command:

    ```
    kubectl run nginx-web --image bitnami/nginx
    ```

2. To create a new service that will use the LoadBalancer type, you can create a new manifest or you can expose the deployment using only kubectl.

    To create a manifest, create a new file called `nginx-lb.yaml` and add the following:

    ```
    apiVersion: v1
    kind: Service
    metadata:
      name: nginx-lb
    spec:
      ports:
      - port: 8080
        targetPort: 8080
      selector:
        run: nginx-web
      type: LoadBalancer
    ```

3. Apply the file to the cluster using kubectl:

    ```
    kubectl apply -f nginx-lb.yaml
    ```

4. To verify that the service was created correctly, list the services using `kubectl get services`:

    ```
    NAME          TYPE           CLUSTER-IP    EXTERNAL-IP      PORT(S)
    AGE
    kubernetes    ClusterIP      10.96.0.1     <none>           443/TCP
    5d18h
    nginx-lb      LoadBalancer   10.104.41.3   172.18.200.100
    8080:30296/TCP              23s
    ```

You will see that a new service was created using the LoadBalancer type and that MetalLB assigned an IP address from the configured pool we created earlier.

A quick look at the controller log will verify that the MetalLB controller assigned the service the IP address:

```
{"caller":"service.go:114","event":"ipAllocated","
ip":"172.18.200.100","msg":"IP address assigned by
controller","service":"default/nginx-lb","ts":"2021-06-
25T12:23:03.132228668Z"}
```

5. Now you can test the service by using `curl` on the Docker host. Using the IP address that was assigned to the service and port **8080**, enter the following command:

```
curl 172.18.200.100:8080
```

You will receive the following output:

```
surovich@buntu20:/$ curl 172.18.200.100:8080
<!DOCTYPE html>
<html>
<head>
<title>Welcome to nginx!</title>
<style>
    body {
        width: 35em;
        margin: 0 auto;
        font-family: Tahoma, Verdana, Arial, sans-serif;
    }
</style>
</head>
<body>
<h1>Welcome to nginx!</h1>
<p>If you see this page, the nginx web server is successfully installed and
working. Further configuration is required.</p>

<p>For online documentation and support please refer to
<a href="http://nginx.org/">nginx.org</a>.<br/>
Commercial support is available at
<a href="http://nginx.com/">nginx.com</a>.</p>

<p><em>Thank you for using nginx.</em></p>
</body>
</html>
```

Figure 4.7: Curl output to the LoadBalancer service running NGINX

Adding MetalLB to a cluster allows you to expose applications that otherwise could not be exposed using a layer 7 balancer. Adding both layer 7 and layer 4 services to your clusters allows you to expose almost any application type you can think of, including databases. What if you wanted to offer different IP pools to services? In the next section, we will explain how to create multiple IP pools that can be assigned to services using an annotation, allowing you to assign an IP range to services.

Adding multiple IP pools to MetalLB

There may be scenarios where you need to provide different subnets to specific workloads on a cluster. One scenario may be that when you created a range on the network for your services, you underestimated how many services would be created and you ran out of IP addresses.

Depending on the original range that you used, you may be able to just increase the range on your configuration. If you cannot extend the existing range, you will need to create a new range before any new LoadBalancer services can be created. You can also add additional IP ranges to the default pool, but for this example, we will create a new pool.

We can edit the configuration file and add the new range information to the file. Using the original YAML file, `metallb-config.yaml`, we need to add the text in bold to the following code:

```
apiVersion: v1
kind: ConfigMap
metadata:
  namespace: metallb-system
  name: config
data:
  config: |
    address-pools:
    - name: default
      protocol: layer2
      addresses:
      - 172.18.200.100-172.18.200.125
    - name: subnet-201
      protocol: layer2
      addresses:
      - 172.18.201.100-172.18.201.125
```

Apply the updated ConfigMap using `kubectl`:

```
kubectl apply -f metallb-config.yaml
```

The updated ConfigMap will create a new pool called `subnet-201`. MetalLB now has two pools that can be used to assign IP addresses to services: the `default` and `subnet-201`.

If a user creates a LoadBalancer service and does not specify a pool name, Kubernetes will attempt to use the default pool. If the requested pool is out of address, the service will sit in a pending state until an address is available.

To create a new service from the second pool, you need to add an annotation to your service request. Using our NGINX deployment, we will create a second service called `nginx-web2` that will request an IP address from the `subnet-201` pool:

1. Create a new file called `nginx-lb2.yaml` with the following content:

   ```
   apiVersion: v1
   kind: Service
   metadata:
     name: nginx-lb2
     annotations:
       metallb.universe.tf/address-pool: subnet-201
   spec:
     ports:
     - port: 8080
       targetPort: 8080
     selector:
       run: nginx-web
     type: LoadBalancer
   ```

2. To create the new service, deploy the manifest using kubectl:

   ```
   kubectl apply -f nginx-lb2.yaml
   ```

3. To verify that the service was created with an IP address from the subnet-201 pool, list all of the services:

   ```
   kubectl get services
   ```

   You will receive the following output:

   ```
   NAME            TYPE           CLUSTER-IP      EXTERNAL-IP
   PORT(S)         AGE
   kubernetes      ClusterIP      10.96.0.1       <none>
   443/TCP         5d18h
   nginx-lb        LoadBalancer   10.104.41.3     172.18.200.100
   8080:30296/TCP         9m16s
   nginx-lb2       LoadBalancer   10.111.34.213   172.18.201.100
   8080:31342/TCP         10s
   ```

   The last service on the list is our newly created `nginx-lb2` service. We can confirm that it has been assigned an external IP address of `172.18.20.100`, which is from the subnet-201 pool.

4. And finally, we can test the service by using a `curl` command on the Docker host, to the assigned IP address on port `8080`:

```
surovich@buntu20:/$ curl 172.18.201.100:8080
<!DOCTYPE html>
<html>
<head>
<title>Welcome to nginx!</title>
<style>
    body {
        width: 35em;
        margin: 0 auto;
        font-family: Tahoma, Verdana, Arial, sans-serif;
    }
</style>
</head>
<body>
<h1>Welcome to nginx!</h1>
<p>If you see this page, the nginx web server is successfully installed and
working. Further configuration is required.</p>

<p>For online documentation and support please refer to
<a href="http://nginx.org/">nginx.org</a>.<br/>
Commercial support is available at
<a href="http://nginx.com/">nginx.com</a>.</p>

<p><em>Thank you for using nginx.</em></p>
</body>
</html>
```

Figure 4.8: Curl NGINX on a LoadBalancer using a second IP pool

Having the ability to offer different address pools allows you to assign a known IP address block to services. You may decide that address pool 1 will be used for web services, address pool 2 for databases, address pool 3 for file transfers, and so on. Some organizations do this to identify traffic based on the IP assignment, making it easier to track communication.

Adding a layer 4 load balancer to your cluster allows you to migrate applications that may not work with simple layer 7 traffic.

As more applications are migrated or refactored for containers, you will run into many applications that require multiple protocols for a single service. Natively, if you attempt to create a service with both TCP and UDP port mapping, you will receive an error that multiple protocols are not supported for the service object. This may not affect many applications, but why should you be limited to a single protocol for a service?

Using multiple protocols

All of our examples so far have used a TCP as the protocol. Of course, MetalLB supports using UDP as the service protocol as well, but what if you had a service that required you to use both protocols?

Multiple protocol issues

Not all service types support assigning multiple protocols to a single service. The following table shows the three service types and their support for multiple protocols:

Service Type	Supports Multiple Protocols
ClusterIP	Yes
NodePort	Yes
LoadBalancer	No

Table 4.6: Service type protocol support

If you attempt to create a service that uses both protocols, you will receive an error message. We have highlighted the error in the following error message:

```
The Service "kube-dns-lb" is invalid: spec.ports: Invalid value:
[]core.ServicePort{core.ServicePort{Name:"dns", Protocol:"UDP",
Port:53, TargetPort:intstr.IntOrString{Type:0, IntVal:53, StrVal:""},
NodePort:0}, core.ServicePort{Name:"dns-tcp", Protocol:"TCP",
Port:53, TargetPort:intstr.IntOrString{Type:0, IntVal:53, StrVal:""},
NodePort:0}}: cannot create an external load balancer with mix
protocols
```

The service we were attempting to create would expose our CoreDNS service to an external IP using a LoadBalancer service. We need to expose the service on port 50 for both TCP and UDP.

MetalLB includes support for multiple protocols bound to a single IP address. The configuration requires the creation of two different services rather than a single service, which may seem a little odd at first. As we have shown previously, the API server will not allow you to create a service object with multiple protocols. The only way to work around this limitation is to create two different services: one that has the TCP ports assigned, and another that has the UDP ports assigned.

Using our CoreDNS example, we will go through the steps to create an application that requires multiple protocols.

Using multiple protocols with MetalLB

To enable support for an application that requires both TCP and UDP, you need to create two separate services. If you have been paying close attention to how services are created, you may have noticed that each service receives an IP address.

Logically, this means that when we create two services for our application, we would receive two different IP addresses.

In our example, we want to expose CoreDNS as a LoadBalancer service, which requires both TCP and UDP protocols. If we created two standard services, one with each protocol defined, we would receive two different IP addresses. How would you configure a system to use a DNS server that requires two different IP addresses for a connection?

The simple answer is, **you can't**.

But we just told you that MetalLB supports this type of configuration. Stay with us— we are building up to explaining this by first explaining the issues that MetalLB will solve for us.

When we created the NGINX service that we pulled from the subnet-201 IP pool earlier, we did so by adding an annotation to the load balancer manifest. MetalLB has added support for multiple protocols by adding an annotation for **shared-IPs**.

Using shared-IPs

Now that you understand the limitations around multiple protocol support in Kubernetes, let's use MetalLB to expose our CoreDNS service to external requests, using both TCP and UDP.

As we mentioned earlier, Kubernetes will not allow you to create a single service with both protocols. To have a single load-balanced IP use both protocols, you need to create a service for both protocols, one for TCP and another for UDP. Each of the services will need an annotation that MetalLB will use to assign the same IP to both services.

For each service, you need to set the same value for the `metallb.universe.tf/allow-shared-ip` annotation. We will cover a complete example to expose CoreDNS to explain the entire process.

 Most Kubernetes distributions use CoreDNS as the default DNS provider, but some of them still use the service name from when kube-dns was the default DNS provider. KinD is one of the distributions that may confuse you at first since the service name is kube-dns, but rest assured, the deployment is using CoreDNS.

So, let's begin:

1. First, look at the services in the `kube-system` namespace:

```
NAME                TYPE                CLUSTER-IP          EXTERNAL-IP
PORT(S)                     AGE
kube-dns        ClusterIP       10.96.0.10          <none>              53/
UDP,53/TCP,9153/TCP     5d18h
```

   The only service we have is the default `kube-dns` service, using the ClusterIP type, which means that it is only accessible internally to the cluster.

   You might have noticed that the service has multiple protocol support, having both port UDP and TCP assigned. Remember that, unlike the LoadBalancer service, a ClusterIP service **can** be assigned multiple protocols.

2. The first step to add LoadBalancer support to our CoreDNS server is to create two manifests, one for each protocol.

   We will create the TCP service first. Create a file called `coredns-tcp.yaml` and add the content from the following example manifest. Note that the internal service for CoreDNS is using the `k8s-app: kube-dns` selector. Since we are exposing the same service, that's the selector we will use in our manifests:

```yaml
apiVersion: v1
kind: Service
metadata:
  name: coredns-tcp
  namespace: kube-system
  annotations:
    metallb.universe.tf/allow-shared-ip: "coredns-ext"
spec:
  selector:
    k8s-app: kube-dns
  ports:
  - name: dns-tcp
    port: 53
    protocol: TCP
    targetPort: 53
  type: LoadBalancer
```

   This file should be familiar by now, with the one exception in the annotations being the addition of the `metallb.universe.tf/allow-shared-ip` value. The use of this value will become clear when we create the next manifest for the UDP services.

3. Create a file called `coredns-udp.yaml` and add the content from the following example manifest.

```
apiVersion: v1
kind: Service
metadata:
  name: coredns-udp
  namespace: kube-system
  annotations:
    metallb.universe.tf/allow-shared-ip: "coredns-ext"
spec:
  selector:
    k8s-app: kube-dns
  ports:
  - name: dns-udp
    port: 53
    protocol: UDP
    targetPort: 53
  type: LoadBalancer
```

Note that we used the same annotation value from the TCP service manifest, `metallb.universe.tf/allow-shared-ip: "coredns-ext"`. This is the value that MetalLB will use to create a single IP address, even though two separate services are being requested.

4. Finally, we can deploy the two services to the cluster using `kubectl apply`:

```
kubectl apply -f coredns-tcp.yaml
kubectl apply -f coredns-udp.yaml
```

5. Once deployed, get the services in the `kube-system` namespace to verify that our services were deployed:

```
NAME            TYPE            CLUSTER-IP       EXTERNAL-IP
PORT(S)
coredns-tcp     LoadBalancer    10.105.87.247    172.18.200.101
53:30324/TCP
coredns-udp     LoadBalancer    10.100.82.206    172.18.200.101
53:30864/UDP
kube-dns        ClusterIP       10.96.0.10       <none>
53/UDP,53/TCP,9153/TCP
```

You should see that two new services were created: the `coredns-tcp` and `coredns-udp` services. Under the `EXTERNAL-IP` column, you can see that both services have been assigned the same IP address, which allows the service to accept both protocols on the same IP address.

Adding MetalLB to a cluster gives your users the ability to deploy any application that they can containerize. It uses IP pools that dynamically assign an IP address for the service so that it is instantly accessible for servicing external requests.

One issue is that MetalLB does not provide name resolution for the service IPs. Users prefer to target an easy-to-remember name rather than random IP addresses when they want to access a service. Kubernetes does not provide the ability to create externally accessible names for services, but it does have an incubator project to enable this feature.

In the next section, we will learn how to use CoreDNS to create service name entries in DNS using an incubator project called external-dns. We will also introduce an exciting new CNCF sandbox project called K8GB that provides a cluster with Kubernetes native global load balancing features.

Enhancing load balancers for the enterprise

In this third, and final section, we will discuss some of the limitations of certain load balancer features and how we can configure a cluster to resolve the limitations. Our examples have been good for learning, but in an enterprise, nobody wants to access a workload running on the cluster using an IP address. Also, in an enterprise, you will commonly run services on multiple clusters to provide some failover for your applications. So far, the options discussed can't address these two key points. In this section, we will explain how to resolve these issues so your enterprise can offer easier access to workloads that are highly available by names, including across multiple clusters.

Making service names available externally

You may have been wondering why we were using the IP addresses to test some of the services that we created, while we used domain names for our Ingress examples.

While a Kubernetes load balancer provides a standard IP address to a service, it does not create an external DNS name for users to connect to the service. Using IP addresses to connect to applications running on a cluster is not very efficient, and manually registering names in DNS for each IP assigned by MetalLB would be an impossible method to maintain. So how would you provide a more cloud-like experience to adding name resolution to our LoadBalancer services?

Similar to the team that maintains KinD, there is a Kubernetes SIG that is working on this feature to Kubernetes called `ExternalDNS`. The main project page can be found on the SIG's GitHub at `https://github.com/kubernetes-sigs/external-dns`.

At the time of writing, the `ExternalDNS` project supports a long list of compatible DNS servers, including the following:

- Google's Cloud DNS
- Amazon's Route 53
- AzureDNS
- Cloudflare
- CoreDNS
- RFC2136
- PowerDNS
- And more…

As you know, our Kubernetes cluster is running CoreDNS to provide cluster DNS name resolution. Many people are not aware that CoreDNS is not limited to providing only internal cluster DNS resolution. It can also provide external name resolution, resolving names for any DNS zone that is managed by a CoreDNS deployment.

Setting up external-dns

Right now, our CoreDNS is only resolving names for internal cluster names, so we need to set up a zone for our new DNS entries. Since FooWidgets wanted all applications to go into `foowidgets.k8s`, we will use that as our new zone.

Integrating external-dns and CoreDNS

The final step to providing dynamic service registration to our cluster is to deploy and integrate `ExternalDNS` with CoreDNS.

To configure `ExternalDNS` and CoreDNS to work in the cluster, we need to configure each to use ETCD for the new DNS zone. Since our clusters are running KinD with a preinstalled ETCD, we will deploy a new ETCD pod dedicated to `ExternalDNS` zones.

The quickest method to deploy a new ETCD service is to use the official ETCD operator Helm chart. If you are new to Helm, it is a tool that makes defining and maintaining Kubernetes applications easier.

It's a powerful tool and you will find that many projects and vendors offer their applications, by default, using Helm charts. You can read more about Helm on their main home page at `https://v3.helm.sh/`.

First, we need to install the Helm binary. We can install Helm quickly using the script provided by the Helm team (if you are using the scripts from the book, Helm was installed when you ran `create-cluster.sh` to create the KinD cluster):

```
curl -fsSL -o get_helm.sh https://raw.githubusercontent.com/helm/helm/
master/scripts/get-helm-3
chmod 700 get_helm.sh
./get_helm.sh
```

Before we can use Helm to deploy a chart, we need to add a chart repository first. To add the standard stable chart repository, you need to run Helm with the `repo add` option, and then update the charts from the repository:

```
helm repo add stable https://charts.helm.sh/stable
helm repo update
```

Now, to show how easy deployment is using Helm, we can create the ETCD cluster that we will integrate with CoreDNS using a single command line. The following command will deploy all of the required components and create the ETCD cluster:

```
helm install etcd-dns --set customResources.createEtcdClusterCRD=true
stable/etcd-operator --namespace kube-system
```

You will see some warnings about CRDs that will be deprecated in K8s 1.22+, but since we are running 1.21, the warnings can be safely ignored.

It will take a few minutes to deploy the operator and the ETCD nodes. You can check on the status by looking at the pods in the `kube-system` namespace. Once fully installed, you will see three ETCD operator pods and three ETCD cluster pods:

NAME	READY
STATUS RESTARTS	
coredns-558bd4d5db-9jbvx	1/1
Running 0	
coredns-558bd4d5db-gz7jm	1/1
Running 0	
etcd-cluster-chxc52qhql	1/1
Running 0	
etcd-cluster-mpstktwhq5	1/1
Running 0	
etcd-cluster-v545bbk8zp	1/1

```
0
etcd-cluster01-control-plane                                    1/1
Running   0
etcd-dns-etcd-operator-etcd-backup-operator-5db56c779b-hjx4k    1/1
Running   0
etcd-dns-etcd-operator-etcd-operator-6b77c4799c-p58lq           1/1
Running   0
etcd-dns-etcd-operator-etcd-restore-operator-6fcdcd5bfb-m7slf   1/1
Running   0
```

Once the deployment has completed, view the services in the `kube-system` namespace to get the IP address of the new ETCD service called `etcd-cluster-client`:

```
etcd-cluster-client      ClusterIP        10.111.196.223    <none>
2379/TCP                 5m56s
```

Make a note of the IP address. We will need the service IP address to configure `ExternalDNS` and the CoreDNS zone file in the next section.

Adding an ETCD zone to CoreDNS

Developers do not have time to wait to test their deployments, and using an IP address may cause issues with proxy servers or internal policies. To help the users speed up their delivery and testing of an application, we need to provide dynamic name resolution for their services.

The first prerequisite to providing this dynamic functionality is that `ExternalDNS` requires the CoreDNS zone to be stored on an ETCD server.

To enable an ETCD-integrated zone for FooWidgets, edit the CoreDNS ConfigMap, and add the following bold lines. To edit the ConfigMap, run the `kubectl edit cm coredns -n kube-system` command.

You may need to change the **endpoint** to the IP address of the new ETCD service that was retrieved on the previous page:

```
apiVersion: v1
data:
  Corefile: |
    .:53 {
       errors
       health {
         lameduck 5s
```

```
    }
    ready
    kubernetes cluster.local in-addr.arpa ip6.arpa {
      pods insecure
      fallthrough in-addr.arpa ip6.arpa
      ttl 30
    }
    prometheus :9153
    forward . /etc/resolv.conf
    etcd foowidgets.k8s {
      stubzones
      path /skydns
      endpoint http://10.96.181.53:2379
    }
    cache 30
    loop
    reload
    loadbalance
  }
kind: ConfigMap
```

The next step is to deploy ExternalDNS to the cluster.

We have provided a manifest in the GitHub repository in the chapter4 directory that will patch the deployment with your ETCD service endpoint. You can deploy ExternalDNS using this manifest by executing the following command, from the chapter4 directory, named external-dns.sh. The following commands will query the service IP for the ETCD cluster and create a deployment file using that IP as the endpoint.

To execute the commands, ensure you are in the chapter4 directory from the book repo, and execute the following commands:

```
ETCD_URL=$(kubectl -n kube-system get svc etcd-cluster-client -o go-
template='{{ .spec.clusterIP }}')
cat external-dns.yaml | sed -E "s/<ETCD_URL>/${ETCD_URL}/" > external-
dns-deployment.yaml
kubectl apply -f external-dns-deployment.yaml
```

The newly created deployment will then install ExternalDNS in your cluster:

To deploy ExternalDNS to your cluster manually, edit the external-dns-deployment.yaml manifest in the chapter4 directory and, at the end of the file, add your ETCD service IP address on the last line:

```
env:
- name: ETCD_URLS
  value: http://10.111.196.223:2379
```

Remember, if your ETCD server's IP address is not 10.96.181.53, change it before deploying the manifest.

Deploy the manifest using kubectl apply -f external-dns-deployment.yaml.

The next step is to expose our external-dns service using a LoadBalancer service.

Creating a LoadBalancer service with external-dns integration

You should still have the NGINX deployment from the beginning of this chapter running. It has a few services tied to it. We will add another one to show you how to create a dynamic registration for the deployment:

1. To create a dynamic entry in the CoreDNS zone, you need to add an annotation to your service manifest. Create a new file called nginx-dynamic. yaml with the following content:

```
apiVersion: v1
kind: Service
metadata:
  annotations:
    external-dns.alpha.kubernetes.io/hostname: nginx.foowidgets.k8s
  name: nginx-ext-dns
  namespace: default
spec:
  ports:
  - port: 8080
    protocol: TCP
    targetPort: 8080
  selector:
    run: nginx-web
  type: LoadBalancer
```

Note the annotation in the file. To instruct ExternalDNS to create a record, you need to add an annotation that has the key external-dns.alpha.kubernetes. io/hostname with the desired name for the service — in this example, nginx. foowidgets.k8s.

2. Create the service using `kubectl apply -f nginx-dynamic.yaml`.

   It takes about a minute for `ExternalDNS` to pick up on DNS changes.

3. To verify that the record was created, check the `external-dns` pod logs using `kubectl logs -n kube-system -l app=external-dns`. Once the record has been picked up by `external-dns`, you will see an entry similar to the following:

```
time="2021-07-02T19:25:16Z" level=info msg="Add/set key /
skydns/k8s/foowidgets/nginx/293e6752 to Host=172.18.200.102,
Text=\"heritage=external-dns,external-dns/owner=default,external-
dns/resource=service/default/nginx-ext-dns\", TTL=0"
```

4. The last step for confirming that ExternalDNS is fully working is to test a connection to the application. Since we are using a KinD cluster, we must test this from a pod in the cluster. We will use a Netshoot container, as we have been doing throughout this book.

> At the end of this section, we will show the steps to integrate a Windows DNS server with our Kubernetes CoreDNS servers. The steps are being provided to provide you with a complete understanding of how you fully integrate the enterprise DNS server with delegation to our CoreDNS service.

5. Run a Netshoot container:

```
kubectl run tmp-shell --rm -i --tty --image nicolaka/netshoot --
/bin/bash
```

6. To confirm that the entry has been created successfully, execute an `nslookup` for the host in a Netshoot shell:

```
bash-5.1# nslookup nginx.foowidgets.k8s
Server:         10.96.0.10
Address:        10.96.0.10#53
Name:   nginx.foowidgets.k8s
Address: 172.18.200.102
```

We can confirm that the DNS server in use is CoreDNS, based on the IP address, which is the IP assigned to the `kube-dns` service. (Again, the service is `kube-dns`, but the pods are running CoreDNS.)

The `172.18.200.102` address is the IP that was assigned to the new NGINX service; we can confirm this by listing the services in the default namespace:

```
NAME              TYPE           CLUSTER-IP       EXTERNAL-IP
PORT(S)               AGE
kubernetes        ClusterIP      10.96.0.1        <none>
443/TCP              5d19h
nginx-ext-dns     LoadBalancer   10.101.166.129   172.18.200.102
8080:31990/TCP      5m50s
```

7. Finally, let's confirm that the connection to NGINX works by connecting to the container using the name. Using a `curl` command in the Netshoot container, `curl` to the DNS name on port `8080`:

```
bash-5.1# curl nginx.foowidgets.k8s:8080
<!DOCTYPE html>
<html>
<head>
<title>Welcome to nginx!</title>
<style>
    body {
        width: 35em;
        margin: 0 auto;
        font-family: Tahoma, Verdana, Arial, sans-serif;
    }
</style>
</head>
<body>
<h1>Welcome to nginx!</h1>
<p>If you see this page, the nginx web server is successfully installed and
working. Further configuration is required.</p>

<p>For online documentation and support please refer to
<a href="http://nginx.org/">nginx.org</a>.<br/>
Commercial support is available at
<a href="http://nginx.com/">nginx.com</a>.</p>

<p><em>Thank you for using nginx.</em></p>
</body>
</html>
```

Figure 4.9: Curl test using the ExternalDNS name

The `curl` output confirms that we can use the dynamically created service name to access the NGINX web server.

We realize that some of these tests aren't very exciting since you can test them using a standard browser. In the next section, we will integrate the CoreDNS running in our cluster with a Windows DNS server.

Integrating CoreDNS with an enterprise DNS

This section will show you how to forward the name resolution of the `foowidgets.k8s` zone to a CoreDNS server running on a Kubernetes cluster.

This section has been included to provide an example of integrating an enterprise DNS server with a Kubernetes DNS service.

Because of the external requirements and additional setup, the steps provided are for reference and **should not be executed** on your KinD cluster.

For this scenario, the main DNS server is running on a Windows 2016 server.

The components deployed are as follows:

- Windows 2016/2019 Server running DNS
- A Kubernetes cluster
- Bitnami NGINX deployment
- LoadBalancer service created and assigned the IP address `10.2.1.74`
- CoreDNS service configured to use hostPort 53
- Deployed add-ons, using the configuration from this chapter such as external-dns, an ETCD cluster for CoreDNS, a CoreDNS ETCD zone added, and MetalLB using an address pool of `10.2.1.60-10.2.1.80`

Now, let's go through the configuration steps to integrate our DNS servers.

Configuring the primary DNS server

The first step is to create a conditional forwarder to the node running the CoreDNS pod.

On the Windows DNS host, we need to create a new conditional forwarder for `foowidgets.k8s` pointing to the host that is running the CoreDNS pod. In our example, the CoreDNS pod has been assigned to the host `10.240.100.102`:

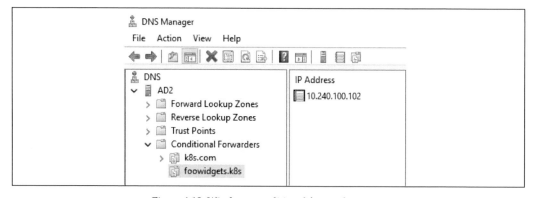

Figure 4.10: Windows conditional forwarder setup

This configures the Windows DNS server to forward any request for a host in the `foowidgets.k8s` domain to the CoreDNS pod.

Testing DNS forwarding to CoreDNS

To test the configuration, we will use a workstation on the main network that has been configured to use the Windows DNS server.

The first test we will run is an `nslookup` of the NGINX record that was created by the MetalLB annotation:

From Command Prompt, we execute an `nslookup nginx.foowidgets.k8s` command:

```
PS C:\> nslookup nginx.foowidgets.k8s
Server:   AD2.hyper-vplanet.com
Address:  10.2.1.14

Non-authoritative answer:
Name:     nginx.foowidgets.k8s
Address:  10.2.1.74
```

Figure 4.11: Nslookup confirmation for a registered name

Since the query returned the IP address we expected for the record, we can confirm that the Windows DNS server is forwarding requests to CoreDNS correctly.

We can do one more additional NGINX test from the laptop's browser:

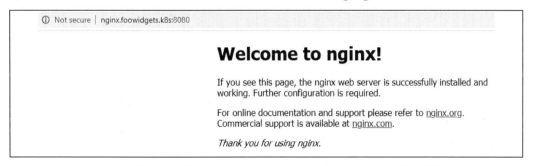

Figure 4.12: Success browsing from an external workstation using CoreDNS

One test confirms that the forwarding works, but we aren't comfortable that the system is fully working.

To test a new service, we deploy a different NGINX server called microbot, with a service that has an annotation assigning the name `microbot.foowidgets.k8s`. MetalLB has assigned the service the IP address of `10.2.1.65`.

Like our previous test, we test the name resolution using nslookup:

```
Non-authoritative answer:
Name:      microbot.foowidgets.k8s
Address:   10.2.1.65
```

Figure 4.13: Nslookup confirmation for an additional registered name

To confirm that the web server is running correctly, we browse to the URL from a workstation:

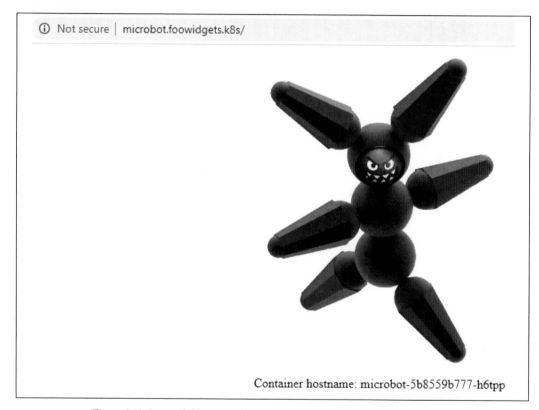

Figure 4.14: Successful browsing from an external workstation using CoreDNS

Success! We have now integrated an enterprise DNS server with a CoreDNS server running on a Kubernetes cluster. This integration provides users with the ability to register service names dynamically by simply adding an annotation to the service.

Load balancing between multiple clusters

Running services in multiple clusters can be configured in multiple ways, usually requiring complex and expensive add-ons such as global load balancers from companies like F5. These are very common in the enterprise, and while many organizations implement clusters using add-ons like F5's **Global Service Load Balancers (GSLB)**, there are projects available that provide similar functionality that are low, or no cost, and native to Kubernetes. These projects do not replace all of the features that the vendor solutions provide, but in many cases, we do not need all of the features from the more expensive solutions – we require only a small subset of the features provided.

A new project that has recently been released is K8GB, a CNCF sandbox project. To learn about the project, browse to the project's main page at `https://www.k8gb.io`.

Since we are using KinD and a single host for our cluster, this section of the book is meant to introduce you to the project and the benefits it provides. This section is for reference only, since it is a complex topic that requires multiple components, some outside of Kubernetes, and we will maintain an example deployment with additional information in the book's repo at `https://github.com/PacktPublishing/Kubernetes---An-Enterprise-Guide-2E/tree/main/chapter4/k8gb-example`.

 This is a sandbox project, which means it is in its early stages and any newer version after the writing of this chapter may have changes to objects and configurations. Even though this may occur, we see the value in the project for enterprises and wanted to introduce it to readers.

Introducing the Kubernetes Global Balancer

Why should you care about a project like K8GB?

One example is an internal enterprise cloud, running a Kubernetes cluster in a production site and a cluster in a disaster recovery data center. To provide a seamless experience to users, we want to have the ability for applications to fail between the data centers, without any human interaction (in other words, no manual DR events or tasks). So, how do we address the enterprise's need to provide high availability for their microservices when multiple clusters are serving the applications?

One answer is **K8GB**.

What makes K8GB an ideal solution for addressing our high availability requirements? As documented on their site, the key features are:

- Load balancing is provided using a timeproof DNS protocol that is extremely reliable and works well for global deployments
- There is no requirement for a management cluster
- There is no single point of failure
- It uses native Kubernetes health checks for load balancing decisions
- Configuring is as simple as a single Kubernetes CRD
- It works with any Kubernetes cluster – on-prem or off-prem
- It's free!!!

Now that we have discussed the key features of K8GB, let's get into the details.

Requirements for K8GB

For a product that provides global load balancing, K8GB doesn't require a lot of complex infrastructure to provide global balancing to your clusters, or too many prerequisites. The latest release, as of this chapter's creation, is 0.0.8 – and there are only two requirements:

- The CoreDNS servers Load Balancer IP address in the main DNZ zone using the naming standard `gslb-ns-<k8gb-name>-gb.foowidgets.k8s`; for example, `gslb-ns-us-nyc-gb.foowidgets.k8s` and `gslb-ns-us-buf-gb.foowidgets.k8s`

 If you are using K8GB with a service like Route 53, Infoblox, or NS1, the CoreDNS servers will be added to the domain automatically. Since our example is using an on-premises DNS server running on a Windows 2019 server, we need to create the records manually.

- An Ingress controller
- A K8GB controller deployed in the cluster, which will deploy:
    - The K8GB controller
    - A CoreDNS server with the CoreDNS CRD plugin configured

Earlier in this chapter, we covered the first requirement, using NGINX as our cluster Ingress controller, and in this section, we will go over the last requirement – deploying and configuring the K8GB controller in a cluster.

Deploying K8GB to a cluster

Installing K8GB has been made very simple – you only need to deploy a single Helm chart using a `values.yaml` file that has been configured for your infrastructure.

To install K8GB, you will need to add the K8GB repository to your Helm list and then update the charts:

```
helm repo add k8gb https://www.k8gb.io
helm repo update
```

With the Helm repository added and updated, we need to customize the Helm `values.yaml` file for the deployment. An example `values.yaml` file is located in the K8GB Git repository: `https://github.com/k8gb-io/k8gb/blob/master/chart/k8gb/values.yaml`.

Understanding K8GB load balancing options

Like most load balancers today, K8GB offers a variety of solutions that can be configured differently for each load-balanced URL. It offers the most commonly required strategies, including round robin, weighted round robin, failover, and manual.

For our example, we will configure K8GB as a failover load balancer between two clusters on-premises; however, K8GB is not limited to just failover. You can configure K8GB load balancing to support any of the strategies:

- **Round Robin**: If you do not specify a strategy, it will default to a simple round robin load balancing configuration. Using round robin means that requests will be split between the configured clusters – request 1 will go to cluster 1, request 2 will go to cluster 2, request 3 will go to cluster 1, request 4 will go to cluster 2, and so on…

- **Weighted Round Robin**: Similar to round robin, but this strategy provides the ability to specify the percentage of traffic to send to a cluster; for example, 75% of traffic will go to cluster 1 and 15% will go to cluster 2 (*as of this writing, this feature is still being worked on*).

- **Failover**: All traffic will go to the primary cluster unless all pods for a deployment become unavailable. If all pods are down in cluster 1, cluster 2 will take over the workload until the pods in cluster 1 become available again, which will then become the primary cluster again.

- **Manual**: Any failover will require manual intervention. If all pods in a cluster become unavailable, any request will return an error until failover is manually executed or the pods in the primary cluster become healthy again (*as of this writing, this feature is still being worked on*).

Now that you know the available strategies, let's go over our infrastructure for our clusters:

Cluster/Server Details	Details

Corporate DNS Server – New York City
 	
IP: `10.2.1.14`
	• Main corporate zone
	    • `foowidgets.k8s`
	• Host records for the CoreDNS servers
	    • `gslb-ns-us-nyc-gb.foowidgets.k8s`
	    • `gslb-ns-us-buf-gb.foowidgets.k8s`
	• Global domain configured delegating to the CoreDNS servers in the clusters
	    • `gb.foowidgets.k8s`

New York City, New York – Cluster 1 Primary Site CoreDNS LB IP: `10.2.1.220` Ingress LB IP: `10.2.1.221`	• NGINX Ingress Controller • CoreDNS deployment exposed using MetalLB
Buffalo, New York – Cluster 2 Secondary Site CoreDNS LB IP: `10.2.1.223` Ingress LB IP: `10.2.1.224`	• NGINX Ingress Controller • CoreDNS deployment exposed using MetalLB

Table 4.7: Cluster details

We will use the details from the above table to explain how we would deploy K8GB in our infrastructure.

With the details of the infrastructure, we can now create our Helm `values.yaml` file for our deployments. In the next section, we will show the values we need to configure using the example infrastructure and then we will explain what each value does.

Customizing the Helm chart values

Each cluster will have a similar values file; the main changes will be the tag values we use. The values file below is for the New York City cluster:

```
# NYC K8GB values.yaml File
```

```
global:
  imagePullSecrets: []

k8gb:
  imageRepo: absaoss/k8gb
  dnsZone: "gb.foowidgets.k8s"
  edgeDNSZone: "foowidgets.k8s"
  edgeDNSServer: "10.2.1.14"
  clusterGeoTag: "us-nyc"
  extGslbClustersGeoTags: "us-buff"
  reconcileRequeueSeconds: 30
  exposeCoreDNS: true
  log:
    format: simple
    level: info
  metricsAddress: "0.0.0.0:8080"

coredns:
  isClusterService: false
  deployment:
    skipConfig: true
  image:
    repository: absaoss/k8s_crd
    tag: "v0.0.4"
  serviceAccount:
    create: true
    name: coredns
```

The same file contents will be used for the Buffalo cluster, but we need to switch the tag values:

```
clusterGeoTag: "us-buff"
extGslbClustersGeoTags: "us-nyc"
```

As you can see, the configuration isn't very lengthy, requiring only a handful of options to configure a usually complex global load balancing configuration. While it's not a large configuration, DNS and K8GB may be fairly new to some readers, so let's go over some of the main details of the values we are using.

The main section that we will explain are the values in the K8GB section, which configures all of the options K8GB will use for load balancing.

Chart Value	Description
imageRepo	The image to use for K8GB. You will need to change this if you are in an air-gapped network.
dnsZone	This is the DNS zone that you will use for K8GB – basically, this is the zone that will be used for the DNS records that will be used by users to access the application.
edgeDNSZone	The main DNS zone that contains the delegated dnsZone from the previous option (dnsZone)
edgeDNSServer	The edge DNS server – usually the main DNS server used for name resolution.
clusterGeoTag	If you have multiple K8GB controllers, this tag is used to specify instances between each other.
extGslbClusterGeoTags	Specifies the other K8GB controllers to pair with.
reconcileRequeueSeconds	The time in seconds for updating records between the cluster CoreDNS servers.
exposeCoreDNS	If set to **true**, a LoadBalancer service will be created, exposing the CoreDNS deployed in the **k8gb** namespace on port 53/UDP for external access.
log	Specifies the log format and the logging level – can be set to simple or JSON format, and a level of panic, fatal, error, warn, info, debug, or trace.
metricsAddress	The address to use for metrics.

Table 4.8: K8GB options

Using Helm to install K8GB

With the overview of K8GB and the Helm values file complete, we can move on to installing K8GB in the clusters.

The first step is to create the **k8gb** namespace in each cluster:

```
kubectl create ns k8gb
```

In the New York City cluster, we can deploy K8GB using the following Helm command (using a values file specific for the NYC cluster):

```
helm install k8gb k8gb/k8gb -n k8gb -f k8gb-nyc-values.yaml
```

Using the Buffalo values file, we can deploy K8GB using the following Helm command (using a values file specific for the Buffalo cluster):

```
helm install k8gb k8gb/k8gb -n k8gb  -f k8gb-buf-values.yaml
```

Once deployed, you will see two pods running in the k8gb namespace, one for the k8gb controller and the other for the CoreDNS server that will be used to resolve load balancing names.

```
NAME                             READY   STATUS    RESTARTS   AGE
k8gb-8d8b4cb7c-mhglb             1/1     Running   0          7h58m
k8gb-coredns-7995d54db5-ngdb2    1/1     Running   0          7h37m
```

We can also verify that the services were created to handle the incoming DNS requests. Since we exposed it using MetalLB, we will see a LoadBalancer type service on port 53 using the UDP protocol. You will also notice the default ClusterIP type that the deployment created in the list:

```
NAME                  TYPE           CLUSTER-IP       EXTERNAL-IP    PORT(S)
AGE
k8gb-coredns          ClusterIP      10.97.178.51     <none>         53/UDP,53/TCP
8h
k8gb-coredns-lb       LoadBalancer   10.98.170.251    10.2.1.213     53:32503/UDP
7h44m
```

With the deployment of K8GB complete and verified in both clusters, let's move on to the next section where we will explain how to deploy an application that has global load balancing.

Deploying a highly available application using K8GB

There are two methods to enable global load balancing for an application. You can create a new record using a custom resource provided by K8GB, or you can annotate an Ingress rule. For our demonstration of K8GB, we will deploy a simple NGINX web server in a cluster and add it to K8GB using the natively supplied custom resource.

Adding an application to K8GB using custom resources

When we deployed K8GB, a new CRD was created called Gslb, which will control the applications that we want to enable global load balancing for. In the object, we provide a spec for the Ingress name, which is identical to a standard Ingress object. The only difference between a standard Ingress and a Gslb object is the last section of the manifest – the strategy.

The strategy defines the type of load balancing we want to use, which is failover for our example, and the primary GeoTag to use for the object. In our example, the NYC cluster is our primary cluster, so our Gslb object will be set to `us-nyc`.

To deploy an application that will leverage load balancing, we need to create the following in both clusters:

1. A standard deployment and service for the application. We will call the deployment `nginx-lb`, using the Bitnami NGINX image

2. A Gslb object in each cluster. For our example, we will use the manifest below, which will designate the Ingress rule and set the strategy to failover using `us-nyc` as the primary K8GB:

```
apiVersion: k8gb.absa.oss/v1beta1
kind: Gslb
metadata:
  name: gslb-nginx
  namespace: web-frontend
spec:
  ingress:
    rules:
      - host: fe.gb.foowidgets.k8s
        http:
          paths:
          - backend:
              serviceName: nginx
              servicePort: 8080
            path: /
  strategy:
    type: failover
    primaryGeoTag: us-nyc
```

When you deploy the manifest for the Gslb object, it will create two Kubernetes objects, the Gslb object, and an Ingress object.

If we look at the web-frontend namespace for the Gslb objects in the NYC cluster, we would see the following:

```
NAME                    STRATEGY        GEOTAG
gslb-failover-nyc       failover        us-nyc
```

And if we looked at the Ingress objects in the NYC cluster, we would see:

```
NAME         CLASS      HOSTS                   ADDRESS      PORTS   AGE
gslb-nginx   <none>     fe.gb.foowidgets.k8s    10.2.1.221   80      4s
```

We would also have similar objects in the Buffalo cluster, which we will explain in the *Understanding how K8GB provides global load balancing* section.

Adding an application to K8GB using Ingress annotations

The second method for adding an application to K8GB is to add two annotations to a standard Ingress rule, which was primarily added to allow developers to add an existing Ingress rule to K8GB.

To add an Ingress object to the global load balancing list, you only need to add two annotations to the Ingress object, `strategy` and `primary-geotag`. An example of the annotations is shown below:

```
k8gb.io/strategy: "failover"
k8gb.io/primary-geotag: "us-nyc"
```

This would add the Ingress to K8GB using the failover strategy using the `us-nyc` geotag as the primary tag.

Now that we have deployed all of the required infrastructure components and all of the required objects to enable global load balancing for an application, let's see it in action.

Understanding how K8GB provides global load balancing

The design of K8GB is complex, but once you deploy an application and understand how K8GB maintains zone files, it will become easier. This is a fairly complex topic, and it does assume some previous knowledge of how DNS works, but by the end of this section, you should be able to explain how K8GB works.

Keeping the K8GB CoreDNS servers in sync

The first topic to discuss is how K8GB manages to keep two, or more, zone files in sync to provide seamless failover for our deployments.

As we mentioned earlier, each K8GB CoreDNS server in the clusters must have an entry in the main DNS server.

This is the DNS server and zone that we configured for the edge values in the `values.yaml` file:

```
edgeDNSZone: "foowidgets.k8s"
edgeDNSServer: "10.2.1.14"
```

So, in the DNS server (`10.2.1.14`), we have a host record for each CoreDNS server using the required K8GB naming convention:

```
gslb-ns-us-nyc-gb.gb.foowidgets.k8s      10.2.1.220   (The NYC CoreDNS
load balancer IP)
gslb-ns-us-buf-gb.gb.foowidgets.k8s      10.2.1.223   (The BUF CoreDNS
load balancer IP)
```

K8GB will communicate between all of the CoreDNS servers, at a defined interval, and update any records that need to be updated due to being added, deleted, or updated. This interval is defined by `reconcileRequeueSeconds` in the `values.yaml` file.

This becomes a little easier to understand with an example. Using our cluster example, we have deployed an NGINX web server and created all of the required objects in both clusters. After deploying, we would have a Gslb and Ingress object in each cluster, as shown below:

Cluster: NYC	Cluster: Buffalo
Deployment: `nginx-web`	Deployment: `nginx-web`
Ingress: `fe.gb.foowidgets.k8s`	Ingress: `fe.gb.foowidgets.k8s`
IP address: `10.2.1.221` (Ingress)	IP address: `10.2.1.224` (Ingress)

Table 4.9: Objects in each cluster

Since the deployment is healthy in both clusters, the CoreDNS servers will have a record for the `fe.gb.foowidgets.k8s` with an IP address of `10.2.1.221`. We can verify this by running a `dig` command on any client machine that uses the main corporate DNS server:

```
surovich@ubuntu-20:~$ dig fe.gb.foowidgets.k8s

; <<>> DiG 9.16.1-Ubuntu <<>> fe.gb.foowidgets.k8s
;; global options: +cmd
;; Got answer:
;; ->>HEADER<<- opcode: QUERY, status: NOERROR, id: 14856
```

```
;; flags: qr rd ra; QUERY: 1, ANSWER: 1, AUTHORITY: 0, ADDITIONAL: 1

;; OPT PSEUDOSECTION:
; EDNS: version: 0, flags:; udp: 65494
;; QUESTION SECTION:
;fe.gb.foowidgets.k8s.            IN       A

;; ANSWER SECTION:
fe.gb.foowidgets.k8s.    30       IN       A        10.2.1.221

;; Query time: 0 msec
;; SERVER: 127.0.0.53#53(127.0.0.53)
;; WHEN: Tue Jul 06 23:49:29 UTC 2021
;; MSG SIZE  rcvd: 65
```

As you can see in the output from `dig`, the host resolved to `10.2.1.221` since the application is healthy in the main cluster.

We will simulate a failure by scaling the replicas for the deployment in the NYC cluster to 0, which will look like a failed application to K8GB. When the K8GB controller in the NYC cluster sees that the application no longer has any healthy endpoints, it will update the CoreDNS record in all servers with the secondary IP address to fail the service over to the secondary cluster.

Once scaled down, we can use `dig` to verify what host is returned:

```
surovich@ubuntu-20:~$ dig fe.gb.foowidgets.k8s

; <<>> DiG 9.16.1-Ubuntu <<>> fe.gb.foowidgets.k8s
;; global options: +cmd
;; Got answer:
;; ->>HEADER<<- opcode: QUERY, status: NOERROR, id: 64563
;; flags: qr rd ra; QUERY: 1, ANSWER: 1, AUTHORITY: 0, ADDITIONAL: 1

;; OPT PSEUDOSECTION:
; EDNS: version: 0, flags:; udp: 65494
;; QUESTION SECTION:
;fe.gb.foowidgets.k8s.            IN       A

;; ANSWER SECTION:
fe.gb.foowidgets.k8s.    30       IN       A        10.2.1.224

;; Query time: 4 msec
```

```
;; SERVER: 127.0.0.53#53(127.0.0.53)
;; WHEN: Tue Jul 06 23:52:10 UTC 2021
;; MSG SIZE  rcvd: 65
```

Note that the IP address returned is now the IP address for the deployment in the Buffalo cluster, the secondary cluster, `10.2.1.224`. This proves that K8GB is working correctly and providing us with a Kubernetes controlled global load balancer.

Once the application becomes healthy in the primary cluster, K8GB will update CoreDNS and any requests will resolve to the main cluster again. To test this, we scaled the deployment in NYC back up to 1 and ran another dig test:

```
surovich@ubuntu-20:~$ dig fe.gb.foowidgets.k8s

; <<>> DiG 9.16.1-Ubuntu <<>> fe.gb.foowidgets.k8s
;; global options: +cmd
;; Got answer:
;; ->>HEADER<<- opcode: QUERY, status: NOERROR, id: 54278
;; flags: qr rd ra; QUERY: 1, ANSWER: 1, AUTHORITY: 0, ADDITIONAL: 1

;; OPT PSEUDOSECTION:
; EDNS: version: 0, flags:; udp: 65494
;; QUESTION SECTION:
;fe.gb.foowidgets.k8s.          IN      A

;; ANSWER SECTION:
fe.gb.foowidgets.k8s.   30      IN      A       10.2.1.221

;; Query time: 4 msec
;; SERVER: 127.0.0.53#53(127.0.0.53)
;; WHEN: Tue Jul 06 23:58:49 UTC 2021
;; MSG SIZE  rcvd: 65
```

We can see that the IP has been updated to reflect the NYC Ingress controller on address `10.2.1.221`, the primary data center location.

K8GB is a unique, and impressive, project from the CNCF that offers global load balancing similar to what other, more expensive, products offer today. It's a project that we are watching carefully and if you have a requirement to deploy applications across multiple clusters, you should consider looking into the K8GB project as it matures.

Summary

In this three-part chapter, you learned about exposing your workloads in Kubernetes to other cluster resources and users.

The first part of the chapter went over services and the multiple types that can be assigned. The three major service types are ClusterIP, NodePort, and LoadBalancer. Remember that the selection of the type of service will configure how your application is exposed.

In the second part, we introduced two load balancer types, layer 4 and layer 7, each having a unique functionality for exposing workloads. Typically, services alone are not the only objects that are used to provide access to applications running in the cluster. You will often use a ClusterIP service along with an Ingress controller to provide access to services that use layer 7. Some applications may require additional communication, which is not provided by a layer 7 load balancer. These applications may require a layer 4 load balancer to expose their services to users. In the load balancing section, we demonstrated the installation and use of MetalLB, a popular, open source, layer 4 load balancer.

In the last section, we moved on to how to add additional enterprise features to your load balancing. We explained how to integrate a dynamic CoreDNS zone with an external enterprise DNS server using conditional forwarding. Integrating the two naming systems provides a method to allow the dynamic registration of any layer 4, load-balanced service in the cluster.

The chapter was closed out by introducing a new and powerful project called K8GB. This CNCF sandbox project provides a Kubernetes native global load balancer, allowing enterprises to deploy applications to multiple clusters with automatic failover or load balancing between the configured clusters.

Now that you know how to expose services on the cluster to users, how do we control who has access to the cluster to create a new service? In the next chapter, we will explain how to integrate authentication with your cluster. We will deploy an OIDC provider into our KinD clusters and connect with an external SAML2 lab server for identities.

Questions

1. How does a service know what pods should be used as endpoints for the service?

    a. By the service port

    b. By the namespace

    c. By the author

    d. By the selector label

2. What kubectl command helps you to troubleshoot services that may not be working properly?

    a. `kubectl get services <service name>`

    b. `kubectl get ep <service name>`

    c. `kubectl get pods <service name>`

    d. `kubectl get servers <service name>`

3. All Kubernetes distributions include support for services that use the `LoadBalancer` type.

    a. `True`

    b. `False`

4. Which load balancer type supports all TCP/UDP ports and accepts traffic regardless of the packet's contents?

    a. Layer 7

    b. Cisco layer

    c. Layer 2

    d. Layer 4

5. Without any added components, you can use multiple protocols using which of the following service types?

    a. `NodePort` and `ClusterIP`

    b. `LoadBalancer` and `NodePort`

    c. `NodePort`, `LoadBalancer`, and `ClusterIP`

    d. `LoadBalancer` and `ClusterIP`

Join our book's Discord space

Join the book's Discord workspace for a monthly *Ask me Anything* session with the authors: `https://packt.link/K8EntGuide`

5

Integrating Authentication into Your Cluster

Once a cluster has been built, users will need to interact with it securely. For most enterprises, this means authenticating individual users and making sure they can only access what they need in order to do their jobs. With Kubernetes, this can be challenging because a cluster is a collection of APIs, not an application with a frontend that can prompt for authentication.

In this chapter, you'll learn how to integrate enterprise authentication into your cluster using the OpenID Connect protocol and Kubernetes impersonation. We'll also cover several anti-patterns and explain why you should avoid using them.

In this chapter, we will cover the following topics:

- Understanding how Kubernetes knows who you are
- Understanding OpenID Connect
- Configuring KinD for OpenID Connect
- How cloud Kubernetes knows who you are
- Configuring your cluster for impersonation
- Configuring impersonation without OpenUnison
- Authenticating pipelines to your cluster

Let's get started!

Technical requirements

To complete the exercises in this chapter, you will require the following:

- An Ubuntu 20.04 server with 8 GB of RAM
- A KinD cluster running with the configuration from *Chapter 2, Deploying Kubernetes Using KinD*

You can access the code for this chapter at the following GitHub repository: `https://github.com/PacktPublishing/Kubernetes---An-Enterprise-Guide-2E/tree/main/chapter5`.

Understanding how Kubernetes knows who you are

In the 1999 sci-fi film *The Matrix*, Neo talks to a child about the Matrix as he waits to see the Oracle. The child explains to him that the trick to manipulating the Matrix is to realize that "*There is no spoon.*"

This is a great way to look at users in Kubernetes, because they don't exist. With the exception of service accounts, which we'll talk about later, there are no objects in Kubernetes called "User" or "Group." Every API interaction must include enough information to tell the API server who the user is and what groups the user is a member of. This assertion can take different forms, depending on how you plan to integrate authentication into your cluster.

In this section, we will get into the details of the different ways Kubernetes can associate a user with a cluster.

External users

Users who are accessing the Kubernetes API from outside the cluster will usually do so using one of two authentication methods:

- **Certificate**: You can assert who you are using a client certificate that has information about you, such as your username and groups. The certificate is used as part of the TLS negotiation process.
- **Bearer token**: Embedded in each request, a bearer token can either be a self-contained token that contains all the information needed to verify itself or a token that can be exchanged by a webhook in the API server for that information.

You can also use service accounts to access the API server outside the cluster, though it's strongly discouraged. We'll cover the risks and concerns around using service accounts in the *Other authentication options* section.

Groups in Kubernetes

Different users can be assigned the same permissions without creating `RoleBinding` objects for each user individually via groups. Kubernetes includes two types of groups:

- **System assigned**: These groups start with the `system:` prefix and are assigned by the API server. An example group is `system:authenticated`, which is assigned to all authenticated users. Another example of system-assigned groups is the `system:serviceaccounts:namespace` group, where `Namespace` is the name of the namespace that contains all the service accounts for the namespace named in the group.

- **User-asserted groups**: These groups are asserted by the authentication system either in the token provided to the API server or via the authentication webhook. There are no standards or requirements for how these groups are named. Just as with users, groups don't exist as objects in the API server. Groups are asserted at authentication time by external users and tracked locally for system-generated groups. When asserting a user's groups, the primary difference between a user's unique ID and groups is that the unique ID is expected to be unique, whereas groups are not.

You may be authorized for access by groups, but all access is still tracked and audited based on your user's unique ID.

Service accounts

Service accounts are objects that exist in the API server to track which pods can access the various APIs. Service account tokens are called **JSON Web Tokens**, or **JWTs**, and depending on how the token was generated, there are two ways to obtain a service account:

- The first is from a secret that was generated by Kubernetes when the service account was created.

- The second is via the `TokenRequest` API, which is used to inject a secret into pods via a mount point or used externally from the cluster. All service accounts are used by injecting the token as a header in the request into the API server. The API server recognizes it as a service account and validates it internally.

Unlike users, service accounts **CANNOT** be assigned to arbitrary groups. Service accounts are members of pre-built groups only; you can't create a group of specific service accounts for assigning roles.

Now that we have explored the fundamentals of how Kubernetes identifies users, we'll explore how this framework fits into the **OpenID Connect (OIDC)** protocol. OIDC provides the security most enterprises require and is standards-based, but Kubernetes doesn't use it in a way that is typical of many web applications. Understanding these differences and why Kubernetes needs them is an important step in integrating a cluster into an enterprise security environment.

Understanding OpenID Connect

OpenID Connect is a standard identity federation protocol. It's built on the OAuth2 specification and has some very powerful features that make it the preferred choice for interacting with Kubernetes clusters.

The main benefits of OpenID Connect are as follows:

- **Short-lived tokens**: If a token is leaked, such as via a log message or breach, you want the token to expire as quickly as possible. With OIDC, you're able to specify tokens that can live for 1-2 minutes, which means the token will likely be expired by the time an attacker attempts to use it.

- **User and group memberships**: When we start talking about authorization, we'll see quickly that it's important to manage access by group instead of managing access by referencing users directly. OIDC tokens can embed both the user's identifier and their groups, leading to easier access management.

- **Refresh tokens scoped to timeout policies**: With short-lived tokens, you need to be able to refresh them as needed. The time a refresh token is valid for can be scoped to your enterprise's web application idle timeout policy, keeping your cluster in compliance with other web-based applications.

- **No plugins required for kubectl**: The kubectl binary supports OpenID Connect natively, so there's no need for any additional plugins. This is especially useful if you need to access your cluster from a jump box or VM because you're unable to install the **Command-Line Interface (CLI)** tools directly onto your workstation.

- **More multi-factor authentication options**: Many of the strongest multi-factor authentication options require a web browser. Examples include FIDO U2F and WebAuthn, which use hardware tokens.

OIDC is a peer-reviewed standard that has been in use for several years and is quickly becoming the preferred standard for identity federation.

 Identity federation is the term used to describe the assertion of identity data and authentication without sharing the user's confidential secret or password. A classic example of identity federation is logging into your employee website and being able to access your benefits provider without having to log in again. Your employee website doesn't share your password with your benefits provider. Instead, your employee website *asserts* that you logged in at a certain date and time and provides some information about you. This way, your account is *federated* across two silos (your employee website and benefits portal), without your benefits portal knowing your employee website password.

The OpenID Connect protocol

As you can see, there are multiple components to OIDC. To fully understand how OIDC works, let's begin with understanding the OpenID Connect protocol.

The two aspects of the OIDC protocol we will be focusing on are as follows:

- Using tokens with `kubectl` and the API server
- Refreshing tokens to keep your tokens up to date

We won't focus too much on obtaining tokens. While the protocol to get a token does follow a standard, the login process does not. How you obtain tokens from an identity provider will vary, and it's based on how you choose to implement the OIDC **Identity Provider (IdP)**.

Three tokens are generated from an OIDC login process:

- `access_token`: This token is used to make authenticated requests to web services your identity provider may provide, such as obtaining user information. It is NOT used by Kubernetes and can be discarded. This token does not have a standard form. It may be a JWT, it may not.
- `id_token`: This token is a JWT that encapsulates your identity, including your unique identifier, groups, and expiration information about you that the API server can use to authorize your access. The JWT is signed by your identity provider's certificate and can be verified by Kubernetes simply by checking the JWT's signature. This is the token you pass to Kubernetes for each request to authenticate yourself.

- refresh_token: kubectl knows how to refresh your id_token for you automatically once it expires. To do this, it makes a call to your IdP's token endpoint using a refresh_token to obtain a new id_token. A refresh_token can only be used once and is opaque, meaning that you, as the holder of the token, have no visibility into its format and it really doesn't matter to you. It either works, or it doesn't. The refresh_token never goes to Kubernetes (or any other application). It is only used in communications with the IdP.

Once you have your tokens, you can use them to authenticate with the API server. The easiest way to use your tokens is to add them to the kubectl configuration using command-line parameters:

```
kubectl config set-credentials username --auth-provider=oidc --auth-
provider-arg=idp-issuer-url=https://host/uri --auth-provider-
arg=client-id=kubernetes --auth-provider-arg=refresh-token=$REFRESH_
TOKEN --auth-provider-arg=id-token=$ID_TOKEN
```

config set-credentials has a few options that need to be provided. We have already explained id-token and refresh_token, but there are two additional options:

- idp-issuer-url: This is the same URL we will use to configure the API server and points to the base URL used for the IdP's discovery URL.

- client-id: This is used by your IdP to identify your configuration. This is unique to a Kubernetes deployment and is not considered secret information.

The OpenID Connect protocol has an optional element, known as a client_secret, that is shared between an OIDC client and the IdP. It is used to "authenticate" the client prior to making any requests, such as refreshing a token. While it's supported by Kubernetes as an option, it's recommended to not use it and instead configure your IdP to use a public endpoint (which doesn't use a secret at all).

The client secret has no practical value since you'd need to share it with every potential user and since it's a password, your enterprise's compliance framework will likely require that it is rotated regularly, causing support headaches. Overall, it's just not worth any potential downsides in terms of security.

Kubernetes requires that your identity provider supports the discovery URL endpoint, which is a URL that provides some JSON to tell you where you can get keys to verify JWTs and the various endpoints available. Take any issuer URL and add /.well-known/openid-configuration to see this information.

Following OIDC and the API's interaction

Once `kubectl` has been configured, all of your API interactions will follow the following sequence:

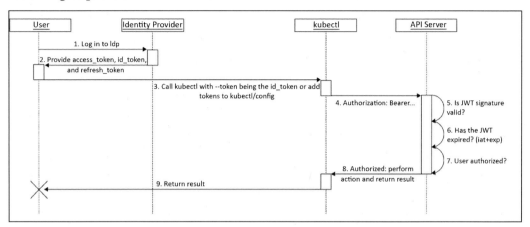

Figure 5.1: Kubernetes/kubectl OpenID Connect sequence diagram

The preceding diagram is from Kubernetes' authentication page at `https://kubernetes.io/docs/reference/access-authn-authz/authentication/#openid-connect-tokens`. Authenticating a request involves doing the following:

1. **Log in to your IdP**: This will be different for each IdP. This could involve providing a username and password to a form in a web browser, a multi-factor token, or a certificate. This will be specific to every implementation.

2. **Provide tokens to the user**: Once authenticated, the user needs a way to generate the tokens needed by `kubectl` to access the Kubernetes APIs. This can take the form of an application that makes it easy for the user to copy and paste them into the configuration file, or can be a new file to download.

3. This step is where `id_token` and `refresh_token` are added to the `kubectl` configuration. If the tokens were presented to the user in the browser, they can be manually added to the configuration. Alternatively, some solutions provide a new `kubectl` configuration to download at this step. There are also `kubectl` plugins that will launch a web browser to start the authentication process and, once completed, generate your configuration for you.

4. **Inject id_token**: Once the `kubectl` command has been called, each API call includes an additional header, called the **Authorization** header, that includes `id_token`.

5. **JWT signature validation**: Once the API server receives `id_token` from the API call, it validates the signature against the public key provided by the identity provider. The API server will also validate whether the issuer matches the issuer for the API server configuration, and also that the recipient matches the client ID from the API server configuration.

6. **Check the JWT's expiration**: Tokens are only good for a limited amount of time. The API server ensures that the token hasn't expired.

7. **Authorization check**: Now that the user has been authenticated, the API server will determine whether the user identified by the provided `id_token` is able to perform the requested action by matching the user's identifier and asserted groups to internal policies.

8. **Execute the API**: All checks are complete and the API server executes the request, generating a response that will be sent back to `kubectl`.

9. **Format the response for the user**: Once the API call is complete (or a series of API calls), the response in JSON is formatted and presented to the user by `kubectl`.

 In general terms, authentication is the process of validating you are you. Most of us encounter this when we put our username and password into a website. We're proving who we are. In the enterprise world, authorization then becomes the decision of whether we're allowed to do something. First, we authenticate and then we authorize. The standards built around API security don't assume authentication and go straight to authorization based on some sort of token. It's not assumed that the caller has to be identified. For instance, when you use a physical key to open a door, the door doesn't know who you are, only that you have the right key. This terminology can become very confusing, so don't feel bad if you get a bit lost. You're in good company!

`id_token` is self-contained; everything the API server needs to know about you is in that token. The API server verifies `id_token` using the certificate provided by the identity provider and verifies that the token hasn't expired. As long as that all lines up, the API server will move on to authorizing your request based on its own RBAC configuration. We'll cover the details of that process later. Finally, assuming you're authorized, the API server provides a response.

Notice that Kubernetes never sees your password or any other secret information that you, and only you, know. The only thing that's shared is the `id_token`, and that's ephemeral. This leads to several important points:

- Since Kubernetes never sees your password or other credentials, it can't compromise them. This can save you a tremendous amount of time working with your security team, because all the tasks and controls related to securing passwords can be skipped!

- The `id_token` is self-contained, which means that if it's compromised, there is nothing you can do, short of re-keying your identity provider, to stop it from being abused. This is why it's so important for your `id_token` to have a short lifespan. At 1-2 minutes, the likelihood that an attacker will be able to obtain an `id_token`, realize what it is, and abuse it is very low.

If, while performing its calls, `kubectl` finds that `id_token` has expired, it will attempt to refresh it by calling the IdP's token endpoint using `refresh_token`. If the user's session is still valid, the IdP will generate a new `id_token` and `refresh_token`, which `kubectl` will store for you in the `kubectl` configuration. This happens automatically with no user intervention. Additionally, a `refresh_token` has a one-time use, so if someone tries to use a previously used `refresh_token`, your IdP will fail the refresh process.

 It's bound to happen. Someone may need to be locked out immediately. It may be that they're being walked out or that their session has been compromised. This is dependent on your IdP, so when choosing an IdP, make sure it supports some form of session revocation.

Finally, if the `refresh_token` has expired or the session has been revoked, the API server will return a `401 Unauthorized` message to indicate that it will no longer support the token.

We've spent a considerable amount of time examining the OIDC protocol. Now, let's take an in-depth look at the `id_token`.

id_token

An `id_token` is a JSON web token that is Base64-encoded and is digitally signed. The JSON contains a series of attributes, known as claims, in OIDC. There are some standard claims in the `id_token`, but for the most part, the claims you will be most concerned with are as follows:

- `iss`: The issuer, which MUST line up with the issuer in your `kubectl` configuration
- `aud`: Your client ID
- `sub`: Your unique identifier

- **groups**: Not a standard claim, but should be populated with groups specifically related to your Kubernetes deployment

 Many deployments attempt to identify you by your email address. This is an anti-pattern as your email address is generally based on your name, and names change. The sub claim is supposed to be a unique identifier that is immutable and will never change. This way, it doesn't matter if your email changes because your name changes. This can make it harder to debug "who is cd25d24d-74b8-4cc4-8b8c-116bf4abbd26?" but will provide a cleaner and easier-to-maintain cluster.

There are several other claims that indicate when an `id_token` should no longer be accepted. These claims are all measured in seconds from epoch (January 1, 1970) UTC time:

- **exp**: When the `id_token` expires
- **iat**: When the `id_token` was created
- **nbf**: The absolute earliest an `id_token` should be allowed

Why doesn't a token just have a single expiration time?

It's unlikely that the clock on the system that created the `id_token` has the exact same time as the system that is evaluating it. There's often a skew and, depending on how the clock is set, it may be a few minutes. Having a not-before in addition to an expiration gives some room for standard time deviation.

There are other claims in an `id_token` that don't really matter but are there for additional context. Examples include your name, contact information, organization, and so on.

While the primary use for tokens is to interact with the Kubernetes API server, they are not limited to only API interaction. In addition to going to the API server, webhook calls may also receive your `id_token`.

You may have deployed OPA as a validating webhook on a cluster. When someone submits a pod creation request, the webhook will receive the user's `id_token`, which can be used for other decisions.

 OPA, the Open Policy Agent, is a tool for validating and authorizing requests. It's often deployed in Kubernetes as an admission controller webhook. If you haven't worked with OPA or admission controllers, we cover both in depth starting in *Chapter 8, Extending Security Using Open Policy Agent*.

One example is that you want to ensure that the PVCs are mapped to specific PVs based on the submitter's organization. The organization is included in the `id_token`, which is passed to Kubernetes, and then onto the OPA webhook. Since the token has been passed to the webhook, the information can then be used in your OPA policies.

Other authentication options

In this section, we focused on OIDC and presented reasons why it's the best mechanism for authentication. It is certainly not the only option, and we will cover the other options in this section and when they're appropriate.

Certificates

This is generally everyone's first experience authenticating to a Kubernetes cluster.

Once a Kubernetes installation is complete, a pre-built `kubectl config` file that contains a certificate and private key is created and ready to be used. Where this file is created is dependent on the distribution. This file should only be used in "break glass in case of emergency" scenarios, where all other forms of authentication are not available. It should be controlled by your organization's standards for privileged access. When this configuration file is used, it doesn't identify the user and can easily be abused since it doesn't allow for an easy audit trail.

While this is a standard use case for certificate authentication, it's not the only use case for certificate authentication. Certificate authentication, when done correctly, is one of the strongest recognized credentials in the industry.

Certificate authentication is used by the US Federal Government for its most important tasks. At a high level, certificate authentication involves using a client key and certificate to negotiate your HTTPS connection to the API server. The API server can get the certificate you used to establish the connection and validate it against a **Certificate Authority (CA)** certificate. Once verified, it maps attributes from the certificate to a user and groups the API server can recognize.

To get the security benefits of certificate authentication, the private key needs to be generated on isolated hardware, usually in the form of a smartcard, and never leave that hardware. A certificate signing request is generated and submitted to a CA that signs the public key, thus creating a certificate that is then installed on the dedicated hardware. At no point does the CA get the private key, so even if the CA were compromised, you couldn't gain the user's private key. If a certificate needs to be revoked, it's added to a revocation list that can either be pulled from an LDAP directory or a file, or it can be checked using the OCSP protocol.

This may look like an attractive option, so why shouldn't you use certificates with Kubernetes?

- Smartcard integration uses a standard called PKCS11, which neither `kubectl` nor the API server support

- The API server has no way of checking certificate revocation lists or using OCSP, so once a certificate has been minted, there's no way to revoke it so that the API server can use it

Additionally, the process to correctly generate a key pair is rarely used. It requires a complex interface to be built that is difficult for users to use combined with command-line tools that need to be run. To get around this, the certificate and key pair are generated for you and you download them or they're emailed to you, negating the security of the process.

The other reason you shouldn't use certificate authentication for users is that it's difficult to leverage groups. While you can embed groups into the subject of the certificate, you can't revoke a certificate. So, if a user's role changes, you can give them a new certificate but you can't keep them from using the old one. While you could reference users directly in your RoleBindings and ClusterRoleBindings, this is an anti-pattern that will make it difficult to keep track of access across even small clusters.

As stated in the introduction to this section, using a certificate to authenticate in "break glass in case of emergency" situations is a good use of certificate authentication. It may be the only way to get into a cluster if all other authentication methods are experiencing issues.

Service accounts

Service accounts appear to provide an easy access method. Creating them is easy. The following command creates a service account object and a secret to go with it that stores the service account's token:

```
kubectl create sa mysa -n default
```

Next, the following command will retrieve the service account's token in JSON format and return only the value of the token. This token can then be used to access the API server:

```
kubectl get secret $(kubectl get sa mysa -n default -o json | jq -r
'.secrets[0].name') -o json | jq -r '.data.token' | base64 -d
```

To show an example of this, let's call the API endpoint directly, without providing any credentials (make sure you use the port for your own local control plane):

```
curl -v --insecure https://0.0.0.0:32768/api
```

You will receive the following:

```
.
.
.
{
  "kind": "Status",
  "apiVersion": "v1",
  "metadata": {
  },
  "status": "Failure",
  "message": "forbidden: User \"system:anonymous\" cannot get path
\"/api\"",
  "reason": "Forbidden",
  "details": {
  },
  "code": 403
* Connection #0 to host 0.0.0.0 left intact
```

By default, most Kubernetes distributions do not allow anonymous access to the API server, so we receive a *403 error* because we didn't specify a user.

Now, let's add our service account to an API request:

```
export KUBE_AZ=$(kubectl get secret $(kubectl get sa mysa -n default -o
json | jq -r '.secrets[0].name') -o json | jq -r '.data.token' | base64
-d)
curl  -H "Authorization: Bearer $KUBE_AZ" --insecure
https://0.0.0.0:32768/api
{
  "kind": "APIVersions",
  "versions": [
    "v1"
  ],
  "serverAddressByClientCIDRs": [
    {
      "clientCIDR": "0.0.0.0/0",
      "serverAddress": "172.17.0.3:6443"
    }
```

```
    ]
  }
```

Success! This was an easy process, so you may be wondering, "Why do I need to worry about all the complicated OIDC mess?" This solution's simplicity brings multiple security issues:

- **Secure transmission of the token**: Service accounts are self-contained and need nothing to unlock them or verify ownership, so if a token is taken in transit, you have no way of stopping its use. You could set up a system where a user logs in to download a file with the token in it, but you now have a much less secure version of OIDC.

- **No expiration**: When you decode a legacy service account token, there is nothing that tells you when the token expires. That's because the token never expires. You can revoke a token by deleting the service account and recreating it, but that means you need a system in place to do that. Again, you've built a less capable version of OIDC.

- **Auditing**: The service account can easily be handed out by the owner once the key has been retrieved. If there are multiple users using a single key, it becomes very difficult to audit the use of the account.

In addition to these issues, you can't put a service account into arbitrary groups. This means that RBAC bindings have to either be direct to the service account or use one of the pre-built groups that service accounts are a member of. We'll explore why this is an issue when we talk about authorization, so just keep it in mind for now.

Finally, service accounts were never designed to be used outside of the cluster. It's like using a hammer to drive in a screw. With enough muscle and aggravation, you will drive it in, but it won't be pretty and no one will be happy with the result.

TokenRequest API

The TokenRequest API is the future of service account integration. It went into beta in 1.12 and will be GA in 1.22. This API eliminates the use of static legacy service accounts and instead projects accounts into your pods. These projected tokens are short-lived and unique for each individual pod. Finally, these tokens become invalid once the pods they're associated with are destroyed. This makes service account tokens embedded into a pod much more secure.

This API provides another great feature: you can use it with third-party services. One example is using HashiCorp's Vault secret management system to authenticate pods without having to do a token review API call against the APIs server to validate it.

This feature makes it much easier, and more secure, for your pods to call external APIs.

The `TokenRequest` API lets you request a short-lived service account for a specific scope. While it provides slightly better security since it will expire and has a limited scope, it's still bound to a service account, which means no groups, and there's still the issue of securely getting the token to the user and auditing its use.

Starting in 1.21, all service account tokens are projected into pods via the `TokenRequest` API by default. The new tokens are good for a year though, so not very short-lived! That said, even if a token is set up to expire quickly, the API server won't reject it. It will log that someone is using an expired token. This is intended to make the transition from unlimited-life tokens to short-lived tokens easier.

Some people may be tempted to use tokens for user authentication; however, tokens generated by the `TokenRequest` API are still built for pods to talk to your cluster or for talking to third-party APIs; they are not meant to be used by users.

Custom authentication webhooks

If you already have an identity platform that doesn't use an existing standard, a custom authentication webhook will let you integrate it without having to customize the API server. This feature is commonly used by cloud providers who host managed Kubernetes instances.

You can define an authentication webhook that the API server will call with a token to validate it and get information about the user. Unless you manage a public cloud with a custom IAM token system that you are building a Kubernetes distribution for, don't do this. Writing your own authentication is like writing your own encryption – just don't do it. Every custom authentication system we've seen for Kubernetes boils down to either a pale imitation of OIDC or "pass the password." Much like the analogy of driving a screw in with a hammer, you could do it, but it will be very painful. This is mostly because instead of driving the screw through a board, you're more likely to drive it into your own foot.

Keystone

Those familiar with OpenStack will recognize the name Keystone as an identity provider. If you are not familiar with Keystone, it is the default identity provider used in an OpenStack deployment.

Keystone hosts the API that handles authentication and token generation. OpenStack stores users in Keystone's database.

While using Keystone is more often associated with OpenStack, Kubernetes can also be configured to use Keystone for username and password authentication, with some limitations:

- The main limitation of using Keystone as an IdP for Kubernetes is that it only works with Keystone's LDAP implementation. While you could use this method, you should consider that only username and password are supported, so you're creating an identity provider with a non-standard protocol to authenticate to an LDAP server, which pretty much any OIDC IdP can do out of the box.

- You can't leverage SAML or OIDC with Keystone, even though Keystone supports both protocols for OpenStack, which limits how users can authenticate, thus cutting you off from multiple multi-factor options.

- Few, if any, applications know how to use the Keystone protocol outside of OpenStack. Your cluster will have multiple applications that make up your platform, and those applications won't know how to integrate with Keystone.

Using Keystone is certainly an appealing idea, especially if you're deploying on OpenStack, but ultimately, it's very limiting and you will likely put in just as much work getting Keystone integrated as just using OIDC.

The next section will take the details we've explored here and apply them to integrating authentication into a cluster. As you move through the implementation, you'll see how kubectl, the API server, and your identity provider interact to provide secure access to the cluster. We'll tie these features back to common enterprise requirements to illustrate why the details for understanding the OpenID Connect protocol are important.

Configuring KinD for OpenID Connect

For our example deployment, we will use a scenario from our customer, FooWidgets. FooWidgets has a Kubernetes cluster that they would like integrated using OIDC. The proposed solution needs to address the following requirements:

- Kubernetes must use our central authentication system, Active Directory
- We need to be able to map Active Directory groups into our RBAC RoleBinding objects
- Users need access to the Kubernetes Dashboard
- Users need to be able to use the CLI
- All enterprise compliance requirements must be met

- Additional cluster management applications need to be managed centrally as well

Let's explore each of these in detail and explain how we can address the customer's requirements.

Addressing the requirements

Our enterprise's requirements require multiple moving parts, both inside and outside our cluster. We'll examine each of these components and how they relate to building an authenticated cluster.

Using LDAP and Active Directory with Kubernetes

Most enterprises today use Active Directory from Microsoft™ to store information about users and their credentials. Depending on the size of your enterprise, it's not unusual to have multiple domains or forests where users' data is stored. We'll need a solution that knows how to talk to each domain. Your enterprise may have one of many tools and products for OpenID Connect integration, or you may just want to connect via LDAP. **LDAP**, the **Lightweight Directory Access Protocol**, is a standard protocol that has been used for over thirty years and is still the standard way to talk directly to Active Directory. Using LDAP, you can look up users and validate their passwords. It's also the simplest way to start because it doesn't require integration with an identity provider. All you need is a service account and credentials!

For FooWidgets, we're going to connect directly to our Active Directory for all authentication.

> Don't worry – you don't need Active Directory ready to go to run this exercise. We'll walk through deploying a demo directory into our KinD cluster.

Mapping Active Directory groups to RBAC RoleBindings

This will become important when we start talking about authorization. Active Directory lists all the groups a user is a member of in the `memberOf` attribute. We can read this attribute directly from our logged-in user's account to get their groups. These groups will be embedded into our `id_token` in the `groups` claim and can be referenced directly in RBAC bindings.

Kubernetes Dashboard access

The dashboard is a powerful way to quickly access information about your cluster and make quick updates. When deployed correctly, the dashboard does not create any security issues. The proper way to deploy the dashboard is with no privileges, instead relying on the user's own credentials. We'll do this with a reverse proxy that injects the user's OIDC token on each request, which the dashboard will then use when it makes calls to the API server. Using this method, we'll be able to constrain access to our dashboard the same way we would with any other web application.

There are a few reasons why using the `kubectl` built-in proxy and port-forward aren't a great strategy for accessing the dashboard. Many enterprises will not install CLI utilities locally, forcing you to use a jump box to access privileged systems such as Kubernetes, meaning port forwarding won't work. Even if you can run `kubectl` locally, opening a port on loopback (`127.0.0.1`) means anything on your system can use it, not just you from your browser. While browsers have controls in place to keep you from accessing ports on loopback using a malicious script, that won't stop anything else on your workstation. Finally, it's just not a great user experience.

We'll dig into the details of how and why this works in *Chapter 7, Deploying a Secured Kubernetes Dashboard*.

Kubernetes CLI access

Most developers want to be able to access `kubectl` and other tools that rely on the `kubectl` configuration. For instance, the Visual Studio Code Kubernetes plugin doesn't require any special configuration. It just uses the `kubectl` built-in configuration. Most enterprises tightly constrain what binaries you're able to install, so we want to minimize any additional tools and plugins we want to install.

Enterprise compliance requirements

Being cloud-native doesn't mean you can ignore your enterprise's compliance requirements. Most enterprises have requirements such as having 20-minute idle timeouts, may require multi-factor authentication for privileged access, and so on. Any solution we put in place has to make it through the control spreadsheets needed to go live. Also, this goes without saying, but everything needs to be encrypted (and I do mean everything).

Pulling it all together

To fulfill these requirements, we're going to use OpenUnison. It has prebuilt configurations to work with Kubernetes, the Dashboard, the CLI, and Active Directory.

It's also pretty quick to deploy, so we don't need to concentrate on provider-specific implementation details and instead focus on Kubernetes' configuration options. Our architecture will look like this:

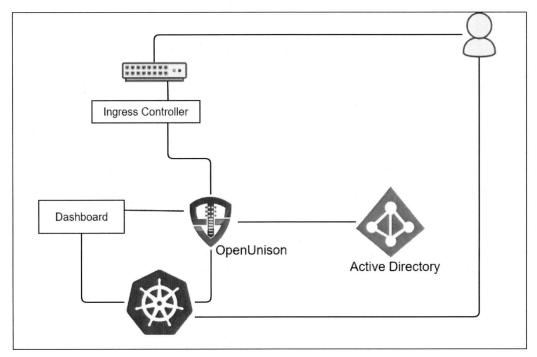

Figure 5.2: Authentication architecture

For our implementation, we're going to use two hostnames:

- `k8s.apps.X-X-X-X.nip.io`: Access to the OpenUnison portal, where we'll initiate our login and get our tokens

- `k8sdb.apps.X-X-X-X.nip.io`: Access to the Kubernetes dashboard

 As a quick refresher, `nip.io` is a public DNS service that will return an IP address from the one embedded in your hostname. This is really useful in a lab environment where setting up DNS can be painful. In our examples, `X-X-X-X` is the IP of your Docker host.

When a user attempts to access `https://k8s.apps.X-X-X-X.nip.io/`, they'll be asked for their username and password. After the user hits submit, OpenUnison will look up the user against Active Directory, retrieving the user's profile information. At that point, OpenUnison will create user objects in the OpenUnison namespace to store the user's information and create OIDC sessions.

Earlier, we described how Kubernetes doesn't have user objects. Kubernetes lets you extend the base API with **Custom Resource Definitions (CRDs)**. OpenUnison defines a User CRD to help with high availability and to avoid needing a database to store state in. These user objects can't be used for RBAC.

Once the user is logged into OpenUnison, they can get their `kubectl` configuration to use the CLI or use the Kubernetes Dashboard, `https://kubernetes.io/docs/tasks/access-application-cluster/web-ui-dashboard/`, to access the cluster from their browser. Once the user is ready, they can log out of OpenUnison, which will end their session and invalidate their `refresh_token`, making it impossible for them to use `kubectl` or the dashboard until after they log in again. If they walk away from their desk for lunch without logging out, when they return, their `refresh_token` will have expired, so they'll no longer be able to interact with Kubernetes without logging back in.

Now that we have walked through how users will log in and interact with Kubernetes, we'll deploy OpenUnison and integrate it into the cluster for authentication.

Deploying OpenUnison

The Dashboard is a popular feature for many users. It provides a quick view of resources without needing to use the `kubectl` CLI. Over the years, it has received some bad press for being insecure, but when deployed correctly, it is very secure. Most of the stories you may have read or heard about come from a Dashboard deployment that was not set up correctly. We will cover this topic in *Chapter 7, Deploying a Secured Kubernetes Dashboard*:

1. First, we'll deploy the dashboard from `https://github.com/kubernetes/dashboard`:

```
kubectl apply -f https://raw.githubusercontent.com/kubernetes/
dashboard/v2.2.0/aio/deploy/recommended.yaml

namespace/kubernetes-dashboard created
serviceaccount/kubernetes-dashboard created
service/kubernetes-dashboard created
secret/kubernetes-dashboard-certs created
secret/kubernetes-dashboard-csrf created
secret/kubernetes-dashboard-key-holder created
configmap/kubernetes-dashboard-settings created
role.rbac.authorization.k8s.io/kubernetes-dashboard created
clusterrole.rbac.authorization.k8s.io/kubernetes-dashboard
created
rolebinding.rbac.authorization.k8s.io/kubernetes-dashboard
```

```
created
clusterrolebinding.rbac.authorization.k8s.io/Kubernetes
dashboard created
deployment.apps/kubernetes-dashboard created
service/dashboard-metrics-scraper created
deployment.apps/dashboard-metrics-scraper created
```

2. Second, deploy our testing "Active Directory." This is an ApacheDS instance that has the same schema as Active Directory, so you'll be able to see how Kubernetes would integrate with Active Directory without needing to deploy it yourself! After running the following `kubectl` command, wait until the pod is running in the `activedirectory` namespace:

```
kubectl create -f chapter5/apacheds.yaml
```

3. Next, we need to add the repository that contains OpenUnison to our Helm list. To add the Tremolo chart repository, use the `helm repo add` command:

```
helm repo add tremolo https://nexus.tremolo.io/repository/helm/
https://nexus.tremolo.io/repository/helm/"tremolo" has been
added to your repositories
```

4. Once added, you need to update the repository using the `helm repo update` command:

```
helm repo update
Hang tight while we grab the latest from your chart
repositories...
...Successfully got an update from the "tremolo" chart
repository
Update Complete. Happy Helming!
```

You are now ready to deploy the OpenUnison operator using the Helm chart.

5. First, we want to deploy OpenUnison in a new namespace called `openunison`. We need to create the namespace before deploying the Helm chart:

```
kubectl create ns openunison
```

6. Next, we need to add a ConfigMap that will tell OpenUnison how to talk to our "Active Directory":

```
kubectl create -f chapter5/myvd-book.yaml
```

7. With the namespace created, you can deploy the chart into the namespace using Helm. To install a chart using Helm, use helm install <name> <chart> <options>:

```
helm install openunison tremolo/openunison-operator --namespace
```

```
openunison
NAME: openunison
LAST DEPLOYED: Fri Apr 17 15:04:50 2020
NAMESPACE: openunison
STATUS: deployed
REVISION: 1
TEST SUITE: None
```

The operator will take a few minutes to finish deploying.

 An operator is a concept that was pioneered by CoreOS with the goal of encapsulating many of the tasks an administrator may perform that can be automated. Operators are implemented by watching for changes to a specific CRD and acting accordingly. The OpenUnison operator looks for objects of the OpenUnison type and will create any objects that are needed. A secret is created with a PKCS12 file; Deployment, Service, and Ingress objects are all created too. As you make changes to an OpenUnison object, the operator makes updates to the Kubernetes object as needed. For instance, if you change the image in the OpenUnison object, the operator updates the Deployment, which triggers Kubernetes to roll out new pods. For SAML, the operator also watches metadata so that if it changes, the updated certificates are imported.

8. Once the operator has been deployed, we need to create a secret that will store passwords used internally by OpenUnison. Make sure to use your own values for the keys in this secret (remember to Base64-encode them):

```
kubectl create -f - <<EOF
apiVersion: v1
type: Opaque
metadata:
   name: orchestra-secrets-source
   namespace: openunison
data:
   K8S_DB_SECRET: c3RhcnQxMjM=
   unisonKeystorePassword: cGFzc3dvcmQK
   AD_BIND_PASSWORD: c3RhcnQxMjM=
kind: Secret
EOF
secret/orchestra-secrets-source created
```

From here on out, we'll assume you're using the testing "Active Directory." You can customize values and examples, though, to work with your own Active Directory if you want.

9. Now, we need to create a `values.yaml` file that will be used to supply configuration information when we deploy OpenUnison. This book's GitHub repository contains the file to customize in `chapter5/openunison-values.yaml`:

```
network:
    openunison_host: "k8sou.apps.XX-XX-XX-XX.nip.io"
    dashboard_host: "k8sdb.apps.XX-XX-XX-XX.nip.io"
    api_server_host: ""
    session_inactivity_timeout_seconds: 900
    k8s_url: https://0.0.0.0:6443
```

You need to change the following values for your deployment:

   - Network: `openunison_host`: This value should use the IP address of your cluster, which is the IP address of your Docker host; for example, `k8sou.apps.192-168-2-131.nip.io`

   - Network: `dashboard_host`: This value should also use the IP address of your cluster, which is the IP address of your Docker host; for example, `k8sdb.apps.192-168-2-131.nip.io`

After you've edited or created the file using your own entries, save the file and move on to deploying OpenUnison provider

10. To deploy OpenUnison using your `openunison-values.yaml` file, execute a `helm install` command that uses the `-f` option to specify the `openunison-values.yaml` file:

```
helm install orchestra tremolo/orchestra --namespace openunison
-f ./chapter5/openunison-values.yaml
NAME: orchestra
LAST DEPLOYED: Tue Jul 6 16:20:00 2021
NAMESPACE: openunison
STATUS: deployed
REVISION: 1
TEST SUITE: None
```

11. In a few minutes, OpenUnison will be up and running. Check the deployment status by getting the pods in the `openunison` namespace:

```
kubectl get pods -n openunison
NAME                                      READY  STATUS   RESTARTS
AGE
openunison-operator-858d496-zzvvt         1/1    Running  0
5d6h
openunison-orchestra-57489869d4-88d2v     1/1    Running  0
85s
```

12. The last step is to deploy our portal configuration:

```
helm install orchestra-login-portal tremolo/orchestra-login-
portal --namespace openunison -f ./chapter5/openunison-values.
yaml
NAME: orchestra-login-portal
LAST DEPLOYED: Tue Jul 6 16:22:00 2021
NAMESPACE: openunison
STATUS: deployed
REVISION: 1
TEST SUITE: None
```

You can log into the OIDC provider using any machine on your network by using the assigned nip.io address. Since we will test access using the dashboard, you can use any machine with a browser. Navigate your browser to `network.openunison_host` in your `openunison-values.yaml` file. When prompted, use the username `mmosley` and the password `start123` and click on **Sign in**.

Figure 5.3: OpenUnison login screen

When you do, you'll see this screen:

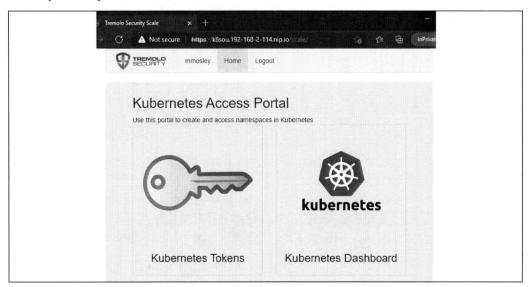

Figure 5.4: OpenUnison home screen

Let's test the OIDC provider by clicking on the **Kubernetes Dashboard** link. Don't panic when you look at the initial dashboard screen – you'll see something like the following:

Figure 5.5: Kubernetes Dashboard before SSO integration has been completed with the API server

That looks like a lot of errors! We're in the dashboard, but nothing seems to be authorized. That's because the API server doesn't trust the tokens that have been generated by OpenUnison yet. The next step is to tell Kubernetes to trust OpenUnison as its OpenID Connect Identity Provider.

Configuring the Kubernetes API to use OIDC

At this point, you have deployed OpenUnison as an OIDC provider and it's working, but your Kubernetes cluster has not been configured to use it as a provider yet.

To configure the API server to use an OIDC provider, you need to add the OIDC options to the API server and provide the OIDC certificate so that the API will trust the OIDC provider.

Since we are using KinD, we can add the required options using a few `kubectl` and `docker` commands.

To provide the OIDC certificate to the API server, we need to retrieve the certificate and copy it over to the KinD master server. We can do this using two commands on the Docker host:

1. The first command extracts OpenUnison's TLS certificate from its secret. This is the same secret referenced by OpenUnison's Ingress object. We use the `jq` utility to extract the data from the secret and then Base64-decode it:

    ```
    kubectl get secret ou-tls-certificate -n openunison -o json | jq
    -r '.data["tls.crt"]' | base64 -d > ou-ca.pem
    ```

2. The second command will copy the certificate to the master server into the `/etc/kubernetes/pki` directory:

    ```
    docker cp ou-ca.pem cluster01-control-plane:/etc/kubernetes/pki/
    ou-ca.pem
    ```

3. As we mentioned earlier, to integrate the API server with OIDC, we need to have the OIDC values for the API options. To list the options we will use, describe the `api-server-config` ConfigMap in the `openunison` namespace:

    ```
    kubectl describe configmap api-server-config -n openunison
    Name:          api-server-config
    Namespace:     openunison
    Labels:        <none>
    Annotations:   <none>
    Data
    ====
    oidc-api-server-flags:
    ----
    --oidc-issuer-url=https://k8sou.apps.192-168-2-131.nip.io/auth/
    idp/k8sIdp
    --oidc-client-id=Kubernetes
    --oidc-username-claim=sub
    --oidc-groups-claim=groups
    --oidc-ca-file=/etc/kubernetes/pki/ou-ca.pem
    ```

4. Next, edit the API server configuration. OpenID Connect is configured by changing flags on the API server. This is why managed Kubernetes generally doesn't offer OpenID Connect as an option, but we'll cover that later in this chapter. Every distribution handles these changes differently, so check with your vendor's documentation. For KinD, shell into the control plane and update the manifest file:

```
docker exec -it cluster01-control-plane bash
apt-get update
apt-get install vim
vi /etc/kubernetes/manifests/kube-apiserver.yaml
```

5. Add the flags from the output of the ConfigMap under command. Make sure to add spacing and a dash (-) in front. It should look something like this when you're done:

```
    - --kubelet-preferred-address-types=InternalIP,ExternalIP,Ho
stname
    - --oidc-issuer-url=https://k8sou.apps.192-168-2-131.nip.io/
auth/idp/k8sIdp
    - --oidc-client-id=Kubernetes
    - --oidc-username-claim=sub
    - --oidc-groups-claim=groups
    - --oidc-ca-file=/etc/kubernetes/pki/ou-ca.pem
    - --proxy-client-cert-file=/etc/kubernetes/pki/front-proxy-
client.crt
```

6. Exit vim and the Docker environment (*Ctrl + D*) and then take a look at the api-server pod:

```
kubectl get pod kube-apiserver-cluster01-control-plane -n kube-
system
NAME                                              READY   STATUS
RESTARTS   AGE
kube-apiserver-cluster-auth-control-plane   1/1       Running        0
73s
```

Notice that it's only 73s old. That's because KinD saw that there was a change in the manifest and restarted the API server.

 The API server pod is known as a static pod. This pod can't be changed directly; its configuration has to be changed from the manifest on disk. This gives you a process that's managed by the API server as a container, but without giving you a situation where you need to edit pod manifests in etcd directly if something goes wrong.

Verifying OIDC integration

Once OpenUnison and the API server have been integrated, we need to test that the connection is working:

1. To test the integration, log back into OpenUnison and click on the **Kubernetes Dashboard** link again.

2. Click on the bell in the upper right and you'll see a different error:

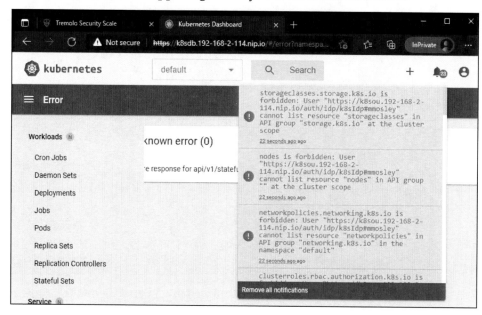

Figure 5.6: SSO enabled but the user is not authorized to access any resources

SSO between OpenUnison and Kubernetes is working! However, the new error, `service is forbidden: User https://...`, is an authorization error, **not** an authentication error. The API server knows who we are, but isn't letting us access the APIs.

3. We'll dive into the details of RBAC and authorizations in the next chapter, but for now, create this RBAC binding:

```
kubectl create -f - <<EOF
apiVersion: rbac.authorization.k8s.io/v1
kind: ClusterRoleBinding
```

```
metadata:
    name: ou-cluster-admins
subjects:
- kind: Group
  name: cn=k8s-cluster-admins,ou=Groups,DC=domain,DC=com
  apiGroup: rbac.authorization.k8s.io
roleRef:
  kind: ClusterRole
  name: cluster-admin
  apiGroup: rbac.authorization.k8s.io
EOF
clusterrolebinding.rbac.authorization.k8s.io/ou-cluster-admins
created
```

4. Finally, go back to the Dashboard and you'll see that you have full access to your cluster and all the error messages are gone.

The API server and OpenUnison are now connected. Additionally, an RBAC policy has been created to enable our test user to manage the cluster as an administrator. Access was verified by logging into the Kubernetes dashboard, but most interactions will take place using the kubectl command. The next step is to verify we're able to access the cluster using kubectl.

Using your tokens with kubectl

 This section assumes you have a machine on your network that has a browser and kubectl running.

Using the Dashboard has its use cases, but you will likely interact with the API server using kubectl, rather than the Dashboard, for the majority of your day. In this section, we will explain how to retrieve your JWT and how to add it to your Kubernetes config file:

1. You can retrieve your token from the OpenUnison dashboard. Navigate to the OpenUnison home page and click on the key that says **Kubernetes Tokens**. You'll see a screen that looks as follows:

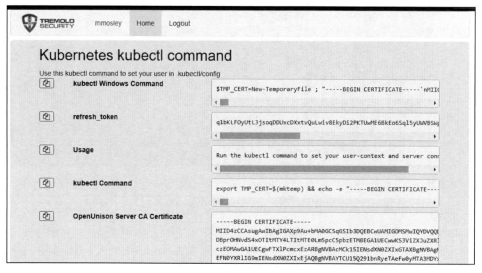

Figure 5.7: OpenUnison kubectl configuration tool

OpenUnison provides a command line that you can copy and paste into your host session that adds all the required information to your config.

2. First, click on the double documents button next to the `kubectl` command (or `kubectl` Windows command if you're on Windows) to copy your `kubectl` command into your buffer. Leave the web browser open in the background.

3. You may want to back up your original config file before pasting the `kubectl` command from OpenUnison:

```
cp .kube/config .kube/config.bak
export KUBECONFIG=/tmp/k
kubectl get nodes
W0423 15:46:46.924515    3399 loader.go:223] Config not found:
/tmp/k error: no configuration has been provided, try setting
KUBERNETES_MASTER environment variable
```

4. Then, go to your host console and paste the command into the console (the following output has been shortened, but your paste will start with the same output):

```
export TMP_CERT=$(mktemp) && echo -e "-----BEGIN CER. . .
Cluster "kubernetes" set.
Context "kubernetes" modified.
User "mmosley@kubernetes" set.
```

```
Switched to context "kubernetes".
```

5. Now, verify that you can view the cluster nodes using `kubectl get nodes`:

```
kubectl get nodes

NAME                          STATUS   ROLES     AGE    VERSION
cluster-auth-control-plane    Ready    master    60m    v1.21.1
cluster-auth-worker           Ready    <none>    61m    v1.21.1
```

6. You are now using your login credentials instead of the master certificate! As you work, the session will refresh. Log out of OpenUnison and watch the list of nodes. Within a minute or two, your token will expire and no longer work:

```
kubectl get nodes
Unable to connect to the server: failed to refresh token:
oauth2: cannot fetch token: 401 Unauthorized
```

Congratulations! You've now set up your cluster so that it does the following:

- Authenticates using LDAP using your enterprise's existing authentication system

- Uses groups from your centralized authentication system to authorize access to Kubernetes (we'll get into the details of how in the next chapter)

- Gives access to your users to both the CLI and the dashboard using the centralized credentials

- Maintains your enterprise's compliance requirements by having short-lived tokens that provide a way to time out

- Everything uses TLS, from the user's browser, to the Ingress Controller, to OpenUnison, the Dashboard, and finally, the API server

Next, you'll learn how to integrate centralized authentication into your managed clusters.

Introducing impersonation to integrate authentication with cloud-managed clusters

It's very popular to use managed Kubernetes services from cloud vendors such as Google, Amazon, Microsoft, and DigitalOcean (among many others).

When it comes to these services, they are generally very quick to get up and running, and they all share a common thread: they mostly don't support OpenID Connect (Amazon's EKS does support OpenID Connect now, but the cluster must be running on a public network and have a commercially signed TLS certificate).

Earlier in this chapter, we talked about how Kubernetes supports custom authentication solutions through webhooks and that you should never, ever, use this approach unless you are a public cloud provider or some other host of Kubernetes systems. It turns out that pretty much every cloud vendor has its own approach to using these webhooks that uses their own identity and access management implementations. In that case, why not just use what the vendor provides? There are several reasons why you may not want to use a cloud vendor's IAM system:

- **Technical**: You may want to support features not offered by the cloud vendor, such as the dashboard, in a secure fashion.

- **Organizational**: Tightly coupling access to managed Kubernetes with that cloud's IAM puts an additional burden on the cloud team, which means that they may not want to manage access to your clusters.

- **User experience**: Your developers and admins may have to work across multiple clouds. Providing a consistent login experience makes it easier on them and requires learning fewer tools.

- **Security and compliance**: The cloud implementation may not offer choices that line up with your enterprise's security requirements, such as short-lived tokens and idle timeouts.

All that being said, there may be reasons to use the cloud vendor's implementation. You'll need to balance out the requirements, though. If you want to continue to use centralized authentication and authorization with hosted Kubernetes, you'll need to learn how to work with Impersonation.

What is Impersonation?

Kubernetes Impersonation is a way of telling the API server who you are without knowing your credentials or forcing the API server to trust an OpenID Connect IdP.

When you use `kubectl`, instead of the API server receiving your `id_token` directly, it will receive a service account or identifying certificate that will be authorized to impersonate users, as well as a set of headers that tell the API server who the proxy is acting on behalf of:

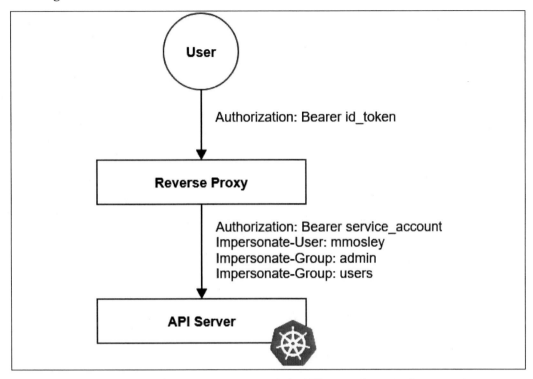

Figure 5.8: Diagram of how a user interacts with the API server when using Impersonation

The reverse proxy is responsible for determining how to map from the `id_token`, which the user provides (or any other token, for that matter), to the `Impersonate-User` and `Impersonate-Group` HTTP headers. The dashboard should never be deployed with a privileged identity, which the ability to impersonate falls under.

To allow Impersonation with the 2.x dashboard, use a similar model, but instead of going to the API server, you go to the dashboard:

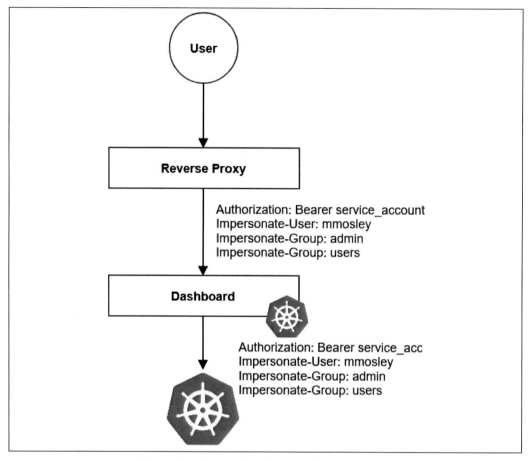

Figure 5.9: Kubernetes Dashboard with Impersonation

The user interacts with the reverse proxy just like any web application. The reverse proxy uses its own service account and adds the impersonation headers. The dashboard passes this information through to the API server on all requests. The dashboard never has its own identity.

Security considerations

The service account has a certain superpower: it can be used to impersonate **anyone** (depending on your RBAC definitions). If you're running your reverse proxy from inside the cluster, a service account is OK, especially if combined with the TokenRequest API to keep the token short-lived.

Earlier in the chapter, we talked about the legacy tokens for `ServiceAccount` objects having no expiration. That's important here because if you're hosting your reverse proxy off cluster, then if it were compromised, someone could use that service account to access the API service as anyone. Make sure you're rotating that service account often. If you're running the proxy off cluster, it's probably best to use a shorter-lived certificate instead of a service account.

When running the proxy on a cluster, you want to make sure it's locked down. It should run in its own namespace at a minimum. Not `kube-system` either. You want to minimize the number of people who have access. Using multi-factor authentication to get to that namespace is always a good idea, as is using network policies that control what pods can reach out to the reverse proxy.

Based on the concepts we've just learned about regarding impersonation, the next step is to update our cluster's configuration to use impersonation instead of using OpenID Connect directly. You don't need a cloud-managed cluster to work with impersonation.

Configuring your cluster for impersonation

Let's deploy an impersonating proxy for our cluster. Assuming you're reusing your existing cluster, we'll upgrade our existing orchestra Helm deployment with an updated `openunison-values.yaml` file:

1. First, delete the current TLS secret for OpenUnison since it doesn't have the right configuration for Impersonation. When we update the orchestra Helm chart, the operator will generate a new certificate for us.

   ```
   kubectl delete secret ou-tls-certificate -n openunison
   ```

2. Next, update our Helm chart to use impersonation. Edit the `openunison-values.yaml` file, update `network.api_server_host` as shown in the following snippet, and set `enable_impersonation` to `true`:

   ```
   network:
       openunison_host: "k8sou.apps.192-168-2-131.nip.io"
       dashboard_host: "k8sdb.apps.192-168-2-131.nip.io"
       api_server_host: "k8sapi.apps.192-168-2-131.nip.io"
       session_inactivity_timeout_seconds: 900
       k8s_url: https://192.168.2.131:32776
   enable_impersonation: true
   ```

We have made two changes here:

- Added a host for the API server proxy
- Enabled impersonation

These changes enable OpenUnison's impersonation features and generate an additional RBAC binding to enable impersonation on OpenUnison's service account.

3. Upgrade the orchestra Helm chart with the new `openunison-values.yaml` file:

```
helm upgrade orchestra tremolo/orchestra -n openunison -f
chapter5/openunison-values.yaml
NAME: orchestra
LAST DEPLOYED: Wed Jul  7 02:45:36 2021
NAMESPACE: openunison
STATUS: deployed
REVISION: 1
TEST SUITE: None
```

4. Once the `openunison-orchestra` pod is running, upgrade the `orchestra-login-portal` Helm chart with the new `openunison-values.yaml` file too:

```
helm upgrade orchestra-login-portal tremolo/orchestra-login-
portal -n openunison -f chapter5/openunison-values.yaml
NAME: orchestra-login-portal
LAST DEPLOYED: Wed Jul  7 02:47:03 2021
NAMESPACE: openunison
STATUS: deployed
REVISION: 1
TEST SUITE: None
```

The new OpenUnison deployment is configured as a reverse proxy for the API server and is still integrated with our Active Directory. There are no cluster parameters to set because Impersonation doesn't need any cluster-side configuration. The next step is to test the integration.

Testing Impersonation

Now, let's test our Impersonation setup. Follow these steps:

1. In a browser, enter the URL for your OpenUnison deployment. This is the same URL you used for your initial OIDC deployment.

2. Log into OpenUnison and then click on the dashboard. You should recall that the first time you opened the dashboard on your initial OpenUnison deployment, you received a lot of errors until you created the new RBAC role, which granted access to the cluster.

   After you've enabled impersonation and opened the dashboard, you shouldn't see any error messages, even though you were prompted for new certificate warnings and didn't tell the API server to trust the new certificates you're using with the dashboard.

3. Click on the little circular icon in the upper right-hand corner to see who you're logged in as.

4. Next, go back to the main OpenUnison dashboard and click on the **Kubernetes Tokens** badge.

   Notice that the `--server` flag being passed to `kubectl` no longer has an IP. Instead, it has the hostname from `network.api_server_host` in the `values.yaml` file. This is Impersonation. Instead of interacting directly with the API server, you're now interacting with OpenUnison's reverse proxy.

5. Finally, let's copy and paste our `kubectl` command into a shell:

```
export TMP_CERT=$(mktemp) && echo -e "-----BEGIN CERTIFI...
Cluster "kubernetes" set.
Context "kubernetes" created.
User "mmosley@kubernetes" set.
Switched to context "kubernetes".
```

6. To verify you have access, list the cluster nodes:

```
kubectl get nodes
NAME                          STATUS   ROLES     AGE     VERSION
cluster-auth-control-plane    Ready    master    6h6m    v1.21.1
cluster-auth-worker           Ready    <none>    6h6m    v1.21.1
```

7. Just like when you integrated the original deployment of OpenID Connect, once you've logged out of the OpenUnison page, within a minute or two, the tokens will expire and you won't be able to refresh them:

```
kubectl get nodes
Unable to connect to the server: failed to refresh token:
oauth2: cannot fetch token: 401 Unauthorized
```

You've now validated that your cluster is working correctly with Impersonation. Instead of authenticating directly to the API server, the impersonating reverse proxy (OpenUnison) is forwarding all requests to the API server with the correct impersonation headers. You're still meeting your enterprise's needs by providing both a login and logout process and integrating your Active Directory groups.

You'll also notice that you can now access your cluster from any system on your network! This might make doing the rest of the examples throughout the book easier.

Configuring Impersonation without OpenUnison

The OpenUnison operator automated a couple of key steps to get impersonation working. There are other projects designed specifically for Kubernetes, such as Jetstack's OIDC proxy (`https://github.com/jetstack/kube-oidc-proxy`), that are designed to make using Impersonation easier. You can use any reverse proxy that can generate the correct headers. There are two critical items to understand when doing this on your own.

Impersonation RBAC policies

RBAC will be covered in the next chapter, but for now, the correct policy to authorize a service account for Impersonation is as follows:

```
apiVersion: rbac.authorization.k8s.io/v1
kind: ClusterRole
metadata:
  name: impersonator
rules:
- apiGroups:
  - ""
  resources:
  - users
  - groups
  verbs:
  - impersonate
```

To constrain what accounts can be impersonated, add `resourceNames` to your rule.

Default groups

When impersonating a user, Kubernetes does not add the default group, `system:authenticated`, to the list of impersonated groups. When using a reverse proxy that doesn't specifically know to add the header for this group, configure the proxy to add it manually. Otherwise, simple acts such as calling the `/api` endpoint will fail as this will be unauthorized for anyone except cluster administrators.

We've focused the bulk of this chapter on authenticating users who will interact with the API server. A major advantage of Kubernetes and the APIs it provides is to automate your systems. Next, we'll look at how you apply what we've learned so far to authenticating those automated systems.

Authenticating from pipelines

This chapter so far has focused exclusively on authentication to Kubernetes by users. Whether an operator or a developer, a user will often interact with a cluster to update objects, debug issues, view logs, and so on. This doesn't quite handle all use cases, though. Most Kubernetes deployments are partnered with pipelines, a process by which code is moved from source to binaries to containers and ultimately into a running cluster. We'll cover pipelines in more detail in *Chapter 14, Provisioning a Platform*. For now, the main question is "How will your pipeline talk to Kubernetes securely?"

If your pipeline runs in the same cluster as being updated, this is a simple question to answer. You would grant access to the pipeline's service account via RBAC to do what it needs to do. This is why service accounts exist, to provide identity to processes inside the cluster.

What if your pipeline runs outside of the cluster? Kubernetes is an API, and all the options presented in this chapter apply to a pipeline as they would to a user. Service account tokens don't provide an expiration and can easily be abused. The `TokenRequest` API could give you a short-lived token, but you still need to be authenticated to get it. If your cluster is running on the same cloud provider as your pipeline, you may be able to use its integrated IAM system. For instance, you can generate an IAM role in Amazon CodeBuild that can talk to an EKS cluster without having a static service account. The same is true for Azure DevOps and AKS.

If a cloud's IAM capabilities won't cover your needs, there are two options. The first is to dynamically generate a token for a pipeline the same way you would for a user by authenticating to an identity provider and then using the returned `id_token` with your API calls. The second is to generate a certificate that can be used with your API server. Let's look at both options and see how our pipelines can use them.

Using tokens

Kubernetes doesn't distinguish between an API call from a human or a pipeline. A short-lived token is a great way to interact with your API server as a pipeline. Most of the client SDKs for Kubernetes know how to refresh these tokens. The biggest issue is how do you get a token your pipeline can use?

Most enterprises already have some kind of service account management system. Here, the term "service account" is generic and means an account used by a service of some kind instead of being the ServiceAccount object in Kubernetes. These service account management systems often have their own way of handling tasks, such as credential rotation and authorization management. They also have their own compliance tools, making it easier to get through your security review processes!

Assuming you have an enterprise service account for your pipeline, how do you translate that credential into a token? We are generating tokens based on credentials in our OIDC integrated identity provider; it would be great to use that from our pipelines too! With OpenUnison, this is pretty easy because the page that gave us our token is just a frontend for an API. The next question to answer is how to authenticate to OpenUnison. We could write some code to simulate a browser and reverse engineer the login process, but that's just ugly. And if the form changes, our code would break. It would be better to configure the API to authenticate with something that is more API friendly, such as HTTP Basic authentication.

OpenUnison can be extended by creating configuration custom resources. In fact, most of OpenUnison is configured using these custom resources. You deployed them in the third Helm chart we used to stand up OpenUnison. The current token service assumes you are authenticating using the default OpenUnison form login mechanism, instead of a basic authentication that would be helpful from a pipeline. In order to tell OpenUnison to support API authentication, we need to tell it to:

1. Enable authentication via HTTP Basic authentication by defining an authentication mechanism

2. Create an authentication chain that uses the basic authentication mechanism to complete the authentication process

3. Define an application that can provide the token API, authenticating using the newly created chain

We won't go through the details of how to make this work in OpenUnison, instead focusing on the end results. The chapter5 folder contains a Helm chart that was created for you to configure this API. Run it using the same openunison-values.yaml file you used to deploy OpenUnison:

```
helm install orchestra-token-api chapter5/token-login -n openunison -f
chapter5/openunison-values.yaml
Release "orchestra-token-api" has been installed. Happy Helming!
NAME: orchestra-token-api
LAST DEPLOYED: Wed Jul  7 15:04:21 2021
NAMESPACE: openunison
STATUS: deployed
```

```
REVISION: 5
TEST SUITE: None
```

Once deployed, we can test using `curl`:

```
export KUBE_AZ=$(curl --insecure -u 'pipeline_svc_account:start123'
https://k8sou.192-168-2-114.nip.io/k8s-api-token/token/user | jq -r
'.token.id_token')
curl --insecure   -H "Authorization: Bearer $KUBE_AZ"
https://0.0.0.0:6443/api
{
  "kind": "APIVersions",
  "versions": [
    "v1"
  ],
  "serverAddressByClientCIDRs": [
    {
      "clientCIDR": "0.0.0.0/0",
      "serverAddress": "172.18.0.2:6443"
    }
  ]
}
```

Now, wait a minute or two and try the `curl` command again, and you'll see you're not authenticated anymore. This example is great if you're running a single command, but most pipelines run multiple steps and a single token's lifetime isn't enough. We could write code to make use of the `refresh_token`, but most of the SDKs will do that for us. Instead of getting just the `id_token`, let's generate an entire `kubectl` configuration:

```
export KUBECONFIG=/tmp/r
kubectl get nodes
W0707 15:18:50.646390 1512400 loader.go:221] Config not found: /tmp/r
The connection to the server localhost:8080 was refused - did you
specify the right host or port?
curl --insecure -u 'pipeline_svc_account:start123' https://
k8sou.192-168-2-114.nip.io/k8s-api-token/token/user 2>/dev/null | jq -r
'.token["kubectl Command"]' | bash
Cluster "kubernetes" set.
Context "kubernetes" created.
User "pipelinex-95-xsvcx-95-xaccount@kubernetes" set.
Switched to context "kubernetes".
kubectl get nodes
NAME                    STATUS   ROLES              AGE
```

```
VERSION
cluster01-control-plane    Ready    control-plane,master    2d15h
v1.21.1
cluster01-worker           Ready    <none>                  2d15h
v1.21.1
```

We're getting a short-lived token securely, while also interacting with the API server using our standard tools! This solution only works if your service accounts are stored and accessed via an LDAP directory. If that's not the case, you can extend OpenUnison's configuration to support any number of configuration options. To learn more, visit OpenUnison's documentation at `https://openunison.github.io/`.

This solution is specific to OpenUnison because there is no standard to convert a user's credentials into an `id_token`. That is a detail left to each identity provider. Your identity provider may have an API for generating an `id_token` easily, but it's more likely you'll need something to act as a broker since an identity provider won't know how to generate a full `kubectl` configuration.

Using certificates

The preceding process works well, but requires OpenUnison or something similar. If you wanted to take a vendor-neutral approach you could use certificates as your credential instead of trying to generate a token. Earlier in the chapter, I said that certificate authentication should be avoided for users because of Kubernetes' lack of revocation support and the fact that most certificates aren't deployed correctly. Both of these issues are generally easier to mitigate with pipelines because the deployment can be automated.

If your enterprise requires you to use a central store for service accounts, this approach may not be possible. Another potential issue with this approach is that you may want to use an enterprise CA to generate the certificates for service accounts, but Kubernetes doesn't know how to trust third-party CAs. There are active discussions about enabling the feature but it's not there yet.

Finally, you can't generate certificates for many managed clusters. Most managed Kubernetes distributions, such as EKS, do not make the private keys needed to sign requests via the built-in API available to clusters directly. In that case, you'll be unable to mint certificates that will be accepted by your cluster.

With all that said, let's walk through the process:

1. First, we'll generate a keypair and **certificate signing request (CSR)**:

    ```
    openssl req -out sa_cert.csr -new -newkey rsa:2048 -nodes
    -keyout sa_cert.key -subj '/O=k8s/O=sa-cluster-admins/CN=sa-
    ```

```
cert/'
Generating a RSA private key
..........+++++
...............................+++++
writing new private key to 'sa_cert.key'
-----
```

Next, we'll submit the CSR to Kubernetes:

```
cat <<EOF | kubectl apply -f -
apiVersion: certificates.k8s.io/v1
kind: CertificateSigningRequest
metadata:
  name: sa-cert
spec:
  request: $(cat sa_cert.csr | base64 | tr -d '\n')
  signerName: kubernetes.io/kube-apiserver-client
  usages:
  - digital signature
  - key encipherment
  - client auth
EOF
```

2. Once the CSR is submitted to Kubernetes, we need to approve the submission:

```
kubectl certificate approve sa-cert
certificatesigningrequest.certificates.k8s.io/sa-cert approved
```

After being approved, we download the minted certificate into a pem file:

```
kubectl get csr sa-cert -o jsonpath='{.status.certificate}' |
base64 --decode > sa_cert.crt
```

3. Next, we'll configure kubectl to use our newly approved certificate

```
cp ~/.kube/config ./sa-config
export KUBECONFIG=./sa-config
kubectl config set-credentials kind-cluster01 --client-key=./
sa_cert.key --client-certificate=./sa_cert.crt
kubectl get nodes
Error from server (Forbidden): nodes is forbidden: User "sa-
cert" cannot list resource "nodes" in API group "" at the
cluster scope
```

The API server has accepted our certificate, but has not authorized it. Our CSR had an "o" in the subject called `sa-cluster-admins`, which Kubernetes translates to "the user `sa-cert` is in the group `sa-cluster-admins`". We need to authorize that group to be a cluster admin next:

```
export KUBECONFIG=
kubectl create -f chapter5/sa-cluster-admins.yaml
export KUBECONFIG=./sa-config
kubectl get nodes
NAME                         STATUS     ROLES                    AGE
VERSION
cluster01-control-plane      Ready      control-plane,master     2d17h
v1.21.1
cluster01-worker             Ready      <none>                   2d17h
v1.21.1
```

You now have a key pair that can be used from your pipelines with your cluster! Beware while automating this process. The CSR submitted to the API server can set any groups it wants, including `system:masters`. If a certificate is minted with `system:masters` as an "o" in the subject it will not only be able to do anything on your cluster, it will bypass all RBAC authorization. It will bypass all authorization!

If you're going to go down the certificate route, think about potential alternatives, such as using certificates with your identity provider instead of going directly to the API server. This is similar to our token-based authentication, but instead of using a username and password in HTTP Basic authentication, you use a certificate. This gives you a strong credential that can be issued by your enterprise certificate authority while avoiding having to use passwords.

Having discussed how to properly authenticate to your cluster from your pipeline, let's examine some anti-patterns with pipeline authentication.

Avoiding anti-patterns

It turns out most of the anti-patterns that apply to user authentication also apply to pipeline authentication. Given the nature of code that authenticates, there are some specific things to look out for.

First, don't use a person's account for a pipeline. It will likely violate your enterprise's policies and can expose your account, and maybe your employment, to issues. Your enterprise account (and that assigned to everyone else in the enterprise) generally has several rules attached to it. Simply using it in code can breach these rules. The other anti-patterns we'll discuss add to the risk.

Next, never put your service account's credentials into Git, even when encrypted. It's popular to include credentials directly in objects stored in Git because you now have change control, but it's just so easy to accidentally push a Git repository out to a public space. Much of security is protecting users from accidents that can leak sensitive information. Even encrypted credentials in Git can be abused if the encryption keys are also stored in Git. Every cloud provider has a secret management system that will synchronize your credentials into Kubernetes Secret objects. You can do this with Vault as well. This is a much better approach as these tools are specifically designed to manage sensitive data. Git is meant to make it easy to share and collaborate, which makes for poor secret management.

Finally, don't use legacy service account tokens from outside of your cluster. I know, I've said this a dozen times in this chapter, but it's incredibly important. When using a bearer token, anything that carries that token is a potential attack vector. There have been network providers that leak tokens as an example. It's a common anti-pattern. If a vendor tells you to generate a service account token, push back: you're putting your enterprise's data at risk.

Summary

This chapter detailed how Kubernetes identifies users and what groups their members are in. We detailed how the API server interacts with identities and explored several options for authentication. Finally, we detailed the OpenID Connect protocol and how it's applied to Kubernetes.

Learning how Kubernetes authenticates users and the details of the OpenID Connect protocol is an important part of building security into a cluster. Understanding the details and how they apply to common enterprise requirements will help you decide the best way to authenticate to clusters, and also provide justification regarding why the anti-patterns we explored should be avoided.

In the next chapter, we'll apply our authentication process to authorizing access to Kubernetes resources. Knowing who somebody is isn't enough to secure your clusters. You also need to control what they have access to.

Questions

1. OpenID Connect is a standard protocol with extensive peer review and usage.
    a. True
    b. False
2. Which token does Kubernetes use to authorize your access to an API?
    a. `access_token`
    b. `id_token`

    c.   `refresh_token`

    d.   `certificate_token`

3. In which situation is certificate authentication a good idea?

    a.   Day-to-day usage by administrators and developers

    b.   Access from external CI/CD pipelines and other services

    c.   Break glass in case of emergency when all other authentication solutions are unavailable

4. How should you identify users accessing your cluster?

    a.   Email address

    b.   Unix login ID

    c.   Windows login ID

    d.   An immutable ID not based on a user's name

5. Where are OpenID Connect configuration options set in Kubernetes?

    a.   Depends on the distribution

    b.   In a ConfigMap object

    c.   In a secret

    d.   Set as flags on the Kubernetes API server executable

6. When using Impersonation with your cluster, the groups your user brings are the only ones needed.

    a.   True

    b.   False

7. The dashboard should have its own privileged identity to work properly.

    a.   True

    b.   False

Join our book's Discord space

Join the book's Discord workspace for a monthly *Ask me Anything* session with the authors: `https://packt.link/K8EntGuide`

6

RBAC Policies and Auditing

Authentication is only the first step in managing access to a cluster. Once access to a cluster is granted, it's important to limit what accounts can do, depending on whether an account is for an automated system or a user. Authorizing access to resources is an important part of protecting against both accidental issues and bad actors looking to abuse a cluster.

In this chapter, we're going to detail how Kubernetes authorizes access via its **Role-Based Access Control (RBAC)** model. The first part of this chapter will be a deep dive into how Kubernetes RBAC is configured, what options are available, and mapping the theory onto practical examples. Debugging and troubleshooting RBAC policies will be the focus of the second half.

In this chapter, we will cover the following topics:

- Introduction to RBAC
- Mapping enterprise identities to Kubernetes to authorize access to resources
- Namespace multi-tenancy
- Kubernetes auditing
- Using `audit2rbac` to debug policies

Once you have completed this chapter you'll have the tools needed to manage access to your cluster and debug issues when they arise. Next, let's dive into the technical requirements for this chapter.

Technical requirements

This chapter has the following technical requirements:

- A KinD cluster running with the configuration from *Chapter 5, Integrating Authentication into Your Cluster*

You can access the code for this chapter at the following GitHub repository: `https://github.com/PacktPublishing/Kubernetes---An-Enterprise-Guide-2E/tree/main/chapter6`.

Introduction to RBAC

Before we jump into RBAC, let's take a quick look at the history of Kubernetes and access controls.

Before Kubernetes 1.6, access controls were based on **Attribute-Based Access Control (ABAC)**. As the name implies, ABAC provides access by comparing a rule against attributes, rather than roles. The assigned attributes can be assigned any type of data, including user attributes, objects, environments, and locations.

In the past, to configure a Kubernetes cluster for ABAC, you had to set two values on the API server:

- `--authorization-policy-file`
- `--authorization-mode=ABAC`

`authorization-policy-file` is a local file on the API server. Since it's a local file on each API server, any changes to the file require privileged access to the host and will require you to restart the API server. As you can imagine, the process to update ABAC policies becomes difficult and any immediate changes will require a short outage as the API servers are restarted.

Starting in Kubernetes 1.6, RBAC became the preferred method of authorizing access to resources. Unlike ABAC, RBAC uses Kubernetes native objects, and updates are reflected without restarting the API servers. RBAC is also compatible with different authentication methods. From here, our focus will be on how to develop RBAC policies and apply them to your cluster.

What's a Role?

In Kubernetes, a Role is a way to tie together permissions into an object that can be described and configured.

Roles have rules, which are a collection of resources and verbs. Working backward, we have the following:

- **Verbs**: The actions that can be taken on an API, such as reading (`get`), writing (`create`, `update`, `patch`, and `delete`), or listing and watching.
- **Resources**: Names of APIs to apply the verbs to, such as `services`, `endpoints`, and so on. Specific sub-resources may be listed as well. Specific resources can be named to provide very specific permissions on an object.

A Role does not say who can perform the verbs on the resources—that is handled by `RoleBindings` and `ClusterRoleBindings`. We will learn more about these in the *RoleBindings and ClusterRoleBindings* section.

> The term "role" can have multiple meanings, and RBAC is often used in other contexts. In the enterprise world, the term "role" is often associated with a business role and used to convey entitlements to that role instead of a specific person. As an example, an enterprise may assign all accounts payable staff the ability to issue checks instead of creating a specific assignment for each member of the accounts' payable department the specific permission in order to issue a check. When someone moves between roles, they lose the permissions from their old role and gain permissions for their new role. In the instance of moving from accounts payable to accounts receivable the user would lose the ability to make payments and gain the ability to accept payment. By tying the permissions to roles, instead of individuals, the change in permissions happens automatically with the role change instead of having to manually toggle permissions for each user. This is the more "classic" use of the term RBAC.

Each resource that a rule will be built of is identified by the following:

- `apiGroups`: A list of groups the resources are a member of
- `resources`: The name of the object type for the resource (and potentially sub-resources)
- `resourceNames`: An optional list of specific objects to apply this rule to

Each rule *must* have a list of `apiGroups` and `resources`. `resourceNames` is optional.

Once the resource is identified in a rule, verbs can be specified. A verb is an action that can be taken on the resource, providing access to the object in Kubernetes.

If the desired access to an object should be `all`, you do not need to add each verb; instead, the wildcard character may be used to identify all the `verbs`, `resources`, or `apiGroups`.

Identifying a Role

The Kubernetes authorization page (`https://kubernetes.io/docs/reference/access-authn-authz/rbac/`) uses the following Role as an example to allow someone to get the details of a Pod and its logs:

```
apiVersion: rbac.authorization.k8s.io/v1
kind: Role
metadata:
  namespace: default
  name: pod-and-pod-logs-reader
rules:
- apiGroups: [""]
  resources: ["pods", "pods/log"]
  verbs: ["get", "list"]
```

Working backward to determine how this Role was defined, we will start with `resources`, since it is the easiest aspect to find. All objects in Kubernetes are represented by URLs. If you want to pull all the information about the Pods in the default namespace, you would call the `/api/v1/namespaces/default/pods` URL, and if you wanted the logs for a specific Pod, you would call the `/api/v1/namespaces/default/pods/mypod/log` URL.

The URL pattern will be true of all namespace-scoped objects. `pods` lines up to `resources`, as does `pods/log`. When trying to identify which resources you want to authorize, use the `api-reference` document from the Kubernetes API documentation at `https://kubernetes.io/docs/reference/#api-reference`.

If you are trying to access an additional path component after the name of the object (such as with status and logs on Pods), it needs to be explicitly authorized. Authorizing Pods does not immediately authorize logs or status.

Based on the use of URL mapping to `resources`, your next thought may be that the `verbs` field is going to be HTTP verbs. This is not the case. There is no `GET` verb in Kubernetes. Verbs are instead defined by the schema of the object in the API server. The good news is that there's a static mapping between HTTP verbs and RBAC verbs (`https://kubernetes.io/docs/reference/access-authn-authz/authorization/#determine-the-request-verb`). Looking at this URL, notice that there are verbs on top of the HTTP verbs for `PodSecurityPolicies` and impersonation. That's because the RBAC model is used beyond authorizing specific APIs and is also used to authorize who can impersonate users and how to assign a `PodSecurityPolicy` object. The focus of this chapter is going to be on the standard HTTP verb mappings.

The final component to identify is `apiGroups`. APIs will be in an API group and that group will be part of their URL. You can find the group by looking at the API documentation for the object you are looking to authorize or by using the `kubectl api-resources` command. For instance, to get the `apiGroups` for the `Ingress` object you could run:

```
kubectl api-resources -o wide | grep Ingress
ingresses ing extensions/v1beta1 true Ingress [create delete
deletecollection get list patch update watch]
ingressclasses networking.k8s.io/v1 false IngressClass [create delete
deletecollection get list patch update watch]
ingresses ing networking.k8s.io/v1 true Ingress [create delete
deletecollection get list patch update watch]
```

The second example gives you what you would see in the `apiVersion` of a YAML version of an `Ingress` object. Use this for `apiGroups`, but without the version number. In the preceding case, `apiGroups` would be `networking.k8s.io`.

The inconsistencies in the RBAC model can make debugging difficult, to say the least. The last lab in this chapter will walk through the debugging process and take much of the guesswork out of defining your rules.

Now that we've defined the contents of a Role and how to define specific permissions, it's important to note that Roles can be applied at both the namespace and cluster level.

Roles versus ClusterRoles

RBAC rules can be scoped either to specific namespaces or to the entire cluster. Taking our preceding example, if we defined it as a ClusterRole instead of a Role, and removed the namespace, we would have a Role that authorizes someone to get the details and logs of all pods across the cluster. This new Role could alternatively be used in individual namespaces to assign the permissions to the Pods in a specific namespace:

```
apiVersion: rbac.authorization.k8s.io/v1
kind: ClusterRole
metadata:
  name: cluster-pod-and-pod-logs-reader
rules:
- apiGroups: [""]
  resources: ["pods", "pods/log"]
  verbs: ["get", "list"]
```

Whether this permission is applied globally across a cluster or within the scope of a specific namespace depends on how it's bound to the subjects it applies to. This will be covered in the *RoleBindings and ClusterRoleBindings* section.

In addition to applying a set of rules across the cluster, ClusterRoles are used to apply rules to resources that aren't mapped to a namespace, such as `PersistentVolume` and `StorageClass` objects.

After learning how a Role is defined, let's explore the different ways Roles can be designed for specific purposes. In the next sections, we'll look at different patterns for defining Roles and their application in a cluster.

Negative Roles

One of the most common requests for authorization is *"can I write a Role that lets me do everything EXCEPT xyz?"*. In RBAC, the answer is *NO*. RBAC requires either every resource to be allowed or specific resources and verbs to be enumerated. There are two reasons for this in RBAC:

- **Better security through simplicity**: Being able to enforce a rule that says *every Secret except this one* requires a much more complex evaluation engine than RBAC provides. The more complex an engine, the harder it is to test and validate, and the easier it is to break. A simpler engine is just simpler to code and keep secure.

- **Unintended consequences**: Allowing someone to do everything *except* xyz leaves the door open for issues in unintended ways as the cluster grows and new capabilities are added.

On the first point, an engine with this capability is difficult to build and maintain. It also makes the rules much harder to keep track of. To express this type of rule, you need to not only have authorization rules but also an order to those rules. For instance, to say *I want to allow everything except this Secret*, you would first need a rule that says *allow everything* and then a rule that says *deny this secret*. If you switch the rules to say *deny this secret* then *allow everything*, the first rule would be overridden. You could assign priorities to different rules, but that now makes it even more complex.

There are ways to implement this pattern, either by using a custom authorization webhook or by using a controller to dynamically generate RBAC `Role` objects. These should both be considered security anti-patterns and so won't be covered in this chapter.

The second point deals with unintended consequences. It's becoming more popular to support the provisioning of infrastructure that isn't Kubernetes using the operator pattern, where a custom controller looks for new instances of a **CustomResourceDefinition (CRD)** to provision infrastructure such as databases.

Amazon Web Services publishes an operator for this purpose (`https://github.com/aws/aws-controllers-k8s`). These operators run in their own namespaces with administrative credentials for their cloud looking for new instances of their objects to provision resources. If you have a security model that allows everything "except…", then once deployed, anyone in your cluster can provision cloud resources that have real costs and can create security holes. Enumerating your resources, from a security perspective, is an important part of knowing what is running and who has access.

The trend in Kubernetes clusters is to provide more control over infrastructure outside of the cluster via the custom resource API. You can provision anything from VMs to additional nodes, to any kind of API-driven cloud infrastructure. There are other tools you can use besides RBAC to mitigate the risk of someone creating a resource they shouldn't, but these should be secondary measures.

Aggregated ClusterRoles

ClusterRoles can become confusing quickly and be difficult to maintain. It's best to break them up into smaller ClusterRoles that can be combined as needed. Take the admin ClusterRole, which is designed to let someone do generally anything inside of a specific namespace. When we look at the admin ClusterRole, it enumerates just about every resource there is. You may think someone wrote this ClusterRole so that it would contain all those resources, but that would be really inefficient, and what happens as new resource types get added to Kubernetes? The admin ClusterRole is an aggregated ClusterRole. Take a look at the ClusterRole:

```
kind: ClusterRole
apiVersion: rbac.authorization.k8s.io/v1
metadata:
  name: admin
  labels:
    kubernetes.io/bootstrapping: rbac-defaults
  annotations:
    rbac.authorization.kubernetes.io/autoupdate: 'true'
rules:
  .
  
  .
  
  .
  
aggregationRule:
  clusterRoleSelectors:
    - matchLabels:
        rbac.authorization.k8s.io/aggregate-to-admin: 'true'
```

The key is the `aggregationRule` section. This section tells Kubernetes to combine the rules for all ClusterRoles where the `rbac.authorization.k8s.io/aggregate-to-admin` label is `true`. When a new CRD is created, an admin is not able to create instances of that CRD without adding a new ClusterRole that includes this label. To allow namespace admin users to create an instance of the new `myapi/superwidget` objects, create a new ClusterRole:

```
apiVersion: rbac.authorization.k8s.io/v1
kind: ClusterRole
metadata:
  name: aggregate-superwidget-admin
  labels:
    # Add these permissions to the "admin" default role.
    rbac.authorization.k8s.io/aggregate-to-admin: "true"
rules:
- apiGroups: ["myapi"]
  resources: ["superwidgets"]
  verbs: ["get", "list", "watch", "create", "update", "patch",
"delete"]
```

The next time you look at the admin ClusterRole, it will include `myapi/superwidgets`. You can also reference this ClusterRole directly for more specific permissions.

RoleBindings and ClusterRoleBindings

Once a permission is defined, it needs to be assigned to something to enable it. "Something" can be a user, a group, or a service account. These options are referred to as subjects. Just as with Roles and ClusterRoles, a RoleBinding binds a Role or ClusterRole to a specific namespace, and a ClusterRoleBinding will apply a ClusterRole across the cluster. A binding can have many subjects but may only reference a single Role or ClusterRole. To assign the `pod-and-pod-logs-reader` Role created earlier in this chapter to a service account called `mysa` in the default namespace, a user named `podreader`, or anyone with the `podreaders` group, create a RoleBinding:

```
apiVersion: rbac.authorization.k8s.io/v1
kind: RoleBinding
metadata:
  name: pod-and-pod-logs-reader
  namespace: default
subjects:
- kind: ServiceAccount
  name: mysa
```

```
  namespace: default
  apiGroup: rbac.authorization.k8s.io
- kind: User
  name: podreader
- kind: Group
  name: podreaders
roleRef:
  kind: Role
  name: pod-and-pod-logs-reader
  apiGroup: rbac.authorization.k8s.io
```

The preceding RoleBinding lists three different subjects:

- `ServiceAccount`: Any service account in the cluster can be authorized
  to a RoleBinding. The namespace must be included since a RoleBinding
  can authorize a service account in any namespace, not just the one the
  RoleBinding is defined in.

- `User`: A user is asserted by the authentication process. Remember from
  Chapter 5, Integrating Authentication into Your Cluster, that there are no objects
  in Kubernetes that represent users.

- `Group`: Just as with users, groups are asserted as part of the authentication
  process and have no object associated with them.

Finally, the Role we created earlier is referenced. In a similar fashion, to assign
the same subjects the ability to read pods and their logs across the cluster, a
ClusterRoleBinding can be created to reference the `cluster-pod-and-pod-logs-
reader` ClusterRole created earlier in the chapter:

```
apiVersion: rbac.authorization.k8s.io/v1
kind: ClusterRoleBinding
metadata:
  name: cluster-pod-and-pod-logs-reader
subjects:
- kind: ServiceAccount
  name: mysa
  namespace: default
  apiGroup: rbac.authorization.k8s.io
- kind: User
  name: podreader
- kind: Group
  name: podreaders
roleRef:
```

```
kind: ClusterRole
name: cluster-pod-and-pod-logs-reader
apiGroup: rbac.authorization.k8s.io
```

The ClusterRoleBinding is bound to the same subjects, but is bound to a ClusterRole instead of a namespace-bound Role. Now, instead of being able to read Pod details and Pod/logs in the default namespace, these users can read all Pod details and Pod/logs in all namespaces.

Combining ClusterRoles and RoleBindings

We have a use case where a log aggregator wants to pull logs from Pods in multiple namespaces, but not all namespaces. A ClusterRoleBinding is too broad. While the Role could be recreated in each namespace, this is inefficient and a maintenance headache. Instead, define a ClusterRole but reference it from a RoleBinding in the applicable namespaces. This allows the reuse of permission definitions while still applying those permissions to specific namespaces. In general, note the following:

- ClusterRole + ClusterRoleBinding = cluster-wide permission
- ClusterRole + RoleBinding = namespace-specific permission

To apply our ClusterRoleBinding in a specific namespace, create a Role, referencing the ClusterRole instead of a namespaced Role object:

```
apiVersion: rbac.authorization.k8s.io/v1
kind: RoleBinding
metadata:
  name: pod-and-pod-logs-reader
  namespace: default
subjects:
- kind: ServiceAccount
  name: mysa
  namespace: default
  apiGroup: rbac.authorization.k8s.io
- kind: User
  name: podreader
- kind: Group
  name: podreaders
roleRef:
  kind: ClusterRole
  name: cluster-pod-and-pod-logs-reader
  apiGroup: rbac.authorization.k8s.io
```

The preceding RoleBinding lets us reuse the existing ClusterRole. This cuts down on the number of objects that need to be tracked in the cluster and makes it easier to update permissions across the cluster if the ClusterRole permissions need to change.

Having built our permissions and defined how to assign them, next we'll look at how to map enterprise identities into cluster policies.

Mapping enterprise identities to Kubernetes to authorize access to resources

One of the benefits of centralizing authentication is leveraging the enterprise's existing identities instead of having to create new credentials that users that interact with your clusters need to remember. It's important to know how to map your policies to these centralized users. In *Chapter 5, Integrating Authentication into Your Cluster*, you created a cluster and integrated it with an "enterprise Active Directory." To finish the integration, the following ClusterRoleBinding was created:

```
apiVersion: rbac.authorization.k8s.io/v1
kind: ClusterRoleBinding
metadata:
  name: ou-cluster-admins
subjects:
- kind: Group
  name: cn=k8s-cluster-admins,ou=Groups,DC=domain,DC=com
  apiGroup: rbac.authorization.k8s.io
roleRef:
  kind: ClusterRole
  name: cluster-admin
  apiGroup: rbac.authorization.k8s.io
```

This binding allows all users that are members of the `cn=k8s-cluster-admins,ou=Groups,DC=domain,DC=com` group to have full cluster access. At the time, the focus was on authentication, so there weren't many details provided as to why this binding was created.

What if we wanted to authorize our users directly? That way, we have control over who has access to our cluster. Our RBAC ClusterRoleBinding would look different:

```
apiVersion: rbac.authorization.k8s.io/v1
kind: ClusterRoleBinding
```

```
metadata:
  name: ou-cluster-admins
subjects:
- kind: User
  name: https://k8sou.apps.192-168-2-131.nip.io/auth/idp/k8sIdp#mmosley
  apiGroup: rbac.authorization.k8s.io
roleRef:
  kind: ClusterRole
  name: cluster-admin
  apiGroup: rbac.authorization.k8s.io
```

Using the same ClusterRole as before, this ClusterRoleBinding will assign the `cluster-admin` privileges only to my testing user.

The first issue to point out is that the user has the URL of our OpenID Connect issuer in front of the username. When OpenID Connect was first introduced, it was thought that Kubernetes would integrate with multiple identity providers and different types of identity providers, so the developers wanted you to be able to easily distinguish between users from different identity sources. For instance, `mmosley` in domain 1 is a different user then `mmosley` in domain 2. To ensure that a user's identity doesn't collide with another user across identity providers, Kubernetes requires the identity provider's issuer to be prepended to your username. This rule doesn't apply if the username claim defined in your API server flags is `mail`. It also doesn't apply if you're using certificates or impersonation.

Beyond the inconsistent implementation requirements, this approach can cause problems in a few ways:

- **Changing your identity provider URL**: Today, you're using an identity provider at one URL, but tomorrow you decide to move it. Now, you need to go through every ClusterRoleBinding and update them.
- **Audits**: You can't query for all RoleBindings associated with a user. You need to instead enumerate every binding.
- **Large bindings**: Depending on how many users you have, your bindings can get quite large and difficult to track.

While there are tools you can use to help manage these issues, it's much easier to associate your bindings with groups instead of individual users. You could use the `mail` attribute to avoid the URL prefix, but that is considered an anti-pattern and will result in equally difficult changes to your cluster if an email address changes for any reason.

So far in this chapter, we have learned how to define access policies and map those policies to enterprise users. Next, we need to determine how clusters will be divided into tenants.

Implementing namespace multi-tenancy

Clusters deployed for multiple stakeholders, or tenants, should be divided up by namespace. This is the boundary that was designed into Kubernetes from the very beginning. When deploying namespaces, there are generally two ClusterRoles that are assigned to users in the namespace:

- `admin`: This aggregated ClusterRole provides access to every verb and nearly every resource that ships with Kubernetes, making the `admin` user the ruler of their namespace. The exception to this is any namespace-scoped object that could affect the entire cluster, such as `ResourceQuotas`.
- `edit`: Similar to `admin`, but without the ability to create RBAC Roles or RoleBindings.

It's important to note that the `admin` ClusterRole can't make changes to the namespace object by itself. Namespaces are cluster-wide resources, so they can only be assigned permissions via a ClusterRoleBinding.

Depending on your strategy for multi-tenancy, the `admin` ClusterRole may not be appropriate. The ability to generate RBAC Role and RoleBinding objects means that a namespace admin may grant themselves the ability to change resource quotas or run elevated PodSecurityPolicy privileges. This is where RBAC tends to fall apart and needs some additional options:

- **Don't grant access to Kubernetes**: Many cluster owners want to keep Kubernetes out of the hands of their users and limit their interaction to external CI/CD tools. This works well with microservices but begins to fall apart on multiple lines. First, more legacy applications being moved into Kubernetes means more legacy administrators needing to directly access their namespace. Second, if the Kubernetes team keeps users out of the clusters, they are now responsible. The people who own Kubernetes may not want to be the reason things aren't happening the way application owners want them to and often, the application owners want to be able to control their own infrastructure to ensure they can handle any situation that impacts their own performance.
- **Treat access as privileged**: Most enterprises require a privileged user to access infrastructure. This is typically done using a privileged access model where an admin has a separate account that needs to be "checked out" in order to use it and is only authorized at certain times, as approved by a "change board" or process. The use of these accounts is closely monitored. This is a good approach if you already have a system in place, especially one that integrates with your enterprise's central authentication system.

- **Give each tenant a cluster**: This model moves multi-tenancy from the cluster to the infrastructure layer. You haven't eliminated the problem, only moved where it is addressed. This can lead to sprawl that becomes unmanageable and costs can skyrocket depending on how you are implementing Kubernetes.

- **Admission controllers**: These augment RBAC by limiting which objects can be created. For instance, an admission controller can decide to block an RBAC policy from being created, even if RBAC explicitly allows it. This topic will be covered in *Chapter 8, Extending Security Using Open Policy Agent*.

In addition to authorizing access to namespaces and resources, a multi-tenant solution needs to know how to provision tenants. This topic will be covered in the final chapter, *Chapter 14, Provisioning a Platform*.

Now that we have a strategy for implementing authorization policies, we'll need a way to debug those policies as we create them and also to know when those policies are violated. Kubernetes provides an audit capability that will be the focus of the next section, where we will add the audit log to our KinD cluster and debug the implementation of RBAC policies.

Kubernetes auditing

The Kubernetes audit log is where you track what is happening in your cluster from an API perspective. It's in JSON format, which makes reading it directly more difficult, but makes it much easier to parse using tools such as Elasticsearch. In *Chapter 10, Auditing Using Falco, DevOps AI, and ECK*, we will cover how to create a full logging system using the **Elasticsearch, Fluentd, and Kibana (EFK)** stack.

Creating an audit policy

A policy file is used to control what events are recorded and where to store the logs, which can be a standard log file or a webhook. We have included an example audit policy in the chapter6 directory of the GitHub repository, and we will apply it to the KinD cluster that we have been using throughout the book.

An audit policy is a collection of rules that tell the API server which API calls to log and how. When Kubernetes parses the policy file, all rules are applied in order and only the initial matching policy event will be applied. If you have more than one rule for a certain event, you may not receive the expected data in your log files. For this reason, you need to be careful that your events are created correctly.

Policies use the `audit.k8s.io` API and the manifest kind of `Policy`. The following example shows the beginning of a policy file:

```
apiVersion: audit.k8s.io/v1
kind: Policy
rules:
  - level: Request
    userGroups: ["system:nodes"]
    verbs: ["update","patch"]
    resources:
      - group: "" # core
        resources: ["nodes/status", "pods/status"]
    omitStages:
      - "RequestReceived"
```

 While a policy file may look like a standard Kubernetes manifest, you do not apply it using `kubectl`. A policy file is used with the `--audit-policy-file` API flag on the API server(s). This will be explained in the *Enabling auditing on a cluster* section.

To understand the rule and what it will log, we will go through each section in detail.

The first section of the rule is `level`, which determines the type of information that will be logged for the event. There are four levels that can be assigned to events:

Audit level	Logging details
None	Does not log any data
Metadata	Only logs metadata – does not include the request or the request response
Request	Logs metadata and the request, but not the request response
RequestResponse	Logs metadata, the request, and the request response

Table 6.1: Kubernetes auditing levels

The `userGroups`, `verbs`, and `resources` values tell the API server the object and action that will trigger the auditing event. In this example, only requests from `system:nodes` that attempt an action of `update` or `patch` on a `node/status` or `pod/status` on the `core` API will create an event.

`omitStages` tells the API server to skip any logging events during a stage, which helps you to limit the amount of data that is logged. There are four stages that an API request goes through:

API stage	Stage details
`RequestReceived`	This is the stage where the API receives a request.
`ResponseStarted`	This stage is only used with certain requests and it starts before the response is sent in the `ResponseComplete` stage.
`ResponseComplete`	This is the stage where the API server responds to a request.
`Panic`	Event created if a panic occurs.

Table 6.2: Auditing stages

In our example, we have set the event to ignore the `RequestReceived` event, which tells the API server not to log any data for the incoming API request.

Every organization has its own auditing policy, and policy files can become long and complex. Don't be afraid to set up a policy that logs everything until you get a handle on the types of events that you can create. Logging everything is not a good practice since the log files become very large. Fine-tuning an audit policy is a skill that is learned over time and as you learn more about the API server, you will start to learn what events are most valuable to audit.

Policy files are just the start of enabling cluster auditing, and now that we have an understanding of the policy file, let's explain how to enable auditing on a cluster.

Enabling auditing on a cluster

Enabling auditing is specific to each distribution of Kubernetes. In this section, we will enable the audit log in KinD to understand the low-level steps. As a quick refresher, the finished product of the last chapter was a KinD cluster with impersonation enabled (instead of directly integrating with OpenID Connect). The rest of the steps and examples in this chapter assume this cluster is being used. If you haven't run through *Chapter 5, Integrating Authentication into Your Cluster*, start with a fresh cluster and run the `chapter6/openunison/depeploy_openunison_imp.sh` script:

```
$ cd chapter6/openunison
$ ./deploy_openunison_imp.sh
Helm Repo Name tremolo
Helm Repo URL https://nexus.tremolo.io/repository/helm
Deploying the Kubernetes Dashboard
namespace/kubernetes-dashboard unchanged
```

```
.
.
.
Deploying the login portal
NAME: orchestra-login-portal
LAST DEPLOYED: Fri Oct 22 13:37:48 2021
NAMESPACE: openunison
STATUS: deployed
REVISION: 1
TEST SUITE: None
OpenUnison is deployed!
```

Next, we're going to configure the API server to send audit log data to a file. This is more complex than setting a switch because kubeadm, the installer that KinD is built on, runs the API server as a static Pod(s). The API server is a container inside of Kubernetes! This means that in order for us to tell the API server where to write log data to, we first have to have storage to write it to and then configure the API server's Pod to use that location as a volume. We're going to walk through this process manually to give you experience with modifying the API server's context.

You can follow the steps in this section manually or you can execute the included script, `enable-auditing.sh`, in the `chapter6` directory of the GitHub repository:

1. First, copy the example audit policy from the `chapter6` directory to the API server:

   ```
   $ cd chapter6
   $ docker exec -ti cluster01-control-plane mkdir /etc/kubernetes/
   audit
   $ docker cp k8s-audit-policy.yaml cluster01-control-plane:/etc/
   kubernetes/audit/
   ```

2. Next, create the directories to store the audit log and policy configuration on the API server. We will `exec` into the container since we need to modify the API server file in the next step:

   ```
   $ docker exec -ti cluster01-control-plane mkdir /var/log/k8s
   ```

   At this point, you have the audit policy on the API server and you can enable the API options to use the file.

3. On the API server, edit the kubeadm configuration file (you will need to install an editor such as vi by running `apt-get update; apt-get install vim`), /etc/kubernetes/manifests/kube-apiserver.yaml, which is the same file that we updated to enable OpenID Connect. To enable auditing, we need to add three values.

4. It's important to note that many Kubernetes clusters may only require the file and the API options. We need the second and third steps since we are using a KinD cluster for our testing.

5. First, add bold command-line flags for the API server that enable the audit logs. Along with the policy file, we can add options to control the log file rotation, retention, and maximum size:

```
- --tls-private-key-file=/etc/kubernetes/pki/apiserver.key
- --audit-log-path=/var/log/k8s/audit.log
- --audit-log-maxage=1
- --audit-log-maxbackup=10
- --audit-log-maxsize=10
- --audit-policy-file=/etc/kubernetes/audit/k8s-audit-policy.yaml
```

Notice that the option is pointing to the policy file that you copied over in the previous step.

6. Next, add the bold directories that store the policy configuration and the resulting logs to the volumeMounts section:

```
- mountPath: /usr/share/ca-certificates
  name: usr-share-ca-certificates
  readOnly: true
- mountPath: /var/log/k8s
  name: var-log-k8s
  readOnly: false
- mountPath: /etc/kubernetes/audit
  name: etc-kubernetes-audit
  readOnly: true
```

7. Finally, add the bold hostPath configurations to the volumes section so that Kubernetes knows where to mount the local paths to:

```
- hostPath:
    path: /usr/share/ca-certificates
    type: DirectoryOrCreate
  name: usr-share-ca-certificates
- hostPath:
    path: /var/log/k8s
    type: DirectoryOrCreate
  name: var-log-k8s
- hostPath:
    path: /etc/kubernetes/audit
    type: DirectoryOrCreate
  name: etc-kubernetes-audit
```

8. Save and exit the file.

9. Like all API option changes, you need to restart the API server for the changes to take effect; however, KinD will detect that the file has changed and restart the API server's pod automatically.

   Exit the attached shell and check the pods in the `kube-system` namespace:

   ```
   $ kubectl get pod kube-apiserver-cluster01-control-plane -n
   kube-system
   NAME                                       READY    STATUS
   RESTARTS    AGE
   kube-apiserver-cluster01-control-plane     1/1      Running       0
   47s
   ```

   The API server is highlighted to have been running for only 47 seconds, showing that it successfully restarted.

10. Having verified that the API server is running, let's look at the audit log to verify that it's working correctly. To check the log, you can use `docker exec` to tail `audit.log`:

    ```
    $ docker exec cluster01-control-plane  tail /var/log/k8s/audit.
    log
    ```

    This command generates the following log data:

    ```
    {"kind":"Event","apiVersion":"audit.k8s.io/v1","level":"Meta
    data","auditID":"451ddf5d-763c-4d7c-9d89-7afc6232e2dc","stag
    e":"ResponseComplete","requestURI":"/apis/discovery.k8s.io/
    v1/namespaces/default/endpointslices/kubernetes","verb":"get
    ","user":{"username":"system:apiserver","uid":"7e02462c-26d1-
    4349-92ec-edf46af2ab31","groups":["system:masters"]},"sourc
    eIPs":["::1"],"userAgent":"kube-apiserver/v1.21.1 (linux/amd64)
    kubernetes/5e58841","objectRef":{"resource":"endpointslices","n
    amespace":"default","name":"kubernetes","apiGroup":"discovery.
    k8s.io","apiVersion":"v1"},"responseStatus":{"metadata":{},"cod
    e":200},"requestReceivedTimestamp":"2021-07-12T08:53:55.345776Z
    ","stageTimestamp":"2021-07-12T08:53:55.365609Z","annotations":
    {"authorization.k8s.io/decision":"allow","authorization.k8s.io/
    reason":""}}
    ```

There is quite a bit of information in this JSON, and it would be challenging to find a specific event looking at a log file directly. Luckily, now that you have auditing enabled, you can forward events to a central logging server. We will do this in *Chapter 10, Auditing Using Falco and EFK,* where we will deploy an EFK stack.

Now that we have auditing enabled, the next step is to practice debugging RBAC policies.

Using audit2rbac to debug policies

There is a tool called `audit2rbac` that can reverse engineer errors in the audit log into RBAC policy objects. In this section, we'll use this tool to generate an RBAC policy after discovering that one of our users can't perform an action they need to be able to do. This is a typical RBAC debugging process and learning how to use this tool can save you hours trying to isolate RBAC issues:

1. In the previous chapter, a generic RBAC policy was created to allow all members of the `cn=k8s-cluster-admins,ou=Groups,DC=domain,DC=com` group to be administrators in our cluster. If you're logged into OpenUnison, log out.

2. Now, log in again with the username `jjackson` and the password `start123`.

3. Next, click on **Sign In**. Once you're logged in, go to the dashboard. Just as when OpenUnison was first deployed, there won't be any namespaces or other information because the RBAC policy for cluster administrators doesn't apply any more.

4. Next, copy your `kubectl` configuration from the token screen, making sure to paste it into a window that isn't your main KinD terminal so you do not overwrite your master configuration.

5. Once your tokens are set, attempt to create a namespace called `not-going-to-work`:

```
PS C:\Users\mlb> kubectl create ns not-going-to-work
Error from server (Forbidden): namespaces is forbidden: User
"jjackson" cannot create resource "namespaces" in API group ""
at the cluster scope
```

There's enough information here to reverse engineer an RBAC policy.

6. In order to eliminate this error message, create a ClusterRole with a resource for `"namespaces"`, `apiGroups` set to `""`, and a verb of `"create"` using your KinD administrative user:

```
apiVersion: rbac.authorization.k8s.io/v1
kind: ClusterRole
metadata:
  name: cluster-create-ns
rules:
- apiGroups: [""]
  resources: ["namespaces"]
  verbs: ["create"]
```

7. Next, create a ClusterRoleBinding for the user and this ClusterRole:

```
apiVersion: rbac.authorization.k8s.io/v1
kind: ClusterRoleBinding
metadata:
  name: cluster-create-ns
subjects:
- kind: User
  name: jjackson
  apiGroup: rbac.authorization.k8s.io
roleRef:
  kind: ClusterRole
  name: cluster-create-ns
  apiGroup: rbac.authorization.k8s.io
```

8. Once the ClusterRole and ClusterRoleBinding are created, try running the command again, and it will work:

```
PS C:\Users\mlb> kubectl create ns not-going-to-work
namespace/not-going-to-work created
```

Unfortunately, this is not likely how most RBAC debugging will go. Most of the time, debugging RBAC will not be this clear or simple. Typically, debugging RBAC means getting unexpected error messages between systems. For instance, if you're deploying the kube-prometheus project for monitoring, you'll generally want to monitor by Service objects, not by explicitly naming Pods. In order to do this, the Prometheus ServiceAccount needs to be able to list the Service objects in the namespace of the service you want to monitor. Prometheus won't tell you this needs to happen; you just won't see your services listed. A better way to debug is to use a tool that knows how to read the audit log and can reverse engineer a set of roles and bindings based on the failures in the log.

The audit2rbac tool is the best way to do this. It will read the audit log and give you a set of policies that will work. It may not be the exact policy that's needed, but it will provide a good starting point. Let's try it out:

1. First, attach a shell to the control-plane container of your cluster and download the tool from GitHub (https://github.com/liggitt/audit2rbac/releases):

```
root@cluster01-control-plane:/# curl -L https://github.com/
liggitt/audit2rbac/releases/download/v0.8.0/audit2rbac-linux-
amd64.tar.gz 2>/dev/null > audit2rbac-linux-amd64.tar.gz
root@cluster01-control-plane:/# tar -xvzf audit2rbac-linux-
amd64.tar.gz
```

2. Before using the tool, make sure to close the browser with the Kubernetes dashboard in it to avoid polluting the logs. Also, remove the `cluster-create-ns` ClusterRole and ClusterRoleBinding created previously. Finally, try creating the `still-not-going-to-work` namespace:

```
PS C:\Users\mlb> kubectl create ns still-not-going-to-work
Error from server (Forbidden): namespaces is forbidden: User
"jjackson" cannot create resource "namespaces" in API group ""
at the cluster scope
```

3. Next, use the `audit2rbac` tool to look for any failures for your test user:

```
root@cluster01-control-plane:/# ./audit2rbac --filename=/var/
log/k8s/audit.log  --user=jjackson
Opening audit source...
Loading events...
Evaluating API calls...
Generating roles...
apiVersion: rbac.authorization.k8s.io/v1
kind: ClusterRole
metadata:
  annotations:
    audit2rbac.liggitt.net/version: v0.8.0
  labels:
    audit2rbac.liggitt.net/generated: "true"
    audit2rbac.liggitt.net/user: jjackson
  name: audit2rbac:jjackson
rules:
- apiGroups:
  - ""
  resources:
  - namespaces
  verbs:
  - create
---
apiVersion: rbac.authorization.k8s.io/v1
kind: ClusterRoleBinding
metadata:
  annotations:
    audit2rbac.liggitt.net/version: v0.8.0
  labels:
    audit2rbac.liggitt.net/generated: "true"
```

```
        audit2rbac.liggitt.net/user: jjackson
    name: audit2rbac:jjackson
roleRef:
    apiGroup: rbac.authorization.k8s.io
    kind: ClusterRole
    name: audit2rbac:jjackson
subjects:
- apiGroup: rbac.authorization.k8s.io
    kind: User
    name: jjackson
Complete!
```

This command generated a policy that will allow the test user to create namespaces. This becomes an anti-pattern, though, of explicitly authorizing access to users.

4. In order to better leverage this policy, it would be better to use our group:

```
apiVersion: rbac.authorization.k8s.io/v1
kind: ClusterRole
metadata:
    name: create-ns-audit2rbac
rules:
- apiGroups:
    - ""
    resources:
    - namespaces
    verbs:
    - create
---
apiVersion: rbac.authorization.k8s.io/v1
kind: ClusterRoleBinding
metadata:
    name: create-ns-audit2rbac
roleRef:
    apiGroup: rbac.authorization.k8s.io
    kind: ClusterRole
    name: create-ns-audit2rbac
subjects:
- apiGroup: rbac.authorization.k8s.io
    kind: Group
    name: cn=k8s-create-ns,ou=Groups,DC=domain,DC=com
```

The major change is highlighted. Instead of referencing the user directly, the ClusterRoleBinding is now referencing the `cn=k8s-create-ns,ou=Groups,DC=domain,DC=com` group so that any member of that group can now create namespaces.

Summary

This chapter's focus was on RBAC policy creation and debugging. We explored how Kubernetes defines authorization policies and how it applies those policies to enterprise users. We also looked at how these policies can be used to enable multi-tenancy in your cluster. Finally, we enabled the audit log in our KinD cluster and learned how to use the `audit2rbac` tool to debug RBAC issues.

Using Kubernetes' built-in RBAC policy management objects lets you enable access that's needed for operational and development tasks in your clusters. Knowing how to design policies can help limit the impact of issues, providing the confidence to let users do more on their own.

In the next chapter, *Chapter 7, Deploying a Secured Kubernetes Dashboard*, we'll be learning about how to secure the Kubernetes dashboard, as well as how to approach security for other infrastructure applications that make up your cluster. You'll learn how to apply what we've learned about authentication and authorization to the applications that make up your cluster, providing your developers and infrastructure team with a better and more secure experience.

Questions

1. True or false – ABAC is the preferred method of authorizing access to Kubernetes clusters.

    a. True

    b. False

2. What are the three components of a Role?

    a. Subject, noun, and verb

    b. Resource, action, and group

    c. `apiGroups`, resources, and verbs

    d. Group, resource, and sub-resource

3. Where can you go to look up resource information?

    a. Kubernetes API reference

    b. The library

    c. Tutorials and blog posts

4. How can you reuse Roles across namespaces?

    a. You can't; you need to re-create them.

    b. Define a ClusterRole and reference it in each namespace as a RoleBinding.

    c. Reference the Role in one namespace with the RoleBindings of other namespaces.

    d. None of the above.

5. How should bindings reference users?

    a. Directly, listing every user.

    b. RoleBindings should only reference service accounts.

    c. Only ClusterRoleBindings should reference users.

    d. Whenever possible, RoleBindings and ClusterRoleBindings should reference groups.

6. True or false – RBAC can be used to authorize access to everything except for one resource.

    a. True

    b. False

7. True or false – RBAC is the only method of authorization in Kubernetes.

    a. True

    b. False

Join our book's Discord space

Join the book's Discord workspace for a monthly *Ask me Anything* session with the authors: `https://packt.link/K8EntGuide`

7

Deploying a Secured Kubernetes Dashboard

Kubernetes clusters are made up of more than the API server and the kubelet. Clusters are generally made up of additional applications that need to be secured, such as container registries, source control systems, pipeline services, GitOps applications, and monitoring systems. The users of your cluster will often need to interact with these applications directly.

While many clusters are focused on authenticating access to user-facing applications and services, cluster solutions are not given the same first-class status. Users often are asked to use kubectl's **port-forward** or **proxy** capability to access these systems. This method of access is an anti-pattern from a security and user experience standpoint. The first exposure users and administrators will have to this anti-pattern is the Kubernetes Dashboard. This chapter will detail why this method of access is an anti-pattern and how to properly access Dashboard. We'll walk you through how not to deploy a secure web application and point out the issues and risks.

We'll use the Kubernetes Dashboard as a way to learn about web application security and how to apply those patterns in your own cluster. These lessons will work with not just the dashboard, but other cluster-focused applications such as the Kiali dashboard for Istio, Grafana, Prometheus, and other cluster management applications.

Finally, we'll spend some time talking about local dashboards and how to evaluate their security. This is a popular trend, but not universal. It's important to understand the security of both approaches, and we'll explore them in this chapter.

In this chapter, we will cover the following topics:

- How does the dashboard know who you are?
- Is the dashboard insecure?
- Deploying the dashboard with a reverse proxy
- Integrating the dashboard with OpenUnison

Having covered what we'll work through in this chapter, next let's work through the technical requirements for this chapter.

Technical requirements

To follow the exercises in this chapter, you will require a fresh KinD cluster from *Chapter 2, Deploying Kubernetes Using KinD*.

You can access the code for this chapter at the following GitHub repository: `https://github.com/PacktPublishing/Kubernetes---An-Enterprise-Guide-2E/tree/main/chapter7`.

How does the dashboard know who you are?

The Kubernetes Dashboard is a powerful web application for quickly accessing your cluster from inside a browser. It lets you browse your namespaces and view the status of nodes, and even provides a shell you can use to access Pods directly. There is a fundamental difference between using the dashboard and kubectl. The dashboard, being a web application, needs to manage your session, whereas kubectl does not. This means there's a different set of security issues during deployment that are often not accounted for, leading to severe consequences. In this section, we'll explore how the dashboard identifies users and interacts with the API server.

Dashboard architecture

Before diving into the specifics of how the dashboard authenticates a user, it's important to understand the basics of how the dashboard works. The dashboard at a high level has three layers:

- **User interface**: This is the Angular + HTML frontend that is displayed in your browser and that you interact with

- **Middle tier**: The frontend interacts with a set of APIs hosted in the dashboard's container to translate calls from the frontend into Kubernetes API calls

- **API server**: The middle tier API interacts directly with the Kubernetes API server

This three-layered architecture of the Kubernetes Dashboard can be seen in the following diagram:

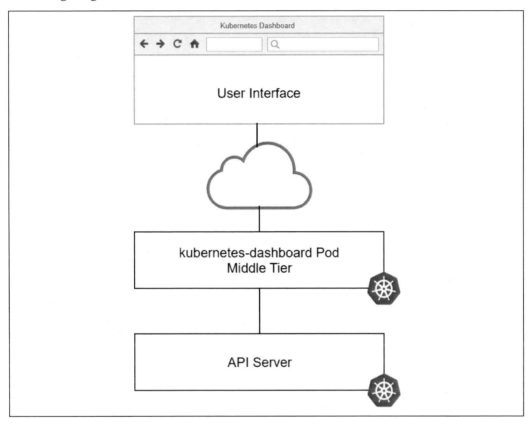

Figure 7.1: Kubernetes Dashboard architecture

When a user interacts with the dashboard, the user interface makes calls to the middle tier, which in turn makes calls to the API server. The dashboard doesn't know how to collect credentials, using which most of the applications users would generally get access. There's no place to put a username or password. It has a very simple session mechanism system based on cookies, but for the most part, the dashboard doesn't really know, or care, who the currently logged-in user is. The only thing the dashboard cares about is what token to use when communicating with the API server.

So, how does the dashboard know who you are? Let's walk through the options.

Authentication methods

There are three ways that the dashboard can determine who a user is:

- **No credentials**: The dashboard can be told not to collect any tokens or credentials. When this happens, the dashboard will interact with the API server using the container's own service account with whatever privileges it is assigned via RBAC.

- **Token from login/uploaded kubectl configuration**: The dashboard can prompt the user for their kubectl configuration file or for a bearer token to use. Once a token is provided (or extracted from the configuration file uploaded to the dashboard), an encrypted cookie is created to store the token. This cookie is decrypted by the middle tier, and the token inside is passed to the API server.

- **Token from a reverse proxy**: If there's an authorization header containing a bearer token in requests from the user interface to the middle tier, the middle tier will use that bearer token in requests to the API server. This is the most secure option and the implementation that will be detailed in this chapter.

Throughout the rest of this chapter, the first two options will be explored as anti-patterns for accessing the dashboard, and we will explain why the reverse proxy pattern is the best option for accessing a cluster's dashboard implementation from a security standpoint and a user experience standpoint.

Understanding dashboard security risks

The question of the dashboard's security often comes up when setting up a new cluster. Securing the dashboard boils down to how the dashboard is deployed, rather than if the dashboard itself is secure. Going back to the architecture of the dashboard application, there is no sense of "security" being built in. The middle tier simply passes a token to the API server.

When talking about any kind of IT security, it's important to look at it through the lens of *defense in depth*. This is the idea that any system should have multiple layers of security. If one fails, there are other layers to fill the gap until the failed layers can be addressed. A single failure doesn't give an attacker direct access.

The most often cited incident related to the dashboard's security was the breach of Tesla in 2018 by crypto-miners. Attackers were able to access Pods running in Tesla's clusters because the dashboard wasn't secured.

The cluster's Pods had access to tokens that provided the attackers with access to Tesla's cloud providers where the attackers ran their crypto-mining systems.

Dashboards in general are often an attack vector because they make it easy to find what attackers are looking for and can easily be deployed insecurely. Illustrating this point, at KubeCon NA 2019 a **Capture the Flag (CTF)** was presented where one of the scenarios was a developer "accidentally" exposing the cluster's dashboard.

 The CTF is available as a home lab at `https://securekubernetes.com/`. It's a highly recommended resource for anyone learning Kubernetes security. In addition to being educational, and terrifying, it's also really fun!

Since the Tesla breach, it's become harder to deploy the dashboard without credentials. It's no longer the default and requires updates to both the dashboard and the cluster. To demonstrate just how dangerous this can be, let's go through the steps to do it and see what damage can be done.

Going through these steps might bring about the thought "does anyone really go through all these steps to get to the dashboard?" The answer is probably something no one wants to talk about. In the previous chapter, multiple options for authorizing access to a cluster and designing multi-tenancy were discussed. One of the options was tenancy at the cluster layer, where each tenant gets its own cluster. Unfortunately, many of these deployments include cluster-admin access for the tenants, which would give them the ability to perform these steps. Cluster administrators are a few Google searches away from instructions to easily bypass that pesky VPN developers don't like using from home.

Deploying an insecure dashboard

While this may sound crazy, it's something that we have seen in the wild far too often. The recommended Dashboard installation states multiple times not to use this type of configuration outside of an isolated development lab. The downfall is that since it does make deploying the dashboard so easy, many newer administrators use it since it's easy to set up, and they often use the same deployment in a production cluster.

Now, let's show how easy it is to attack a Dashboard instance that is deployed without security in mind:

1. First, deploy the dashboard to your cluster:

   ```
   kubectl apply -f https://raw.githubusercontent.com/kubernetes/
   dashboard/v2.3.1/aio/deploy/recommended.yaml
   ```

2. The first step is to tell the dashboard to allow users to bypass authentication. Edit the `kubernetes-dashboard` deployment in the `kubernetes-dashboard` namespace:

```
kubectl edit deployment kubernetes-dashboard -n kubernetes-
dashboard
```

3. Look for the `args` option for the container, add - `--enable-skip-login`, then save:

Figure 7.2: Enabling skip-login on the dashboard

4. Now we need to expose the dashboard to the network by creating a new Ingress rule. Create a new Ingress manifest called `insecure-dashboard.yaml` with the following YAML. Remember to replace the IP address in the `host` section with your Docker host's IP address:

```
apiVersion: networking.k8s.io/v1
kind: Ingress
metadata:
  name: dashboard-external-auth
  namespace: kubernetes-dashboard
  annotations:
    kubernetes.io/ingress.class: nginx
    nginx.ingress.kubernetes.io/affinity: cookie
    nginx.ingress.kubernetes.io/backend-protocol: https
    nginx.ingress.kubernetes.io/secure-backends: "true"
    nginx.org/ssl-services: kubernetes-dashboard
spec:
  rules:
```

```
    - host: k8s-secret-dashboard.apps.192-168-2-129.nip.io
      http:
        paths:
        - backend:
            service:
              name: kubernetes-dashboard
              port:
                number: 443
          path: /
          pathType: Prefix
```

5. Create the Ingress rule by deploying the manifest using `kubectl`. Since we added the namespace value to the manifest, we do need to add `-n` to the `kubectl` command:

```
kubectl create -f insecure-dashboard.yaml
```

6. Once the Ingress is created, open a browser and go to your secret dashboard using the `nip.io` name specified in the `host` section of the Ingress rule.

7. You will see an authentication screen that asks for a token or a kubeconfig file, but since we enabled the option to skip the login when we edited the dashboard, you can simply skip the login by clicking on **Skip**:

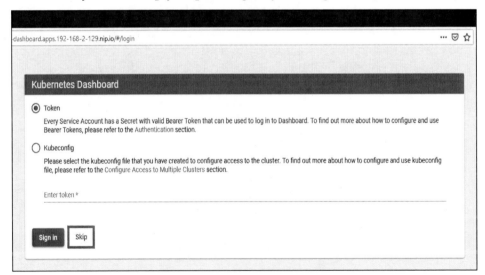

Figure 7.3: Kubernetes Dashboard with login disabled

8. Once in the dashboard, the default service account doesn't have access to anything:

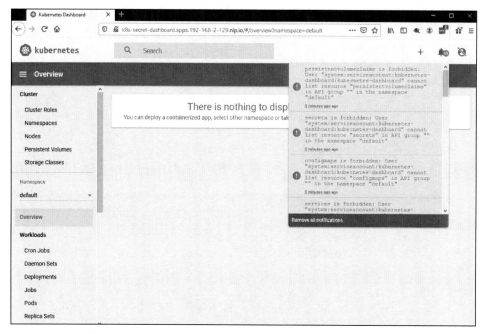

Figure 7.4: Kubernetes Dashboard with the default service account

So far this may not look too bad. You will see access forbidden errors, so right now the dashboard will not allow you to do any damage. Unfortunately, many people get to this point and go the extra step to change the permissions that the default service account has on the cluster.

9. Right now, the service account isn't authorized for access to the cluster, so change that by creating a new `ClusterRoleBinding` to the cluster-admin `ClusterRole`.

    Create a new file called `dashboard-role.yaml` with the following contents:

    ```
    apiVersion: rbac.authorization.k8s.io/v1
    kind: ClusterRoleBinding
    metadata:
      name: secret-dashboard-cluster-admin
    roleRef:
      apiGroup: rbac.authorization.k8s.io
      kind: ClusterRole
    ```

```
    name: cluster-admin
subjects:
- apiGroup: ""
    kind: ServiceAccount
    namespace: kubernetes-dashboard
    name: kubernetes-dashboard
```

10. Create the new `ClusterRoleBinding` by applying it using `kubectl`:

```
kubectl create -f dashboard-role.yaml
```

Congratulations! The secret dashboard is now available for anyone who may want to use it!

Now, you may be thinking *"Who can find my dashboard? They would need to know the URL, and I'm not telling anyone what it is."* You feel secure because nobody else knows the URL or the IP address to your dashboard. This is called Security by Obscurity and is generally seen to be a terrible approach to securing a system.

Let's use a scenario of how someone may exploit the dashboard without you knowing.

You are a big Reddit fan, and one day you come across a Reddit post titled *This is a great tool for securing your Kubernetes Dashboard*. The post seems to be legit and you are excited to test this new tool out. After reading the post, you see the link at the bottom to the utility and the command to run it: You can download it from `https://raw.githubusercontent.com/PacktPublishing/Kubernetes---An-Enterprise-Guide-2E/master/chapter7/kubectl-secure-my-dashboard.go` to give it a try!

To fully experience this example, you can run the tool on your KinD cluster by executing the following command from your cloned repository in the `chapter7` directory. Be sure to change the URL to your dashboard's Ingress host:

```
$ apt-get update
$ apt-get install golang
.
.
.
$ go run kubectl-secure-my-dashboard.go https://k8s-secret-dashboard.
apps.192-168-2-129.nip.io
Running analysis on https://k8s-secret-dashboard.apps.192-168-2-129.
nip.io
Your dashboard has been secured!
```

Now, let's see review what just happened. Open a browser and go to your secret dashboard site to view what's been changed:

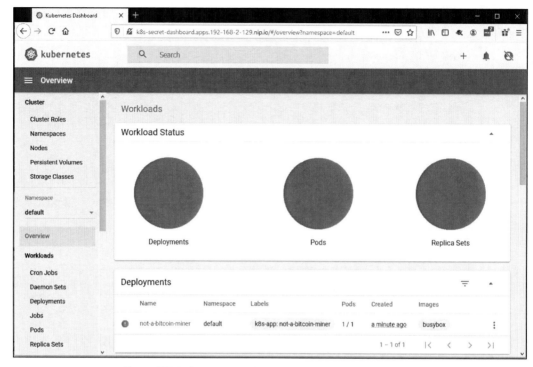

Figure 7.5: Kubernetes Dashboard showing malware deployed

It appears our hardening plugin was a ruse to deploy a bitcoin miner. How rude!

Now that you have seen how easily an insecure Dashboard can be exploited, delete the bitcoin miner deployment using `kubectl`:

```
$ kubectl delete deployments --all -n default
deployment.apps "not-a-bitcoin-miner" deleted
```

While this attack could be mitigated by preauthorizing registries with approved images (this topic will be covered when `OpenPolicyAgent` is covered in *Chapter 8, Extending Security Using Open Policy Agent*), at that point the security is reactive, trying to respond to threats instead of preventing them. Using an admission controller won't stop someone from extracting secrets from your Dashboard either.

This was the simplest way to get access to the dashboard insecurely, it's not the only way. The kubectl utility includes two features that can make accessing the dashboard easy.

The port-forward utility is often used to create a tunnel to a pod inside the cluster. This utility creates a TCP stream to a specific port on your pod, making it accessible to your local host (or more if you wanted). This still bypasses authentication in the dashboard, requiring that the dashboard's service account has access via RBAC to perform whichever tasks are needed. While it is true that the user must have RBAC authorization to port-forward to a pod, this leaves the dashboard open via two attack vectors:

- **External**: Any script running on a user's local workstation can access the forwarded network tunnel
- **Internal**: Any pod inside of the cluster can access the dashboard pod

For internal access, network policies can be used to limit which namespaces and Pods can access the dashboard's API. It's a good idea to use network policies to begin with, but that's a single point of failure in this instance. One misconfigured policy will open the dashboard to attack.

Threats from external sources will likely come in the form of scripts you (or another tool you use) may decide to run. Web browsers aren't able to access the ports opened by port-forwarding from a page hosted outside your local system, but any script running on your workstation can. For instance, while you could access a port-forwarded host by opening your browser and going directly to that port, a web page with malicious JavaScript that loads from a remote site can't open a connection to your local host. Attempt to run the hardening script from earlier in the section against a forwarded port and the same result will occur, an unwanted pod on your infrastructure.

Another technique for providing access is to use the API server's integrated proxy utility. Running `kubectl proxy` creates a local network tunnel to the API server that can then be used to proxy HTTP requests to any pod, including the dashboard. This has the same drawbacks as `kubectl port-forward` and will open your cluster up to attacks from any script running locally.

The common thread among these methods is they have a single point of failure in their security. Even with mitigations put in place to limit what images can be deployed, an unsecured dashboard can still be used to access Secret objects, delete deployments, and even remote shell into Pods via the terminal integrated into the dashboard.

Having explored how to bypass all authentication on the dashboard, and its implications, next we'll look at how to provide a token to the dashboard without deploying additional infrastructure.

Using a token to log in

A user may upload a token or kubectl configuration file to the dashboard as a login to avoid the perils of a secret dashboard. As discussed earlier, the dashboard will take the user's bearer token and use it with all requests to the API server. While this may appear to solve the problem of giving the dashboard its own privileged service account, it brings its own issues. The dashboard isn't kubectl and doesn't know how to refresh tokens as they expire. This means that a token would need to be fairly long-lived to be useful. This would require either creating service accounts that can be used or making your OpenID Connect `id_tokens` longer-lived. Both options would negate much of the security put in place by leveraging OpenID Connect for authentication.

So far, we've only focused on the wrong way to deploy the dashboard. While it is important to understand this, what is the correct method? In the next section, we'll detail the correct way to deploy the dashboard using a reverse proxy.

Deploying the dashboard with a reverse proxy

Proxies are a common pattern in Kubernetes. There are proxies at every layer in a Kubernetes cluster. The proxy pattern is also used by most service mesh implementations on Kubernetes, creating side cars that will intercept requests. The difference between the reverse proxy described here and these proxies is in their intent. Microservice proxies often do not carry a session, whereas web applications need a session to manage state.

The following diagram shows the architecture of a Kubernetes Dashboard with a reverse proxy:

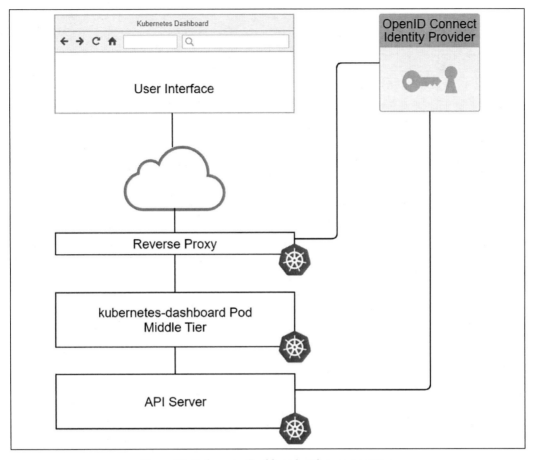

Figure 7.6: Kubernetes Dashboard with a reverse proxy

The reverse proxy shown in *Figure 7.6* performs three roles:

- **Authentication**: The reverse proxy intercepts unauthenticated requests (or stale sessions) and triggers the authentication process with an OpenID Connect identity provider to authenticate the user.

- **Session management**: Kubernetes' Dashboard is a user-facing application. It should have the typical controls put in place to support session timeouts and revocation. Be wary of a reverse proxy that stores all session data in a cookie. These methods are difficult to revoke.

- **Identity injection**: Once the proxy has authenticated a user, it needs to be able to inject an HTTP authorization header on each request that is a JWT identifying the logged-in user, is signed by the same OpenID Connect identity provider, and has the same issuer and recipient as the API server. The exception to this is using impersonation, which, as discussed in *Chapter 5, Integrating Authentication into Your Cluster*, injects specific headers into the requests.

The reverse proxy does not need to run on the cluster. Depending on your setup, it may be advantageous to do so, especially when utilizing impersonation with your cluster. When using impersonation, the reverse proxy uses a service account's token, so it's best for that token to never leave the cluster.

The focus of this chapter has been on the Kubernetes project's dashboard. There are multiple options for dashboard functionality. Next, we'll explore how these dashboards interact with the API server and how to evaluate their security.

Local dashboards

A common theme among third-party dashboards is to run locally on your workstation and use a Kubernetes SDK to interact with the API server the same way kubectl would. These tools offer the benefit of not having to deploy additional infrastructure to secure them.

Visual Studio Code's Kubernetes plugin is an example of a local application leveraging direct API server connections. When launching the plugin, Visual Studio Code accesses your current kubectl configuration and interacts with the API server using that configuration. It will even refresh an OpenID Connect token when it expires:

Figure 7.7: Visual Studio Code with the Kubernetes plugin

The Kubernetes plugin for Visual Studio Code is able to refresh its OpenID Connect token because it's built with the client-go SDK, the same client libraries used by kubectl. When evaluating a client dashboard, make sure it works with your authentication type even if it isn't OpenID Connect. Many of the SDKs for Kubernetes don't support OpenID Connect token refreshes. The Java and Python SDKs only recently (as of the published date of this book) began supporting the refresh of OpenID Connect tokens the way the client-go SDK does. When evaluating a local dashboard, make sure it's able to leverage your short-lived tokens and can refresh them as needed, just like kubectl can.

There is no shortage of different dashboards in the Kubernetes ecosystem all with their own spins on management. I don't want to simply provide a list of these dashboards without giving you an in-depth review of their benefits and security impacts. Instead, let's focus on what's important when evaluating which dashboard you want to use:

- If the dashboard is web-based:

    - Does it support OpenID Connect directly?

    - Can it run behind a reverse proxy and accept both tokens and impersonation headers?

    - Does it require any permissions for its own `ServiceAccount`? Do these permissions adhere to a least-privilege approach?

- If the dashboard is local:

    - Does the client SDK support OpenID Connect, with the ability to automatically refresh tokens as kubectl does using the client-go SDK?

These are important evaluation questions not just for the Kubernetes Dashboard, but for dashboards that you may use for other cluster management applications. As an example, in *Chapter 14, Provisioning a Platform*, we'll deploy the TektonCD dashboard, which is a web application for managing your pipelines. This deployment involved deleting several RBAC bindings to make sure the dashboard had to use the user's identity and couldn't be co-opted to using its `ServiceAccount` identity.

Other cluster-level applications

The introduction of this chapter discussed how a cluster is made up of several applications besides Kubernetes. Other applications will likely follow the same model as the dashboard for security, and the reverse proxy method is a better method for exposing those applications than kubectl port-forwarding, even when the application has no built-in security. Take the common Prometheus stack as an example. Grafana has support for user authentication, but Prometheus and Alert Manager do not.

How would you track who had access to these systems or when they were accessed using port-forwarding?

Using a reverse proxy, logs of each URL and the user that was authenticated to access the URL can be forwarded to a central log management system and analyzed by a **Security Information and Event Manager (SIEM)** providing an additional layer of visibility into a cluster's usage.

Just as with the dashboard, using a reverse proxy with these applications provides a layered security approach. It offloads sessions management from the application in question and provides the capability to have enhanced authentication measures in place such as multi-factor authentication and session revocation. These benefits will lead to a more secure, and easier-to-use, cluster.

Integrating the dashboard with OpenUnison

The topic of how OpenUnison injected identity headers using impersonation was covered in *Chapter 5, Integrating Authentication into Your Cluster*, but not how OpenUnison injected user's identity into the dashboard with an OpenID Connect integrated cluster. It worked, but it wasn't explained. This section will use the OpenUnison implementation as an example of how to build a reverse proxy for the dashboard. Use the information in this section to get a better understanding of API security or to build your own solution for dashboard authentication.

The OpenUnison deployment comprises two integrated applications:

- **The OpenID Connect Identity Provider & Login Portal**: This application hosts the login process and the discovery URLs used by the API server to get the keys needed to validate an `id_token`. It also hosts the screens where you can obtain your token for kubectl.

- **The dashboard**: A reverse proxy application that authenticates to the integrated OpenID Connect identity provider and injects the user's `id_token` into each request.

This diagram shows how the dashboard's user interface interacts with its server-side component with a reverse proxy injecting the user's `id_token`:

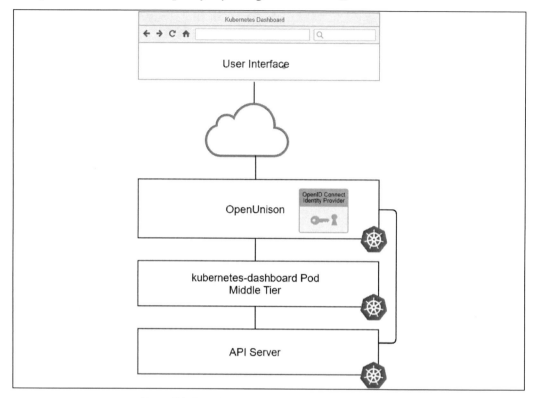

Figure 7.8: OpenUnison integration with the dashboard

The dashboard uses the same OpenID Connect identity provider as the API server but doesn't use the `id_token` provided by it. Instead, OpenUnison has a plugin that will generate a new `id_token` independent of the identity provider with the user's identity data in it. OpenUnison can do this because the key used to generate an `id_token` for the OpenID Connect identity provider, used by kubectl and the API server, is stored in OpenUnison.

A new, short-lived token is generated separate from the OpenID Connect session used with kubectl. This way, the token can be refreshed independently of a kubectl session. This process provides the benefits of 1- to 2-minute token life with the convenience of a direct login process.

If you have an eye for security, you may point out that this method has a glaring single point of failure in the security model: a user's credentials! Just as with the Secret dashboard built earlier in this chapter in the *Understanding dashboard security risks* section, an attacker generally just needs to ask for credentials in order to get them.

This is often done via email in an attack called phishing, where an attacker sends a victim a link to a page that looks like their login page but really just collects credentials. This is why multi-factor authentication is so important for infrastructure systems.

In a 2019 study, Google showed multi-factor authentication stopped 99% of automated and phishing attacks (`https://security.googleblog.com/2019/05/new-research-how-effective-is-basic.html`). Adding multi-factor authentication to the identity provider OpenUnison authenticates against, or integrating it directly into OpenUnison, is one of the most effective ways to secure the dashboard and your cluster.

Summary

In this chapter, we explored the security of the Kubernetes Dashboard in detail. First, we walked through the architecture and how the dashboard passes your identity information on to the API server. We then explored how the dashboard gets compromised, and finally we detailed how to correctly deploy the dashboard securely.

With this knowledge, you can now provide a secured tool to your users. Many users prefer the simplicity of accessing the dashboard via a web browser. Adding multi-factor authentication adds an additional layer of security and peace of mind. When your security team questions the security of the dashboard, you'll have the answers needed to satisfy their concerns.

The previous three chapters focused on the security of the Kubernetes APIs. Next, in *Chapter 8, Extending Security Using Open Policy Agent*, we'll explore securing the soft underbelly of every Kubernetes deployment, nodes!

Questions

1. The dashboard is insecure.

    a. True

    b. False

2. How can the dashboard identify a user?

    a. The options are either no authentication, or a token injected from a reverse proxy

    b. Username and password

    c. ServiceAccount

    d. Multi-factor authentication

3. How does the dashboard track session state?

    a. Sessions are stored in etc

    b. Sessions are stored in custom resource objects called `DashboardSession`

    c. There are no sessions

    d. If a token is uploaded, it's encrypted and stored in the browser as a cookie

4. When using a token, how often can the dashboard refresh it?

    a. Once a minute

    b. Every thirty seconds

    c. When the token expires

    d. None of the above

5. What's the best way to deploy the dashboard?

    a. Using `kubectl port-forward`

    b. Using `kubectl proxy`

    c. With a secret Ingress host

    d. Behind a reverse proxy

6. The dashboard doesn't support impersonation.

    a. True

    b. False

7. OpenUnison is the only reverse proxy that supports the dashboard.

    a. True

    b. False

Join our book's Discord space

Join the book's Discord workspace for a monthly *Ask me Anything* session with the authors: `https://packt.link/K8EntGuide`

8

Extending Security Using Open Policy Agent

So far, we have covered Kubernetes' built-in authentication and authorization capabilities, which help to secure a cluster. While this will cover most use cases, it doesn't cover all of them. Several security best practices that Kubernetes can't handle are pre-authorizing container registries and ensuring that resource requests are on all Pod objects.

These tasks are left to outside systems and are called dynamic admission controllers. **Open Policy Agent (OPA)**, and its Kubernetes native sub-project, Gatekeeper, is one of the most popular ways to handle these use cases. This chapter will detail the deployment of OPA and Gatekeeper, how OPA is architected, and how to develop policies.

In this chapter, we will cover the following topics:

- Introduction to validating webhooks
- What is OPA and how does it work?
- Using Rego to write policies
- Enforcing memory constraints
- Enforcing Pod security policies using OPA

Once you've completed this chapter, you'll be on your way to developing and implementing important policies for your cluster and workloads.

Technical requirements

To complete the hands-on exercises in this chapter, you will require an Ubuntu 20.04 server, running a KinD cluster with the configuration from *Chapter 6, RBAC Policies and Auditing*.

You can access the code for this chapter at the following GitHub repository: `https://github.com/PacktPublishing/Kubernetes---An-Enterprise-Guide-2E/tree/main/chapter8`.

Introduction to dynamic admission controllers

There are two ways to extend Kubernetes:

- Build a custom resource definition so that you can define your own objects and APIs.

- Implement a webhook that listens for requests from the API server and responds with the necessary information. You may recall that in *Chapter 5, Integrating Authentication into Your Cluster*, we explained that a custom webhook could be used to validate tokens.

Starting in Kubernetes 1.9, a webhook can be defined as a dynamic admission controller, and in 1.16, the dynamic admission controller API became **Generally Available (GA)**.

 There are two types of dynamic admission controllers, validating and mutating. Validating admission controllers verify that a new object, update, or delete can move forward. Mutation allows a webhook to change the payload of an object's creation, deletion, or update. This section will focus on the details of admission controllers. We'll talk more about mutation controllers in the next chapter, *Chapter 9, Node Security with GateKeeper*.

The protocol is very straightforward. Once a dynamic admission controller is registered for a specific object type, the webhook is called with an HTTP post every time an object of that type is created or edited. The webhook is then expected to return JSON that represents whether it is allowed or not.

As of 1.16, `admission.k8s.io/v1` is at GA. All examples will use the GA version of the API.

The request submitted to the webhook is made up of several sections. We're not including an example here because of how large an `Admission` object can get, but we'll use `https://github.com/PacktPublishing/Kubernetes---An-Enterprise-Guide-2E/blob/main/chapter8/example_admission_request.json` as an example:

- **Object Identifiers**: The `resource` and `subResource` attributes identify the object, API, and group. If the version of the object is being upgraded, then `requestKind`, `requestResource`, and `requestSubResource` are specified. Additionally, `namespace` and `operation` are provided to provide the location of the object and whether it is a `CREATE`, `UPDATE`, `DELETE`, or `CONNECT` operation. In our example, a `Deployment` resource with a `subResource` of `Scale` is being created to scale our `Deployment` up in the `my-namespace` namespace.

- **Submitter Identifiers**: The `userInfo` object identifies the user and groups of the submitter. The submitter and the user who created the original request are not always the same. For instance, if a user creates a `Deployment`, then the `userInfo` object won't be for the user who created the original `Deployment`; it will be for the `ReplicaSet` controller's service account because the `Deployment` creates a `ReplicaSet` that creates the `Pod`. In our example, a user with the `uid` of admin submitted the scaling request.

- **Object**: `object` represents the JSON of the object being submitted, where `oldObject` represents what is being replaced if this is an update. Finally, `options` specifies additional options for the request. In our example, the new `Pod` with the new number of replicas after the scaling operation is submitted.

The response from the webhook will simply have two attributes, the original `uid` from the request and `allowed`, which can be `true` or `false`. For instance, to allow our scaling operation to complete:

```
{
   "uid": "705ab4f5-6393-11e8-b7cc-42010a800002"
   "allowed": true
}
```

The `userInfo` object can create complications quickly. Since Kubernetes often uses multiple layers of controllers to create objects, it can be difficult to track usage creation based on a user who interacts with the API server.

It's much better to authorize based on objects in Kubernetes, such as namespace labels or other objects.

A common use case is to allow developers to have a "sandbox" that they are administrators in, but that has very limited capacity. Instead of trying to validate the fact that a particular user doesn't try to request too much memory, annotate a personal namespace with a limit so that the admission controller has something concrete to reference regardless of whether the user submits a `Pod` or a `Deployment`. This way, the policy will check the annotation on the `namespace` instead of the individual user. To ensure that only the user who owns the namespace is able to create something in it, use RBAC to limit access.

One final point on generic validating webhooks: there is no way to specify a key or password. It's an anonymous request. While in theory, a validating webhook could be used to implement updates, it is not recommended.

Now that we've covered how Kubernetes implements dynamic access controllers, we'll look at one of the most popular options in OPA.

What is OPA and how does it work?

OPA is a lightweight authorization engine that fits well in Kubernetes. It didn't get its start in Kubernetes, but it's certainly found a home there. There's no requirement to build dynamic admission controllers in OPA, but it's very good at it and there are extensive resources and existing policies that can be used to start your policy library.

This section provides a high-level overview of OPA and its components with the rest of the chapter getting into the details of an OPA implementation in Kubernetes.

OPA architecture

OPA comprises three components – the HTTP listener, the policy engine, and the database:

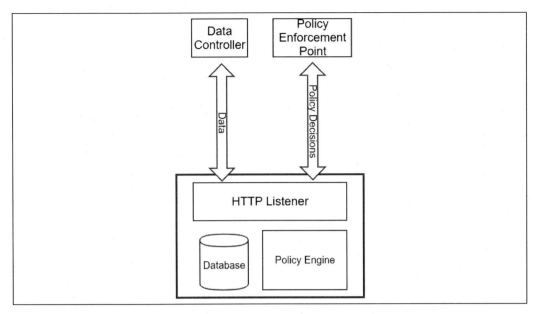

Figure 8.1: OPA architecture

The database used by OPA is in memory and ephemeral. It doesn't persist information used to make policy decisions. On the one hand, this makes OPA very scalable since it is essentially an authorization microservice. On the other hand, this means that every instance of OPA must be maintained on its own and must be kept in sync with authoritative data:

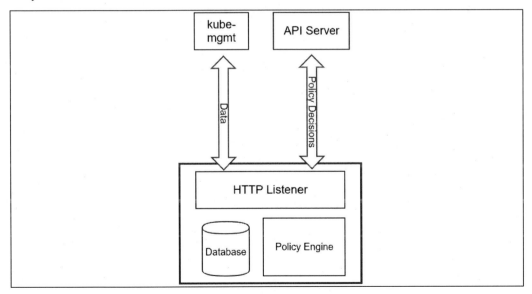

Figure 8.2: OPA in Kubernetes

When used in Kubernetes, OPA populates its database using a sidecar, called `kube-mgmt`, which sets up watches on the objects you want to import into OPA. As objects are created, deleted, or changed, `kube-mgmt` updates the data in its OPA instance. This means that OPA is "eventually consistent" with the API server, but it won't necessarily be a real-time representation of the objects in the API server. Since the entire etcd database is essentially being replicated over and over again, great care needs to be taken in order to refrain from replicating sensitive data, such as `Secrets`, in the OPA database.

Rego, the OPA policy language

We'll cover the details of Rego in the next section in detail. The main point to mention here is that Rego is a policy evaluation language, not a generic programming language. Rego can be difficult for developers who are used to languages such as Golang, Java, or JavaScript, which support complex logic such as iterators and loops. Rego is designed to evaluate policy and is streamlined as such. For instance, if you wanted to write code in Java to check that all the container images in a `Pod` started with one of a list of registries, it would look something like the following:

```
public boolean validRegistries(List<Container> containers,List<String>
allowedRegistries) {
   for (Container c : containers) {
         boolean imagesFromApprovedRegistries = false;
      for (String allowedRegistry : allowedRegistries) {
                imagesFromApprovedRegistries =
                imagesFromApprovedRegistries  || c.getImage().
startsWith(allowedRegistry);
      }
      if (! imagesFromApprovedRegistries) {
      return false;
      }
   }
   return true;
}
```

This code iterates over every container and every allowed registry to make sure that all of the images conform to the correct policy. The same code in Rego is much smaller:

```
invalidRegistry {
   ok_images = [image | startswith(input_images[j],input.parameters.
registries[_]) ; image = input_images[j] ]
   count(ok_images) != count(input_images)
}
```

The preceding rule will evaluate to `true` if any of the images on the containers come from unauthorized registries. We'll cover the details as to how this code works later in the chapter. The key to understanding why this code is so much more compact is that much of the boilerplate of loops and tests is inferred in Rego. The first line generates a list of conforming images, and the second line makes sure that the number of conforming images matches the number of total images. If they don't match, then one or more of the images must come from invalid registries. The ability to write compact policy code is what makes Rego so well suited to admission controllers.

Gatekeeper

Thus far, everything discussed has been generic to OPA. It was mentioned at the beginning of the chapter that OPA didn't get its start in Kubernetes. Early implementations had a sidecar that kept the OPA database in sync with the API server, but you had to manually create policies as `ConfigMap` objects and manually generate responses for webhooks. In 2018, Microsoft debuted Gatekeeper, `https://github.com/open-policy-agent/gatekeeper`, to provide a Kubernetes-native experience.

In addition to moving from `ConfigMap` objects to proper custom resources, Gatekeeper adds an audit function that lets you test policies against existing objects. If an object violates a policy, then a violation entry is created to track it. This way, you can get a snapshot of the existing policy violations in your cluster or know whether something was missed during Gatekeeper downtime due to an upgrade.

A major difference between Gatekeeper and generic OPA is that in Gatekeeper, OPA's functionality is not exposed via an API anyone can call. OPA is embedded, with Gatekeeper calling OPA directly to execute policies and keep the database up to date. Decisions can only be made based on data in Kubernetes or by pulling data at evaluation time.

Deploying Gatekeeper

The examples that will be used will assume the use of Gatekeeper instead of a generic OPA deployment. Based on the directions from the Gatekeeper project, use the following command:

```
$ kubectl apply -f https://raw.githubusercontent.com/open-policy-agent/
gatekeeper/release-3.5/deploy/gatekeeper.yaml
```

This launches the Gatekeeper namespace `Pods`, and creates the validating webhook. Once deployed, move on to the next section. We'll cover the details of using Gatekeeper throughout the rest of this chapter.

Automated testing framework

OPA has a built-in automated testing framework for your policies. This is one of the most valuable aspects of OPA. Being able to test policies consistently before deployment can save you hours of debugging time. When writing policies, have a file with the same name as your policies file, but with _test in the name. For instance, to have test cases associated with `mypolicies.rego`, have the test cases in `mypolicies_test.rego` in the same directory. Running `opa test` will then run your test cases. We'll show how to use this to debug your code in the next section.

Having covered the basics of OPA and how it is constructed, the next step is to learn how to use Rego to write policies.

Using Rego to write policies

Rego is a language specifically designed for policy writing. It is different from most languages you have likely written code in. Typical authorization code will look something like the following:

```
//assume failure
boolean allowed = false;
//on certain conditions allow access
if (someCondition) {
  allowed = true;
}
//are we authorized?
if (allowed) {
  doSomething();
}
```

Authorization code will generally default to unauthorized, with a specific condition having to happen in order to allow the final action to be authorized. Rego takes a different approach. Rego is generally written to authorize everything unless a specific set of conditions happens.

Another major difference between Rego and more general programming languages is that there are no explicit `if/then/else` control statements. When a line of Rego is going to make a decision, the code is interpreted as "if this line is false, stop execution." For instance, the following code in Rego says "if the image starts with `myregistry.lan/`, then stop execution of the policy and pass this check, otherwise generate an error message":

```
not startsWith(image,"myregistry.lan/")
msg := sprintf("image '%v' comes from untrusted registry", [image])
```

The same code in Java might look as follows:

```
if (! image.startsWith("myregistry.lan/")) {
    throw new Exception("image " + image + " comes from untrusted
registry");
}
```

This difference between inferred control statements and explicit control statements is often the steepest part of the learning curve when learning Rego. While this can produce a steeper learning curve than other languages, Rego more than makes up for it by making it easy to test and build policies in an automated and manageable way.

OPA can be used to automate the testing of policies. This is incredibly important when writing code that the security of your cluster relies upon. Automating your testing will help speed up your development and will increase your security by catching any bugs introduced into previously working code by means of new working code. Next, let's work through the life cycle of writing an OPA policy, testing it, and deploying it to our cluster.

Developing an OPA policy

A common example of using OPA is to limit which registries a Pod can come from. This is a common security measure in clusters to help restrict which Pods can run on a cluster. For instance, we've mentioned Bitcoin miners a few times. If the cluster won't accept `Pods` except from your own internal registry, then that's one more step that needs to be taken for a bad actor to abuse your cluster. First, let's write our policy, taken from the OPA documentation website (`https://www.openpolicyagent.org/docs/latest/kubernetes-introduction/`):

```
package k8sallowedregistries
invalidRegistry {
  input_images[image]
  not startswith(image, "quay.io/")
}
input_images[image] {
  image := input.review.object.spec.containers[_].image
}
input_images[image] {
  image := input.review.object.spec.template.spec.containers[_].image
}
```

The first line in this code declares the `package` our policy is in. Everything is stored in OPA in a package, both data and policies.

Packages in OPA are like directories on a filesystem. When you place a policy in a package, everything is relative to that package. In this case, our policy is in the k8sallowedregistries package.

The next section defines a rule. This rule ultimately will be undefined if our Pod has an image that comes from quay.io. If the Pod doesn't have an image from quay.io, the rule will return true, signifying that the registry is invalid. Gatekeeper will interpret this as a failure and return false to the API server when the Pod is evaluated during a dynamic admission review.

The next two rules look very similar. The first of the input_images rules says "evaluate the calling rule against every container in the object's spec.container," matching Pod objects directly submitted to the API server, and extracting all the image values for each container. The second input_images rule states: "evaluate the calling rule against every container in the object's spec.template.spec.containers" to short circuit Deployment objects and StatefulSets.

Finally, we add the rule that Gatekeeper requires to notify the API server of a failed evaluation:

```
violation[{"msg": msg, "details": {}}] {
    invalidRegistry
    msg := "Invalid registry"
}
```

This rule will return an empty msg if the registry is valid. It's a good idea to break up your code into code that makes policy decisions and code that responds with feedback. This makes it easier to test, which we'll do next.

Testing an OPA policy

Once we have written our policy, we want to set up an automated test. Just as with testing any other code, it's important that your test cases cover both expected and unexpected input. It's also important to test both positive and negative outcomes. It's not enough to corroborate that our policy allowed a correct registry; we also need to make sure it stops an invalid one. Here are eight test cases for our code:

```
package k8sallowedregistries
test_deployment_registry_allowed {
    not invalidRegistry with input as {"apiVersion"...
}
test_deployment_registry_not_allowed {
    invalidRegistry with input as {"apiVersion"...
}
```

```
test_pod_registry_allowed {
    not invalidRegistry with input as {"apiVersion"...
}
test_pod_registry_not_allowed {
    invalidRegistry with input as {"apiVersion"...
}
test_cronjob_registry_allowed {
    not invalidRegistry with input as {"apiVersion"...
}
test_cronjob_registry_not_allowed {
    invalidRegistry with input as {"apiVersion"...
}
test_error_message_not_allowed {
    control := {"msg":"Invalid registry","details":{}}
    result = violation with input as {"apiVersion":"admissi…
    result[_] == control
}
test_error_message_allowed {
    result = violation with input as {"apiVersion":"admissi…
    result == set()
}
```

There are eight tests in total; two tests to make sure that the proper error message is returned when there's an issue, and six tests covering two use cases for three input types. We're testing simple `Pod` definitions, `Deployment`, and `CronJob`. To validate success or failure as expected, we have included definitions that have `image` attributes that include `docker.io` and `quay.io` for each input type. The code is abbreviated for print, but can be downloaded from `https://github.com/PacktPublishing/Kubernetes---An-Enterprise-Guide-2E/tree/main/chapter8/simple-opa-policy/rego/`.

To run the tests, first install the OPA command-line executable as per the OPA website – `https://www.openpolicyagent.org/docs/latest/#running-opa`. Once downloaded, go to the `simple-opa-policy/rego` directory and run the tests:

```
$ opa test .
data.kubernetes.admission.test_cronjob_registry_not_allowed: FAIL
(248ns)
-----------------------------------------------------------------
PASS: 7/8
FAIL: 1/8
```

Seven of the tests passed, but `test_cronjob_registry_not_allowed` failed. The `CronJob` submitted as `input` should not be allowed because its `image` uses `docker.io`. The reason it snuck through was that `CronJob` objects follow a different pattern to `Pods` and `Deployments`, so our two `input_image` rules won't load any of the container objects from the `CronJob`. The good news is that when the `CronJob` ultimately submits the `Pod`, Gatekeeper will not validate it, thereby preventing it from running. The bad news is that no one will know this until the `Pod` was supposed to be run. Making sure we pick up `CronJob` objects in addition to our other objects with containers in them will make it much easier to debug because the `CronJob` won't be accepted.

To get all tests passing, add a new `input_container` rule to the `limitregistries.rego` file in the GitHub repo that will match the container used by a `CronJob`:

```
input_images[image] {
    image := input.review.object.spec.jobTemplate.spec.template.spec.
containers[_].image
}
```

Now, running the tests will show that everything passes:

```
$ opa test .
PASS: 8/8
```

With a policy that has been tested, the next step is to integrate the policy into Gatekeeper.

Deploying policies to Gatekeeper

The policies we've created need to be deployed to Gatekeeper, which provides Kubernetes custom resources that policies need to be loaded into. The first custom resource is `ConstraintTemplate`, which is where the Rego code for our policy is stored. This object lets us specify parameters in relation to our policy enforcement, and we'll cover this next. To keep things simple, create a template with no parameters:

```
apiVersion: templates.gatekeeper.sh/v1beta1
kind: ConstraintTemplate
metadata:
  name: k8sallowedregistries
spec:
  crd:
    spec:
      names:
```

```
   kind: K8sAllowedRegistries
   validation: {}
targets:
  - target: admission.k8s.gatekeeper.sh
    rego: |
      package k8sallowedregistries

      .

      .

      .
```

The entire source code for this template is available at `https://raw.githubusercontent.com/PacktPublishing/Kubernetes---An-Enterprise-Guide-2E/main/chapter8/simple-opa-policy/yaml/gatekeeper-policy-template.yaml`.

Once created, the next step is to apply the policy by creating a constraint based on the template. Constraints are objects in Kubernetes based on the configuration of `ConstraintTemplate`. Notice that our template defines a custom resource definition. This gets added to the `constraints.gatekeeper.sh` API group. If you look at the list of CRDs on your cluster, you'll see `k8sallowedregistries` listed:

```
PS C:\Users\mlb> kubectl get crds
NAME                                                          CREATED AT
bgpconfigurations.crd.projectcalico.org                       2020-07-04T17:14:08Z
bgppeers.crd.projectcalico.org                                2020-07-04T17:14:08Z
blockaffinities.crd.projectcalico.org                         2020-07-04T17:14:06Z
clusterinformations.crd.projectcalico.org                     2020-07-04T17:14:08Z
configs.config.gatekeeper.sh                                  2020-07-04T17:45:26Z
constraintpodstatuses.status.gatekeeper.sh                    2020-07-04T17:45:26Z
constrainttemplatepodstatuses.status.gatekeeper.sh           2020-07-04T17:45:26Z
constrainttemplates.templates.gatekeeper.sh                   2020-07-04T17:45:26Z
felixconfigurations.crd.projectcalico.org                     2020-07-04T17:14:06Z
globalnetworkpolicies.crd.projectcalico.org                   2020-07-04T17:14:08Z
globalnetworksets.crd.projectcalico.org                       2020-07-04T17:14:08Z
hostendpoints.crd.projectcalico.org                           2020-07-04T17:14:08Z
ipamblocks.crd.projectcalico.org                              2020-07-04T17:14:06Z
ipamconfigs.crd.projectcalico.org                             2020-07-04T17:14:07Z
ipamhandles.crd.projectcalico.org                             2020-07-04T17:14:06Z
                                                              2020-07-04T17:14:08Z
k8sallowedregistries.constraints.gatekeeper.sh                2020-07-06T11:09:46Z
                                                              2020-07-04T17:14:08Z
networksets.crd.projectcalico.org                             2020-07-04T17:14:08Z
oidc-sessions.openunison.tremolo.io                           2020-07-04T17:20:20Z
openunisons.openunison.tremolo.io                             2020-07-04T17:20:20Z
users.openunison.tremolo.io                                   2020-07-04T17:20:20Z
PS C:\Users\mlb>
```

Figure 8.3: CRD created by ConstraintTemplate

Creating the constraint means creating an instance of the object defined in the template.

To keep from causing too much havoc in our cluster, we're going to restrict this policy to the openunison namespace:

```
apiVersion: constraints.gatekeeper.sh/v1beta1
kind: K8sAllowedRegistries
metadata:
  name: restrict-openunison-registries
spec:
  match:
    kinds:
      - apiGroups: [""]
        kinds: ["Pod"]
      - apiGroups: ["apps"]
        kinds:
        - StatefulSet
        - Deployment
      - apiGroups: ["batch"]
        kinds:
        - CronJob
    namespaces: ["openunison"]
```

The constraint limits the policy we wrote to just Deployment, CronJob, and Pod objects in the openunison namespace. Once created, if we try to kill the openunison-operator Pod, it will fail to successfully be recreated by the replica set controller because the image comes from dockerhub.io, not quay.io:

```
PS C:\Users\mlb> kubectl get pods -n openunison
NAME                                      READY   STATUS      RESTARTS   AGE
check-certs-orchestra-1593914400-pd5f5    0/1     Completed   0          40h
check-certs-orchestra-1594000800-zxjxr    0/1     Completed   0          16h
openunison-operator-858d496-5p4dm         1/1     Running     0          7h
openunison-orchestra-57489869d4-f46rm     1/1     Running     0          2d
PS C:\Users\mlb> kubectl delete pod -l app=openunison-operator -n openunison
pod "openunison-operator-858d496-5p4dm" deleted
PS C:\Users\mlb> kubectl get pods -n openunison
NAME                                      READY   STATUS      RESTARTS   AGE
check-certs-orchestra-1593914400-pd5f5    0/1     Completed   0          40h
check-certs-orchestra-1594000800-zxjxr    0/1     Completed   0          16h
openunison-orchestra-57489869d4-f46rm     1/1     Running     0          2d
PS C:\Users\mlb> kubectl get events -n openunison
LAST SEEN   TYPE      REASON        OBJECT                                      MESSAGE
26s         Normal    Killing       pod/openunison-operator-858d496-5p4dm       Stopping container openunison-operator
8s          Warning   FailedCreate  replicaset/openunison-operator-858d496      Error creating: admission webhook "validat
ion.gatekeeper.sh" denied the request: [denied by restrict-openunison-registries] Invalid registry
PS C:\Users\mlb>
```

Figure 8.4: Pod fails to create because of Gatekeeper policy

Next, look at the policy object. You will see that there are several violations in the status section of the object:

```
totalViolations: 6
violations:
- enforcementAction: deny
  kind: CronJob
  message: Invalid registry
  name: check-certs-orchestra
  namespace: openunison
- enforcementAction: deny
  kind: Deployment
  message: Invalid registry
  name: openunison-operator
  namespace: openunison
- enforcementAction: deny
  kind: Deployment
  message: Invalid registry
  name: openunison-orchestra
  namespace: openunison
- enforcementAction: deny
  kind: Pod
  message: Invalid registry
  name: check-certs-orchestra-1593914400-pd5f5
  namespace: openunison
- enforcementAction: deny
  kind: Pod
  message: Invalid registry
  name: check-certs-orchestra-1594000800-zxjxr
  namespace: openunison
- enforcementAction: deny
  kind: Pod
  message: Invalid registry
  name: openunison-orchestra-57489869d4-f46rm
  namespace: openunison
```

Figure 8.5: List of objects that violate the image registry policy

Having deployed your first Gatekeeper policy, you may quickly notice it has a few issues. The first is that the registry is hardcoded. This means that we'd need to replicate our code for every change of registry. It's also not flexible for the namespace. All of Tremolo Security's images are stored in `docker.io/tremolosecurity`, so instead of limiting a specific registry server, we may want flexibility for each namespace and to allow multiple registries. Next, we'll update our policies to provide this flexibility.

Building dynamic policies

Our current registry policy is limiting. It is static and only supports a single registry. Both Rego and Gatekeeper provide functionality to build a dynamic policy that can be reused in our cluster and configured based on individual namespace requirements. This gives us one code base to work from and debug instead of having to maintain repetitive code. The code we're going to use is in `https://github.com/packtpublishing/Kubernetes---An-Enterprise-Guide-2E/blob/main/chapter8/parameter-opa-policy/`.

When inspecting `rego/limitregistries.rego`, the main difference between the code in `parameter-opa-policy` and `simple-opa-policy` comes down to the `invalidRegistry` rule:

```
invalidRegistry {
   ok_images = [image | startswith(input_images[i],input.parameters.
registries[_]) ; image = input_images[i] ]
   count(ok_images) != count(input_images)
}
```

The goal of the first line of the rule is to determine which images come from approved registries using a comprehension. Comprehensions provide a way to build out sets, arrays, and objects based on some logic. In this case, we want to only add images to the `ok_images` array that start with any of the allowed registries from `input.parameters.registries`.

To read a comprehension, start with the type of brace. Ours starts with a square bracket, so the result will be an array. Objects and sets can also be generated. The word between the open bracket and the pipe character (|) is called the head and this is the variable that will be added to our array if the right conditions are met. Everything to the right of the pipe character (|) is a set of rules used to determine what `image` should be and if it should have a value at all. If any of the statements in the rule resolve to undefined or false, the execution exits for that iteration.

The first rule of our comprehension is where most of the work is done. The `startswith` function is used to determine whether each of our images starts with the correct registry name. Instead of passing two strings to the function, we instead pass arrays. The first array has a variable we haven't declared yet, `i`, and the other uses an underscore (_) where the index would usually be. The `i` is interpreted by Rego as "do this for each value in the array, incrementing by 1, and let it be referenced throughout the comprehension." The underscore is shorthand in Rego for "do this for all values." Since we specified two arrays, every combination of the two arrays will be used as input to the `startswith` function.

That means that if there are two containers and three potential pre-approved registries, then `startswith` will be called six times. When any of the combinations return `true` from `startswith`, the next rule is executed. That sets the `image` variable to `input_image` with index `i`, which then means that image is added to `ok_images`. The same code in Java would look something like the following:

```java
ArrayList<String> okImages = new ArrayList<String>();
for (int i=0;i<inputImages.length;i++) {
  for (int j=0;j<registries.length;j++) {
    if (inputImages[i].startsWith(registries[j])) {
      okImages.add(inputImages[i]);
    }
  }
}
```

One line of Rego eliminated seven lines of mostly boilerplate code.

The second line of the rule compares the number of entries in the `ok_images` array with the number of known container images. If they are equal, we know that every container contains a valid image.

With our updated Rego rules for supporting multiple registries, the next step is to deploy a new policy template (if you haven't done so already, delete the old `k8sallowedregistries` `ConstraintTemplate` and `restrict-openunison-registries` `K8sAllowedRegistries`). Here's our updated `ConstraintTemplate`:

```yaml
apiVersion: templates.gatekeeper.sh/v1beta1
kind: ConstraintTemplate
metadata:
  name: k8sallowedregistries
spec:
  crd:
    spec:
      names:
        kind: K8sAllowedRegistries
      validation:
        openAPIV3Schema:
          properties:
            registries:
              type: array
              items: string
  targets:
    - target: admission.k8s.gatekeeper.sh
      rego: |
        package k8sallowedregistries
```

.

.

.

Beyond including our new rules, the highlighted section shows that we added a schema to our template. This will allow for the template to be reused with specific parameters. This schema goes into the CustomResourceDefinition that will be created and is used to validate input for the K8sAllowedRegistries objects we'll create in order to enforce our pre-authorized registry lists.

Finally, let's create our policy for the openunison namespace. Since the only containers that are running in this namespace should come from Tremolo Security's dockerhub.io registry, we'll limit all Pods to docker.io/tremolosecurity/ using the following policy:

```
apiVersion: constraints.gatekeeper.sh/v1beta1
kind: K8sAllowedRegistries
metadata:
  name: restrict-openunison-registries
spec:
  match:
    kinds:
      - apiGroups: [""]
        kinds: ["Pod"]
      - apiGroups: ["apps"]
        kinds:
        - StatefulSet
        - Deployment
      - apiGroups: ["batch"]
        kinds:
        - CronJob
    namespaces: ["openunison"]
  parameters:
    registries: ["docker.io/tremolosecurity/"]
```

Unlike our previous version, this policy specifies which registries are valid instead of embedding the policy data directly into our Rego. With our policies in place, let's try to run the busybox container in the openunison namespace to get a shell:

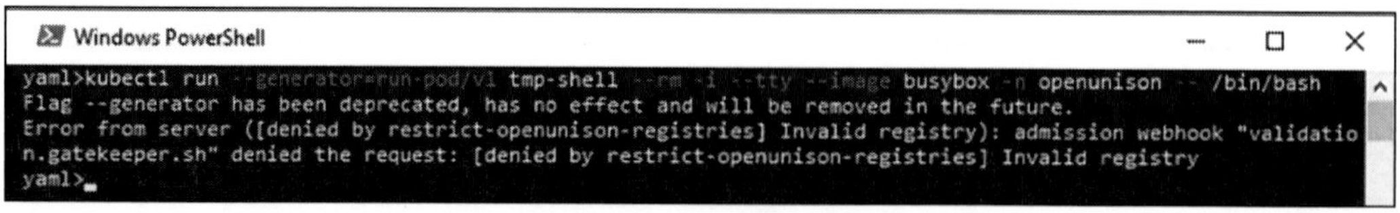

```
Windows PowerShell                                                        —   □   ×
yaml>kubectl run --generator=run-pod/v1 tmp-shell --rm -i --tty --image busybox -n openunison -- /bin/bash
Flag --generator has been deprecated, has no effect and will be removed in the future.
Error from server ([denied by restrict-openunison-registries] Invalid registry): admission webhook "validatio
n.gatekeeper.sh" denied the request: [denied by restrict-openunison-registries] Invalid registry
yaml>
```

Figure 8.6: Failed busybox shell

Using this generic policy template, we can restrict which registries the namespaces are able to pull from. As an example, in a multi-tenant environment, you may want to restrict all Pods to the owner's own registry. If a namespace is being used for a commercial product, you can stipulate that only that vendor's containers can run in it. Before moving on to other use cases, it's important to understand how to debug your code and handle Rego's quirks.

Debugging Rego

Debugging Rego can be challenging. Unlike more generic programming languages such as Java or Go, there's no way to step through code in a debugger. Take the example of the generic policy we just wrote for checking registries. All the work was done in a single line of code. Stepping through it wouldn't do much good.

To make Rego easier to debug, the OPA project provides a trace of all failed tests when verbose output is set on the command line. This is another great reason to use OPA's built-in testing tools.

To make better use of this trace, Rego has a function called trace that accepts a string. Combining this function with sprintf lets you more easily track where your code is not working as expected. In the chapter8/parameter-opa-policy-fail/rego directory, there's a test that will fail. There is also an invalidRegistry rule with multiple trace options added:

```
invalidRegistry {
  trace(sprintf("input_images : %v",[input_images]))
  ok_images = [image |
    trace(sprintf("image %v",[input_images[j]]))
    startswith(input_images[j],input.parameters.registries[_]) ;
    image = input_images[j]
  ]
  trace(sprintf("ok_images %v",[ok_images]))
  trace(sprintf("ok_images size %v / input_images size %v",[count(ok_
images),count(input_images)]))
  count(ok_images) != count(input_images)
}
```

When the test is run, OPA will output a detailed trace of every comparison and code path. Wherever it encounters the trace function, a "note" is added to the trace. This is the equivalent of adding print statements in your code to debug. The output of the OPA trace is very verbose, and far too much text to include in print. Running opa test . -v in this directory will give you the full trace you can use to debug your code.

Using existing policies

Before moving into more advanced use cases for OPA and Gatekeeper, it's important to understand the implications of how OPA is built and used. If you inspect the code we worked through in the previous section, you might notice that we aren't checking for an `initContainer`. We're only looking for the primary containers. An `initContainer` is a special container that is run before the containers listed in a `Pod` are expected to end. They're often used to prepare the filesystem of a volume mount and for other "initial" tasks that should be performed before the containers of a `Pod` have run. If a bad actor tried to launch a `Pod` with an `initContainer` that pulls in a Bitcoin miner (or worse), our policy wouldn't stop it.

It's important to be very detailed in the design and implementation of policies. One of the ways to make sure you're not missing something when building policies is to use policies that already exist and have been tested. The Gatekeeper project maintains several libraries of pre-tested policies and how to use them in its GitHub repo at `https://github.com/open-policy-agent/gatekeeper-library`. Before attempting to build one of your own policies, see whether one already exists there first.

This section provided an overview of Rego and how it works in policy evaluation. It didn't cover everything, but should give you a good point of reference for working with Rego's documentation. Next, we'll learn how to build policies that rely on data from outside our request, such as other objects in our cluster.

Enforcing memory constraints

So far in this chapter, we've built policies that are self-contained. When checking whether an image is coming from a pre-authorized registry, the only data we needed was from the policy and the containers. This is often not enough information to make a policy decision. In this section, we'll work on building a policy that relies on other objects in your cluster to make policy decisions.

Before diving into the implementation, let's talk about the use case. It's a good idea to include at least memory requirements on any `Pod` submitted to the API server. There are certain namespaces though where this doesn't make as much sense. For instance, many of the containers in the `kube-system` namespace don't have CPU and memory resource requests.

There are multiple ways we could handle this. One way is to deploy a constraint template and apply it to every namespace we want to enforce memory resource requests on. This can lead to repetitive objects or require us to explicitly update policies to apply them to certain namespaces.

Another method is to add a label to the namespace that lets OPA know it needs all `Pod` objects to have memory resource requests. Since Kubernetes already has `ResourceQuota` objects for managing memory, we can also establish whether a namespace has a `ResourceQuota` and, if it does, then we know there should be memory requests.

For our next example, we'll write a policy that says any `Pod` created in a namespace that has a `ResourceQuota` must have a memory resource request. The policy itself should be pretty simple. The pseudocode will look something like this:

```
if (hasResourceQuota(input.review.object.metdata.namespace) &&
containers.resource.requests.memory == null) {
    generate error;
}
```

The hard part here is understanding if the namespace has a `ResourceQuota`. Kubernetes has an API, which you could query, but that would mean either embedding a secret into the policy so it can talk to the API server or allowing anonymous access. Neither of those options is a good idea. Another issue with querying the API server is that it's difficult to automate testing since you are now reliant on an API server being available wherever you run your tests.

We discussed earlier that OPA can replicate data from the API server in its own database. Gatekeeper uses this functionality to create a "cache" of objects that can be tested against. Once this cache is populated, we can replicate it locally to provide test data for our policy testing.

Enabling the Gatekeeper cache

The Gatekeeper cache is enabled by creating a `Config` object in the `gatekeeper-system` namespace. Add this configuration to your cluster:

```yaml
apiVersion: config.gatekeeper.sh/v1alpha1
kind: Config
metadata:
  name: config
  namespace: "gatekeeper-system"
spec:
  sync:
    syncOnly:
      - group: ""
        version: "v1"
        kind: "Namespace"
```

```
- group: ""
  version: "v1"
  kind: "ResourceQuota"
```

This will begin replicating `Namespace` and `ResourceQuota` objects in Gatekeeper's internal OPA database. Let's create a `Namespace` with a `ResourceQuota` and one without a `ResourceQuota`:

```
apiVersion: v1
kind: Namespace
metadata:
  name: ns-with-no-quota
spec: {}
---
apiVersion: v1
kind: Namespace
metadata:
  name: ns-with-quota
spec: {}
---
kind: ResourceQuota
apiVersion: v1
metadata:
  name: memory-quota
  namespace: ns-with-quota
spec:
  hard:
    requests.memory: 1G
    limits.memory: 1G
```

After a moment, the data should be in the OPA database and ready to query.

 The Gatekeeper service account has read access to everything in your cluster with its default installation. This includes secret objects. Be careful what you replicate in Gatekeeper's cache as there are no security controls from inside a Rego policy. Your policy could very easily log secret object data if you are not careful. Also, make sure to control who has access to the `gatekeeper-system` namespace. Anyone who gets hold of the service account's token can use it to read any data in your cluster.

Mocking up test data

In order to automate the testing of our policy, we need to create test data. In the previous examples, we used data injected into the `input` variable. Cache data is stored in the `data` variable. Specifically, in order to access our resource quota, we need to access `data.inventory.namespace["ns-with-quota"]["v1"]` `["ResourceQuota"]["memory-quota"]`. This is the standard way for you to query data from Rego in Gatekeeper. Just as we did with the input, we can inject a mocked-up version of this data by creating a data object. Here's what our JSON will look like:

```json
{
    "inventory": {
        "namespace":{
            "ns-with-no-quota" : {},
            "ns-with-quota":{
                "v1":{
                    "ResourceQuota": {
                        "memory-quota":{
                            "kind": "ResourceQuota",
                            "apiVersion": "v1",
                            "metadata": {
                                "name": "memory-quota",
                                "namespace": "ns-with-quota"
                            },
                            "spec": {
                                "hard": {
                                "requests.memory": "1G",
                                "limits.memory": "1G"
                            }}}}}}}}
```

When you look at `chapter8/enforce-memory-request/rego/enforcememory_test.` `rego`, you'll see the tests have `with input as {…} with data as {…}` with the preceding document as our control data. This lets us test our policies with data that would exist in GateKeeper without having to deploy our code in a cluster.

Building and deploying our policy

Just as before, we've written test cases prior to writing our policy. Next, we'll examine our policy:

```
package k8senforcememoryrequests
violation[{"msg": msg, "details": {}}] {
   invalidMemoryRequests
```

```
    msg := "No memory requests specified"
}
invalidMemoryRequests {
    data.inventory.namespace[input.review.object.metadata.namespace]
["v1"]["ResourceQuota"]
    containers := input.review.object.spec.containers
    ok_containers = [ok_container |
      containers[j].resources.requests.memory ;
      ok_container = containers[j]  ]

    count(containers) != count(ok_containers)
}
```

This code should look familiar. It follows a similar pattern as our earlier policies. The first rule, `violation`, is the standard reporting rule for Gatekeeper. The second rule is where we test our `Pod`. The first line will fail and exit out if the namespace for the specified `Pod` doesn't contain a `ResourceQuota` object. The next line loads all of the containers of the `Pod`. After this, a composition is used to construct a list of containers that has memory requests specified. Finally, the rule will only succeed if the number of compliant containers doesn't match the total number of containers. If `invalidMemoryRequests` succeeds, this means that one or more containers does not have memory requests specified. This will force `msg` to be set and `violation` to inform the user of the issue.

To deploy, add `chapter8/enforce-memory-request/yaml/gatekeeper-policy-template.yaml` and `chapter8/enforce-memory-request/yaml/gatekeeper-policy.yaml` to your cluster. To test this, create a `Pod` without memory requests in both our `ns-with-quota` and `ns-with-no-quota` namespaces:

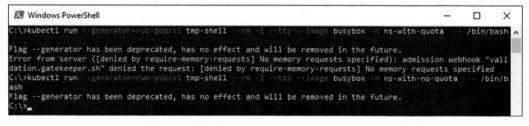

Figure 8.7: Creating pods without memory requests

The first attempt to create a `Pod` in the `ns-with-quota` namespace fails because our `require-memory-requests` policy rejected it since `ns-with-quota` has a `ResourceQuota` in it. The second attempt succeeds because it is running in a namespace with no `ResourceQuota`.

Most of this chapter has been spent writing policies. The final use case for OPA will focus on using Gatekeeper's prebuilt policies to replace Pod security policies.

Mutating objects and default values

To this point, everything we have discussed has been about how to use Gatekeeper to enforce a policy. Kubernetes has another feature called mutating admission webhooks that allow a webhook to change, or mutate, an object before the API server processes it and runs validating admission controllers.

A common usage of a mutating webhook is to explicitly set security context information on pods that don't have it set. For instance, if you create a Pod with no `spec.securityContext.runAsUser` then the Pod will run as the user the Docker container was built to run as using the `USER` directive (or root by default) when it was built. This is insecure, since it means you could be running as root, especially if the container in question is from Docker Hub. While you can have a policy that blocks running as root, you could also have a mutating webhook that will set a default user ID if it's not specified to make it a default. This makes for a better developer experience because now, as a developer, I don't have to worry about which user my container was built to run as so long as it was designed to work with any user.

This brings up a common question of defaults vs explicit configuration. There are two schools of thought. The first is that you should provide sane defaults wherever possible to minimize what developers have to know to get a typical workload running. This creates consistency and makes it easier to spot outliers. The other school of thought is to require explicit configuration of security contexts so that it's known looking at a glance what the workload expects. This can make auditing easier, especially if paired with GitOps to manage your manifests, but creates quite a bit of repetitive YAML.

I'm personally a fan of sane defaults. The vast majority of workloads will not require any privilege and should be treated as such. It doesn't mean you don't still need enforcement, just that it's a better experience for your developers. It also makes it easier to make global changes. Want to change the default user ID or security context? You make the change in your mutating webhook instead of across tens, hundreds, or even thousands of manifests. Most of Kubernetes is built this way. You don't create `Pod` objects directly; you create `Deployments` and `StatefulSets` with controllers that create `Pods`. Going back to our discussions on RBAC, aggregate roles work this way too. Instead of creating a massive `ClusterRole` for namespace administrators, Kubernetes uses a controller to generate the `ClusterRole` dynamically based on label selectors, making it easier to maintain. In my experience, this example should be applied to security defaults as well.

Gatekeeper's mutation support is in alpha when this book is being published. Its mutation isn't built on Rego the way its validation policies are. While you can write mutating webhooks in Rego, and I can say this from experience, it's not well suited to it. What makes Rego a great policy definition language makes it very hard to build mutations.

Now that we know what mutations are useful for and that we can use Gatekeeper, let's build a mutation that will configure all containers to run as a default user if none is specified. First, we'll update Gatekeeper to run mutations:

```
kubectl apply -f https://raw.githubusercontent.com/open-policy-agent/
gatekeeper/release-3.5/deploy/experimental/gatekeeper-mutation.yaml
```

This will redeploy Gatekeeper with mutation enabled. Now, we can deploy the policy in `chapter8/defaultUser/addDefaultUser.yaml`:

```
apiVersion: mutations.gatekeeper.sh/v1alpha1
kind: Assign
metadata:
  name: default-user
spec:
  applyTo:
  - groups: [""]
    kinds: ["Pod"]
    versions: ["v1"]
  match:
    scope: Namespaced
    excludedNamespaces:
    - kube-system
  location: "spec.securityContext.runAsUser"
  parameters:
    assign:
      value:  70391
    pathTests:
      - subPath: "spec.securityContext.runAsUser"
        condition: MustNotExist
```

Let's walk through this mutation. The first part of the `spec`, `applyTo`, tells Gatekeeper what objects you want this mutation to act on. For us, we want it to work on all `Pods`.

The next section, `match`, gives you the chance to specify conditions on which Pods we want the mutation to apply to. In our case we're applying to all of them except in the `kube-system` namespace. In general, I tend to avoid making changes to anything in the `kube-system` namespace because it's the domain of whoever is managing your clusters.

Making changes there can have permanent impacts on your cluster. In addition to specifying which namespaces you don't want to apply your mutation to, you can also specify additional conditions:

- `kind` – What kind of object to match on
- `labelSelectors` – Labels on the object that must match
- `namespaces` – List of namespaces to apply the mutation policy to
- `namespaceSelector` – Labels on the container namespaces

We'll talk more about label matching in *Chapter 9, Node Security with GateKeeper.*

After defining how to match objects to mutate we specify what mutation to perform. For us, we want to set `spec.securityContext.runAsUser` to a randomly chosen user ID if one isn't specified. The last part, `pathTests`, is what lets us set this value if the `spec.securityContext.runAsUser` isn't already set.

Once you've applied your mutation policy, verify that the OpenUnison operator isn't running as a specific user:

```
kubectl get pods -l app=openunison-operator -o jsonpath='{.items[0].
spec.securityContext}' -n openunison
{}
```

Now, delete the operator pod and check again:

```
kubectl delete pods -l app=openunison-operator -n openunison
pod "openunison-operator-f87f994b6-zfts5" deleted
kubectl get pods -l app=openunison-operator -o jsonpath='{.items[0].
spec.securityContext}' -n openunison
{"runAsUser":70391}
```

Our operator is now running as user `70391`! Now, let's edit our deployment so that the user is set the user identity:

```
kubectl patch deployment openunison-operator --patch '{"spec":{"templat
e":{"spec":{"securityContext":{"runAsUser":19307}}}}}' -n openunison
deployment.apps/openunison-operator patched
kubectl get pods -l app=openunison-operator -o jsonpath='{.items[0].
spec.securityContext}' -n openunison
{"runAsUser":19307}
```

Our mutation didn't apply because we already had a user specified in our Deployment object.

One last note on setting values: you'll often find that you want to set a value for an object in a list. For instance, you may want to create a policy that will set any container as unprivileged unless specifically set to be privileged. In `chapter8/defaultUser/yaml/setUnprivileged.yaml` our `location` (and `subPath`) have changed:

```
location: "spec.containers[image:*].securityContext.privileged"
```

This reads as "match all objects in the list `spec.containers` that have an attribute called `image`." Since every container must have an image, this will match on all containers. Apply this object and test it out again on the OpenUnison operator:

```
kubectl get pods -l app=openunison-operator -o jsonpath='{.items[0].
spec.containers[0].securityContext}' -n openunison

kubectl delete pods -l app=openunison-operator -n openunison
pod "openunison-operator-96759f67-qklnd" deleted
kubectl get pods -l app=openunison-operator -o jsonpath='{.items[0].
spec.containers[0].securityContext}' -n openunison
{"privileged":false}
```

Now our Pod is marked as unprivileged!

In this section we looked at how you can set defaults using Gatekeeper's built-in mutation support. We discussed the benefits of mutating webhooks that set defaults, enabled Gatekeeper's support for mutations, and built policies that set a default user identity and disable privileged containers. Using what you've learned in this section you can use Gatekeeper not only to enforce your policies but also to set sane defaults to make compliance easier for your developers.

Summary

In this chapter, we explored how to use Gatekeeper as a dynamic admission controller to provide additional authorization policies on top of Kubernetes' built-in RBAC capabilities. We looked at how Gatekeeper and OPA are architected. Then, we learned how to build, deploy, and test policies in Rego. Finally, you were shown how to use Gatekeeper's built-in mutation support to create default configuration options in pods.

Extending Kubernetes' policies leads to a stronger security profile in your clusters and provides greater confidence in the integrity of the workloads you are running.

Using Gatekeeper can also help catch previously missed policy violations through its application of continuous audits. Using these capabilities will provide a stronger foundation for your cluster.

This chapter focused on whether or not to launch a Pod based on our specific policies. In the next chapter, we'll learn how to protect your nodes from the processes running in those Pods.

Questions

1. Are OPA and Gatekeeper the same thing?

    a. Yes

    b. No

2. How is Rego code stored in Gatekeeper?

    a. It is stored as ConfigMap objects that are watched

    b. Rego has to be mounted to the Pod

    c. Rego needs to be stored as secret objects

    d. Rego is saved as a ConstraintTemplate

3. How do you test Rego policies?

    a. In production

    b. Using an automated framework built directly into OPA

    c. By first compiling to WebAssembly

4. In Rego, how do you write a for loop?

    a. You don't need to; Rego will identify iterative steps.

    b. By using the for all syntax.

    c. By initializing counters in a loop.

    d. There are no loops in Rego.

5. What is the best way to debug Rego policies?

    a. Use an IDE to attach to the Gatekeeper container in a cluster

    b. In production

    c. Add trace functions to your code and run the opa test command with -v to see execution traces

    d. Include System.out statements

6. Constraints all need to be hardcoded.

   a. True

   b. False

7. Gatekeeper can replace Pod security policies.

   a. True

   b. False

Join our book's Discord space

Join the book's Discord workspace for a monthly *Ask me Anything* session with the authors: https://packt.link/K8EntGuide

9
Node Security with GateKeeper

Most of the security discussed so far has focused on protecting Kubernetes APIs. Authentication has meant the authentication of API calls. Authorization has meant authorizing access to certain APIs. Even the discussion on the dashboard centered mostly around how to securely authenticate to the API server by way of the dashboard.

This chapter will be different as we will now shift our focus to securing our nodes. We will learn how to use the GateKeeper project to protect the nodes of a Kubernetes cluster. Our focus will be on how containers run on the nodes of your cluster and how to keep those containers from having more access than they should. We'll get into the details of impacts in this chapter by looking at how exploits can be used to gain access to a cluster when the nodes aren't protected. We'll also explore how these scenarios can be exploited even in code that doesn't need node access.

In this chapter, we will cover the following topics:

- What is node security?
- Enforcing node security with GateKeeper

When done, you'll have a better understanding of how Kubernetes interacts with the nodes that run your workloads and how those nodes can be better protected.

Technical requirements

To follow the examples in this chapter, make sure you have a KinD cluster running with the configuration from *Chapter 8, Extending Security Using Open Policy Agent.*

You can access the code for this chapter at the following GitHub repository: `https://github.com/PacktPublishing/Kubernetes---An-Enterprise-Guide-2E/tree/main/chapter9`.

What is node security?

Each Pod that is launched in your cluster runs on a node. That node could be a VM, a "bare metal" server, or even another kind of compute service that is itself a container. Every process started by a Pod runs on that node, and depending on how it is launched, can have a surprising set of capabilities on that node such as talking to the filesystem, breaking out of the container to get a shell on the node, or even accessing the secrets used by the node to communicate with the API server. It's important to make sure that processes that are going to request special privileges are done so only when authorized and even then, for specific purposes.

Many people have experience with physical and virtual servers, and most know how to secure workloads running on them. Containers need to be considered differently when you talk about securing each workload. To understand why Kubernetes security tools such as the **Open Policy Agent (OPA)** exist, you need to understand how a container is different from a **virtual machine (VM)**.

Understanding the difference between containers and VMs

A container is a lightweight VM is often how containers are described to those new to containers and Kubernetes. While this makes for a simple analogy, from a security standpoint, it's a dangerous comparison. A container at runtime is a process that runs on a node. On a Linux system, these processes are isolated by a series of Linux technologies that limit their visibility to the underlying system.

Go to any node in a Kubernetes cluster and run the `top` command and all of the processes from containers are listed. As an example, even though Kubernetes is running in KinD, running `ps -A -elf | grep java` will show the OpenUnison and operator container processes:

```
4 S k8s       1193507 1193486  1  80   0 - 3446501 -      Oct07 ?
06:50:33 java -classpath /usr/local/openunison/work/webapp/
```

```
WEB-INF/lib/*:/usr/local/openunison/work/webapp/WEB-INF/classes:/
tmp/quartz -Djava.awt.headless=true -Djava.security.egd=file:/dev/./
urandom -DunisonEnvironmentFile=/etc/openunison/ou.env -Djavax.net.ssl.
trustStore=/etc/openunison/cacerts.jks com.tremolosecurity.openunison.
undertow.OpenUnisonOnUndertow /etc/openunison/openunison.yaml
0 S k8s       2734580 2730582  0  80   0 -  1608 pipe_w 13:13 pts/0
00:00:00 grep --color=auto java
```

In contrast, a VM is, as the name implies, a complete virtual system. It emulates its own hardware, has an isolated kernel, and so on. The hypervisor provides isolation for VMs down to the silicon layer, whereas by comparison, there is very little isolation between every container on a node.

There are container technologies that will run a container on their own VM. The container is still just a process.

When containers aren't running, they're simply a "tarball of tarballs," where each layer of the filesystem is stored in a file. The image is still stored on the host system, or multiple host systems, wherever the container has been run or pulled previously.

A "tarball" is a file created by the **tar** Unix command. It can also be compressed.

A VM, on the other hand, has its own virtual disk that stores the entire OS. While there are some very lightweight VM technologies, there's often an order of magnitude difference between the size of a VM and that of a container.

While some people refer to containers as lightweight VMs, that couldn't be further from the truth. They aren't isolated in the same way and require more attention to be paid to the details of how they are run on a node.

From this section, you may think that we are trying to say that containers are not secure. Nothing could be further from the truth. Securing a Kubernetes cluster, and the containers running on it, requires attention to detail and an understanding of how containers differ from VMs. Since so many people do understand VMs, it's easy to attempt to compare them to containers, but doing so puts you at a disadvantage since they are very different technologies.

Once you understand the limitations of a default configuration and the potential dangers that come from it, you can remediate the "issues."

Container breakouts

A container breakout is when the process of your container gets access to the underlying node. Once on the node, an attacker now has access to all the other Pods and any capability the node has in your environment. A breakout can also be a matter of mounting the local filesystem into your container. An example from `https://securekubernetes.com`, originally pointed out by Duffie Cooley, Field CTO at Isovalent, uses a container to mount the local filesystem. Running this on a KinD cluster opens both reads and writes to the node's filesystem:

```
kubectl run r00t --restart=Never -ti --rm --image lol --overrides
'{"spec":{"hostPID": true, "containers":[{"name":"1","image":"alpine","
command":["nsenter","--mount=/proc/1/ns/mnt","--","/bin/bash"],"stdin":
true,"tty":true,"imagePullPolicy":"IfNotPresent","securityContext":{"pr
ivileged":true}}]}}'
If you don't see a command prompt, try pressing Enter.
```

The `run` command in the preceding code started a container that added an option that is key to the example, `hostPID: true`, which allows the container to share the host's process namespace. You may see a few other options, such as `-mount` and a security context setting that sets `privileged` to `true`. All of the options combined will allow us to write to the host's filesystem.

Now that you are in the container, execute the `ls` command to look at the filesystem. Notice how the prompt is `root@r00t:/#`, confirming you are in the container and not on the host:

```
root@r00t:/# ls
bin  boot  build  dev  etc  home  kind  lib  lib32  lib64  libx32
media  mnt  opt  proc  root  run  sbin  srv  sys  tmp  usr  var
```

To prove that we have mapped the host's filesystem to our container, create a file called `this_is_from_a_container` and exit the container:

```
root@r00t:/# touch this_is_from_a_container
root@r00t:/# exit
```

Finally, let's look at the host's filesystem to see whether the container created the file. Since we are running KinD with a single worker node, we need to use Docker to `exec` into the worker node. If you are using the KinD cluster from the book, the worker node is called `cluster01-worker`:

```
docker exec -ti cluster01-worker ls /
bin  boot  build  dev  etc  home  kind  lib  lib32  lib64  libx32
media  mnt  opt  proc  root  run  sbin  srv  sys  this_is_from_a_
container  tmp  usr  var
```

There it is! In this example, a container was run that mounted the local filesystem. From inside the pod, the `this_is_from_a_container` file was created. After exiting the pod and entering the node container, the file was there. Once an attacker has access to the node's filesystem, they also have access to the kubelet's credentials, which can open the entire cluster up.

It's not hard to envision a string of events that can lead to a Bitcoin miner (or worse) running on a cluster. A phishing attack gets the credentials a developer is using for their cluster. Even though those credentials only have access to one namespace, a container is created to get the kubelet's credentials, and from there, containers are launched to stealthily deploy miners across the environment. There are certainly multiple mitigations that could be used to prevent this attack, including the following:

- Multi-factor authentication, which would have kept the phished credentials from being used
- Pre-authorizing only certain containers
- A GateKeeper policy, which would have prevented this attack by stopping a container from running as `privileged`
- A properly secured image

We've already talked about authentication in previous chapters and the importance of multi-factor authentication. We even used port forwarding to set up a miner through our dashboard! This is another example of why authentication is such an important topic in Kubernetes.

The next two approaches listed can be done using GateKeeper. We covered pre-authorizing containers and registries in *Chapter 8, Extending Security Using Open Policy Agent*. This chapter will focus on using GateKeeper to enforce node-centric policies, such as whether a Pod should be privileged.

Finally, at the core of security is a properly designed image. In the case of physical machines and VMs, this is accomplished by securing the base OS. When you install an OS, you don't select every possible option during installation. It is considered poor practice to have anything running on a server that is not required for its role or function. This same practice needs to be carried over to the images that will run on your clusters, which should only contain the necessary binaries that are required for your application.

Given how important it is to properly secure images on your cluster, the next section explores container design from a security standpoint. While not directly related to GateKeeper's policy enforcement, it's an important starting point for node security. It's also important to understand how to build containers securely in order to better debug and manage your node security policies. Building a locked-down container makes managing the security of the nodes much easier.

Properly designing containers

Before exploring how to protect your nodes using GateKeeper, it's important to address how containers are designed. Often, the hardest part of using a policy to mitigate attacks on the node is the fact that so many containers are built and run as root. Once a restricted policy is applied, the container won't start on reload even if it was running fine after the policy was applied. This is problematic at multiple levels. System administrators have learned over the decades of networked computing not to run processes as root, especially services such as web servers that are accessed anonymously over untrusted networks.

All networks should be considered "untrusted." Assuming all networks are hostile leads to a more secure approach to implementation. It also means that services that need security need to be authenticated. This concept is called zero trust. It has been used and advocated by identity experts for years but was popularized in the DevOps and cloud-native worlds by Google's BeyondCorp whitepaper (`https://cloud.google.com/beyondcorp`). The concept of zero trust should apply inside your clusters too!

Bugs in code can lead to access to underlying compute resources, which can then lead to breakouts from a container. Running as root in a privileged container when not needed can lead to a breakout if exploited via a code bug.

The Equifax breach in 2017 used a bug in the Apache Struts web application framework to run code on the server that was then used to infiltrate and extract data. Had this vulnerable web application been running on Kubernetes with a privileged container, the bug could have led to the attackers gaining access to the cluster.

When building containers, at a minimum, the following should be observed:

- **Run as a user other than root**: The vast majority of applications, especially microservices, don't need root. Don't run as root.

- **Only write to volumes**: If you don't write to a container, you don't need write access. Volumes can be controlled by Kubernetes. If you need to write temporary data, use an `emptyVolume` object instead of writing to the container's filesystem.

- **Minimize binaries in your container**: This can be tricky. There are those that advocate for "distro-less" containers that only contain the binary for the application, statically compiled. No shells, no tools. This can be problematic when trying to debug why an application isn't running as expected. It's a delicate balance.

- **Scan containers for known Common Vulnerability Exposures (CVEs); rebuild often**: One of the benefits of a container is that it can be easily scanned for known CVEs. There are several tools and registries that will do this for you. Once CVEs have been patched, rebuild. A container that hasn't been rebuilt in months, or years even, is every bit as dangerous as a server that hasn't been patched.

> Scanning for CVEs is a standard way to report security issues. Application and OS vendors will update CVEs with patches to their code that fix the issues. This information is then used by security scanning tools to act on when a container has a known issue that has been patched.

At the time of writing, the most restrictive defaults for any Kubernetes distribution on the market belong to Red Hat's OpenShift. In addition to sane default policies, OpenShift runs pods with a random user ID, unless the pod definition specifies an ID.

It's a good idea to test your containers on OpenShift, even if it's not your distribution for production use. If a container will run on OpenShift, it's likely to work with almost any security policy a cluster can throw at it. The easiest way to do this is with Red Hat's CodeReady Containers (`https://developers.redhat.com/products/codeready-containers`). This tool can run on your local laptop and launches a minimal OpenShift environment that can be used for testing containers.

> While OpenShift has very tight security controls out of the box, it doesn't use **Pod Security Policies** (**PSPs**) or GateKeeper. It has its own policy system that pre-dates PSPs, called **Security Context Constraints** (**SCCs**). SCCs are similar to PSPs but don't use RBAC for associating with pods.

Enforcing node security with GateKeeper

So far, we've seen what can happen when containers are allowed to run on a node without any security policies in place. We've also examined what goes into building a secure container, which will make enforcing node security much easier. The next step is to examine how to design and build policies using GateKeeper to lock down your containers.

What about Pod security policies?

Doesn't Kubernetes have a built-in mechanism for enforcing node security? It does, but it's going away. In 2018, the Kubernetes project decided that the PSP API would never leave beta. The configuration was too confusing, being a hybrid of Linux-focused configuration options and RBAC assignments. It was determined that the fix would likely mean an incompatible final release from the current release. Instead of marking a complex and difficult-to-manage API as generally available, the project made a difficult decision to deprecate the API.

At the time, it was stated that the PSP API would not be removed until a replacement was ready for release. This changed in 2020 when the project adopted a new policy that no API can stay in beta for more than three releases. This forced the project to re-evaluate how to move forward with replacing PSPs. In April 2021, Tabitha Sable wrote a blog post on the future of PSPs (`https://kubernetes.io/blog/2021/04/06/ podsecuritypolicy-deprecation-past-present-and-future/`). The short version is that they are officially deprecated as of 1.21 and will be removed in 1.25. There's a replacement planned for alpha in 1.22.

Since PSPs have been deprecated, and the replacement won't likely be ready for production for at least a year, we thought it would be a good idea to replace this book's implementation of PSPs with GateKeeper. The rest of this chapter will focus on implementing node security using GateKeeper. We'll also point out the differences between using GateKeeper and PSPs to make it easier to migrate your workloads from PSP to GateKeeper.

What are the differences between PSPs and GateKeeper?

Before diving into the implementation of node security with GateKeeper, let's look at how they're different. If you're familiar with PSP, this will be a helpful guide for migrating. If you have never worked with PSPs, this can give you a good idea as to where to look when things don't work as expected.

The one area that both PSPs and GateKeeper have in common is that they're implemented as admission controllers. As we learned in *Chapter 8, Extending Security Using Open Policy Agent*, an admission controller is used to provide additional checks beyond what the API server provides natively. In the case of GateKeeper and PSPs, the admission controller makes sure that the Pod definition has the correct configuration to run with the least privileges needed. This usually means running as a non-root user, limiting access to the host, and so on. If the required security level isn't met, the admission controller fails, stopping the Pod from running.

While both technologies run as admission controllers, they implement their functionality in very different ways. PSPs are applied by first defining a `PodSecurityPolicy` object, and then defining RBAC `Role` and `RoleBinding` objects to allow a `ServiceAccount` to run with a policy. The PSP admission controller would make a decision based on whether the "user" who created the Pod, or the `ServiceAccount` the `Pod` runs as, is authorized based on the RBAC bindings. This led to difficulties in designing and debugging the policy application. It's difficult to authorize if a user can submit a `Pod` because users usually don't create `Pod` objects anymore. They create Deployments or StatefulSets or Jobs. There are then controllers that run with their own `ServiceAccounts` that then create `Pods`. The PSP admission controller never knows who submitted the original object. In the last chapter, we covered how GateKeeper binds policies via namespace and label matching; this doesn't change with node security policies. Later on, we'll do a deep dive into how to assign policies.

In addition to assigning policies differently, GateKeeper and PSPs handle overlapping policies differently too. PSPs would try to take the *best* policy based on the account and capabilities being requested. This allowed you to define a high-level blanket policy that denies all privileges and then create specific policies for individual use cases such as letting the Nginx Ingress Controller run on port 443. GateKeeper, on the other hand, requires all policies to pass. There's no such thing as a *best* policy; all policies must pass. This means that you can't apply a blanket policy and then carve out exceptions. You have to explicitly define your policies for each use case.

Another difference between the two approaches is how policies are defined. The PSP specification is a Kubernetes object that is mostly based on Linux's built-in security model. The object itself has been assembled with new properties as needed in an inconsistent way. This led to a confusing object that didn't fit the addition of Windows containers. GateKeeper, on the other hand, has a series of policies that have been pre-built and are available from their GitHub repo: `https://github. com/open-policy-agent/gatekeeper-library/tree/master/library/pod-security-policy`. Instead of having one policy, each policy needs to be applied separately.

Finally, the PSP admission controller had some built-in mutations. For instance, if your policy didn't allow root and your Pod didn't define what user to run as, the PSP admission controller would set a user ID of 1. GateKeeper has a mutating capability (which we covered in *Chapter 8, Extending Security Using Open Policy Agent*), but that capability needs to be explicitly configured to set defaults.

Having examined the differences between PSPs and GateKeeper, let's next dive into how to authorize node security policies in your cluster.

Authorizing node security policies

In the previous section, we discussed the differences between authorizing policies between GateKeeper and PSPs. Now we'll look at how to define your authorization model for policies. Before we go too far, we should discuss what we mean by "authorizing policies."

When you create a Pod, usually through a Deployment or StatefulSet, you choose what node-level capabilities you want with settings on your Pod inside of the securityContext sections. You may request specific capabilities or a host mount. GateKeeper examines your Pod definition and decides, or authorizes, that your Pod definition meets the policy's requirements by matching an applicable ConstraintTemplate via its constraint's match section. GateKeeper's match section lets you match on the namespace, kind of object, and labels on the object. At a minimum, you'll want to include namespaces and object types. Labels can be more complicated.

A large part of deciding whether labels are an appropriate way to authorize a policy is based on who can set the labels and why. In a single-tenant cluster, labels are a great way to create constrained deployments. You can define specific constraints that can be applied directly via a label. For instance, you may have an operator in a namespace that you don't want to have access to a host mount but a Pod that does. Creating a policy with specific labels will let you apply more stringent policies to the operator than the Pod.

The risk with this approach lies in multi-tenant clusters where you, as the cluster owner, cannot limit what labels can be applied to a Pod. Kubernetes' RBAC implementation doesn't provide any mechanism for authorizing specific labels. You could implement something using GateKeeper, but that would be 100% custom. Since you can't stop a namespace owner from labeling a Pod, a compromised namespace administrator's account can be used to launch a privileged Pod without there being any checks in place from GateKeeper.

Since labels can't be enforced from a security standpoint, it doesn't really add any value from a security standpoint. If you need to have Pods run with different privilege levels, it's best to split them up among different namespaces.

This way you have an enforceable boundary between node security policies.

In *Chapter 8, Extending Security Using Open Policy Agent*, we learned how to build policies in Rego and deploy them using GateKeeper. In this chapter, we've discussed the importance of securely building images, the differences between PSPs and GateKeeper for node security, and finally how to authorize policies in your clusters. Next, we'll lock down our testing cluster.

Deploying and debugging node security policies

Having gone through much of the theory in building node security policies in GateKeeper, let's dive into locking down our test cluster. The first step is to clean out our cluster. The easiest way to do this is to just remove GateKeeper and redeploy:

```
kubectl delete -f https://raw.githubusercontent.com/open-policy-agent/
gatekeeper/release-3.5/deploy/experimental/gatekeeper-mutation.yaml
kubectl apply -f https://raw.githubusercontent.com/open-policy-agent/
gatekeeper/release-3.5/deploy/experimental/gatekeeper-mutation.yaml
```

Next, we'll want to deploy our node's `ConstraintTemplate` objects. The GateKeeper project builds and maintains a library of templates that replicate the existing `PodSecurityPolicy` object at `https://github.com/open-policy-agent/gatekeeper-library/tree/master/library/pod-security-policy`. For our cluster, we're going to deploy all of the policies except the read-only filesystem seccomp, selinux, apparmor, flexvolume, and host volume policies. I chose to not deploy the read-only filesystem because it's still really common to write to a container's filesystem even though the data is ephemeral, and enforcing this would likely cause more harm than good. The seccomp, apparmor, and selinux policies weren't included because we're running on a KinD cluster. Finally, we ignored the volumes because it's not a feature we plan on worrying about. That said, it's a good idea to look at all these policies to see whether they should be applied to your cluster. The `chapter9` folder has a script that will deploy all our templates for us. Run `chapter9/deploy_gatekeeper_psp_policies.sh`. Once that's done, we have our `ConstraintTemplate` objects deployed, but they're not being enforced because we haven't set up any policy implementation objects. Before we do that, we should set up some sane defaults.

Generating security context defaults

In *Chapter 8, Extending Security Using Open Policy Agent*, we discussed the trade-offs between having a mutating webhook generating sane defaults for your cluster versus explicit configuration.

I'm a fan of sane defaults since it leads to a better developer experience and makes it easier to keep things secure. The GateKeeper project has a set of example mutations for this purpose at `https://github.com/open-policy-agent/gatekeeper-library/tree/master/library/experimental/mutation/pod-security-policy`. For this chapter, I took them and tweaked them a bit. Let's deploy them, and then recreate all our pods so that they have our "sane defaults" in place before rolling out our constraint implementations:

```
kubectl create -f chapter9/default_mutations.yaml
assign.mutations.gatekeeper.sh/k8spspdefaultallowprivilegeescalation
created
assign.mutations.gatekeeper.sh/k8spspfsgroup created
assign.mutations.gatekeeper.sh/k8sprunasnonroot created
assign.mutations.gatekeeper.sh/k8sprunasgroup created
assign.mutations.gatekeeper.sh/k8sprunasuser created
assign.mutations.gatekeeper.sh/k8spspsupplementalgroups created
assign.mutations.gatekeeper.sh/k8spspcapabilities created
sh chapter9/delete_all_pods_except_gatekeeper.sh
activedirectory
pod "apacheds-7bfcccbd8b-ndvpb" deleted
calico-system
pod "calico-kube-controllers-7f58dbcbbd-ckshb" deleted
pod "calico-node-g5cwp" deleted
.
.
.
```

With our pods deleted and recreated, we can check to see whether the pods running in the openunison namespace have a default `securityContext` configuration:

```
kubectl get pod -o jsonpath='{$.items[0].spec.containers[0].
securityContext}' -l app=openunison-operator -n openunison | jq -r
{
  "allowPrivilegeEscalation": false,
  "capabilities": {
    "drop": [
      "all"
    ]
  },
  "runAsGroup": 2000,
  "runAsNonRoot": true,
  "runAsUser": 1000
}
```

Compared with the original OpenUnison operator `Deployment`, the `Pod` now has a `securityContext` that determines what user the container should run as, if it's privileged, and if it needs any special capabilities. If, for some reason, in the future we wanted containers to run as a different process, instead of changing every manifest, we can now change our mutation configuration. Now that our defaults are in place and applied, the next step is to implement instances of our `ConstraintTemplates` to enforce our policies.

Enforcing cluster policies

With our mutations deployed, next we can deploy our constraint implementations. Just as with the `ConstraintTemplate` objects, the GateKeeper project provides example template implementations for each template. I put together a condensed version for this chapter in `chapter9/minimal_gatekeeper_constraints.yaml` that is designed to have a minimum set of privileges across the cluster, ignoring kube-system and calico-system. Deploy this YAML file and wait a few minutes:

```
kubectl apply -f chapter9/minimal_gatekeeper_constraints.yaml
k8spspallowprivilegeescalationcontainer.constraints.gatekeeper.sh/
privilege-escalation-deny-all created
k8spspcapabilities.constraints.gatekeeper.sh/capabilities-drop-all
created
k8spspforbiddensysctls.constraints.gatekeeper.sh/psp-forbid-all-sysctls
created
k8spsphostfilesystem.constraints.gatekeeper.sh/psp-deny-host-filesystem
created
k8spsphostnamespace.constraints.gatekeeper.sh/psp-bloack-all-host-
namespace created
k8spsphostnetworkingports.constraints.gatekeeper.sh/psp-deny-all-host-
network-ports created
k8spspprivilegedcontainer.constraints.gatekeeper.sh/psp-deny-all-
privileged-container created
k8spspprocmount.constraints.gatekeeper.sh/psp-proc-mount-default
created
k8spspallowedusers.constraints.gatekeeper.sh/psp-pods-allowed-user-
ranges created
```

Remember from *Chapter 8, Extending Security Using Open Policy Agent*, that a key feature of GateKeeper over generic OPA is its ability to not just act as a validating webhook, but also audit existing objects against policies. We're waiting so that GateKeeper has a chance to run its audit against our cluster. Audit violations are listed in the `status` of each implementation of each `ConstraintTemplate`.

To make it easier to see how compliant our cluster is, I wrote a small script that will list the number of violations per `ConstraintTemplate`:

```
sh chapter9/show_constraint_violations.sh
k8spspallowedusers.constraints.gatekeeper.sh 8
k8spspallowprivilegeescalationcontainer.constraints.gatekeeper.sh 1
k8spspcapabilities.constraints.gatekeeper.sh 1
k8spspforbiddensysctls.constraints.gatekeeper.sh 0
k8spsphostfilesystem.constraints.gatekeeper.sh 1
k8spsphostnamespace.constraints.gatekeeper.sh 0
k8spsphostnetworkingports.constraints.gatekeeper.sh 1
k8spspprivilegedcontainer.constraints.gatekeeper.sh 0
k8spspprocmount.constraints.gatekeeper.sh 0
k8spspreadonlyrootfilesystem.constraints.gatekeeper.sh null
```

We have several violations. The next step is debugging and correcting them.

Debugging constraint violations

With our constraint implementations in place, we have several violations that need to be remediated. Let's take a look at the privilege escalation policy violation:

```
kubectl get k8spspallowprivilegeescalationcontainer.constraints.
gatekeeper.sh -o jsonpath='{$.items[0].status.violations}' | jq -r
[
  {
    "enforcementAction": "deny",
    "kind": "Pod",
    "message": "Privilege escalation container is not allowed:
controller",
    "name": "ingress-nginx-controller-744f97c4f-msmkz",
    "namespace": "ingress-nginx"
  }
]
```

GateKeeper is telling us that the `ingress-nginx-controller-744f97c4f-msmkz` Pod in the `ingress-nginx` namespace is attempting to elevate its privileges. Looking at its `securityContext` reveals the following:

```
kubectl get pod ingress-nginx-controller-744f97c4f-msmkz -n ingress-
nginx -o jsonpath='{$.spec.containers[0].securityContext}' | jq -r
{
  "allowPrivilegeEscalation": true,
```

```
  "capabilities": {
    "add": [
      "NET_BIND_SERVICE"
    ],
    "drop": [
      "all"
    ]
  },
  "runAsGroup": 2000,
  "runAsNonRoot": true,
  "runAsUser": 101
}
```

Nginx is requesting to be able to escalate its privileges and to add the NET_BIND_SERVICE privilege so that it can run on port 443 without being a root user. Going back to our list of constraint violations, in addition to having a privilege escalation violation, there was also a capabilities violation. If we inspect that violation:

```
kubectl get k8spspcapabilities.constraints.gatekeeper.sh -o
jsonpath='{$.items[0].status.violations}' | jq -r
[
  {
    "enforcementAction": "deny",
    "kind": "Pod",
    "message": "container <controller> has a disallowed capability.
Allowed capabilities are []",
    "name": "ingress-nginx-controller-744f97c4f-msmkz",
    "namespace": "ingress-nginx"
  }
]
```

It's the same container violating both constraints. Having determined which Pods are out of compliance, next we'll fix their configurations.

Earlier in this chapter, we discussed the difference between PSPs and GateKeeper, with one of the key differences being that while PSPs attempt to apply the "best" policy, GateKeeper will evaluate against all applicable constraints. This means that while in PSP you can create a "blanket" policy (often referred to as a "Default Restrictive policy) and then create more relaxed policies for specific Pods, GateKeeper will not let you do that. In order to keep these violations from stopping Nginx from running the constraint implementations, they must be updated to ignore our Nginx Pods. The easiest way to do this is to add ingress-nginx to our list of excludedNamespaces.

I did this for all of our constraint implementations in `chapter9/make_cluster_work_policies.yaml`. Deploy using the `apply` command:

```
kubectl apply -f chapter9/make_cluster_work_policies.yaml
k8spsphostnetworkingports.constraints.gatekeeper.sh/psp-deny-all-host-
network-ports configured
k8spsphostfilesystem.constraints.gatekeeper.sh/psp-deny-host-filesystem
configured
k8spspcapabilities.constraints.gatekeeper.sh/capabilities-drop-all
configured
k8spspallowprivilegeescalationcontainer.constraints.gatekeeper.sh/
privilege-escalation-deny-all configured
```

After a few minutes, let's run our violation check:

```
sh ./chapter9/show_constraint_violations.sh
k8spspallowedusers.constraints.gatekeeper.sh 8
k8spspallowprivilegeescalationcontainer.constraints.gatekeeper.sh 0
k8spspcapabilities.constraints.gatekeeper.sh 0
k8spspforbiddensysctls.constraints.gatekeeper.sh 0
k8spsphostfilesystem.constraints.gatekeeper.sh 0
k8spsphostnamespace.constraints.gatekeeper.sh 0
k8spsphostnetworkingports.constraints.gatekeeper.sh 0
k8spspprivilegedcontainer.constraints.gatekeeper.sh 0
k8spspprocmount.constraints.gatekeeper.sh 0
k8spspreadonlyrootfilesystem.constraints.gatekeeper.sh null
```

The only violations left are for our allowed users' constraint. These violations all come from `gatekeeper-system` because the GateKeeper pods don't have users specified in their `securityContext`. These Pods haven't received any of our sane defaults because, in the GateKeeper `Deployment`, the `gatekeeper-system` namespace is ignored. Even though it's ignored, it's still listed as a violation even though it won't be enforced.

Now that we have eliminated the violations, we're done right? Not quite. Even though Nginx isn't generating any errors, we aren't making sure it's running with least privilege. If someone were to launch a `Pod` in the `ingress-nginx` namespace, it could request privileges and additional capabilities without being blocked by GateKeeper. We'll want to make sure that any pod launched in the `ingress-nginx` namespace can't escalate beyond what it needs. In addition to eliminating the `ingress-nginx` namespace from our cluster-wide policy, we need to create a new constraint implementation that limits which capabilities can be requested by pods in the `ingress-nginx` namespace.

We know that Nginx requires the ability to escalate privileges and to request NET_
BIND_SERVICE so we can create a constraint implementation:

```
---
apiVersion: constraints.gatekeeper.sh/v1beta1
kind: K8sPSPCapabilities
metadata:
  name: capabilities-ingress-nginx
spec:
  match:
    kinds:
      - apiGroups: [""]
        kinds: ["Pod"]
      namespaces: ["ingress-nginx"]
    parameters:
      requiredDropCapabilities: ["all"]
      allowedCapabilities: ["NET_BIND_SERVICE"]
```

We created a constraint implementation that mirrors the Deployment's required
securityContext section. We didn't create a separate constraint implementation for
privilege escalation because that ConstraintTemplate has no parameters. It's either
enforced or it isn't. There's no additional work to be done for that constraint in the
ingress-nginx namespace once the namespace has been removed from the blanket
policy.

I repeated this debugging process for the other violations and added them to
chapter9/enforce_node_policies.yaml. You can deploy them to finish the process.

You may be wondering why we are enforcing at the namespace level and not with
specific labels to isolate individual pods? We discussed authorization strategies
earlier in this chapter and continuing the themes here, I don't see the addition of
additional label-based enforcement as adding much value. Anyone who can create a
Pod in this namespace can set the labels. Limiting the scope more doesn't add much
in the way of security.

The process for deploying and debugging policies is very detail-oriented. In a single-
tenant cluster, this may be a one-time action or a rare action, but in a multi-tenant
cluster, the process does not scale. Next, we'll look at strategies for applying node
security in multi-tenant clusters.

Scaling policy deployment in multi-tenant clusters

In the previous examples, we took a "small batch" approach to our node security. We created a single cluster-wide policy and then added exceptions as needed. This approach doesn't scale in a multi-tenant environment for a few reasons:

1. The `excludedNamespaces` attribute in a constraint's `match` section is a list and is difficult to patch in an automated way. Lists need to be patched, including the original, so it's more than a simple "apply this JSON."

2. You don't want to make changes to global objects in multi-tenant systems. It's easier to add new objects and to link them to a source of truth. It's easier to trace why a new constraint implementation was created using labels than to figure out why a global object was changed.

3. You want to minimize the likelihood of a change on a global object being able to affect other tenants. Adding new objects specifically for each tenant minimizes that risk.

In an ideal world, we'd create a single global policy and then create objects that can be more specific for individual namespaces that need elevated privileges.

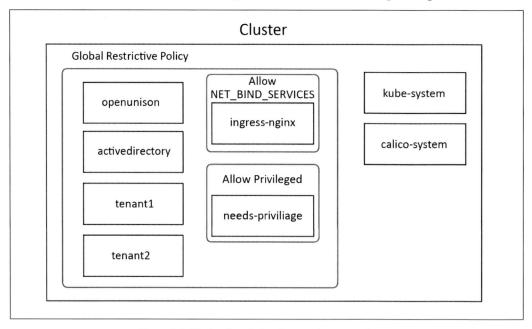

Figure 9.1: Ideal policy design for a multi-tenant cluster

The above diagram illustrates what I mean by having a blanket policy. The large, red box with rounded corners is a globally restrictive policy that minimizes what a Pod is capable of. Then, the smaller red rounded corner boxes are carveouts for specific exceptions. As an example, the `ingress-nginx` namespace would be created with restrictive rights, and a new policy would be added that is scoped specifically to the `ingress-nginx` namespace that would grant Nginx the ability to run with the `NET_BIND_SERVICES` capabilities. By adding an exception for a specific need to a cluster-wide restrictive policy, you're decreasing the likelihood that a new namespace will expose the entire cluster to a vulnerability if a new policy isn't added. The system is built to fail "closed."

The above scenario is not how GateKeeper works. Every policy that matches must succeed, there's no way to have a global policy. In order to effectively manage a multi-tenant environment, we need to:

1. Have policies for system-level namespaces that cluster administrators can own

2. Create policies for each namespace that can be adjusted as needed

3. Ensure that namespaces have policies before Pods can be created

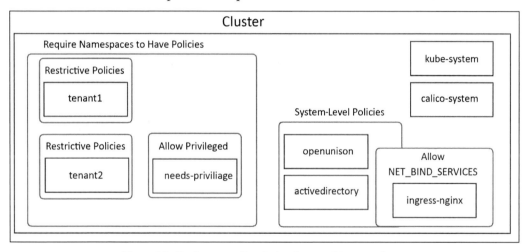

Figure 9.2: Gatekeeper policy design for a multi-tenant cluster

I visualized these goals in *Figure 9.2*. The policies we already created need to be adjusted to be "system-level" policies. Instead of saying that they need to apply globally and then make exceptions, we apply them specifically to our system-level namespaces. We're including `openunison` and `activedirectory` here as system-level namespaces because they're part of running our development cluster. The policies that grant nginx the ability to bind to port 443 are part of the system-level policies because the ingress is a system-level capability.

For individual tenants, goal #2 requires that each tenant gets its own set of constraint implementations. These individual constraint template implementation objects are represented by the rounded corner red boxes circling each tenant. This seems repetitive because it is. You are likely to have very repetitive objects that grant the same capabilities to each namespace. There are multiple strategies you can put in place to make this easier to manage:

1. Define a base restrictive set of constraint template implementations, and add each new namespace to the namespaces list of the match section. This cuts down on the clutter, but makes it harder to automate because of having to deal with patches on lists. It is also harder to track because you can't add any metadata to a single property like you can an object.

2. Automate the creation of constraint template implementations when namespaces are created. This is the approach we will take in *Chapter 14, Provisioning a Platform*. In that chapter, we will automate the creation of namespaces from a self-service portal. The workflow will provision namespaces, RBAC bindings, Tekton pipelines, keys, and so on. It will also provide the constraint templates needed to ensure restricted access.

3. Create a controller to replicate constraint templates based on labels. This is similar to how Fairwinds RBAC Manager (`https://github.com/FairwindsOps/rbac-manager`) generates RBAC bindings using a custom resource definition. I've not seen a tool directly for GateKeeper constraint implementations, but the same principle would work here.

When it comes to managing this automation, the above three options are not mutually exclusive. At KubeCon EU 2021, I presented a session called "I Can RBAC and So Can You!" (`https://www.youtube.com/watch?v=k6J9_P-gnro`) where I demoed using options #2 and #3 together to make "teams" that had multiple namespaces, cutting down on the number of RBAC bindings that needed to be created with each namespace.

Finally, we'll want to ensure that every namespace that isn't a system-level namespace has constraint implementations created. Even if we're automating the creation of namespaces, we don't want a rouge namespace to get created that doesn't have node security constraints in place. That's represented by the large, red, round cornered box around all of the tenants. Now that we've explored the theory behind building node security policies for a multi-tenant cluster, let's build our policies out.

The first step is to clear out our old policies:

```
kubectl delete -f chapter9/enforce_node_policies.yaml
kubectl delete -f chapter9/make_cluster_work_policies.yaml
kubectl delete -f chapter9/minimal_gatekeeper_constraints.yaml
```

This will get us back to a state where there are no policies. The next step is to create our system-wide policies:

```
kubectl create -f chapter9/multi-tenant/yaml/minimal_gatekeeper_
constraints.yaml
k8spspallowprivilegeescalationcontainer.constraints.gatekeeper.sh/
system-privilege-escalation-deny-all created
k8spspcapabilities.constraints.gatekeeper.sh/system-capabilities-drop-
all created
k8spspforbiddensysctls.constraints.gatekeeper.sh/system-psp-forbid-all-
sysctls created
k8spsphostfilesystem.constraints.gatekeeper.sh/system-psp-deny-host-
filesystem created
k8spsphostnamespace.constraints.gatekeeper.sh/system-psp-bloack-all-
host-namespace created
k8spsphostnetworkingports.constraints.gatekeeper.sh/system-psp-deny-
all-host-network-ports created
k8spspprivilegedcontainer.constraints.gatekeeper.sh/system-psp-deny-
all-privileged-container created
k8spspprocmount.constraints.gatekeeper.sh/system-psp-proc-mount-default
created
k8spspallowedusers.constraints.gatekeeper.sh/system-psp-pods-allowed-
user-ranges created
k8spsphostfilesystem.constraints.gatekeeper.sh/psp-tigera-operator-
allow-host-filesystem created
k8spspcapabilities.constraints.gatekeeper.sh/capabilities-ingress-nginx
created
```

Take a look at the policies in `chapter9/multi-tenant/yaml/minimal_gatekeeper_ constraints.yaml` and you'll see that instead of excluding namespaces in the `match` section, we're explicitly naming them:

```
---
apiVersion: constraints.gatekeeper.sh/v1beta1
kind: K8sPSPAllowPrivilegeEscalationContainer
metadata:
  name: system-privilege-escalation-deny-all
spec:
  match:
    kinds:
      - apiGroups: [""]
        kinds: ["Pod"]
    namespaces:
    - default
```

```
      - kube-node-lease
      - kube-public
      - kubernetes-dashboard
      - local-path-storage
      - tigera-operator
      - openunison
      - activedirectory
```

With our system constraint implementations in place, we'll next want to enforce the fact that all tenant namespaces have node security policies in place before any Pods can be created. There are no pre-existing ConstraintTemplates to implement this policy, we will need to build our own. Our Rego for our ConstraintTemplate will need to make sure that all of our required ConstraintTemplate implementations (in other words, privilege escalation, capabilities, and so on) have at least one instance for a namespace before a Pod is created in that namespace. The full code and test cases for the rego are in chapter9/multi-tenant/opa. Here's a snippet:

```
# capabilities
violation[{"msg": msg, "details": {}}] {
  checkForCapabilitiesPolicy
  msg := "No applicable K8sPSPCapabilities for this namespace"
}
checkForCapabilitiesPolicy {
    policies_for_namespace = [policy_for_namespace |
                             data.inventory.cluster["constraints.
gatekeeper.sh/v1beta1"].K8sPSPCapabilities[j].spec.match.namespaces[_]
== input.review.object.metadata.namespace ;
                             policy_for_namespace = data.inventory.
cluster["constraints.gatekeeper.sh/v1beta1"].K8sPSPCapabilities[j] ]
    count(policies_for_namespace)  == 0
}
# sysctls
violation[{"msg": msg, "details": {}}] {
  checkForSysCtlsPolicy
  msg := "No applicable K8sPSPForbiddenSysctls for this namespace"
}
checkForSysCtlsPolicy {
    policies_for_namespace = [policy_for_namespace |
                        data.inventory.cluster["constraints.gatekeeper.
sh/v1beta1"].K8sPSPForbiddenSysctls[j].spec.match.namespaces[_] ==
input.review.object.metadata.namespace ;
                             policy_for_namespace = data.inventory.
cluster["constraints.gatekeeper.sh/v1beta1"].K8sPSPForbiddenSysctls[j]
```

```
]
    count(policies_for_namespace)  == 0
}
```

The first thing to notice is that each constraint template check is in its own rule and has its own violation. Putting all of these rules in one `ConstraintTemplate` will result in them all having to pass in order for the entire `ConstraintTemplate` to pass.

Next, let's look at `checkForCapabilitiesPolicy`. The rule creates a list of all `K8sPSPCapabilities` that list the namespace from our `Pod` in its `match.namespaces` attribute. If this list is empty, the rule will continue to the violation and the `Pod` will fail to create. To create this template, first we need to sync our constraint templates into GateKeeper. Then create our constraint template and implementation:

```
kubectl apply -f chapter9/multi-tenant/yaml/gatekeeper-config.yaml
kubectl create -f chapter9/multi-tenant/yaml/require-psp-for-namespace-
constrainttemplate.yaml
kubectl create -f chapter9/multi-tenant/yaml/require-psp-for-namespace-
constraint.yaml
```

With our new policy in place, let's attempt to create a namespace and launch a `Pod`:

```
kubectl create ns check-new-pods
namespace/check-new-pods created
kubectl run echo-test -ti -n check-new-pods --image busybox
--restart=Never --command -- echo "hello world"
Error from server ([k8srequirepspfornamespace] No applicable
K8sPSPAllowPrivilegeEscalationContainer for this namespace
[k8srequirepspfornamespace] No applicable K8sPSPCapabilities for this
namespace
[k8srequirepspfornamespace] No applicable K8sPSPForbiddenSysctls for
this namespace
.
.
.
```

Our requirement that namespaces have node security policies in place stopped the Pod from being created! Let's fix this by applying restrictive node security policies from `chapter9/multi-tenant/yaml/check-new-pods-psp.yaml`:

```
kubectl create -f chapter9/multi-tenant/yaml/check-new-pods-psp.yaml
kubectl run echo-test -ti -n check-new-pods --image busybox
--restart=Never --command -- echo "hello world"
hello world
```

Now, whenever a new namespace is created on our cluster, node security policies must be in place before we can launch any pods.

In this section, we looked at the theory behind designing node security policies using GateKeeper and put that theory into practice for both a single-tenant and a multi-tenant cluster. We also built out sane defaults for our `securityContexts` using GateKeeper's built-in mutation capabilities. With this information, you have what you need to begin deploying node security policies to your clusters using GateKeeper.

Summary

In this chapter, we began by exploring the importance of protecting nodes, the differences between containers and VMs from a security standpoint, and how easy it is to exploit a cluster when nodes aren't protected. We also looked at secure container design, and finally, we implemented and debugged node security policies using GateKeeper.

Locking down the nodes of your cluster provides one less vector for attackers. Encapsulating the policy makes it easier to explain to your developers how to design their containers and makes it easier to build secure solutions.

So far, all of our security has been built to prevent workloads from being malicious. What happens when those measures fail? How do you know what's going on inside of your `Pods`? In the next chapter, we'll find out using Falco!

Questions

1. True or false – containers are "lightweight VMs."

   a. True

   b. False

2. Can a container access resources from its host?

   a. No, it's isolated.

   b. If marked as privileged, yes.

   c. Only if explicitly granted by a policy.

   d. Sometimes.

3. How could an attacker gain access to a cluster through a container?

    a. A bug in the container's application can lead to a remote code execution, which can be used in a breakout of a vulnerable container, and is then used to get the kubelet's credentials.

    b. Compromised credentials with the ability to create a container in one namespace can be used to create a container that mounts the node's filesystem to get the kubelet's credentials.

    c. Both of the above.

4. How does the `PodSecurityPolicy` admission controller determine which policy to apply to a Pod?

    a. By reading an annotation on the Pod's definition

    b. By comparing the Pod's requested capabilities and the policies authorized via the union of the Pod's creator and its own `ServiceAccount`

    c. By comparing the Pod's requested capabilities and the policies authorized for its own `ServiceAccount`

    d. By comparing the Pod's requested capabilities and the policies authorized for the Pod's creator

5. What mechanism enforces `ConstraintTemplates`?

    a. An admission controller that inspects all pods upon creation and updating

    b. The `PodSecurityPolicy` API

    c. The OPA

    d. GateKeeper

6. True or false – the `PodSecurityPolicy` API will be removed by version 1.25.

    a. True

    b. False

7. True or false – containers should generally run as root.

    a. True

    b. False

Join our book's Discord space

Join the book's Discord workspace for a monthly *Ask me Anything* session with the authors: `https://packt.link/K8EntGuide`

10

Auditing Using Falco, DevOps AI, and ECK

Bad people do bad things.

Good people do bad things.

Accidents happen.

The preceding statements have one thing in common: when any one of them occurs, you need to find out what happened and who did it.

Too often, auditing is considered only when we think of some form of attack. While we certainly require auditing to find "bad people," we also need to audit everyday standard system interactions.

Kubernetes includes logs for most of the important system events that you will need to audit, but it doesn't include everything. As we discussed in previous chapters, all API interactions will be logged by the system, which includes the majority of events you need to audit. However, there are tasks that users execute that will not go through the API server and may go undetected if you are relying on API logs for all of your auditing.

There are tools to address the gaps in the native logging functionality. Open source projects such as Falco will provide enhanced auditing for your pods, providing details for events that are logged by the API server.

Logs without a logging system are not very useful. Like many components in Kubernetes, there are many open source projects that provide a full logging system. One of the most popular systems is the ECK operator, which stands for Elastic Cloud on Kubernetes, which includes Elasticsearch, Filebeat, and Kibana.

Finally, logging systems are a great tool, but they are only useful if you are watching logs or alerting on events. Increasingly, enterprises are automating every aspect of their infrastructure, including automating responses to events that are captured by logging systems. Creating automation to address events increases your cluster security by decreasing the time required to remediate an issue. Falco and Falco Sidekick can forward events to a number of systems that can be used to enable DevOps AI.

All of these projects will be covered in detail throughout this chapter. You will deploy each of these components to gain hands-on experience and to reinforce the material covered in this chapter.

In this chapter, we will cover the following topics:

- Exploring auditing
- Introducing Falco
- Exploring Falco's configuration files
- Deploying Falco
- Using Falco Sidekick to enable DevOps AI
- Overserving Falco logs

By the end of the chapter, you will know how to deploy Falco into a Kubernetes cluster and how to use the data captured by Falco for a full view into any pod events that may be malicious.

Technical requirements

To complete the exercises in this chapter, you will need to meet the following technical requirements:

- An Ubuntu 20.04 server with a minimum of 8 GB of RAM and at least 5 GB of free disk space for persistent volumes
- A KinD cluster installed using the instructions in *Chapter 2, Deploying Kubernetes Using KinD*
- Helm3 binary (you should already have this installed from *Chapter 4, Services, Load Balancing, ExternalDNS, and Global Balancing*)

You can access the code for this chapter by going to this book's GitHub repository: https://github.com/PacktPublishing/Kubernetes---An-Enterprise-Guide-2E/tree/main/chapter10.

Exploring auditing

In most environments where you run Kubernetes clusters, you will need to have an auditing system in place. While Kubernetes has some auditing features, they are often too limited for an enterprise to rely on for a complete audit trail, and logs are often only stored on each host filesystem.

In order to correlate events, you are required to pull all the logs you want to search through on your local system, and manually look through logs or pull them into a spreadsheet and attempt to create some macros to search and tie information together.

Fortunately, there are many third-party logging systems available for Kubernetes. Optional paid systems such as Splunk and Datadog are popular solutions and open source systems including the EFK stack are commonly used and included with many Kubernetes distributions. All of these systems include some form of a log forwarder that allows you to centralize your Kubernetes logs so you can create alerts, custom queries, and dashboards.

Another limitation of native auditing is the limited scope of events, which are limited to API access. While this is important to audit, most enterprises will need to augment or customize the base set of auditing targets beyond simple API events. Extending the base auditing features can be a challenge and most companies will not have the expertise or time to create their own auditing add-ons.

One area of auditing that Kubernetes is missing concerns pod events. As we mentioned, the base auditing capabilities of Kubernetes focus on API access. Most tasks performed by users will trigger a call to the API server. Let's take an example of a user executing a shell on a pod to look at a file. The user would use `kubectl exec -it <pod name> bash` to spawn a bash shell on the pod in interactive mode. This actually sends a request to the API server, the main call of which to execute is as follows:

```
I0216 11:42:58.872949   13139 round_trippers.go:420] POST
https://0.0.0.0:32771/api/v1/namespaces/ingress-nginx/pods/nginx-
ingress-controller-7d6bf88c86-knbrx/exec?command=bash&container=nginx-
ingress-controller&stdin=true&stdout=true&tty=true
```

Looking at the event, you can see that an `exec` command was sent to the `nginx-ingress-controller` pod to run the bash process.

There may be good reasons that someone is running a shell, for example, to look at an error log or to fix an issue quickly. But the issue here is that, once inside the running pod, any command that is executed does not access the Kubernetes API, and therefore, you will not receive any logged events for the actions executed in the pod. To most enterprises, this is a large hole in the auditing system since no end-to-end audit trail would exist if the action conducted in the container were malicious.

Auditing all shell access to pods would lead to many false-positive leads, and in the event that a pod was restarted, you would lose any local audit files in the pod. Instead, you may ignore simple shell access, but you want to log an event if someone tries to execute certain tasks from the shell, such as modifying the `/etc/passwd` file.

So, you may ask, "What is the solution?" The answer is to use Falco.

Introducing Falco

Falco is an open source system from Sysdig that adds anomaly detection functionality for pods in Kubernetes clusters. Out of the box, Falco includes a base set of powerful, community-created rules that can monitor a number of potentially malicious events, including the following:

- When a user attempts to modify a file under `/etc`
- When a user spawns a shell on a pod
- When a user stores sensitive information in a secret
- When a pod attempts to make a call to the Kubernetes API server
- Any attempts to modify a system ClusterRole
- Or any other custom rule you create to meet your needs

When Falco is running on a Kubernetes cluster it watches events, and based on a set of rules, it logs events on the Falco pod that can be picked up by a system such as Fluentd, which would then forward the event to an external logging system.

In this chapter, we will explain the configuration of Falco using the technical requirements for our company scenario for FooWidgets. By the end of the chapter, you will know how to set up Falco on a Kubernetes cluster using custom configuration options. You will also understand the rules used by Falco and how to create rules when you need to audit an event that is not included in the base rules. Finally, you will forward events to Elasticsearch using Filebeat and then use Kibana to visualize the events generated by Falco.

Exploring Falco's configuration files

Before you install Falco, you need to understand the configuration options that are available, and that starts with the initial configuration file that will be used to configure how Falco creates events.

The Falco project includes a set of base configuration files that you can use for your initial auditing. It is highly likely that you will want to change the base configuration to fit your specific enterprise requirements. In this section, we will go over a Falco deployment and provide a basic understanding of the configuration files.

Falco is a powerful system that can be customized to fit almost any requirement you may have for security. Since it is so extensible, it's not possible to cover every detail of the configuration in a single chapter, but like many popular projects, there is an active GitHub community at `https://github.com/falcosecurity/falco` where you can post issues or join their Slack channel.

Recent versions of Falco can be deployed using Helm, which makes the deployment very easy to customize and deploy. Customizing the installation is easy since Helm can use a `values.yaml` file containing all configuration options. Once deployed, Falco has additional base configuration files that define the events that will be audited. These are stored in a ConfigMap located in the Falco namespace and it includes:

- `falco_rules.yaml`
- `falco_rules.local.yaml`
- `k8s_audit_rules.yaml`
- `rules.d`

The included configuration files will work out of the box, but you may want to change or add certain rules to address your logging requirements. Falco allows you to add additional rules by adding rules files that contain your customized events to the base rulesets.

In this section, we will explain the most important configuration options in detail.

The Helm Values file

The first file you will need to edit is the base `values.yaml` file to configure how Falco handles audited events. It allows you to customize the base settings of Falco, including the event output format, timestamp configuration, and endpoint targets such as a Slack channel. Let's have a detailed walkthrough of this file and try to understand it bit by bit.

We have included a custom `values.yaml` in the Git repository under the `Chapter10` folder called `values-falco.yaml` that we will use to deploy Falco. The next section will cover the most common settings that you may want to change. For any settings that aren't covered in this chapter, you can view all of the options here: `https://github.com/falcosecurity/charts/tree/master/falco`.

Customizing the Helm Values

We will start with the `image` section, which tells the deployment which image to use. By default, the image is configured to pull from `docker.io`, but if you have an internal registry you want to use, you can edit the values to pull the image from your own registry. The example below would configure the deployment to use an image that is local to our organization:

```
image:
  registry: harbor.foowidgets.com
  repository: falco/falco
  tag: 0.30.0
  pullPolicy: IfNotPresent
  pullSecrets: []
```

Falco supports Docker and ContainerD runtimes. The next section of the values files allows you to enable or disable either option:

```
docker:
  enabled: true
  socket: /var/run/docker.sock

containerd:
  enabled: true
  socket: /run/containerd/containerd.sock
```

The next sections are often left at the default values, so we will jump to the next important setting, the fake generator event. This will deploy a container that will generate events for testing purposes and is a great option for anyone who is new to Falco. We have enabled this for this chapter so the Falco log will have enough events for the EKF section:

```
fakeEventGenerator:
  enabled: true
  args:
    - run
    - --loop
```

```
    - ^syscall
  replicas: 1
```

Next, we jump to the eBFP section. Falco can run using one of three different drivers. The first uses kernel modules, the second leverages eBPF, and the last uses `pdig`. Each option has its own use case, which is usually based on the operating system and configuration of the host. You can read about the pros and cons on Falco's site at `https://falco.org/blog/choosing-a-driver/`.

The eBPF driver is one of the most popular drivers to use for Falco, and it's the driver we will use for our deployment. It's important to note that your Linux kernel must be at least version 4.4, with a preferred version of 4.9, to use the eBPF driver.

For our deployment, we have set this value to `true`, which will enable eBPF, and for performance, we also enable the `hostNetwork` option.

```
ebpf:
  enabled: true
  path:

  settings:
    hostNetwork: true
```

Falco can also collect requests and responses to the Kubernetes API server. The rules that Falco uses for these events are located in `k8s_audit_rules.yaml`. For this chapter, we will leave this set to false, but you can read more about enabling the audit feature and what it provides on Falco's main page: `https://falco.org/docs/event-sources/kubernetes-audit/`.

If you decide to enable this option, it is more involved than simply enabling it in the values file. You will also need to configure your API server to support the dynamic auditing feature by enabling the following API flags:

```
--audit-dynamic-configuration
--feature-gates=DynamicAuditing=true
--runtime-config=auditregistration.k8s.io/v1alpha1=true
```

And in the Falco values, you would set the `enabled` option to `true`:

```
auditLog:
  enabled: true
```

The next section contains the main configuration options for Falco, including rules files, the event output format, time format, logging levels, and more.

The first option sets the rules files that Falco will use to generate events. Each of the rules files will be explained in greater detail in the next section:

```
rulesFile:
  - /etc/falco/falco_rules.yaml
  - /etc/falco/falco_rules.local.yaml
  - /etc/falco/k8s_audit_rules.yaml
  - /etc/falco/rules.d
```

The next set of values will configure how Falco outputs events, including the time format, and the option to output events as text or JSON.

By default, the `time_format_iso_8601` value is set to `false`, which tells Falco to use the local `/etc/localtime` format. Setting the value to `true` tells Falco to stamp each event using the date format of YYYY-MM-DD, a time format using a 24-hour clock, and a time zone of UTC.

Selecting the appropriate format is a decision for your organization. If you have a global organization, it may be beneficial to set all of your logging to use the ISO 8601 format. However, if you have a regional organization, you may be more comfortable using your local date-and-time format since you may not need to worry about correlating events against logging systems in other time zones:

```
time_format_iso_8601: false
```

The next two lines allow you to configure the output of events as either text or JSON format. The default value is set to `false`, which tells Falco to output events in text format. If the first key is set to `false`, the second value will not be evaluated since JSON is not enabled:

```
json_output: false
json_include_output_property: true
```

You may need to output the events in JSON format, depending on the format that your logging system requires. As an example, if you were going to send Falco events to an Elasticsearch server, you might want to enable JSON to allow Elasticsearch to parse the alerts field. Elasticsearch does not require the events to be sent in JSON format and for the lab in this module, we will leave this set to the default value, `false`.

The following are some examples of the same type of event in both text format and JSON format:

- The Falco text log output looks as follows:

```
19:17:23.139089915: Notice A shell was spawned in a container
with an attached terminal (user=root k8s.ns=default k8s.
pod=falco-daemonset-9mrn4 container=0756e87d121d shell=bash
parent=runc cmdline=bash terminal=34816 container_
id=0756e87d121d image=<NA>) k8s.ns=default k8s.pod=falco-
daemonset-9mrn4 container=0756e87d121d k8s.ns=default k8s.
pod=falco-daemonset-9mrn4 container=0756e87d121d
```

- The Falco JSON log output looks as follows:

```
{"output":"20:47:39.535071657: Notice A shell was spawned
in a container with an attached terminal (user=root k8s.
ns=default k8s.pod=falco-daemonset-mjv2d container=daeaaf1c0551
shell=bash parent=runc cmdline=bash terminal=34816 container_
id=daeaaf1c0551 image=<NA>) k8s.ns=default k8s.pod=falco-
daemonset-mjv2d container=daeaaf1c0551 k8s.ns=default k8s.
pod=falco-daemonset-mjv2d container=daeaaf1c0551","priority"
:"Notice","rule":"Terminal shell in container","time":"2020-
02-13T20:47:39.535071657Z", "output_fields": {"container.
id":"daeaaf1c0551","container.image.repository":null,"evt.
time":1581626859535071657,"k8s.ns.name":"default","k8s.pod.
name":"falco-daemonset-mjv2d","proc.cmdline":"bash","proc.
name":"bash","proc.pname":"runc","proc.tty":34816,"user.
name":"root"}}
```

Continuing on, the next two options tell Falco to log **Falco-level** events to `stderr` and `syslog`:

```
log_stderr: true
log_syslog: true
```

This setting does not have any impact on the events that your rules file will be monitoring, but rather configures how **Falco system events** will be logged:

```
log_stderr: true
log_syslog: true
log_level: info
```

The default for both options is `true`, so all events will be logged to `stderr` and `syslog`.

Next is the logging level you want to capture, with accepted values including `emergency`, `alert`, `critical`, `error`, `warning`, `notice`, `info`, and `debug`.

Continuing on, the priority level specifies the rulesets that will be used by Falco. Any ruleset that has a rule priority equal to or higher than the configured value will be evaluated by Falco to generate alerts:

```
priority: debug
```

The default value is debug. Other values that can be set are emergency, alert, critical, error, warning, notice, and info.

Next up is the value to enable or disable buffered_outputs. By default, buffered_outputs is set to false:

```
buffered_outputs: false
```

To pass system calls, Falco uses a shared buffer that can fill up, and when the value is set to true, the buffer can be configured to tell Falco how to react. The default values are usually a good starting value for an initial configuration. The Falco team has a detailed explanation of dropped events on their main documentation page at https://falco.org/docs/event-sources/dropped-events/.

The syscall_events_drops setting can be set to ignore, log, alert, and exit. The rate configures how often Falco will execute the configured actions. The value is actions per second, so this example tells Falco to execute one action every 30 seconds:

```
syscall_event_drops:
  actions:
    - log
    - alert
  rate: .03333
  max_burst: 10
```

The outputs section allows you to throttle the notifications from Falco, containing two values, rate and max_burst:

```
outputs:
  rate: 1
  max_burst: 1000
```

The syslog_output section tells Falco to output events to syslog. By default, this value is set to true:

```
syslog_output:
  enabled: true
```

In certain use cases, you may want to configure Falco to output events to a file in addition to, or as a replacement for, stdout. By default, this is set to false, but you can enable it by setting it to true and providing a filename.

The keep_alive value is set to false by default, which configures Falco to keep the file open and write data continuously without closing the file. If it is set to false, the file is opened for each event as it occurs, and closed once the events have been written:

```
file_output:
  enabled: false
  keep_alive: false
  filename: ./events.txt
```

By default, Falco will output events to stdout, so it is set to true. If you have a requirement to disable logging events to stdout, you can change this value to false:

```
stdout_output:
  enabled: true
```

The webserver configuration is used to integrate Kubernetes audit events with Falco. By default, it is enabled to listen on port 8765 using HTTP.

You can enable secure communication by changing the ssl_enabled value to true, and supplying a certificate for the ssl_certificate value:

```
webserver:
  enabled: true
  listen_port: 8765
  k8s_audit_endpoint: /k8s_audit
  ssl_enabled: false
  ssl_certificate: /etc/falco/falco.pem
```

Falco can be configured to alert other systems. In our example configuration, we show an example using jq and curl to send an alert to a Slack channel. By default, this section is disabled, but if you want to call an external program when alerts are triggered, you can enable the option and provide the program to be executed. Similar to the file output described previously, the keep_alive option defaults to false, which tells Falco to run the program for each event:

```
program_output:
  enabled: false
  keep_alive: false
  program: "jq '{text: .output}' | curl -d @- -X POST https://hooks.
slack.com/services/XXX"
```

Falco can send alerts to an HTTP endpoint. We will be deploying an add-on for Falco called `Falcosidekick`, which runs a web server to receive requests from the Falco pod. It is disabled by default, but we have enabled it and set it to the name of the service that will be created later in the chapter when we deploy `Falcosidekick`:

```
http_output:
  enabled: true
  url: http://falcosidekick:2801
```

The remaining sections of the file are used to enable and configure a gRPC server. This is not a common configuration when using Falco with Kubernetes, and is only provided here since it's in the base `falco-values.yaml` file:

```
grpc:
    enabled: false
    threadiness: 0

    # gRPC unix socket with no authentication
    unixSocketPath: "unix:///var/run/falco/falco.sock"

    # gRPC over the network (mTLS) / required when unixSocketPath is
empty
    listenPort: 5060
    privateKey: "/etc/falco/certs/server.key"
    certChain: "/etc/falco/certs/server.crt"
    rootCerts: "/etc/falco/certs/ca.crt"

  grpcOutput:
    enabled: false
```

Earlier in the chapter, we mentioned that you can create your own Falco rules, which can be defined in the `customRules` section.

Finally, we can jump down to the last section, `falcosidekick`. This section can be used to enable the Falco sidekick as part of the Falco deployment.

For the chapter, we will deploy `falcosidekick` using a dedicated Helm chart and values file, so we will set the values to false.

```
falcosidekick:
  # enable falcosidekick deployment
  enabled: false
  fullfqdn: false
```

The base configuration is just the initial configuration file for a Falco deployment. In the next section, we will explain how to configure the files used to create Falco alerts.

Falco rules config files

Recall that in our values file, there was a section that had a key called `rules_files` and the key had multiple values. The rules will be mounted using a `configmap`, telling Falco what to audit and how to alert on a given event.

Rules files can contain three types of elements:

- `Rules`: Configure Falco alerts
- `Macros`: Create a function that can shorten definitions in a rule
- `Lists`: A collection of items that can be used in a rule

In the upcoming subsections, we'll go over each of these elements.

Understanding rules

Falco includes a set of example Kubernetes rules that you can use as is, or you can modify the existing rules to fit your specialized requirements.

Falco is a powerful auditing system that enhances cluster security. Like any system that provides auditing, creating rules to monitor systems can become complex, and Falco Kubernetes is no exception. To use Falco effectively, you need to understand how it uses rules files and how you can correctly customize the rules to fit your requirements.

A default Falco installation will include three rulesets:

Rules File	Overview
`falco_rules.yaml`	The base rules provided by Falco. This base ruleset should not be edited since the file may be replaced by future Falco deployments. Any changes or additional rules should be added to the `falco_rules.local.yaml` file.
`falco_rules.local.yaml`	This contains custom rules required by your organization. Also used to modify rules that are included in the base `falco_rules.yaml` file.
`k8s_audit_rules.yaml`	This contains rules that are used when Falco is integrated with Kubernetes audit events. The file is included and added to the `configmap`, but the integration is not configured by default.

Table 10.1: Rules files overview

Each of the rules files has the same syntax, so before explaining each file in greater detail, let's explain how rules, macros, and lists work together to create rules.

Our first example will generate an alert when a pod that is not part of Kubernetes itself tries to contact the API server. This type of activity may signal that an attacker is looking to exploit the Kubernetes API server. To accomplish the most efficient alert, we don't want to generate alerts from pods that are part of the Kubernetes cluster that need to communicate with the API server.

The included rules list includes this event. In the `falco_rules.yaml` file, there is a rule for API server communication:

```
- rule: Contact K8S API Server From Container
  desc: Detect attempts to contact the K8S API Server from a container
  condition: evt.type=connect and evt.dir=< and (fd.typechar=4 or
fd.typechar=6) and container and not k8s_containers and k8s_api_server
  output: Unexpected connection to K8s API Server from container
(command=%proc.cmdline %container.info image=%container.image.
repository:%container.image.tag connection=%fd.name)
  priority: NOTICE
  tags: [network, k8s, container, mitre_discovery]
```

You can see that a rule may contain multiple conditions and values.

Falco includes a large set of conditions that can be checked, so let's start by explaining this rule in detail.

To explain how this rule works, we break down each section in the following table:

Rule Option	Description
rule	Provides a name for our rule. In the example, the name is Contact K8S API Server From Container.
desc:	Provides a description for our rule, which should be more descriptive than the rule option. In our example, the description is Detect attempts to contact the K8S API Server from a container.
condition	This contains the logic that will decide whether a rule is to be triggered. The example rule will be explained in detail in the next section.
output	This creates the output that will be sent to the log.

Table 10.2: Parts of a Falco rule

Most of the table is fairly straightforward, but the `condition` section has some complex logic that may not make much sense to you. Like most logging systems, Falco uses its own syntax for creating rule conditions.

Since rules can be difficult to create, the Falco community has provided an extensive list of premade rules. Many people will find that the community rules will fully meet their needs, but there are scenarios where you might need to create custom rules or need to change one of the existing rules to reduce alerts for events you may not be concerned about. Before you attempt to create or change an event, you need to understand the full logic of a condition.

Covering all of the logic and syntax that Falco offers is beyond the scope of this book, but understanding the example rule is the first step to creating or editing existing rules.

Understanding conditions (fields and values)

The example condition contains a few different conditions that we will break down here into three sections to describe each part of the condition in steps.

The first component of a condition is the class fields. A condition can contain multiple class fields and can be evaluated using standard `and`, `not`, or `equals` conditions.

Breaking down the example condition, we are using the event (evt) and file descriptor (fd) class fields:

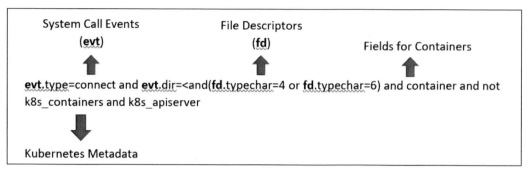

Figure 10.1: Class field example

Each class may have a field value:

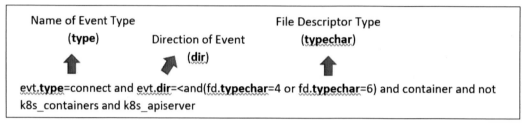

Figure 10.2: Class field value

Finally, each field type will have a value:

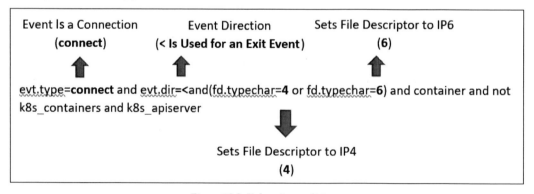

Figure 10.3: Values in conditions

You can get a complete list of the available classes from Falco's website at https://falco.org/docs/rules/supported-fields/.

Falco has a number of class fields and values for rules. There are too many classes to explain in a single chapter, but to help with creating your own custom rules, we have provided an explanation using the original example condition:

```
condition: evt.type=connect and evt.dir=< and (fd.typechar=4 or
fd.typechar=6) and container and not k8s_containers and k8s_api_server
```

The following table explains the event class and its values:

Event (EVT) Class	
Value	**Description**
type	The type of event. In our example, the type value is set to connect, since the event we want to watch for will use a network connection.
dir	The direction of the event. This sets the direction to either enter (>) or exit (<). In the example, it's watching for a connection that is exiting the pod.

Table 10.3: Event class example

Along with using the event class, the rule also uses the file descriptor class, which is explained as follows:

File Descriptor (FD) Class	
Value	**Description**
typechar	Sets the type of class to watch for. The values can be (f) file, (4) IPv4, (6) IPv6, (u) unix, (p) pipe, (e) eventfd, (s) signalfd, (l) eventpoll, (i) notify, or (o) unknown. In the example, the value uses an or statement of 4 or 6. Setting it to both will trigger an alert based on either IPv4 or IPv6.

Table 10.4: File descriptor example

The last part of the rule that starts with the and `container` value will include any container. However, since we do not want to send alerts for valid communications from Kubernetes itself, the value and `not k8s_containers and k8s_api_server` tells the condition to omit the Kubernetes container and the `api_server`. The values in this example use macros that have been defined in the `falco_rules.yaml` file.

In the next section, we will discuss macros, which can make creating rules easier.

Using macros

Macros allow you to create a collection to make rule creation quicker and easier. In the previous example, the condition used two macros, k8s_containers and k8s_api_server.

The k8s_containers macro has been defined to contain the condition:

```
# In a local/user rules file, list the namespace or container images that are
# allowed to contact the K8s API Server from within a container. This
# might cover cases where the K8s infrastructure itself is running
# within a container.
- macro: k8s_containers
  condition: >
    (container.image.repository in (gcr.io/google_containers/hyperkube-amd64,
      gcr.io/google_containers/kube2sky, sysdig/agent, sysdig/falco,
      sysdig/sysdig, falcosecurity/falco) or (k8s.ns.name = "kube-system"))
```

Macros, like rules, use classes to create conditions. To evaluate the k8s_containers condition, macros use two classes:

- The container.image.repository class field, which validates the repositories for the condition
- The k8s.ns.name class field, which is used to include any containers running in the kube-system namespace

The k8s_api_server has been defined to contain the condition:

```
- macro: k8s_api_server
  condition: (fd.sip.name="kubernetes.default.svc.cluster.local")
```

For the k8s_api_server condition, macros use a single class field to evaluate the condition – the fd.sip.name class field, which checks the domain name of the **server IP (SIP)**. If it is equal to kubernetes.default.svc.cluster.local it is considered a match.

Using both of the preceding macros for the rule condition will stop any Kubernetes cluster pods from generating alerts when communicating with the API server.

Understanding lists

Lists allow you to group items into a single object that can be used in rules, macros, or nested in other lists.

A list only requires two keys in a rules file, `list` and `items`. For example, rather than listing a number of binaries on a condition, you could group the binaries into a `list`:

```
- list: editors
  items: [vi, nano, emacs]
```

Using lists allows you to use a single entry, rather than including multiple items in a condition.

Rules can be challenging, but as you read more of the included rules and start to create your own, it will become easier. So far, we have introduced the basics of how to create rules, macros, and lists. With a basic understanding of these objects under our belts, we will move on to the next configuration file where you will create and append Falco rules.

Creating and appending to custom rules

Falco comes with a number of base rules that are located in the `falco_rules.yaml` file. This file should **never** be edited – if you need to change or create a new rule, you should edit the `falco_rules.local.yaml` file or add additional sets by adding additional rules to a new rules file.

Editing an existing rule

 You are not limited to only appending to rules. Falco allows you to append rules, macros, and lists.

The included `falco_rules.local.yaml` is empty by default. You only need to edit this file if an existing rule needs to be modified or removed or a new rule needs to be added. Since the file is used to change or add values to the base `falco_rules.yaml` file, the order in which the files are used by Falco is very important.

Falco will build rules based on the name from all rules files. The files are read and evaluated in the order that they are referenced in the base Falco configuration file. The base file that we used as an example at the beginning of this chapter has the following order for its rules files:

```
rules_file:
  - /etc/falco/falco_rules.yaml
  - /etc/falco/falco_rules.local.yaml
  - /etc/falco/k8s_audit_rules.yaml
```

Notice that the `falco.rules.local.yaml` file is after the base `falco_rules.yaml` file. Keeping control of the order of the files will help you to track any expected/unexpected behaviors of your rules.

Using an example from the Falco documentation, let's show how to append to a rule.

The original rule from `falco_rules.yaml` is shown in the following code block:

```
- rule: program_accesses_file
  desc: track whenever a set of programs opens a file
  condition: proc.name in (cat, ls) and evt.type=open
  output: a tracked program opened a file (user=%user.name
command=%proc.cmdline file=%fd.name)
  priority: INFO
```

As the description states, this rule will trigger whenever a set of programs opens a file. The condition will trigger when `cat` or `ls` is used to open a file.

The current rule does not omit the open operation from any users. You have decided that you do not need to know when the root user uses either `cat` or `ls` to open a file, and you want to stop Falco from generating alerts for `root`.

In the `falco_rules.local.yaml` file, you need to create an append for the existing rule. To append to a rule, you must use the same rule name, then add `append: true` and any changes you want to make to the rule. An example is shown in the following snippet:

```
- rule: program_accesses_file
  append: true
  condition: and not user.name=root
```

Creating a new rule is easier than appending to an existing rule. Let's see how it works.

Creating a new rule

As mentioned previously, you should not edit the base rules that are included with Falco, instead, you should add custom rules to an additional rules file. In the book repository, under the `chapter10` directory, we have provided an example custom rule that will alert on changes to the `conf` directory in a Bitnami NGINX container, called `custom-nginx.yaml`. The rules file is explained below.

```
customRules:
  rules-nginx-write.yaml: |-
```

```
   - rule: Detected NGINX Directory Change
     desc: Detect any writes to the NGINX conf directory
     condition: evt.dir = < and open_write and fd.directory in (/opt/
bitnami/nginx/conf)
     output: There has been a change under the NGINX conf directory
(command=%proc.cmdline pid=%proc.pid connection=%fd.name sport=%fd.
sport user=%user.name %container.info image=%container.image)
     priority: NOTICE
```

This rule will watch for any write events under the `/opt/bitnami/nginx/conf` folder. We will deploy this rule for our DevOps AI example in the *Understand automatic responses to events* section of this chapter, but first, we need to install Falco into our KinD cluster. In the next section, we explain how to deploy Falco, and you will finally get to see it in action.

Deploying Falco

We have included a script to deploy Falco, called `install-falco.sh`, in the GitHub repository in the `chapter10` folder.

The two most popular methods of deploying Falco to a Kubernetes cluster are using the official Helm chart or a DaemonSet manifest from the Falco repo. For the purposes of this module, we will deploy Falco using Helm and a `custom values.yaml` from the book's GitHub repository.

To deploy Falco using the included script, execute the script from within the `chapter10` folder by executing `./install-falco.sh`.

The steps that the script performs are detailed in the following list and will be explained in additional detail in this section.

The script executes the following tasks:

1. Creates the Falco namespace
2. Adds the charts from the `falcosecurity.github.io/charts` repository
3. Installs Falco using Helm in the falco namespace using the custom values file along with the custom rules file for our NGINX example

Falco logs use standard output, so we can easily forward the logs to any third-party logging system. While there are many options that we could select as our logging server, we have chosen to forward our logs using **Elasticsearch, Fluentd, and Kibana (EFK)** along with Falcosidekick.

Introducing Falcosidekick

As you have seen, Falco is a powerful detection system. However, like any logging system, it's only valuable if the events are being monitored and acted on. Unlike many standard events, events captured by Falco could mean that a security breach is in progress, and any delay in acting on an event may mean the difference between a hacker being successful or unsuccessful in their attempts.

Falcosidekick extends base Falco logging by providing the ability to connect to a number of external systems including Slack, Teams, Datadog, Prometheus, AlertManager, ElasticSearch, Loki, Lamba, Kubeless, GCP Cloud Run, GCP Pub/Sub, and more. The graphic below shows the categories and products that are supported by Falcosidekick at the time of writing.

We would like to thank Thomas Labarussias from the Falcosidekick project for allowing us to use the Falcosidekick graphics in this section.

Figure 10.4: Falcosidekick integration

To show the flow between the different components, the Falcosidekick team has created the diagram below.

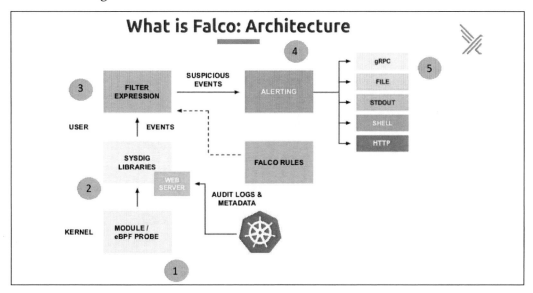

Figure 10.5: Falco architecture

Let's follow the flow of an event:

1. The module or eBPF probe on the worker node will forward information to the Falco POD.

2. Falco receives the activity from the module or eBPF probe and, if configured, the Kubernetes API server.

3. Falco will use the events that are defined by the Falco rulesets to compare the activity that was passed from *step 1*.

4. Falco will log an event based on any rule that is triggered.

5. Output can be to a single or multiple endpoints. By default, the output from events uses STDOUT.

Now that you understand how Falco and Kubeless extend the basic outputs of Falco, let's move on to the next section, where we will install Falcosidekick in our KinD cluster.

Installing Falcosidekick

We have included a custom `values.yaml` file in the book repository under the `chapter10` directory called `values-sidekick.yaml`.

Similar to the values file we used for the Falco deployment, we will explain the most important options, highlighting the options we have configured for the chapter exercises.

The beginning of the file tells the installation what image to use for the Falcosidekick POD(s).

```
image:
  registry: docker.io
  repository: falcosecurity/falcosidekick
  tag: 2.23.1
  pullPolicy: IfNotPresent
```

Since the values file contains all of the possible options for connections, we will jump to the config section, focusing on the section that will configure Falcosidekick to forward events.

```
kubeless:
  function: "falco-functions"
  namespace: "kubeless"
  port: 8080
  minimumpriority: ""
  mutualtls: false
  checkcert: false
```

The `kubeless` block configures Falcosidekick to forward events to a function called `falco-functions` in the `kubeless` namespace, running on port `8080`. When an event is triggered, it will still be logged by Falco, but in addition to the basic logging, it will also forward the event and the information to the function.

```
helm install falcosidekick falcosecurity/falcosidekick -f values-
sidekick.yaml --namespace falco
```

Next, we need to install Kubeless since we will use that, along with Falcosidekick, to create an automatic response to a Falco event.

Understanding Kubeless

You might have heard about **Functions as a Service (FaaS)** or serverless. Kubeless provides the framework to provide serverless computing to your Kubernetes cluster. It allows you to deploy your own code to a Kubernetes cluster without needing to build a container from scratch. You only need to create your code and push it to Kubeless using their CLI, or you can package the code into a native Kubernetes manifest using a custom resource call function, which is provided by Kubeless.

Kubeless supports multiple runtime options for handling functions. Currently, it supports a number of runtimes, including: ballerina0.981.0, dotnetcore2.0, dotnetcore2.1, dotnetcore2.2, dotnetcore3.1, go1.13, go1.14, java1.8, java11, nodejs10, nodejs12, nodejs14, php7.2, php7.3, php7.4, python3.6, python3.7, python3.8, ruby2.3, ruby2.4, ruby2.5, ruby2.6, jvm1.8, nodejs_distroless8, nodejsCE8, and vertx1.8.

We selected Kubeless for this chapter due to its ease of deployment and how easy it is to integrate it with Falcosidekick to create automatic functions that can act on Falco events. By the end of this section, you will know how to install Kubeless and how to create a manifest that will deploy a Python script that we will use to react to a specific Falco event.

The first step is to deploy Kubeless into your cluster. In the next section, we will detail how easy it is to deploy Kubeless.

 This section is only meant to provide a high-level overview of Kubeless. If you would like to learn more about Kubeless, visit the Kubeless home page at `https://kubeless.io/`.

Installing Kubeless

To add Kubeless to a cluster, you only need to execute 2 steps:

1. Create a new namespace, typically using the name `kubeless`
2. Deploy the Kubeless manifest

To make this even easier, we have included a script that will create the namespace and deploy Kubeless using a manifest located in the book repository in the `chapter10/kubeless` directory called `install-kubeless.sh`.

The installation script will execute the following for you:

1. Creates the `kubeless` namespace

2. Deploys Kubeless into the `kubeless` namespace using a custom deployment manifest

3. Creates a service account and `clusterrolebinding` that is bound to the `cluster-admin` `clusterrole`

You can also install Kubeless directly from a manifest that is downloaded directly from the Kubeless Git repo, but at the time of writing, the CronJob triggers image does not run correctly on Kubernetes versions greater than 1.18. For a successful deployment, the manifest in the book repository has been edited to only deploy the base Kubeless engine and the HTTP triggers image.

To install Kubeless, execute the script in the `chapter10/kubeless` directory.

```
./install-kubeless.sh
```

The installation will not take long, and to verify Kubeless was successfully deployed, list the pods in the kubeless namespace. This will return a single POD running two containers:

```
NAME                                             READY    STATUS
RESTARTS     AGE
kubeless-controller-manager-58dc8f698d-jqkz4     2/2      Running
0            19s
```

Along with the Kubeless server, two CRDs were created: `functions.kubeless.io` and `httptriggers.kubeless.io`. We will not use the `httptriggers` custom resource in this chapter, but we will use the standard functions resource to deploy our Python script.

In the next section, we will explain how to deploy a function using a standard Kubernetes manifest that will use the function's custom resource.

Deploying a function using Kubeless

Now that we have Kubeless running, it's time to deploy a function that we will use to automatically remediate a potential security event that has been logged by Falco.

We realize that many readers may not be coders, so we have included a functions manifest in the repository in the `chapter10/kubeless` directory called `isolate-pod.yaml`. This function uses the standard Kubernetes Python client to create a network policy based on any attempt to modify an NGINX `conf` directory. If a file is modified under the conf directory, we will assume it's an attempt to take over our web server and we will isolate the Pod by denying all ingress and egress traffic to the Pod(s).

The script contains some documentation to help explain how it works, but at a high level the script performs the following:

1. Falcosidekick will send all events to Kubeless, using the `falco-functions` function (remember that we configured the Kubeless section of the falcosidekick values file).

2. The function has been configured to watch for a single event. There has been a change under the NGINX conf directory.

3. When this event is seen by the function, it will retrieve the offending Pod name.

4. A network policy is then created using one of the Pod's labels, rather than only isolating a single Pod, since a deployment may have multiple Pods running. We want to isolate any Pod that may answer for the deployed service.

Now, let's deploy the Kubeless function so we can see all of this in action.

Deploy the function as you would any manifest using `kubectl` in the `kubeless` namespace:

```
kubectl create -f isolate-pod.yaml -n kubeless
```

You can verify that the function was deployed by retrieving the functions in the kubeless namespace using `kubectl get functions -n kubeless`:

```
NAME                AGE
falco-functions     11s
```

This is where it gets interesting…

When we introduced Kubeless, we said that you can deploy code without creating your own complete images. Well, we just deployed a function, so let's look at what was actually created in the `kubeless` namespace.

Recall that the `kubeless` namespace had a single pod running, the Kubeless server. Now that we have deployed a function, retrieve the pods in the `kubeless` namespace again.

```
NAME                                          READY   STATUS
falco-functions-7c647fbb8f-k9cxs              1/1     Running
kubeless-controller-manager-58dc8f698d-jqkz4  2/2     Running
```

Wait! There are two Pods running now?

This is the magic of Kubeless – all you need to do is provide your code and a few options in your manifest and Kubeless will bundle your code into a Pod with the required runtime and modules. In our example, it creates a new Pod running Python called `falco-functions`, which is the name of the function that we designated in the manifest.

Finally, we have Falco, Falcosidekick, and Kubeless deployed – now, let's see how the three components provide you the ability to automatically react to Falco events.

Introducing DevOPs AI

Our function isn't really an AI function, it's a "dumb" function that only reacts to a certain event and it has no logic to understand if the event should be allowed or not. Our example is only meant to introduce you to using Falcosidekick to increase your security by forwarding events to an external system.

There are no limits to what you can create once events are forwarded – you can forward events to GCP Pub/Sub, and once an event is in GCP you can leverage any of Google's tools to create complex decisions that leverage any of the Google AI tools.

Obviously, AI is an entire series of books by itself, so we decided to stick to a single, static use case. While it's true that AI is much cooler than static checks, you can still create an effective automatic response engine using standard functions.

Now to see this in action!

Understand automatic responses to events

One of the best methods to understand the power of this type of system is to step through the process of an event and how the system protects the cluster. For our exercise, we will pretend to be a hacker attacking a web server in an attempt to edit the NGINX configuration file to serve up a custom application.

To demonstrate the complete system, we will execute the following steps:

1. Deploy a Bitnami NGINX Pod in the `demo` namespace, exposed on port `80`, with an Ingress rule `demo.w.x.y.z.nip.io` (`w.x.y.z` is the IP address of the KinD worker node)

2. Curl or browse to the Ingress URL to confirm the NGINX Pod is running

3. Exec into the Pod and attempt to add a file in the `/opt/bitnami/nginx/conf/` directory

4. Repeat the curl or browse to the Ingress URL, which should fail due to the modification of a file under the NGINX conf folder

Let's break down each deployment step in detail.

Deploy the NGINX server and test connectivity

First, we need a web server and to keep our cluster easy to manage, we will deploy the server into a new namespace called `demo`. We have included a script that will take care of creating the `demo` namespace, deploy an NGINX Pod, expose the service, and create an Ingress rule for testing. The script is located in the `chapter10/kubeless` directory of the repository, called `deploy-nginx.sh`.

Next, let's verify two things – test the NGINX Pod by curling to the Ingress URL that was provided by the deployment script. In our cluster, that would be `demo-hack.10.2.1.162.nip.io`.

```
curl demo-hack.10.2.1.162.nip.io
```

This will return the HTML for the home page, similar to the truncated output below.

```
<!DOCTYPE html>
<html>
<head>
<title>Welcome to nginx!</title>
<style>
    body {
        width: 35em;
        margin: 0 auto;
        font-family: Tahoma, Verdana, Arial, sans-serif;
    }
</style>
</head>
<body>
<h1>Welcome to nginx!</h1>
```

This verifies that the Pod, Service, and Ingress rule were all created correctly and our NGINX server is live on the network. Let's go one step further and verify that there are no network policies for the demo namespace. Check for policies by executing `kubectl get netpol -n demo`, which should return that there are no resources found:

```
No resources found in demo namespace.
```

With the test Pod running, we can move on to simulating an attack on the NGINX server.

Simulating an attack on the Pod

Finally, we get to see Falcosidekick and Kubeless in action.

To trigger the event that we are watching for in our function, exec into the NGINX Pod in the `demo` namespace:

```
kubectl exec -it nginx-hack -n demo -- bash
```

This will put you in the `containers` bash shell. Since our rule will watch for any writing to the NGINX conf folder, we need to create a new file to trigger the event. The easiest test would be to simply touch a file in the directory, and execute a touch to create a file called `badfile` in the `/opt/bitnami/nginx/conf/` directory. At the `I have no name!@nginx-hack:/app$` prompt in the container, create a new file by executing the following command:

```
touch /opt/bitnami/nginx/conf/badfile
```

This will immediately send you back to the bash prompt, and it may appear that nothing has happened. You didn't receive any permission denied messages, or any error messages – so did anything happen?

For the next step, you can either open another session to the Docker host, or you can just exit the running container. Once you have a shell prompt, curl the Ingress name again to verify the status of the NGINX server. Again, in our example the Ingress name is `demo-hack.10.2.1.162.nip.io`.

```
curl demo-hack.10.2.1.162.nip.io
```

You should notice that there is a delay in the reply. It will sit there for a few seconds and eventually return a `504 Gateway Time-out` error.

```
<html>
<head><title>504 Gateway Time-out</title></head>
<body>
<center><h1>504 Gateway Time-out</h1></center>
<hr><center>nginx</center>
</body>
</html>
```

This error shows that the NGINX server is not replying to any connection attempts. Of course, this worked before we created a new file inside of the running container – so let's find out why the server is now denying traffic.

The reason that the connection is being denied is due to Falco alerting that a file in the NGINX conf directory has been created. This triggered the event, then Falcosidekick sent the event to our Kubeless function, which then acted on the event by creating a network policy. Let's look for network policies in the demo namespace again by running `kubectl get netpol -n demo`:

```
NAME                          POD-SELECTOR       AGE
falco-netpol-nginx-hack       run=nginx-hack     7m28s
```

This dynamically created policy will deny all ingress and egress traffic to any pod with the label `run=nginx-hack` in the `demo` namespace. Since this was generated automatically by our Kubeless function, we instantly denied all network traffic after the hacking attempt was executed – securing our cluster without any human interaction.

The one question that is often asked regarding our example is "Why don't you just delete the POD rather than isolate it?". This comes down to one simple answer: we need a view into what was added to the container and if we delete it, rather than isolate it, we would lose any evidence that may be needed for prosecution/etc...

This ends our Falco section of the chapter. Up to this point, you have learned about Falco and what benefits it brings to runtime security in a cluster, including add-on components like Falcosidekick and Kubeless that can be used to automate responses to events.

In the next section, we will explain how to use different observability tools to look at Falco event details. We will explain how to use a new project called `Falcosidkick-ui` for quickly looking at events, and how to forward events to a full logging solution like EFK.

Observing Falco events

Falco uses STDOUT for logging by default. This makes it very easy to forward events to any logging system including enterprise solutions like Sysdig, Datadog, Splunk, or EFK.

Recently, the Falco project added a standalone UI for observing events called `Falcosidekick-ui`.

In this chapter, we will show how each of these systems can be used to observe events, both in real time or historically.

Using Falcosidekick-ui

We can deploy Falcosidekick using a Helm chart and a values file. In the `chapter10` folder, we have included a script called `install-falcosidekick.sh` that will deploy Falcosidekick and an Ingress rule that will use the nip.io format.

Once executed, Falcosidekick will be installed using Helm and an Ingress rule using the name `sidekick-ui.w.x.y.z.nip.io` will be created. On our KinD cluster, it exposed `sidekick-ui.10.2.1.162.nip.io` on port `80`.

You should be able to access the UI from any machine on your network by opening a browser and navigating to the Ingress rule for your cluster adding `/ui` to the URL path.

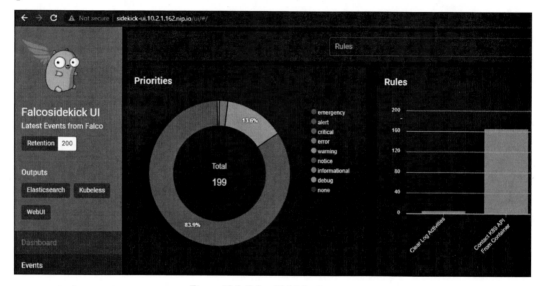

Figure 10.6: Falcosidekick-ui screen

The UI is very useful, allowing you to look at a dashboard that updates in real time and groups events by rules and the timeline, or you can look at the details of events by clicking the **Events** button on the left-hand side pane.

This will change the view to include all events and the details for each.

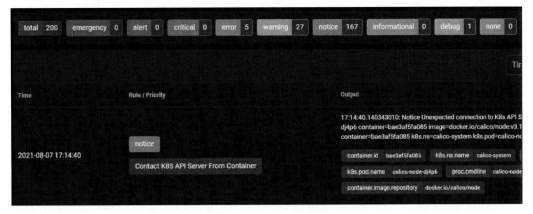

Figure 10.7: Falcosidekick-ui event viewing

Falcosidekick-ui is a great tool for looking at events on smaller clusters, or to have quick access to the most recent events generated by Falco. The team is always updating the project, so watch it for any new features or contribute to the project: `https://github.com/falcosecurity/falcosidekick-ui`.

In an enterprise, we need to have a more robust logging system, and this is where a full logging solution like EFK comes in.

Deploying our logging system

Our first step will be to deploy Elasticsearch to receive event data. To install Elasticsearch, we require persistent storage for the data. Luckily, we are using a KinD cluster so we have persistent storage thanks to Rancher's local provisioner.

To make the deployment easy, we will deploy our stack to the Elastic Cloud Control, which will install Elasticsearch, Filebeat, and Kibana. In the GitHub repository, we have included a script to deploy all of the logging components. The script is called `install-logging.sh` and is located in the `chapter10/logging` directory. Like all of the previous scripts, we will go over the details of the script and the commands that are executed.

Creating a new namespace

Since we may want to delegate access to a centralized logging team, we will create a new namespace called `logging`:

```
kubectl create ns logging
```

Deploying the ECK operator

ECK uses custom resources to create our logging stack components. The operator can deploy a number of logging components, but we will focus on the custom resources to create the Elasticsearch, Beats, and Kibana objects.

You can deploy the CRDs and the operator directly from the Elastic repo, which is what the first two lines of the script perform.

```
kubectl create -f https://download.elastic.co/downloads/eck/1.7.0/crds.yaml
kubectl apply -f https://download.elastic.co/downloads/eck/1.7.0/operator.yaml
```

Before moving on to creating the logging components, we need to confirm that the operator is up and running fully. The included script will watch for the operator to become fully ready before moving on to creating the ECK objects.

Once the operator is in a fully ready state, you can move on to deploying the Elastic logging objects.

Deploying Elasticsearch, Filebeat, and Kibana

We have included a manifest that will create the Elastic components in your cluster, it's in the `chapter10/logging` directory of the repo, called `eck-filebeats.yaml`. It is executed as part of the `install-logging.sh` script, but you can also deploy it manually by using `kubectl create`:

```
kubectl create -f eck-filebeats.yaml -n logging
```

Elasticsearch needs to increase the `vm.max_map_count` kernel setting. To do this, the operator will deploy a privileged `initContainer` that will set the value on our worker node. In a production environment, you may not allow privileged pods to run, which will cause the `initContainer` to fail. If you do not allow privileged pods to run in your cluster (which is a **very** good idea), you will need to set this value manually on each host before deploying Elasticsearch.

You can check the status of the deployment by checking the pods in the `logging` namespace. Using `kubectl`, verify that all of the pods are in a running state before moving on to the next step:

```
kubectl get pods -n logging
```

You should receive the following output:

```
NAME                             READY   STATUS    RESTARTS   AGE
elasticsearch-es-logging-0       1/1     Running   0          11h
filebeat-beat-filebeat-xn5lk     1/1     Running   4          11h
kibana-kb-647fbd8dd9-t4qp6       1/1     Running   0          11h
```

The Elasticsearch POD will also create a PersistentVolumeClaim of 1 GB. We can verify that the PVC was created using `kubectl get pvc -n logging`, producing the following output (abbreviated for formatting):

```
NAME                                                STATUS   VOLUME
elasticsearch-data-elasticsearch-es-logging-0       Bound    pvc-83de97d8-
f06d-4c32-b842-xxxxxx
```

Four ClusterIP services were created since Elasticsearch will only be used by other Kubernetes objects. We can view the services using `kubectl get services -n logging`, producing the following output:

```
NAME                         TYPE        CLUSTER-IP        EXTERNAL-IP
PORT(S)         AGE
elasticsearch-es-http        ClusterIP   10.105.169.185    <none>
9200/TCP        11h
elasticsearch-es-logging     ClusterIP   None              <none>
9200/TCP        11h
elasticsearch-es-transport   ClusterIP   None              <none>
9300/TCP        11h
kibana-kb-http               ClusterIP   10.104.179.136    <none>
5601/TCP        11h
```

By looking at the pods, services, and PVCs, we can confirm that the chart deployment was successful and we can move on to the next component, Filebeat.

Filebeat is similar to another DaemonSet you may have heard of, Fluentd, both are common log forwarders used with Kubernetes to send container logs to a central logging system. We are installing it to forward Kubernetes logs to Elasticsearch to provide a complete example of an ECK deployment.

Since we used the ECK operator for each step of our deployment, we do not need to supply any information for interconnecting the services – the operator takes care of the heavy lifting for integration for us.

Elasticsearch will have a lot of information to sort through to make the data useful. To parse the data and create useful information for the logs, we need to install a system that we can use to create custom dashboards and to search the collected data. This is where Kibana comes in.

Kibana is a log observability tool that provides a graphical view to look at events and to create custom dashboards to present the information. The ECK operator deploys the Kibana POD with automatic integration with the operator-deployed Elasticsearch, making deployment and integration quick and simple.

While ECK will deploy all of the components and services for us, it does need one additional step that we take care of, creating an Ingress rule for the Kibana dashboard. The last section of the installation script will pull the IP address of the Docker host and create an Ingress rule using a nip.io URL that starts with kibana. In our example cluster, the Ingress URL is `kibana.10.2.1.162.nip.io` – you will see the URL and credentials for your cluster in the output after all of the ECK components have been installed.

```
******************************************************************
ECK and all Custom Resources have been deployed
******************************************************************

The Kibana UI has been added to ingress, you can open the UI using
http://kibana.10.2.1.162.nip.io/
To log into Kibana, you will need to use the following credentials:

Username: elastic
Password: 8g57lX4zC03rt32zYcb5EZ6i
******************************************************************
```

Make a note of both the URL and the username/password you will need to log into the Kibana dashboard.

Finally, the step updates the Falcosidekick values file to integrate with Elasticsearch. Since ES requires a username and password, we need to add the generated password to the credentials section of the ES configuration in the values file. We automated this step by reading in the secret from the ES deployment and upgrading the Falcosidekick deployment with the new values file.

```
export PASSWORD=$(kubectl get secret elasticsearch-es-elastic-user -n
logging -o go-template='{{.data.elastic | base64decode}}')

envsubst < values-sidekick-update.yaml | helm upgrade falcosidekick
falcosecurity/falcosidekick -f - --namespace falco
```

The code above will retrieve the ES user password, decrypt it, and store it in an environment variable. This variable is then used in the values file to store the password in the field and then execute a Helm upgrade using the updated values file.

Now that we have Kibana installed, we can open the Kibana dashboard to start configuring our logging solution.

Using the components ECK to view logs

To start configuring Kibana, open the Kibana dashboard by browsing to the Ingress URL that was created during the installation of ECK, and log in with the username `elastic` and the password that you wrote down that was created during the deployment.

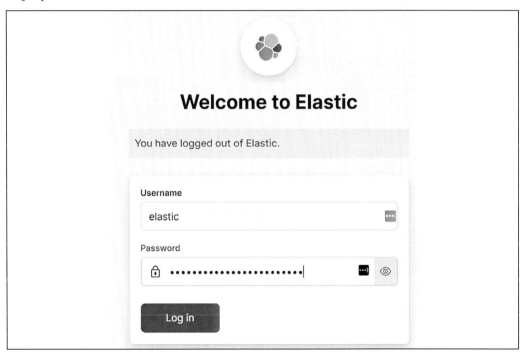

Figure 10.8: Kibana login page

Click on the **Log in** button, and you will be taken to the Kibana **Home** page.

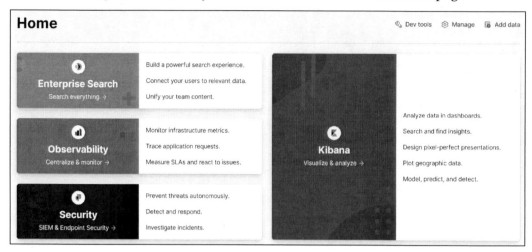

Figure 10.9: Kibana welcome screen

The first step to viewing our logs is to create an index that will use the logs being forwarded by Falcosidekick. We are also receiving logs from all containers via the Filebeat POD in our cluster but we want to focus on only the Falco events for this chapter. You can look around at the other logs as you get comfortable with Kibana.

Creating a Kibana index

To view logs or create visualizations and dashboards, you need to create an index. You can have multiple indexes on a single Kibana server, allowing you to view different logs from a single location. On our example server, we will have two sets of incoming logs, one that starts with `falco` and the other will start with `filebeat`.

First, let's create our index. Click the "hamburger" in the upper-left portion of the **Home** screen.

This will bring up all of the navigation options. Scroll down to the **Management** section, and click on the **Stack Management** link.

In the **Management** section, scroll down and click **Index Patterns** under the **Kibana** section.

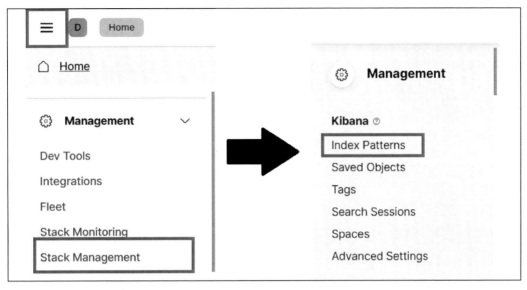

Figure 10.10: Navigating to the index patterns

On this screen, we can create a new index pattern. Click on the **Create index pattern** button to start the process.

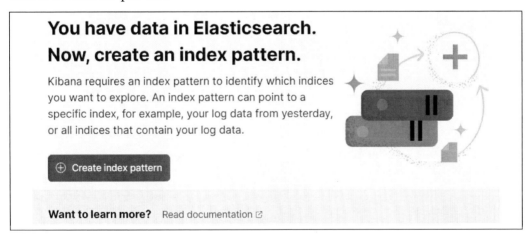

Figure 10.11: Creating a new index pattern

This will start the index creation wizard, starting with step 1, which is to define a pattern. In the **Index pattern name** field, we want to enter `falco*` and then click the **Next step** button.

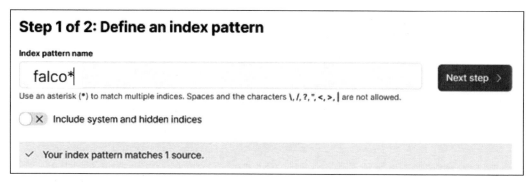

Figure 10.12: Defining an index pattern

Next, we need to select a primary field for the index. From the drop-down box, select **time** and click the **Create index pattern** button.

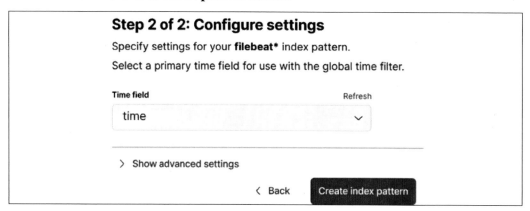

Figure 10.13: Setting a primary field

Finally, we want to set this index to be the default index for our Kibana workspace, so on the last screen, click the star on the upper right-hand side of the screen.

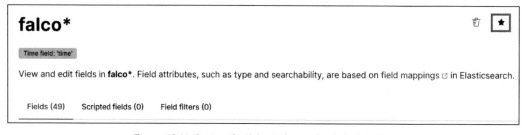

Figure 10.14: Setting the Falco index as the default index

We now have an index that contains all logs starting with `filebeat`, which will be all STDOUT logs from the running containers in the cluster.

Now, let's look at some of our data.

Browsing for events

The first exercise we want to present is the basic discovery mode to look at the logs. To do this, click on the hamburger and then click **Discover**.

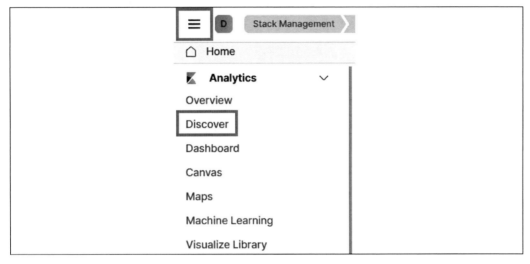

Figure 10.15: Navigating to the Discover page

This will present a new window that shows all of the logged information for our index.

Figure 10.16: Kibana Discover page

You can search for events by typing keywords into the search field. This is helpful if you are looking for a single type of event, and know what value(s) to search for. For example, if you only wanted to see events that only contained the word shell in them, you would just type shell in the search box and Kibana would dynamically update the displayed data. In this case, the information displayed changes to only events that have the word shell in them, which will be highlighted in each event:

Figure 10.17: Example filtered output

The real benefit of logging systems like Kibana is the ability to create custom dashboards that provide a view into multiple events that can be grouped by counts, averages, and more. In the next section, we will explain how to create a dashboard that provides a collection of Falco events.

Creating dashboards is a skill that you need to develop, and it will take time to understand how to group data and what values to use in a dashboard.

This section is meant to provide you with the basic tools you need to start creating dashboards like the following:

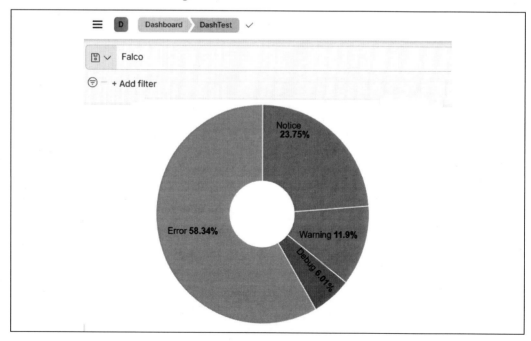

Figure 10.18: Simple example dashboard

People love dashboards, and Kibana provides tools to create dynamic and easily interpreted views of a system. Dashboards can be created using any data that Kibana has access to, including Falco events. Before we create a dashboard, let's understand what *visualization* means.

Visualizations

A visualization is a graphical representation of a collection of data – in our context, from a Kibana index. Kibana includes a set of visualizations that allow you to group data into tables, gauges, horizontal bars, pie charts, vertical bars, and more.

You can create visualizations in two ways: you can create them when creating a dashboard or you can create them before creating a dashboard and store them in the visualization library (located under the hamburger button, analytics, and visualization library).

For our example, we will create them while we are creating a new dashboard to show Falco events.

Creating a dashboard

Dashboards allow you to display visualizations in a collection that is easy to read with information updated every minute:

1. To create a dashboard, click the hamburger button and then, under **Analytics**, click **Dashboard**.

2. This will bring up the **dashboard screen**. Click the **Create dashboard** button in the upper-right corner to start creating your dashboard:

Figure 10.19: Create dashboard

3. You will be presented with a blank dashboard with a screen that says **Add your first visualization** and a few buttons above that caption:

Figure 10.20: Adding a new visualization

4. Click on the **Create visualization** button to create our first visualization for our dashboard. This will bring up an editor that allows you to drag and drop items, and change the type of visualization you will use. Section 1 contains the fields you can use to visualize, and section 2 allows you to change the visualization style (that is, bar graphs, pie charts, and so on).

    The far right of this screen has a third section, and this section allows you to set the values for the axis and how the information will be broken down:

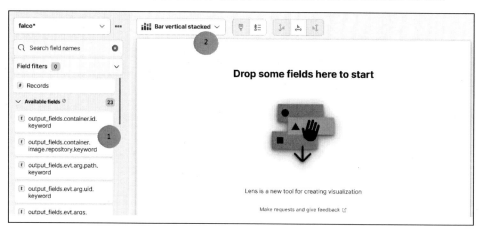

Figure 10.21: Adding visualizations to a dashboard

With a basic understanding of adding visualizations for Kibana, let's add a couple of different visualizations to familiarize you with building custom dashboards.

Creating a visualization for Falco event types

For this visualization, we will use the donut visualization, and we will use the **priority.keyword** field. On the dashboard creation screen, change the visualization type by clicking the default selected **Bar vertical stacked** and selecting **donut**.

We set the Falco index as the default index when we created it, so it should already be the working index. If you forgot to set it as the default, you may need to change the selected index in the upper right-hand section of the visualization screen. If the value is set to **Filebeat**, click the drop-down box and select the **Falco** index.

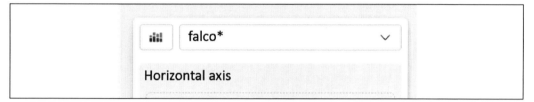

Figure 10.22: Setting the index to Falco

Then we need to add the field to the visualization. This is an easy process. We can search for any event on the left-hand side of the creation screen, in the search box. As you type, Kibana will only display any matching events below the search box.

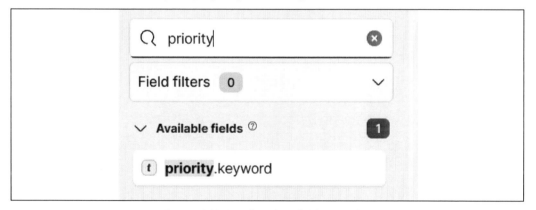

Figure 10.23: Searching for a field to visualize

Once you see the field you would like to add, simply drag it over to the main pane in the middle. Kibana will show you what the final visualization will look like.

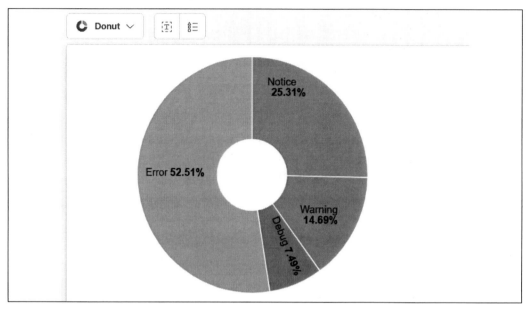

Figure 10.24: Example Kibana visualization

If you are happy with the visualization, you can save it and continue to add additional visualizations by clicking the **Save and return** button in the upper right of the screen.

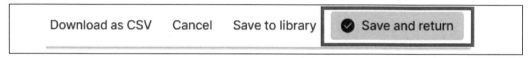

Figure 10.25: Save and return to the main dashboard editor

This will return you to the main dashboard page. Click the **Create visualization** button again. We want to add a new visualization that will show the top keyword for the events that Falco has been logging.

For this visualization, we want to change the type to **table**, and we will use the **rule. keyword** field.

Once you find the field in the search and drag it over to the middle of the screen, you will see something similar to the below screenshot.

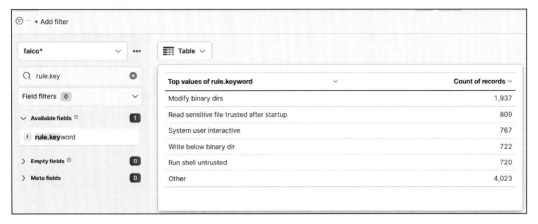

Figure 10.26: Second visualization example

Now, let's save the new visualization and return to the main dashboard screen.

We can save the dashboard by clicking the **Save** button in the upper portion of the dashboard. Call the dashboard **Falco-Events** and click **Save**.

Figure 10.27: Saving a dashboard

Once you save a dashboard, it will be available via the **dashboards** button on the left-hand side of the Kibana home page. This is the same button you used earlier to create the first dashboard.

To exit the editor, click **Switch to view mode** in the upper section of the screen.

Figure 10.28: Switching to view mode

This will exit the editor and you will see your final dashboard.

Figure 10.29: Final example dashboard

As you can imagine, creating dashboards can become very involved and very complex. Most enterprises have dedicated teams that are subject matter experts in logging and creating dashboards. But with time and practice, you can easily create custom dashboards for your clusters.

With the completion of using Kibana to create dashboards, we have come to the end of the Falco and logging chapter.

Summary

This chapter covered how to create an enhanced auditing system for your Kubernetes cluster. We started the chapter by introducing Falco, an auditing add-on that was donated to the CNCF by Sysdig. Falco adds a level of auditing that Kubernetes does not include, and combined with the included auditing functionality, provides an audit trail for everything from API access to actions in a pod.

We explained how Falcosidekick can be used to forward events to other systems to perform complex tasks like creating automated response engines using systems like Kubeless to execute functions based on certain events. This was just a small example, but the possibilities are endless with the integrations that Falcosidekick includes, including Pub/Sub, Cloud Run, Lambda, and more.

Logs aren't beneficial if you can't store them in a logging system that allows you to store logs on persistent storage and offers a management interface to search logs and create dashboards. We installed the common EFK stack on our KinD cluster and created a custom dashboard to show Falco events in Kibana.

With the topics you learned about in this chapter, you should have a strong foundational knowledge of how to add Falco to a cluster and use the ECK operator to store logs and present data in visualizations and dashboards.

While logging and auditing are important, it is equally important to have a process to restore workloads in the event of a disaster. In the next chapter, we will introduce Velero, an open source backup utility from Heptio.

Questions

1. If you need to edit an included Falco rule, which file would you edit?

    a. `falco.yaml`

    b. `falco_rules.yaml`

    c. `falco_rules.changes.yaml`

    d. `falco_rules.local.yaml`

2. Which of the following is a common log forwarder used by Kubernetes?

    a. Kube-forwarder

    b. Fluentd

    c. Forwarder

    d. Kubernetes doesn't use forwarders

3. What is the product that provides a way to present logs using visualizations and dashboards when you deploy the EFK stack?

    a. Fluentd

    b. Elasticsearch

    c. Kibana

    d. Excel

4. Which of the following tools forwards only Falco logs to a central logging system?

    a. Falco

    b. Falcosidekick

    c. The Kubernetes API server

    d. All products forward every log, not just the Falco logs

5. What is the name of the object in Falco that allows you to create a collection of items?

    a. Lists

    b. Rules

    c. Arrays

    d. Collections

Join our book's Discord space

Join the book's Discord workspace for a monthly *Ask me Anything* session with the authors: `https://packt.link/K8EntGuide`

11
Backing Up Workloads

Accidents and disasters happen, and just like you may have insurance for these events in real life, you should have insurance for your cluster and workloads.

Most Kubernetes distributions do not include any components to back up workloads, but there are a number of products available from both the open source community and vendor-supported solutions from companies such as Kasten, Veritas, and Commvault.

In this chapter, we will cover the following topics:

- Understanding Kubernetes backups
- Performing an etcd backup
- Introducing and setting up VMware's Velero
- Using Velero to back up workloads
- Managing Velero using the CLI
- Restoring from a backup

To back up your KinD cluster, we will introduce you to a popular open source backup solution called Velero, which can be used to create full backups of workloads and the persistent data in a cluster. We will explain how to use Velero to back up namespaces and objects, schedule backup jobs, and how to restore workloads.

Technical requirements

To perform the hands-on experiments in this chapter, you will need the following:

- A Docker host installed using the steps from *Chapter 1, Docker and Container Essentials*, with a minimum of 8 GB of RAM
- A KinD cluster configured using the initial scripts from *Chapter 2, Deploying Kubernetes Using KinD*

You can access the code for this chapter by going to this book's GitHub repository: `https://github.com/PacktPublishing/Kubernetes---An-Enterprise-Guide-2E/tree/main/chapter11`.

Understanding Kubernetes backups

Backing up a Kubernetes cluster requires backing up not only the workloads running on the cluster but also the cluster itself. Remember that the cluster state is maintained in an etcd database, making it a very important component that you need to back up to recover from any disasters.

Creating a backup of the cluster and the running workloads allows you to do the following:

- Migrate clusters
- Create a development cluster from a production cluster
- Recover a cluster from a disaster
- Recover data from persistent volumes
- Namespace and deployment recovery

In this chapter, we will provide the details and tools to back up your etcd database and every namespace and object in the cluster.

> Recovering a cluster from a complete disaster in an enterprise usually involves backing up custom SSL certificates for various components, such as Ingress controllers, load-balancers, and the API server.
>
> Since the process to back up all custom components is different for all environments, we will focus on the procedures that are common among most Kubernetes distributions.

As you know, the cluster state is maintained in etcd, and if you lose all of your etcd instances, you will lose your cluster. In a multi-node control plane, you would have a minimum of three etcd instances, providing redundancy for the cluster. If you lose a single instance, the cluster would remain running and you could build a new instance of etcd and add it to the cluster. Once the new instance has been added, it will receive a copy of the etcd database and your cluster will be back to full redundancy.

In the event that you lost all of your etcd servers without any backup of the database, you would lose the cluster, including the cluster state itself and all of the workloads. Since etcd is so important, the `etcdctl` utility includes a built-in backup function.

Performing an etcd backup

Since we are using KinD for our Kubernetes cluster, we can create a backup of the etcd database, but we will not be able to restore it.

Our etcd server is running in a pod on the cluster called `etcd-cluster01-control-plane`, located in the `kube-system` namespace. During the creation of the KinD cluster, we added an extra port mapping for the control plane node, exposing port 2379, which is used to access etcd. In your own production environment, you may not have the etcd port exposed for external requests, but the process of backing up the database will still be similar to the steps explained in this section.

Backing up the required certificates

Most Kubernetes installations store certificates in `/etc/kubernetes/pki`. In this respect, KinD is no different, so we can back up our certificates using the `docker cp` command.

We have included a script in the `chapter11/etcd` directory called `install-etcd-tools.sh` that will execute the steps to download and execute the backup of the etcd database. To execute the script, change your directory to the `chapter11/etcd` directory and execute the installation script.

Let's explain the steps that the script will execute for you so you understand the entire process:

1. First, we need to create a directory to store the certificates required to back up our database. This is included in the cloned repository `chapter11/etcd` folder.

2. To back up the certificates located on the API server, use the following `docker cp` command:

```
docker cp cluster01-control-plane:/etc/kubernetes/pki ./certs
```

This will copy the contents of the `pki` folder contents on the control plane node to your `localhost` in the `chapter11/etcd/certs` folder.

Now that we have the certificates to access etcd, the next step is to create a backup of the database.

Backing up the etcd database

The creators of etcd created a utility to back up and restore the etcd database, called `etcdctl`. For our purposes, we will only use the backup operation; however, since etcd is not exclusive to only Kubernetes, the utility has a number of options that you will not use as a Kubernetes operator or developer. If you want to read more about the utility, you can visit the etcd-io GIT repository at `https://github.com/etcd-io/etcd`.

To back up a database, you will need the `etcdctl` utility and the required certificates to access the database, which we copied from the control plane server.

To back up the etcd database on your KinD cluster, follow these steps (if you executed the install script in the etcd directory, the first three steps have already been completed):

1. You can download the latest version of `etcdctl`. The version we tested for this exercise was 3.5.1, which can be downloaded using the command below:

```
wget https://github.com/etcd-io/etcd/releases/download/v3.5.1/
etcd-v3.5.1-linux-amd64.tar.gz
```

2. Extract the contents of the archive and to make using the utility easier, we will move it to the `/usr/bin` directory.

```
tar xvf etcd-v3.5.1-linux-amd64.tar.gz && sudo cp etcd-v3.5.1-
linux-amd64/etcdctl /usr/bin
```

3. In the etcd pod, back up the etcd database using `etcdctl` (this step is not part of the included script):

```
etcdctl snapshot save etcd-snapshot.db --endpoints=htt
ps://127.0.0.1:2379 --cacert=./certs/ca.crt --cert=./certs/
healthcheck-client.crt --key=./certs/healthcheck-client.key
```

You will receive the following output:

```
{"level":"info","ts":1636769909.8710756,"caller":"snapshot/v3_
snapshot.go:119","msg":"created temporary db file","path":"etcd-
snapshot.db.part"}
{"level":"info","ts":"2021-11-13T02:18:29.891Z","caller":"c
lientv3/maintenance.go:200","msg":"opened snapshot stream;
downloading"}
{"level":"info","ts":1636769909.8919604,"caller":"snapshot/
v3_snapshot.go:127","msg":"fetching snapshot","endpoint":"htt
ps://127.0.0.1:2379"}
{"level":"info","ts":"2021-11-13T02:18:30.119Z","caller":"c
lientv3/maintenance.go:208","msg":"completed snapshot read;
closing"}
{"level":"info","ts":1636769910.1562147,"caller":"snapshot/v3_
snapshot.go:142","msg":"fetched snapshot","endpoint":"https://12
7.0.0.1:2379","size":"4.4 MB","took":0.284949965}
{"level":"info","ts":1636769910.1579342,"caller":"snapshot/v3_
snapshot.go:152","msg":"saved","path":"etcd-snapshot.db"}
Snapshot saved at etcd-snapshot.db
```

 Older versions of `etcdctl` required you to set the API version to 3 using `ETCDCTL_API=3`, since they defaulted to the version 2 API. Etcd 3.4 changed the default API to 3, so we do not need to set that variable before using `etcdctl` commands.

4. Verify that the copy was successful by viewing the contents of the current folder:

```
ls -la
```

You should see the backup file named `etcd-snapshot.db`. If you do not see your backup, repeat the steps again and watch for any errors in the output.

5. Check the status of the backup to verify that the backup was completed:

```
etcdctl --write-out=table snapshot status etcd-snapshot.db
```

This will output an overview of the backup:

HASH	REVISION	TOTAL KEYS	TOTAL SIZE
dd23bff5	7255	1263	4.0 MB

This process only backs up the etcd database once. In the real world, you should create a scheduled process that executes a snapshot of etcd at regular intervals that stores the backup file in a safe, secure location.

 Due to how KinD runs the control plane, we cannot use the restore procedures in this section. We are providing the steps in this section so that you know how to back up an etcd database in an enterprise environment.

Introducing and setting up VMware's Velero

Velero is an open source backup solution for Kubernetes that was originally developed by a company called Heptio. As VMware has enhanced their support for Kubernetes, they have purchased multiple companies and Heptio was one of their acquisitions – bringing Velero into the VMware portfolio.

VMware has moved most of its offerings around Kubernetes under the Tanzu umbrella. This can be a little confusing for some people since the original iteration of Tanzu was a deployment of multiple components that added Kubernetes support to vSphere clusters. Since the initial incarnation of Tanzu, it has come to include components such as Velero, Harbor, and the **Tanzu Application Platform (TAP)**, all of which do not require vSphere to function; they will run natively in any standard Kubernetes cluster.

Even with all of the ownership and branding changes, the base functions of Velero have remained. It offers many features that are only available in commercial products, including scheduling, backup hooks, and granular backup controls – all for no charge.

While Velero is free, it has a learning curve since it does not include an easy-to-use GUI like most commercial products. All operations in Velero are carried out using their command-line utility, an executable called `velero`. This single executable allows you to install the Velero server, create backups, check the status of backups, restore backups, and more. Since every operation for management can be done with one file, restoring a cluster's workloads becomes a very easy process. In this chapter, we will create a second KinD cluster and populate it with a backup from an existing cluster.

But before that, we need to take care of a few requirements.

Velero requirements

Velero consists of a few components to create a backup system:

- **The Velero CLI**: This provides the installation of Velero components. It is used for all backup and restore functions.
- **The Velero server**: Responsible for executing backing up and restore procedures.
- **Storage provider plug-ins**: Used for backup and restoring specific storage systems.

Outside of the base Velero components, you will also need to provide an object storage location that will be used to store your backups. If you do not have an object storage solution, you can deploy MinIO, which is an open source project that provides an S3-compatible object store. We will deploy MinIO in our KinD cluster to demonstrate the backup and restore features provided by Velero.

Installing the Velero CLI

The first step to deploy Velero is to download the latest Velero CLI binary. We have included a script to install the Velero binary in the `chapter11` directory called `install-velero-binary.sh`, which executes the steps below.

To install the CLI, follow these steps:

1. Download the release from the `vmware-tanzu/velero` GitHub repository:
   ```
   wget https://github.com/vmware-tanzu/velero/releases/download/
   v1.6.3/velero-v1.6.3-linux-amd64.tar.gz
   ```

2. Extract the contents of the archive:
   ```
   tar xvf velero-v1.6.3-linux-amd64.tar.gz
   ```

3. Move the Velero binary to `/usr/bin`:
   ```
   sudo mv velero-v1.6.3-linux-amd64/velero /usr/bin
   ```

4. Verify that you can run the Velero CLI by checking the version:
   ```
   velero version
   ```

You should see from the output from Velero that you are running version 1.4.0:

```
Client:
        Version: v1.6.3
        Git commit: 5fe3a50bfddc2becb4c0bd5e2d3d4053a23e95d2
<error getting server version: no matches for kind
"ServerStatusRequest" in version "velero.io/v1">
```

You can safely ignore the last line, which shows an error in finding the Velero server. Right now, all we have installed is the Velero executable and it can't find the server yet. In the next section, we will install the server to complete the installation.

Installing Velero

Velero has minimal system requirements, most of which are easily met:

- A Kubernetes cluster running version 1.12 or higher
- The Velero executable
- Images for the system components
- A compatible storage location
- A volume snapshot plugin (optional)

Depending on your infrastructure, you may not have a compatible location for the backups or snapshotting volumes. Fortunately, if you do not have a compatible storage system, there are open source options that you can add to your cluster to meet the requirements.

In the next section, we will explain the natively supported storage options and since our example will use a KinD cluster, we will install open source options to add compatible storage to use as a backup location.

Backup storage location

Velero requires an S3-compatible bucket to store backups. There are a number of officially supported systems, including all object store offerings from AWS, Azure, and Google.

Along with the officially supported providers, there are a number of community- and vendor-supported providers from companies such as DigitalOcean, Hewlett Packard, and Portworx. The following table lists all of the current providers:

In the following table, the **Backup Support** column means that the plugin provides a compatible location to store Velero backups. **Volume Snapshot Support** means that the plugin supports backing up persistent volumes.

Vendor	Backup Support	Volume Snapshot Support	Support
Amazon	AWS S3	AWS EBS	Official
Various	S3 Compatible	AWS EBS	Official
Google	Google Cloud Storage	GCE Disks	Official
Microsoft	Azure Blob Storage	Azure Managed Disks	Official
VMware	Not Supported	vSphere Volumes	Official
Kubernetes CSI	Not Supported	CSI Volumes	Official
Alibaba Cloud	Alibaba Cloud OSS	Alibaba Cloud	Community
DigitalOcean	DigitalOcean Object Storage	DigitalOcean Volumes Block Storage	Community
HP	Not Supported	HPE Storage	Community
OpenEBS	Not Supported	OpenEBS cStor Volumes	Community
Portworx	Not Supported	Portworkx Volumes	Community
Storj	Storj Object Storage	Not Supported	Community

Table 11.1: Velero storage options

Velero's AWS S3 driver is compatible with many third-party storage systems, including EMC ECS, IBM Cloud, Oracle Cloud, and MinIO.

If you do not have an existing object storage solution, you can deploy the open source S3 provider MinIO.

Now that we have the Velero executable installed, and our KinD cluster has persistent storage, thanks to the auto-provisioner from Rancher, we can move on to the first requirement – adding an S3-compatible backup location for Velero.

Deploying MinIO

MinIO is an open source object storage solution that is compatible with Amazon's S3 cloud services, API. You can read more about MinIO on its GitHub repository at `https://github.com/minio/minio`.

If you install MinIO using a manifest from the internet, be sure to verify what volumes are declared in the deployment before trying to use it as a backup location. Many of the examples on the internet use emptyDir: {}, which is not persistent.

We have included a modified MinIO deployment from the Velero GitHub repository in the chapter11 folder. Since we have persistent storage on our cluster, we edited the volumes in the deployment to use **PersistentVolumeClaims** (**PVCs**), which will use the auto-provisioner for Velero's data and configuration.

To deploy the MinIO server, change directories to chapter11 and execute kubectl create. The deployment will create a Velero namespace, PVCs, and MinIO on your KinD cluster. It may take some time for the deployment to complete. We have seen the deployment take anything from a minute to a few minutes, depending on the host system:

```
kubectl create -f minio-deployment.yaml
```

This will deploy the MinIO server and expose it as minio on port 9000/TCP, and the console on port 9001/TCP as follows:

```
NAME      TYPE        CLUSTER-IP      EXTERNAL-IP   PORT(S)    AGE
console   ClusterIP   10.102.216.91   <none>        9001/TCP   42h
minio     ClusterIP   10.110.216.37   <none>        9000/TCP   42h
```

The MinIO server can be targeted by any pod in the cluster, with correct access keys, using minio.velero.svc on port 9000.

Exposing MinIO and the console

By default, your MinIO storage will only be available inside the cluster it has been deployed in. Since we will demonstrate restoring to a different cluster at the end of the chapter, we need to expose MinIO using an ingress rule. MinIO also includes a dashboard that allows you to browse the contents of the S3 buckets on the server. To allow access to the dashboard, you can deploy an ingress rule that exposes the MinIO console.

We have included a script in the chapter11 folder called create-minio-ingress.sh that will create an ingress rule using the nip.io syntax of minio-console.w.x.y.z.nip.ip and minio.w.x.y.z.nip.ip, with your host IP. You can also create it using the following manifest and steps:

1. Remember to change the host to include the host's IP address in the nip.io URL:

    ```
    apiVersion: networking.k8s.io/v1
    kind: Ingress
    ```

```
metadata:
  name: minio-ingress
  namespace: velero
spec:
  rules:
  - host: "minio-console.[hostip].nip.io"
    http:
      paths:
      - path: /
        pathType: Prefix
        backend:
          service:
            name: console
            port:
              number: 9001
  - host: "minio.[hostip].nip.io"
    http:
      paths:
      - path: /
        pathType: Prefix
        backend:
          service:
            name: minio
            port:
              number: 9000
```

2. Once deployed, you can use a browser on any machine and open the URL you used for the ingress rule. On our cluster, the host IP is `10.2.1.161`, so our URL is `minio-console.10.2.1.161.nip.io`:

Figure 11.1: MinIO dashboard

3. To access the dashboard, supply the access key and secret key from the MinIO deployment. If you used the MinIO installer from the GitHub repository, the username and password have been defined in the manifest. They are `packt/packt123`.

4. Once logged in, you will see a list of buckets and any items that are stored in them. Right now, it will be fairly empty since we haven't created a backup yet. We will revisit the dashboard after we execute a backup of our KinD cluster:

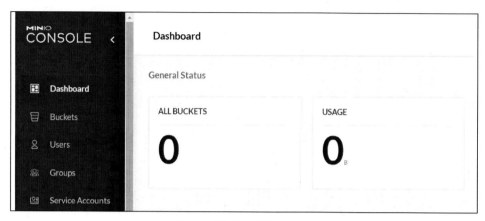

Figure 11.2: MinIO browser

 If you are new to object storage, it is important to note that while this deploys a storage solution in your cluster, it **will not** create a `StorageClass` or integrate with Kubernetes in any way. All pod access to the S3 bucket is done using the URL that we will provide in the next section.

Now that you have an S3-compatible object store running, you need to create a configuration file that Velero will use to target your MinIO server.

Creating the S3 target configuration

Before we configure our Velero server to target a MinIO bucket, we need to create a new bucket. To create a bucket, you need to log in to the MinIO console and, on the left-hand side, select the **Buckets** option.

Once you are in the **Buckets** section, click the **Create Bucket** button, located in the upper right-hand corner of the **Bucket** console. This will bring up the new **Bucket** entry screen.

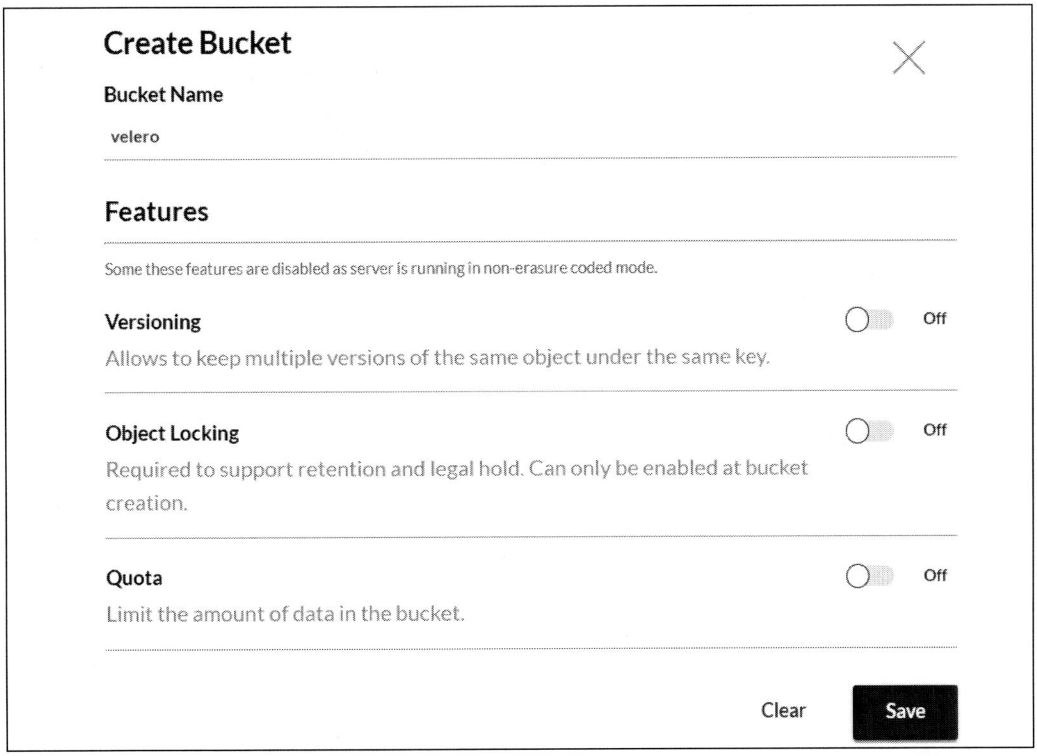

Create Bucket ✕

Bucket Name

velero

Features

Some these features are disabled as server is running in non-erasure coded mode.

Versioning   ◯ Off

Allows to keep multiple versions of the same object under the same key.

Object Locking   ◯ Off

Required to support retention and legal hold. Can only be enabled at bucket

creation.

Quota   ◯ Off

Limit the amount of data in the bucket.

Clear   **Save**

Figure 11.3: Creating a new S3 bucket

We will configure Velero to target a bucket named `velero`, so for the **Bucket Name** value, enter `velero` and click **Save** to create your new S3 bucket.

Next, we need to create a file with credentials to the S3 bucket. When we deployed the MinIO manifest from the `chapter11` folder, it created an initial key ID and access key, `packt/packt123`:

1. Create a new credential file in the `chapter11` folder called `credentials-velero`:

   ```
   vi credentials-velero
   ```

2. Add the following lines to the credentials file and save the file:

   ```
   [default]
   aws_access_key_id = packt
   aws_secret_access_key = packt123
   ```

   Now, we can deploy Velero using the Velero executable and the `install` option.

3. Execute the Velero installation using the following command from inside the `chapter11` folder to deploy Velero:

```
velero install \
     --provider aws \
     --plugins velero/velero-plugin-for-aws:v1.2.0 \
     --bucket velero \
     --secret-file ./credentials-velero \
     --use-volume-snapshots=false \
     --backup-location-config region=minio,s3ForcePathStyle="tru
e",s3Url=http://minio.velero.svc:9000
```

Let's explain the installation options and what the values mean:

Option	Description
`--provider`	Configures Velero to use a storage provider. Since we are using MinIO, which is S3-compatible, we are passing `aws` as our provider.
`--plugins`	Tells Velero the backup plugin to use. For our cluster, since we are using MinIO for object storage, we selected the AWS plugin.
`--bucket`	The name of the S3 bucket that you want to target.
`--secret-file`	Points to the file that contains the credentials to authenticate with the S3 bucket.
`--use-volume-snapshots`	Will enable or disable volume snapshots. Since we do not want to back up persistent disks, we set this value to `false`.
`--backup-location-config`	The S3 target location where Velero will store backups. Since MinIO is running in the same cluster as Velero, we can target S3 using the name `minio.velero.svc:9000`. We will also create an ingress rule to the MinIO service that will allow access to the MinIO dashboard and allow S3 requests externally via the ingress URL.
`--use-restic`	If you want to back up persistent volumes but you don't have a compatible volume snapshot provider, you can enable the restic plugin using this option. For additional details on restic and its features and limitations, see the restic section on the Velero GitHub page at `https://velero.io/docs/v1.4/restic/`.

Table 11.2: Velero install options

When you execute the install, you will see a number of objects being created, including a number of **CustomResourceDefinitions (CRDs)** and secrets that Velero uses to handle backup and restore operations.

If you run into issues with your Velero server starting up correctly, there are a few CRDs and secrets that you can look at that may have incorrect information. In the following table, we explain some of the common objects that you may need to interact with when using Velero:

CustomResourceDefinition	Name	Description
`backups.velero.io`	`backup`	Each backup that is created will create an object called `backup`, which includes the settings for each backup job.
`backupstoragelocations.velero.io`	`BackupStorageLocation`	Each backup storage location creates a `BackupStorageLocation` object that contains the configuration to connect to the storage provider.
`schedules.velero.io`	`Schedule`	Each scheduled backup creates a `Schedule` object that contains the schedule for a backup.
`volumesnapshotlocations.velero.io`	`VolumeSnapshotLocation`	If enabled, the `VolumeSnapshotLocation` object contains the information on the storage used for volume snapshots.

Secret Name	Description
`cloud-credentials`	Contains the credentials to connect to the storage provider in Base64 format. If your Velero pod fails to start up, you may have an incorrect value in the `data.cloud` spec.
`velero-restic-credentials`	If you are using the restic plugin, this will contain your repository password, similar to `cloud-credentials`. If you experience issues connecting to the volume snapshot provider, verify that the repository password is correct.

Table 11.3: Velero's CRDs and Secrets

While most of your interaction with these objects will be through the Velero executable, it is always a good practice to understand how utilities interact with the API server. Understanding the objects and what their functions are is helpful if you do not have access to the Velero executable but you need to view, or potentially change, an object value to address an issue quickly.

Now that we have Velero installed, and a high-level understanding of Velero objects, we can move on to creating different backup jobs for a cluster.

Using Velero to back up workloads

Velero supports running a "one-time" backup with a single command or on a recurring schedule. Whether you chose to run a single backup or a recurring backup, you can back up all objects or only certain objects using `include` and `exclude` flags.

Running a one-time cluster backup

To create an initial backup, you can run a single Velero command that will back up all of the namespaces in the cluster.

Executing a backup without any flags to include or exclude any cluster objects will back up every namespace and all of the objects in the namespace.

To create a one-time backup, execute the `velero` command with the `backup create <backup name>` option. In our example, we have named the backup `initial-backup`:

```
velero backup create initial-backup
```

The only confirmation you will receive from this is that the backup request was submitted:

```
Backup request "initial-backup" submitted successfully.
Run `velero backup describe initial-backup` or `velero backup logs
initial-backup` for more details.
```

Fortunately, Velero also tells you the command to check the backup status and logs. The last line of the output tells us that we can use the `velero` command with the `backup` option and either `describe` or `logs` to check the status of the backup operation.

The `describe` option will show all of the details of the job:

```
Name:          initial-backup
Namespace:     velero
Labels:        velero.io/storage-location=default
Annotations:   velero.io/source-cluster-k8s-gitversion=v1.21.1
               velero.io/source-cluster-k8s-major-version=1
               velero.io/source-cluster-k8s-minor-version=21

Phase:  Completed

Errors:    0
Warnings:  0
```

```
Namespaces:
  Included:   *
  Excluded:   <none>

Resources:
  Included:          *
  Excluded:          <none>
  Cluster-scoped:  auto

Label selector:  <none>

Storage Location:  default

Velero-Native Snapshot PVs:  auto

TTL:  720h0m0s

Hooks:  <none>

Backup Format Version:  1.1.0

Started:    2021-09-29 20:24:07 +0000 UTC
Completed:  2021-09-29 20:24:20 +0000 UTC

Expiration:  2021-10-29 20:24:07 +0000 UTC

Total items to be backed up:  696
Items backed up:                    696

Velero-Native Snapshots: <none included>
```

To reinforce the previous section, where we mentioned some of the CRDs that Velero uses, we also want to explain where the Velero utility retrieves this information from.

Each backup that is created will create a backup object in the Velero namespace. For our initial backup, a new backup object named `initial-backup` was created. Using `kubectl`, we can describe the object to see similar information that the Velero executable will provide.

As shown in the preceding output, the `describe` option shows you all of the settings for the backup job. Since we didn't pass any options to the backup request, the job contains all the namespaces and objects. Some of the most important details to verify are the phase, the total items to be backed up, and the items backed up.

If the status of the phase is anything other than `success`, you may not have all the items that you want in your backup. It's also a good idea to check the backed-up items; if the number of items backed up is less than the items to be backed up, our backup did not back up all of the items.

You may need to check the status of a backup, but you may not have the Velero executable installed. Since this information is in a CR, we can describe the CR to retrieve the backup details. Running `kubectl describe` on the backup object will show the status of the backup:

```
kubectl describe backups initial-backup -n velero
```

If we jump to the bottom of the output from the `describe` command, you will see the following:

```
Spec:
  Default Volumes To Restic:  false
  Hooks:
  Included Namespaces:
    *

  Storage Location:  default
  Ttl:               720h0m0s
Status:
  Completion Timestamp:  2021-09-29T20:24:20Z
  Expiration:            2021-10-29T20:24:07Z
  Format Version:        1.1.0
  Phase:                 Completed
  Progress:
    Items Backed Up:  696
    Total Items:      696
  Start Timestamp:    2021-09-29T20:24:07Z
  Version:            1
Events:               <none>
```

In the output, you can see that the phase is completed, the start and completion times, and the number of objects that were backed up and included in the backup.

It's good practice to use a cluster add-on that can generate alerts based on information in log files or the status of an object, such as AlertManager.

You always want a successful backup, and if a backup fails, you should look into the failure immediately.

To verify that the backup is correctly stored in our S3 target, go back to the MinIO console and if you are not already in the **Bucket** view, click **Buckets** on the left-hand side. If you are already on the **Bucket** screen, press *F5* to refresh your browser to update the view. Once refreshed, you should see that the **velero** bucket has objects stored in it.

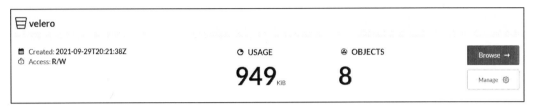

Figure 11.4: Overview of S3 storage

Since the overview of the **velero** bucket shows storage usage and a number of objects, we can safely assume that the initial backup was successful.

Scheduling a cluster backup

Creating a one-time backup is useful if you have a cluster operation scheduled or if there is a major software upgrade in a namespace. Since these events will be rare, you will want to schedule a backup that will back up the cluster at regular intervals, rather than random one-time backups.

To create a scheduled backup, you use the `schedule` option and create a tag with the Velero executable. Along with the schedule and creating the tag, you need to provide a name for the job and the `schedule` flag, which accepts *cron*-based expressions. The following schedule tells Velero to back up at 1 A.M. every day:

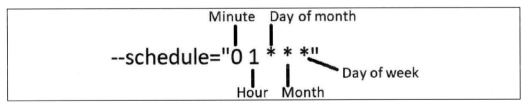

Figure 11.5: Cron scheduling expression

Using the information in *Figure 11.5*, we can create a backup that will run at 1 A.M., using the following `velero schedule create` command:

```
velero schedule create cluster-daily --schedule="0 1 * * *"
```

Velero will reply that a schedule has been successfully created:

```
Schedule "cluster-daily" created successfully.
```

If you are not familiar with cron and the options that are available, you should read the cron package documentation at `https://godoc.org/github.com/robfig/cron`.

cron will also accept some shorthand expressions, which may be easier than using the standard cron expressions. The following table contains the shorthand for predefined schedules:

Shorthand value	Description
@yearly	Executes once a year at midnight on January 1st
@monthly	Executes once a month, on the first day of the month, at midnight
@weekly	Executes once a week, on Sunday morning at midnight
@daily	Executes daily at midnight
@hourly	Executes at the beginning of each hour

Table 11.4: cron shorthand scheduling

Using the values from the shorthand table to schedule a backup job that executes daily at midnight, we use the following Velero command:

```
velero schedule create cluster-daily --schedule="@daily"
```

Scheduled jobs will create a backup object when the job is executed. The backup name will contain the name of the schedule, with a dash and the date and time of the backup. Using the name from the preceding example, our initial backup was created with the name `cluster-daily-20210930010057`. Here, `20210930` is the date the backup ran, and `010057` is the time the backup ran in UTC time. This is the equivalent of `2021-09-30 1:00:57 +0000 UTC`.

All of our examples so far have been configured to back up all of the namespaces and objects in the cluster. You may need to create different schedules or exclude/include certain objects based on your specific clusters.

In the next section, we will explain how to create a custom backup that will allow you to use specific tags to include and exclude namespaces and objects.

Creating a custom backup

When you create any backup job, you can provide flags to customize what objects will be included in or excluded from the backup job. Some of the most common flags are detailed here:

Flag	Description
`--exclude-namespaces`	Comma-separated list of namespaces to exclude from the backup job. *Example*: `--exclude-namespaces web-dev1,web-dev2`
`--exclude-resources`	Comma-separated list of resources to exclude, formatted as `resource.group`. *Example*: `--exclude-resources storageclasses.storage.k8s.io`
`--include-namespaces`	Comma-separated list of namespaces to include in the backup job. *Example*: `--include-namespaces web-dev1,web-dev2`
`--selector`	Configures the backup to include only objects that match a label selector. Accepts a single value only. *Example*: `--selector app.kubernetes.io/name=ingress-nginx`
`--ttl`	Configures how long to keep the backup in hours, minutes, and seconds. By default, the value is set for 30 days or `720h0m0s`. *Example*: `--ttl 24h0m0s` This will delete the backup after 24 hours.

Table 11.5: Velero backup flags

To create a scheduled backup that will run daily and include only Kubernetes system namespaces, we would create a scheduled job using the `--include-namespaces` flag:

```
velero schedule create cluster-ns-daily --schedule="@daily" --include-
namespaces ingress-nginx,kube-node-lease,kube-public,kube-system,local-
path-storage,velero
```

Since Velero commands use a CLI for all operations, we should start by explaining the common commands you will use to manage backup and restore operations.

Managing Velero using the CLI

Right now, all Velero operations must be done using the Velero executable. Managing a backup system without a GUI can be a challenge at first, but once you get comfortable with the Velero management commands, it becomes easy to perform operations.

The Velero executable accepts two options:

- Commands
- Flags

A command is an operation such as backup, restore, install, and get. Most initial commands require a second command to make a complete operation. For example, a backup command requires another command, such as create or delete, to form a complete operation.

There are two types of flags – command flags and global flags. Global flags are flags that can be set for any command, while command flags are specific to the command being executed.

Like many CLI tools, Velero includes built-in help for every command. If you forget some syntax or want to know what flags can be used with a command, you can use the -h flag to get help:

```
velero backup create -h
```

The following is the abbreviated help output for the backup create command:

```
Create a backup
Usage:
velero backup create NAME [flags]
Examples:
  # Create a backup containing all resources.
  velero backup create backup1
  # Create a backup including only the nginx namespace.
  velero backup create nginx-backup --include-namespaces nginx
  # Create a backup excluding the velero and default namespaces.
  velero backup create backup2 --exclude-namespaces velero,default
  # Create a backup based on a schedule named daily-backup.
  velero backup create --from-schedule daily-backup
  # View the YAML for a backup that doesn't snapshot volumes, without
sending it to the server.
  velero backup create backup3 --snapshot-volumes=false -o yaml
  # Wait for a backup to complete before returning from the command.
  velero backup create backup4 --wait
```

We find Velero's help system to be very helpful; once you get comfortable with the Velero basics, you will find that the built-in help provides enough information for most commands.

Using common Velero commands

Since many readers may be new to Velero, we wanted to provide a quick overview of the most commonly used commands to get you comfortable with operating Velero.

Listing Velero objects

As we have mentioned, Velero management is driven by using the CLI. You can imagine that as you create additional backup jobs, it may become difficult to remember what has been created. This is where the `get` command comes in handy.

The CLI can retrieve, or get, a list of the following Velero objects:

- Backup-locations
- Backups
- Plugins
- Restores
- Schedules
- Snapshot locations

As you may expect, executing `velero get <object>` will return a list of the objects managed by Velero:

```
velero get backups
```

Here is the output:

```
NAME                                STATUS      ERRORS   WARNINGS
cluster-daily-20210930010057        Completed   0        0
cluster-daily-20210929203744        Completed   0        0
cluster-ns-daily-20211001000058     Completed   0        0
cluster-ns-daily-20210930000057     Completed   0        0
cluster-ns-daily-20210929203815     Completed   0        0
initial-backup                      Completed   0        0
```

Each `get` command will produce a similar output, containing the names of each object and any unique values for the objects. This command is useful for a quick look at what objects exist, but it's usually used as the first step toward executing the next command, `describe`.

Retrieving details for a Velero object

After you get the name of the object that you want the details for, you can use the `describe` command to get the details of the object. Using the output from the `get` command in the previous section, we want to view the details for the `cluster-daily-20210930010057` backup job:

```
velero describe backup cluster-daily-20210930010057
```

The output of the command provides all the details for the requested object. You will find yourself using the `describe` command to troubleshoot issues such as backup failures.

Creating and deleting objects

Since we have already used the `create` command a few times, we will focus on the `delete` command in this section.

To recap, the `create` command allows you to create objects that will be managed by Velero, including backups, schedules, restores, and locations for backups and snapshots. We have created a backup and a schedule, and in the next section, we will create a restore.

Once an object is created, you may discover that you need to delete it. To delete objects in Velero, you use the `delete` command, along with the object and name you want to delete.

In our `get backups` output example, we had a backup called day2. To delete that backup, we would execute the following `delete` command:

```
velero delete backup day2
```

Since a delete is a one-way operation, you will need to confirm that you want to delete the object. Once confirmed, it may take a few minutes for the object to be removed from Velero since it waits until all associated data is removed:

```
Are you sure you want to continue (Y/N)? y
Request to delete backup "day2" submitted successfully.
The backup will be fully deleted after all associated data (disk
snapshots, backup files, restores) are removed.
```

As you can see in the output, when we delete a backup, Velero will delete all of the objects for the backup, including the snapshot's backup files and restores.

There are additional commands that you can use, but the commands covered in this section are the main commands you need to get comfortable with Velero.

Now that you can create and schedule backups, and know how to use the help system in Velero, we can move on to using a backup to restore objects.

Restoring from a backup

With any luck, you will rarely need to execute a restore of any Kubernetes object.

Even if you haven't been in the IT field long, you have likely experienced a personal situation where you had a drive failure, or accidentally deleted an important file. If you don't have a backup of the data that was lost, it is a very frustrating situation. In the enterprise world, missing data or not having a backup can lead to huge revenue losses, or in some scenarios, large fines in regulated industries.

To run a restore from a backup, you use the `create restore` command with the `--from-backup <backup name>` tag.

Earlier in the chapter, we created a single, one-time backup, called `initial-backup`, which includes every namespace and object in the cluster. If we decided that we needed to restore that backup, we would execute a restore using the Velero CLI:

```
velero restore create --from-backup initial-backup
```

The output from the `restore` command may seem odd:

```
Restore request "initial-backup-20211001002927" submitted successfully.
Run `velero restore describe initial-backup-20211001002927` or `velero
restore logs initial-backup-20211001002927` for more details.
```

At a quick glance, it may seem like a backup request was made since Velero replies with `"initial-backup-20211001002927" submitted successfully`. Velero uses the backup name to create a restore request, and since we named our backup `initial-backup`, the restore job name will use that name and append the date and time of the restore request.

You can view the status of the restore using the `describe` command:

```
velero restore describe initial-backup-20211001002927
```

Depending on the size of the restore, it may take some time to restore the entire backup. During the restore phase, the status of the backup will be `InProgress`. Once completed, the status will change to `Completed`.

Restoring in action

With all of the theory behind us, let's use two examples to see Velero in action. For the examples, we will start with a simple deployment that will delete and restore on the same cluster. The next example will be more complex; we will use the backup for our main KinD cluster and restore the cluster objects to a new KinD cluster.

Restoring a deployment from a backup

For the first example, we will create a simple deployment using an NGINX web server. We will deploy the application, verify that it works as expected, and then delete the deployment. Using the backup, we will restore the deployment and test that the restore worked by browsing to the web server's home page.

We have included a deployment in the chapter11 folder of your cloned repository. This deployment will create a new namespace, the NGINX deployment, a service, and an ingress rule for our exercise. The deployment manifest has also been included.

As with any ingress rule we have created throughout the book, you will need to edit its URL to reflect your host's IP address for nip.io to work correctly. Our lab server has an IP address of 10.2.1.161 – change this IP to your host's IP:

1. Edit the manifest from the GitHub repository under the chapter11 folder called nginx-deployment.yaml to include your nip.io URL. The section you need to change is shown here:

   ```
   spec:
     rules:
     - host: nginx-lab.10.2.1.161.nip.io
   ```

2. Deploy the manifest using kubectl:

   ```
   kubectl apply -f nginx-deployment.yaml
   ```

   This will create the objects we need for the deployment:

   ```
   namespace/nginx-lab created
   pod/nginx-deployment created
   ingress.networking.k8s.io/nginx-ingress created
   service/nginx-lab created
   ```

3. Finally, test the deployment using any browser and open the URL from the ingress rule:

Figure 11.6: Verifying that NGINX is running

Now that you have verified that the deployment works, we need to create a backup using Velero.

Backing up the namespace

Create a one-time backup of the new namespace using the Velero `create backup` command. Assign the backup job the name `nginx-lab`:

```
velero create backup nginx-lab --include-namespaces=nginx-lab
```

Since the namespace only contains a small deployment, the backup should complete quickly. Verify that the backup has completed successfully by using the `describe` command:

```
velero backup describe nginx-lab
```

Verify that the phase status is complete. If you have an error in the phase status, you may have entered the namespace name incorrectly in the `create backup` command.

After you verify that the backup has been successful, you can move on to the next step.

Simulating a failure

To simulate an event that would require a backup of our namespace, we will delete the entire namespace using `kubectl`:

```
kubectl delete ns nginx-lab
```

It may take a minute to delete the objects in the namespace. Once you have returned to a prompt, the deletion should have been completed.

Verify that the NGINX server does not reply by opening the URL in a browser; if you are using the same browser from the initial test, refresh the page. You should receive an error when refreshing or opening the URL:

nginx-lab.10.2.1.161.nip.io

404 Not Found

nginx

Figure 11.7: Verifying NGINX is not running

With the confirmation that the NGINX deployment has been deleted, we will restore the entire namespace and objects from the backup.

Restoring a namespace

Imagine this is a "real-world" scenario. You receive a phone call that a developer has accidentally deleted every object in their namespace and they do not have the source files.

Of course, you are prepared for this type of event. You have several backup jobs running in your cluster and you tell the developer that you can restore it to the state it was in last night from a backup:

1. We know that the backup's name is `nginx-lab`, so using Velero, we can execute a `restore create` command with the `--from-backup` option:

   ```
   velero create restore --from-backup nginx-lab
   ```

2. Velero will return that a restore job has been submitted:

   ```
   Restore request "nginx-lab-20211001003801" submitted
   successfully.
   Run `velero restore describe nginx-lab-20211001003801` or
   `velero restore logs nginx-lab-20211001003801` for more details.
   ```

3. You can check the status using the `velero restore describe` command:

   ```
   velero restore describe nginx-lab-20211001003801
   ```

4. Verify that the phase status shows `completed`, and verify that the deployment has been restored by browsing to the URL or refreshing the page if you already have it open:

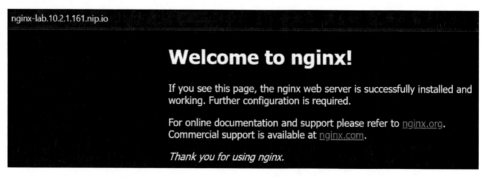

Figure 11.8: Verifying that NGINX has been restored

Congratulations, you just saved the developer a lot of work because you had a backup of the namespace!

Velero is a powerful product that you should consider using in every cluster to protect workloads from disasters.

Using a backup to create workloads in a new cluster

Restoring objects in a cluster is just one use case for Velero. While it is the main use case for most users, you can also use your backup files to restore a workload or all workloads on another cluster. This is a useful option if you need to create a new development or disaster recovery cluster.

 Remember that Velero backup jobs are only the namespaces and objects in the namespaces. To restore a backup to a new cluster, you must have a running cluster running Velero before you can restore any workloads.

Backing up the cluster

By this point in the chapter, we assume that you have seen this process a few times and that you know how to use the Velero CLI. If you need a refresher, you can go back a few pages in the chapter for reference, or use the CLI help function.

First, we should create a few namespaces and add some deployments to each one to make it more interesting (we have included a script in the `chapter11` folder called `create-backup-objects.yaml` that will create the namespaces and the objects for you):

1. Let's create a few demo namespaces:

```
kubectl create ns demo1
kubectl create ns demo2
kubectl create ns demo3
kubectl create ns demo4
```

2. We can add a quick deployment to a namespace using the `kubectl run` command:

```
kubectl run nginx --image=bitnami/nginx -n demo1
kubectl run nginx --image=bitnami/nginx -n demo2
kubectl run nginx --image=bitnami/nginx -n demo3
kubectl run nginx --image=bitnami/nginx -n demo4
```

Now that we have some additional workloads, we need to create a backup of the cluster.

3. Back up the new namespaces using a backup name of `namespace-demo`:

```
velero backup create namespace-demo --include-namespaces=demo1,d
emo2,demo3,demo4
```

Before moving on, verify that the backup has been completed successfully. You can verify the backup by executing the `describe` command against the `namespace-demo` backup:

```
velero backup describe namespace-demo
```

In the output, you will see that the backup includes the four namespaces and the backup has 40 objects in the backup. An abbreviated output is shown below.

```
Namespaces:
  Included:   demo1, demo2, demo3, demo4
  Excluded:   <none>
Started:      2021-10-01 00:44:30 +0000 UTC
Completed:    2021-10-01 00:44:42 +0000 UTC
Expiration:   2021-10-31 00:44:30 +0000 UTC
Total items to be backed up:    40
Items backed up:                40
```

Next, we will deploy a new KinD cluster that we will use to restore our demo backup to.

Building a new cluster

Since we are only demonstrating how Velero can be used to create workloads on a new cluster from a backup, we will create a simple single-node KinD cluster as our restore point:

> This section gets a little complex since you will have two clusters in your `kubeconfig` file. Follow the steps carefully if you're new to switching config contexts.
>
> Once we have completed this exercise, we will delete the second cluster since we will not need to have two clusters.

1. Create a new KinD cluster with the name `velero-restore`:

```
kind create cluster --name velero-restore
```

This will create a new single-node cluster that contains both the control plane and worker node, and it will set your cluster context to the new cluster.

2. Once the cluster has deployed, verify that your context has been switched to the `velero-restore` cluster:

```
kubectl config get-contexts
```

The output is as follows:

```
CURRENT   NAME                CLUSTER               AUTHINFO
          kind-cluster01      kind-cluster01        kind-
cluster01
*         kind-velero-restore kind-velero-restore   kind-velero-
restore
```

3. Verify that the current context is set to the `kind-velero-restore` cluster. You will see an * in the current field of the cluster that is being used.

4. Finally, verify the namespaces in the cluster using `kubectl`. You should only see the default namespaces that are included with a new cluster:

```
NAME                STATUS   AGE
default             Active   4m51s
kube-node-lease     Active   4m54s
kube-public         Active   4m54s
kube-system         Active   4m54s
local-path-storage  Active   4m43s
```

Now that we have a new cluster created, we can start the process to restore the workloads. The first step is to install Velero on the new cluster, pointing to the existing S3 bucket as the backup location.

Restoring a backup to the new cluster

With our new KinD cluster up and running, we need to install Velero to restore our backup. We can use most of the same manifests and settings that we used in the original cluster, but since we are in a different cluster, we need to change the S3 target to the external URL we used to expose MinIO.

Installing Velero in the new cluster

We already have the `credentials-velero` file in the `chapter11` folder, so we can jump right in to installing Velero using the `velero install` command:

1. Be sure to change the IP address in `s3Url target` to your host's IP address:

```
velero install \
    --provider aws \
    --plugins velero/velero-plugin-for-aws:v1.2.0 \
    --bucket velero \
    --secret-file ./credentials-velero \
    --use-volume-snapshots=false \
    --backup-location-config region=minio,s3ForcePathStyle="tru
e",s3Url=http://minio.10.2.1.161.nip.io
```

2. The install will take a few minutes, but once the pod is up and running, view the log files to verify that the Velero server is up and running and connected to the S3 target:

```
kubectl logs deployment/velero -n velero
```

3. If all of your settings were correct, the Velero log will have an entry saying that it has found backups in the backup location that need to be synced with the new Velero server (the number of backups may be different for your KinD cluster):

```
time="2021-10-01T23:53:30Z" level=info msg="Found 9 backups in
the backup location that do not exist in the cluster and need
to be synced" backupLocation=default controller=backup-sync
logSource="pkg/controller/backup_sync_controller.go:204"
```

4. After confirming the installation, verify that Velero can see the existing backup files using `velero get backups`:

```
NAME                                STATUS       ERRORS   WARNINGS
cluster-daily-20211001010058        Completed    0        0
cluster-daily-20210930010057        Completed    0        0
cluster-daily-20210929203744        Completed    0        0
cluster-ns-daily-20211001000058     Completed    0        0
cluster-ns-daily-20210930000057     Completed    0        0
cluster-ns-daily-20210929203815     Completed    0        0
initial-backup                      Completed    0        0
namespace-demo                      Completed    0        0
nginx-lab                           Completed    0        0
```

Your backup list will differ from ours, but you should see the same list that you had in the original cluster.

At this point, we can use any of the backup files to create a restore job in the new cluster.

Restoring a backup in a new cluster

In this section, we will use the backup that was created in the previous section and restore the workloads to a brand new KinD cluster to simulate a workload migration.

The backup that was created of the original cluster, after we added the namespaces and deployment, was called `namespace-demo`:

1. Using that backup name, we can restore the namespaces and objects by running the `velero create restore` command:

    ```
    velero create restore --from-backup=namespace-demo
    ```

2. Wait for the restore to complete before moving on to the next step. To verify that the restore was successful, use the `velero describe restore` command with the name of the restore job that was created when you executed the `create restore` command. In our cluster, the restore job was assigned the name `namespace-demo-20211001235926`:

    ```
    velero restore describe namespace-demo-20211001235926
    ```

3. Once the phase has changed from `InProgress` to `Completed`, verify that your new cluster has the additional demo namespaces using `kubectl get ns`:

    ```
    NAME                 STATUS    AGE
    default              Active    23h
    demo1                Active    89s
    demo2                Active    89s
    demo3                Active    89s
    demo4                Active    89s
    kube-node-lease      Active    23h
    kube-public          Active    23h
    kube-system          Active    23h
    local-path-storage   Active    23h
    velero               Active    7m35s
    ```

4. You will see that the new namespaces were created, and if you look at the pods in each namespace, you will see that each has a pod called `nginx`. You can verify that the pods were created using `kubectl get pods`. For example, to verify the pods in the `demo1` namespace, enter the following: kubectl get pods -n demo1

    The output is as follows:

    ```
    NAME    READY    STATUS     RESTARTS    AGE
    nginx   1/1      Running    0           3m30s
    ```

Congratulations! You have successfully restored objects from one cluster into a new cluster.

Deleting the new cluster

Since we do not need two clusters, let's delete the new KinD cluster that we restored the backup to:

1. To delete the cluster, execute the `kind delete cluster` command:

```
kind delete cluster --name velero-restore
```

2. Set your current context to the original KinD cluster, `kind-cluster01`:

```
kubectl config use-context kind-cluster01
```

This completes the chapter.

Summary

Backing up clusters and workloads is a requirement for any enterprise cluster. In this chapter, we reviewed how to back up the etcd cluster database using `etcdctl` and the snapshot feature. We also went into detail on how to install Velero in a cluster to back up and restore workloads. We closed out the chapter by copying workloads from an existing backup by restoring an existing backup on a new cluster.

Having a backup solution allows you to recover from a disaster or human error. A typical backup solution allows you to restore any Kubernetes object, including namespaces, persistent volumes, RBAC, services, and service accounts. You can also take all of the workloads from one cluster and restore them on a completely different cluster for testing or troubleshooting.

Coming up in the next chapter, we will introduce you to Istio, a popular open source service mesh.

Questions

1. True or false – Velero can only use an S3 target to store backup jobs.

   a. True

   b. False

2. If you do not have an object storage solution, how can you provide an S3 target using a backend storage solution such as NFS?

   a. You can't – there is no way to add anything in front of NFS to present S3.

   b. Kubernetes can do this using native CSI features.

   c. Install MinIO and use the NFS volumes as persistent disks in the deployment.

   d. You don't need to use an object store; you can use NFS directly with Velero.

3. True or false – Velero backups can only be restored on the same cluster where the backup was originally created.

   a. True

   b. False

4. What utility can you use to create an etcd backup?

   a. Velero.

   b. MinIO.

   c. There is no reason to back up the etcd database.

   d. `etcdctl`.

5. Which command will create a scheduled backup that runs every day at 3 A.M.?

   a. `velero create backup daily-backup`

   b. `velero create @daily backup daily-backup`

   c. `velero create backup daily-backup –schedule="@daily3am"`

   d. `velero create schedule daily-backup --schedule="0 3 * * *"`

Join our book's Discord space

Join the book's Discord workspace for a monthly *Ask me Anything* session with the authors: https://packt.link/K8EntGuide

12

An Introduction to Istio

"If it makes it easier for users to use on the frontend, it's probably complex on the backend."

Istio is a large, complex system that provides benefits to your workloads by offering enhanced security, discovery, observability, traffic management, and more – all without requiring application developers to write modules or applications to handle each task.

For most people, it has a large learning curve, but once you have the Istio skills to deploy and operate a service mesh, you will be able to provide very complex offerings to your developers, including the ability to do the following:

- Route traffic based on various requirements
- Secure service-to-service communication
- Traffic shaping
- Circuit breaking
- Service observability

Again, all of these can be used by developers with very little, or no, code changes. When something is simple for users to consume, it usually means the system has a complex backend, and Istio is no different. This chapter will introduce you to installing Istio and the add-on observability project, Kiali. We will also explain the most common custom resources that Istio provides that will allow you to control traffic flow, add security, and expose workloads.

In order to cover Istio completely, we would need to write a second book, dedicated to only Istio custom resources and deployment models. Our goal for this and the next chapter is to provide you with the required base knowledge to feel comfortable installing and using Istio. Since we can't cover every object in complete detail, we encourage you to browse the Istio homepage after reading the chapters at `https://istio.io`.

This chapter will cover:

- Why should you care about a service mesh?
- An introduction to Istio concepts
- Understanding Istio components
- Deploying Istio
- Introducing Istio objects
- Deploying add-on components to provide observability
- Deploying an application into the service mesh

Before we get into the chapter, we wanted to level set the content of the chapter. It's meant to be similar to the Kubernetes bootcamp chapter, providing the details you need to understand how Istio works and the components it includes. Istio is a large topic and it truly justifies a dedicated book, or two, to completely understand all of the components of the service mesh. After you read this chapter and the next chapter, where you will add an application to the mesh, you will have enough knowledge to deploy and operate a basic Istio service mesh.

To close out the introduction, we would like to offer a little Kubernetes trivia – as with most Kubernetes objects, Istio is named after a nautical term; Istio in Greek means **sail**.

Technical requirements

This chapter has the following technical requirements:

- A Docker host installed using the steps from *Chapter 1, Docker and Container Essentials*, with a minimum of 8GB of RAM
- A KinD cluster configured using the initial scripts from *Chapter 2, Deploying Kubernetes Using KinD*
- Installation scripts from this book's GitHub repository

You can access the code for this chapter by going to this book's GitHub repository:
`https://github.com/PacktPublishing/Kubernetes---An-Enterprise-Guide-2E/`
`tree/main/chapter12`.

 To use Istio to expose workloads, we will remove NGINX from the KinD cluster, which will allow Istio to utilize ports **80** and **443** on the host.

Why should you care about a service mesh?

Istio provides a number of features that, without it, would require a developer to create them from scratch and edit their code. If a developer had to create many of the features provided by Istio, they would need to create the code in all of the languages that they are developing in. Need encryption between your services that are written in Java, Python, or Node? You would need to create the code three times – once for each programming language. The same would be true for traffic management, or any of the other features that are provided out of the box by Istio.

So, what can Istio provide you that should make you consider deploying it?

Workload observability

Have you ever tried keeping track of services and finding where the issue is when you have 20, 30, or more services running in your application?

Using the observability and tracing ability provided by Istio and add-on components, you can find and resolve issues faster by viewing the traffic and status between services in real time or playing back recorded information to see where an issue may have occurred hours or days ago.

With components like Prometheus to store metrics, Kiali for observability, and Jaeger for tracing, you will have a troubleshooting arsenal to help you find any issues. In this chapter, we will deploy all three of the add-on components and we will get into the details of Kiali, the main tool for observing the communication between workload services.

Without a service mesh, troubleshooting an issue with a large application that has a number of services can become very difficult. Istio and the features it provides make this a much easier and faster process – and everyone loves when you can find a root cause quickly.

Traffic management

Istio provides advanced traffic management for your workloads, providing you the tools to use any deployment model you require, and all without requiring any network changes – it's all in the hands of you and your developers. It also provides tools to simulate normally random events that may occur when the application is in use, including HTTP errors, delays, timeouts, and retries.

We realize that some readers may be new to deployment models, and understanding the different models available is key to understanding the advantages provided by Istio. Using Istio, developers can leverage deployment models like blue/green and canary deployments.

Blue/Green Deployments

In this model, you deploy two versions to production, directing a certain percentage of traffic to each version of the application, usually sending a low amount of traffic to the "new" (green) release. As you verify that the new deployment is working as expected, you can increase the traffic percentage to the new version until you are eventually sending 100% of the traffic to the new deployment.

For example, you can split the traffic between version 1 of the application and version 2 of the application to verify the functionality of the new version. Once the new version has been verified as functioning correctly, you can increase the percentage between version 1 and version 2, or cut the entire workload to version 2.

Canary Deployments

This term comes from the mining days when miners would put a canary in the mining shaft to verify it was safe to work in the environment. In the case of a deployment, it allows you to deploy an early test version of the application before graduating the release to a new version. Essentially, this is similar to the blue/green deployment, but in a canary deployment, you would direct a very small percentage of traffic to the canary version of the application. Using a small percentage of traffic will minimize any impact that the canary deployment may introduce.

Finding issues before they happen

We can go a step further from deployment models; Istio also provides tools for you to develop resilience and testing for your workloads before you deploy them and learn about issues from customers or end-users.

Have you ever worried about how an application will react to certain unseen events?

Developers need to worry about events that they have little control over, including:

- Application timeouts
- Delays in communication
- HTTP error codes
- Retries

Istio provides objects to assist in dealing with these by allowing you to create an issue with the workload before you move to production. This allows developers to capture and resolve issues in their applications before releasing them to production, creating a better user experience.

Security

In today's world, security is an issue we should all be concerned about. Many of the methods to secure a workload are complex and may require a skillset that many developers do not have. This is truly where Istio shines, providing the tools to easily deploy security and minimize its impact on development.

The first, and most popular security feature in Istio is the ability to provide **mutual TLS (mTLS)** between workloads. Using mTLS, Istio provides not only encryption for communication, but workload identity too. When you visit a website that has an expired certificate or a self-signed certificate your browser will warn you that the site can't be trusted. That's because your browser performs server authentication when establishing a TLS connection by verifying that the certificate presented by the server is trusted by the browser. mTLS verifies trust from the client to the server, but also from the server to the client. That's the mutual part. The server validates that the certificate presented by the client is trusted as well as the client validating the server. When you first start a cluster and use the initial certificate created for you, you're using mTLS. Istio makes this much easier because it will create all of the certificates and identities for you using its built-in sidecar.

You can configure mTLS as a requirement (STRICT), or as an option (PERMISSIVE), for the entire mesh or individual namespaces. If you set either option to STRICT, any communication to the service will require mTLS and if a request fails to provide an identity, the connection will be denied. However, if you set the PERMISSIVE option, traffic that has an identity and requests mTLS will be encrypted, while any request that does not provide an identity or encryption request will still be allowed to communicate.

Another feature provided will give you the ability to secure what communication is allowed to a workload, similar to a firewall, but in a much simpler implementation. Using Istio, you can decide to only allow HTTP GET requests, or only HTTP POST requests, or both – from only defined sources.

Finally, you can use **JSON Web Tokens (JWTs)** for initial user authentication to limit who is authorized to communicate with a workload. This allows you to secure the initial communication attempt by only accepting JWTs that come from an approved token provider.

Now that we have discussed some of the reasons you would want to deploy Istio, let's introduce you to some Istio concepts.

Introduction to Istio concepts

You can break down the concepts of Istio into 4 categories, traffic management, security, observability, and extensibility. Each of these concepts will introduce the components and custom resources that developers will use to leverage the advantages of using Istio.

Understanding the Istio components

Similar to a standard Kubernetes cluster, Istio refers to two separate planes, the control plane and the data plane. Historically, the data plane included 4 different services, Pilot, Galley, Citadel, and Mixer – all broken out in a true microservices design. This design was used for multiple reasons including the flexibility to break out the responsibilities to multiple teams, the ability to use different programming languages, and to scale each service independently of the others.

Istio has evolved quickly since its initial release. The team made the decision that breaking out the core services had little benefit, and in the end, made Istio more complex. This led the team to redesign Istio and starting with Istio 1.5, Istio includes the components that we will discuss in this section.

Making the Control Plane Simple with Istiod

Just as Kubernetes bundled multiple controllers into a single executable, the kube-controller-manager, the Istio team decided to bundle all 4 of the components into a single daemon called istiod. This single daemon has become the control plane, running a single pod that can be scaled as performance is required.

The main advantages to the single daemon are listed in an Istio blog at `https://istio.io/latest/blog/2020/istiod/`. To summarize the team's reasoning, the single process provides:

- Easier and quicker control plane installations
- Easier configuration

- Integration of virtual machines into the service mesh more easily, requiring a single agent and Istio's certificates

- Scaling more easily

- Reduced control plan start-up time

- A reduced amount of overall required resources

We've mentioned the 4 individual components, but we haven't explained what the role of each of them is. In the next section, we will explain the 4 components that are now part of istiod.

Breaking down the istiod pod

Moving to a single binary didn't reduce Istio's functionality or features, it still provides all of the features that the 4 separate components provided, they are all just in a single binary now. Each piece provides a key feature to the service mesh, and in this section, we will explain the 4 components and what they provide to the service mesh.

Pilot – Sidecar management

Before talking about Pilot, we need to introduce another component called Envoy. Envoy is a proxy server and it's the component that provides most of the features to applications. When a workload is deployed to an Istio-enabled namespace, each pod will have an additional container created; this is the Istio sidecar, which is running an Envoy proxy server. All ingress and egress traffic will go through the sidecar, unless you specifically configure additional objects for special use-cases, which we will discuss in the *Introducing Istio resources* section, using Sidecar and Virtual Services.

The first component we will discuss is called Pilot, which is the component that creates and deletes the Envoy proxies for workloads, known as an Istio sidecar. It extends the Kubernetes API, providing additional cluster resources like service discovery, load balancing management, and routing tables.

Pilot makes management of Envoy instances easier than configuring and deploying the sidecar manually. It watches the Kubernetes API for any resource that is offered by Istio and it will take over and configure the complexities and management of using the Envoy proxy as the pod's sidecar.

Galley – Configuration validation

Istio is designed to be platform-independent, although most of the documentation and examples you will see are around integration with Kubernetes. Galley is the component that handles the configuration-specific information for the control plane.

This means that Istio can be used with other orchestration systems other than Kubernetes. For the purpose of this chapter, just remember that Galley is the part of Istiod that validates user-specific information.

Citadel – Certificate Management

Citadel is the component that handles certificate management. As we mentioned earlier in the chapter, Istio can encrypt traffic between services in the mesh – Citadel is responsible for handling the lifecycle of the certificates used to provide mTLS between services.

Mixer – Keeper of security

The last component is Mixer, which is responsible for handling authorization and auditing for the service mesh. Mixer has 3 core features:

- Precondition checking – Checks conditions before allowing a request to a service running in the mesh

- Quota management – Provides fairness between services; one example of a quota is a rate limit

- Telemetry – Provides logging, monitoring, and tracing for the services in the mesh

Mixer sits between the Istio components and the mesh services, where it performs access controls and telemetry capturing.

Understanding the istio-ingressgateway

Moving on from the base Istiod pod, we come to one of the most important components of Istio, the `istio-ingressgateway`. This gateway is what provides incoming access to the service mesh from clients and services that sit outside of the Kubernetes cluster. All clusters will have at least a single deployment of an `istio-ingressgateway`, but you are not limited to a single `ingressgateway`; you can deploy multiple ingress gateways if you have a requirement to do so.

The istio-ingressgateway provides access to applications using two methods:

1. Standard Kubernetes Ingress object support
2. Istio Gateway and VirtualService objects

Since we have already discussed and deployed NGINX as an Ingress controller, we will not cover using Envoy as a standard Ingress controller; we will focus on the second method of using Gateways and Virtual Services for incoming requests.

Using Gateways to expose our services provides more flexibility, customization, and security over a standard Ingress object.

Understanding the istio-egressgateway

The istio-egressgateway can be used to funnel traffic from sidecars to a single or group of pods that centralize egress traffic from the service mesh.

By default, Istio sidecars handle all ingress and egress traffic from a mesh-enabled service. We know that we use the istio-ingressgateway to control incoming traffic to the service mesh, and by adding the istio-egressgateway option to your deployment, you can also control egress traffic.

Both the `ingressgateway` and `egressgateway` objects will be discussed in depth in the *Introducing Istio resources* section.

Now, let's jump into how you install Istio in a cluster.

Installing Istio

There are multiple methods to deploy Istio. The most common method today is to use either `istioctl` or the Istio operator, but there are additional options depending on your organization. You may elect to use one of the alternative installation methods of creating manifests via istoctl or the Helm chart (which as of the time of writing is considered alpha).

A brief list of advantages and disadvantages for each method is detailed in *Table 12.1: Istio deployment methods.*

Deployment method	Advantages	Disadvantages
istioctl	• Configuration validation and health checks • Does not require any privileged pods, increasing cluster security • Multiple configuration options	• Each Istio version requires a new binary

Istio Operator	• Configuration validation and health • Does not require multiple binaries for each Istio version • Multiple configuration options	• Requires a privileged pod running in the cluster
Manifests (via istioctl)	• Generates manifests that can be customized before deploying using kubectl • Multiple configuration options	• Not all checks are performed, which could lead to deployment errors • Error checks and reporting are limited when compared to using istioctl or the Istio operator
Helm	• Helm and charts are well known to most Kubernetes users • Leverages Helm standards, which allow for easy management of deployments	• Offers the least validation checks of all deployment options • Most tasks will require additional work and complexity versus the other deployment models

Table 12.1: Istio deployment methods

For the chapter, we will focus on using the istioctl binary for installation, and in the next section, we will deploy Istio using istioctl.

Downloading Istio

The first thing that we need is to define the version of Istio we want to deploy. We can do this by setting an environment variable, and in our example, we want to deploy Istio 1.10.0:

```
export ISTIO_VERSION=1.10.0
```

Next, we will download the Istio installer using CURL:

```
curl -L https://istio.io/downloadIstio | sh -
```

This will download the installation script and execute it using the ISTIO_VERSION that we defined before executing the curl command. After executing you will have an istio-1.10.0 directory in your current working directory.

Finally, since we will be using executables from the `istio-1.10.0` directory, you should add it to your `path` statement. To make this easier, you should be in the `chapter12` directory from the book repository before setting the `path` variable.

```
export PATH="$PATH:$PWD/istio-1.10.0/bin"
```

Installing Istio using a Profile

To make deploying Istio easier, the team has included a number of pre-defined profiles. Each profile defines which components are deployed and the default configuration. There are six profiles included, but only four profiles are used for most deployments.

Profile	Installed Components
Default	istio-ingressgateway and istiod
Demo	istio-egressgateway, istio-ingressgateway, and istiod
Minimal	istiod
Preview	istio-ingressgateway and istiod

Table 12.2: Istio profiles

If none of the included profiles fit your deployment requirements, you can create a customized deployment. This is beyond the scope of this chapter since we will be using the included demo profile – however, you can read more about customizing the configuration on Istio's site, `https://istio.io/latest/docs/setup/additional-setup/customize-installation/`.

To deploy Istio using the demo profile using istioctl, we simply need to execute a single command:

```
istioctl manifest install --set profile=demo
```

The installer will ask you to verify that you want to deploy Istio using the default profile, which will deploy all of the Istio components:

```
This will install the Istio 1.10.0 demo profile with ["Istio core"
"Istiod" "Ingress gateways" "Egress gateways"] components into the
cluster. Proceed? (y/N)
```

Press the *y* key to say yes to proceed with the deployment. If you want to bypass the confirmation, you can add an option to the istioctl command line, `--skip-confirmation`, which tells istioctl to bypass the confirmation.

If everything went well, you should see a confirmation that each component was installed, and a completion message that thanks you for installing Istio.

```
✔ Istio core installed
✔ Istiod installed
✔ Egress gateways installed
✔ Ingress gateways installed
✔ Installation complete
Thank you for installing Istio 1.10.  Please take a few minutes to tell
us about your install/upgrade experience!
```

The istioctl executable can be used to verify the installation. To verify the installation, you require a manifest and since we used istioctl to deploy Istio directly, we do not have a manifest, so we need to create one to check our installation.

```
istioctl manifest generate --set profile=demo > istio-kind.yaml
```

Then run the `istioctl verify-install` command.

```
istioctl verify-install -f istio-kind.yaml
```

This will verify each component, and once verified, it will provide a summary similar to the output below:

```
Checked 13 custom resource definitions
Checked 3 Istio Deployments
✔ Istio is installed and verified successfully
```

Now that we have verified the installation, let's look at what istioctl created:

- A new namespace called `istio-system`
- Three deployments were created, and a corresponding service for each:
    - `istio-ingressgateway`
    - `istio-egressgateway`
    - `istiod`
- **CustomResourceDefinitions (CRDs)** to provide the Istio resources including:
    - `authorizationpolicies.security.istio.io`
    - `gateways.networking.istio.io`
    - `virtualservices.networking.istio.io`

- `destinationrules.networking.istio.io`
- `peerauthentications.security.istio.io`
- `requestauthentications.security.istio.io`
- `serviceentries.networking.istio.io`
- `sidecars.networking.istio.io`
- `envoyfilters.networking.istio.io`

Don't worry about all of the CRs at this point. We will go into the details of each resource throughout the chapter, and in the next chapter, we will go into the details of deploying an application into the mesh, which will utilize many of the deployed CRs.

With Istio deployed, our next step is to expose it to our network so we can access the applications we'll build. Since we're running on KinD this can be tricky. Docker is forwarding all traffic from port `80` (HTTP) and `443` (HTTPS) on our KinD server to the worker node. The worker node is in turn running the NGINX Ingress controller on ports `443` and `80` to receive that traffic. In a real-world scenario, we'd use an external load balancer, like MetalLB, to expose the individual services via a `LoadBalancer`. For our labs though, we're going to instead focus on simplicity. We created a script in the `chapter12` directory called `expose_istio.sh` that will do two things. First, it will delete the `ingress-nginx` namespace, removing NGINX and freeing up ports `80` and `443` on the Docker host. Second, it will patch the `istio-ingressgateway` Deployment in the `istio-system` namespace so that it runs on ports `80` and `443` on the worker node.

Now that we have Istio deployed and we know the custom resources that Istio includes, let's move on to the next section, which will explain each resource and its use-cases.

Introducing Istio resources

Once you deploy Istio, you will have additional custom resources that provide the Istio features. Each of these resources provides powerful features and each one could be a chapter by itself. In this section, we want to provide enough details so you will have a strong understanding of each object. In the next section, we will deploy a basic application that will explain many of the objects in a real-world application example.

Authorization policies

Authorization policies are used to control access to the deployments in the service mesh. They provide developers with the ability to control access to workloads based on actions including deny, allow, and custom.

Policies are applied in a certain order. Istio will apply custom policies first, then deny policies, and finally, any allow policies.

Understanding how a policy's actions are evaluated is very important, since a misconfigured policy may not provide the expected results. The high-level flow for policy evaluation is:

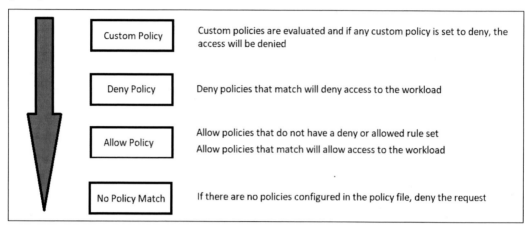

Figure 12.1: Istio policy evaluation flow

If a policy has any conflicting rules, like denying and allowing the same request, the deny policy will evaluate first and the request will be denied since the deny policy is evaluated before the allow policy. It's also very important to note that if you allow a certain action, like an HTTP GET, the GET request would be allowed, but any other operation would be denied since it has not been allowed by the policy.

> Authorization policies can get very complex. The Istio team has created a page with multiple examples on the Istio site at `https://istio.io/latest/docs/reference/config/security/authorization-policy/`.

Policies can be broken down into scope, action, and rules:

- **Scope**: The scope defines what object(s) will be enforced by the policy. You can scope a policy to the entire mesh, a namespace, or any Kubernetes object label like a pod.

- **Actions**: There can be one of two actions defined, ALLOW or DENIED – each either denying or allowing a request based on the defined rules.

- **Rules**: Defines what actions will be allowed or denied by the request. Rules can become very complex, allowing you to define actions based on source and destination, different operations, keys, and more.

To help understand the flow, let's look at a few example authorization policies and what access will be applied when the policy is evaluated.

Example 1: Denying and allowing all access

For our first example, we will create a policy that will deny all requests to the resources in the namespace `marketing`:

```
apiVersion: security.istio.io/v1beta1
kind: AuthorizationPolicy
metadata:
 name: marketing-policy-deny
 namespace: marketing
spec:
  {}
```

This is a very simple policy that defines nothing in the `spec` section, no rules have been provided for the policy, and this will evaluate to no policy matching – which will fall through the flow to the last box in *Figure 12.1: Istio policy evaluation flow*, denying the request.

By adding a single entry to the policy, we can change it from denying all requests to allowing all requests.

```
apiVersion: security.istio.io/v1beta1
kind: AuthorizationPolicy
metadata:
 name: marketing-policy-deny
 namespace: marketing
spec:
  rules:
  - {}
```

When we add the `rules` section to the policy definition, we have created a rule that does not have a matching or allow rule, so this rule will evaluate to the third box in *Figure 12.1*, allowing the request.

You might start to see why we mentioned how not understanding how policies are evaluated in the flow may lead to unexpected access results. This is a prime example of how a single entry, `rules`, changes the policy from denying all requests to allowing all requests.

Example 2: Allowing only GET methods to a workload

Policies can get granular, allowing only certain operations like GET from an HTTP request. This example will allow GET requests, while denying all other request types for pods that are labeled with app=nginx in the marketing namespace.

```
apiVersion: security.istio.io/v1beta1
kind: AuthorizationPolicy
metadata:
  name: nginx-get-allow
  namespace: marketing
spec:
  selector:
    matchLabels:
        app: nginx
  action: ALLOW
  rules:
  - to:
    - operation:
        methods: ["GET"]
```

In this example, the policy accepts the GET request from any source, since we have only defined a to action without a from action. We can get even more granular, accepting (or denying) a request based on the source of the request. In the next section, we will show another example of a policy but we will limit the source to a single IP address.

Example 3: Allowing requests from a specific source

In our last policy example, we will limit what source will be allowed access to a workload using a GET or POST method.

This will increase security by denying any request from a source that is not in the policy source list.

```
metadata:
  name: nginx-get-allow-source
  namespace: marketing
spec:
  selector:
    matchLabels:
        app: nginx
  action: ALLOW
  rules:
  - from:
    - source:
        ipBlocks:
        - 192.168.10.100
```

Unlike the previous examples, this policy has a `source:` section, which allows you to limit access based on different sources, like an IP address. This policy will allow the source IP `192.168.10.100` access to all operations to the NGINX server, and all other sources will be denied access.

Moving on from authorization policies, we will introduce our next custom resource, destination rules.

Gateways

Earlier we mentioned that traffic will come into a central point, the istio-ingressgateway. We didn't explain how the traffic flows from the ingressgateway to a namespace and workloads – this is where gateways come in.

A gateway can be configured at the namespace, so you can delegate the creation and configuration to a team. It is a load balancer that receives incoming and outgoing traffic that can be customized with options like accepted ciphers, TLS versions, certificate handling, and more.

Gateways work along with Virtual Services, which we will discuss in the next topic, but until then, the following figure shows the interaction between the Gateway and VirtualService objects.

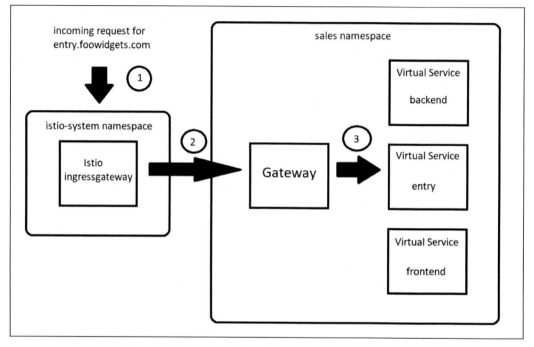

Figure 12.2: Gateway to Virtual Service communication flow

1. An incoming request is sent to the Istio `ingress-gateway` controller, located in the `istio-system` namespace.

2. The `sales` namespace has a Gateway configured that is set to use the ingressgateway with a host of `entry.foowidgets.com`. This tells the ingressgateway to send the request to the gateway object in the `sales` namespace.

3. Finally, the traffic is routed to the service using a Virtual Service object that has been created using the gateway in the `sales` namespace.

To show an example Gateway configuration, we have a namespace called `sales` that has Istio enabled running an application that can be accessed using the URL `entry.foowidgets.com` and we need to expose it for external access. To accomplish this, we would create a gateway using the example manifest below.

```
apiVersion: networking.istio.io/v1alpha3
kind: Gateway
metadata:
```

```
    name: sales-gateway
    namespace: sales
  spec:
    selector:
      istio: ingressgateway
    servers:
    - port:
        number: 443
        name: http
        protocol: HTTP
      hosts:
      - sales.foowidgets.com
      tls:
        mode: SIMPLE
        serverCertificate: /etc/certs/servercert.pem
        privateKey: /etc/certs/privatekey.pem
```

This gateway configuration will tell the ingress gateway to listen on port 443 for requests that are incoming for `sales.foowidgets.com`. It also defines the certificates that will be used to secure the communication for incoming web requests.

You may be wondering, "How does it know to use the ingress gateway that we have running in our cluster?" If you look at the `spec` section, and then the selector, we have configured the selector to use an ingress gateway that has the label `istio=ingressgateway`. This selector and label tell the gateway object which ingress gateway will create our new gateway for incoming connections. When we deployed Istio earlier, the ingress gateways were labeled with the default label `istio=ingressgateway`, as shown highlighted below from a `kubectl get pods -show-labels -n istio-system`.

```
app=istio-ingressgateway,chart=gateways,heritage=Tiller,install.
operator.istio.io/owning-resource=unknown,istio.io/rev=default,istio=in
gressgateway,operator.istio.io/component=IngressGateways,pod-template-
hash=69dc4765b4,release=istio,service.istio.io/canonical-name=istio-
ingressgateway,service.istio.io/canonical-revision=latest,sidecar.
istio.io/inject=false
```

You may be wondering how the gateway will be used to direct traffic to a particular workload since there are no configuration options in the gateway telling it where to direct traffic. That's because the gateway just configures the ingress gateways to accept traffic for a destination URL and the required ports – it does not control how the traffic will flow to a service; that's the job of the next object, the Virtual Service object.

Virtual Services

Gateways and virtual services combine to provide the correct traffic route to a service, or services. Once you have a gateway deployed, you need to create a virtual service object to tell the gateway how to route traffic to your service(s).

Building on the Gateway example, we need to tell the gateway how to route traffic to our webserver running on port 443. The server has been deployed using NGINX in the marketing namespace and it has a label of app-nginx and a service named frontend. To route traffic to the NGINX service, we would deploy the manifest below.

```
apiVersion: networking.istio.io/v1beta1
kind: VirtualService
metadata:
  name: sales-entry-web-vs
  namespace: sales
spec:
  hosts:
  - entry.foowidgets.com
  gateways:
  - sales-gateway
  http:
  - route:
    - destination:
        port:
          number: 443
        host: entry
```

Breaking down the manifest, we specify the host(s) that this VirtualService object will route, and in our example, we only have one host, entry.foowidgets.com. The next field defines which gateway will be used for the traffic, and in the previous section we defined a gateway called marketing-gateway, which was configured to listen on port 443.

Finally, the last section defines which service the traffic will be routed to. The route, destination, and port are all fairly straightforward to understand, but the host section can be misleading. This field actually defines the service that you will route the traffic to. In the example, we are going to route the traffic to a service called entry, so our field is defined with host: entry.

With the knowledge of using gateways and virtual services to route traffic in the service mesh, we can move on to the next topic, destination rules.

Destination rules

Virtual services provide a basic method to direct traffic to a service, but Istio offers an additional object to create complex traffic direction by using Destination rules. Destination rules are applied after Virtual Services. Traffic is initially routed using a Virtual Service and, if defined, a Destination rule can be used to route the request to its final destination.

This may be confusing at first, but it becomes easier when you see an example, so let's dive into an example that can route traffic to different versions of a deployment.

As we learned, incoming requests will use the Virtual Service initially, and then a destination rule, if defined, will route the request to the destination. In this example, we have already created a Virtual Service but we actually have two versions of the application labeled v1 and v2 and we want to direct traffic between both versions of the application using round-robin. To accomplish this, we would create a DestinationRule using the manifest below.

```
apiVersion: networking.istio.io/v1alpha3
kind: DestinationRule
metadata:
  name: nginx
spec:
  host: nginx
  trafficPolicy:
    loadBalancer:
      simple: ROUND_ROBIN
  subsets:
  - name: v1
    labels:
      version: nginx-v1
  - name: v2
    labels:
      version: nginx-v2
```

Using this manifest, incoming requests to the NGINX server will be split between the two versions of the application equally since we defined the loadBalancer policy as ROUND_ROBIN. But what if we wanted to route traffic to the version that had the least number of connections? Destination rules have other options for the loadBalancer options, and to route connections to the version with the least connections, we would set the LEAST_CONN loadBalancer policy.

Peer authentications

Istio's peer authentication object controls how the service mesh controls the mutual TLS settings for workloads, either for the entire service mesh or just a namespace. Each policy can be configured with a value that will either allow both encrypted communication and non-encrypted communication between pods or require encryption between pods.

mTLS mode	Pod communication	Description
STRICT	mTLS required	Any non-encrypted traffic sent to a pod will be denied
PERMISSIVE	mTLS optional	Both encrypted and non-encrypted traffic will be accepted by the pod

Table 12.3: PeerAuthentication options

If you want to set the PeerAuthentication for the entire mesh, you would create a PeerAuthentication in the istio-system namespace. For example, to require mTLS between all pods, you would create the policy shown below:

```
apiVersion: security.istio.io/v1beta1
kind: PeerAuthentication
metadata:
  name: mtls-policy
  namespace: istio-system
spec:
  mtls:
    mode: STRICT
```

To allow both encrypted and non-encrypted traffic, the policy mode just needs to be set to PERMISSIVE, by changing the mode to mode: PERMISSIVE.

Rather than setting the mode for the entire mesh, many enterprises only set the mode to STRICT for namespaces that require additional security. In the example below, we set the mode to STRICT for the sales namespace.

```
apiVersion: security.istio.io/v1beta1
kind: PeerAuthentication
metadata:
  name: mtls-policy
  namespace: sales
spec:
  mtls:
    mode: STRICT
```

Since this policy is configured for the `sales` namespace, rather than the `istio-system` namespace, Istio will only enforce a strict mTLS policy for the namespace rather than the entire service mesh.

This is a great security feature provided by the mesh, but encryption won't stop a request from hitting our workload; it simply encrypts it. The next object we will discuss will add a level of security to a workload by requiring authentication before being allowed access.

Request authentication

Security requires two pieces, first the authentication piece, which is "who you are." The second piece is authorization, which is the actions that are allowed once authentication has been provided, or "what you can do."

`RequestAuthentication` objects are only one part required to secure a workload. To fully secure the workload, you need to create the `RequestAuthentication` object and an `AuthorizationPolicy`. The `RequestAuthorization` policy will determine what identities are allowed access to the workload, and the `AuthorizationPolicy` will determine what permissions are allowed.

A `RequestAuthorization` policy without an `AuthorizationPolicy` can lead to unintentionally allowing access to the resource. If you only create a `RequestAuthorization` policy, the access in *Table 12.4: RequestAuthentication access* shows who would be allowed access.

Token action	Access provided
Invalid token provided	Access will be denied
No token provided	Access will be granted
Valid token provided	Access will be granted

Table 12.4: RequestAuthentication access

As you can see, once we create a policy, any invalid JWT will be denied access to the workload, and any valid token will be allowed access to the workload. However, when no token is provided, many people think that access would be denied, but in reality, access would be allowed. A `RequestAuthentication` policy only verifies the tokens, and if no token is present, the `RequestAuthentication` rule will not deny the request.

An example manifest is shown below. We will use this manifest in the examples section of the chapter, but we wanted to show it in this section to explain the fields.

```
apiVersion: security.istio.io/v1beta1
kind: RequestAuthentication
metadata:
  name: demo-requestauth
  namespace: demo
spec:
  selector:
    matchLabels:
      app: frontend
  jwtRules:
  - issuer: testing@secure.istio.io
    jwksUri: https://raw.githubusercontent.com/istio/istio/
release-1.11/security/tools/jwt/samples/jwks.json
```

This manifest will create a policy that configures a workload with the label `matching app=frontend` in the `demo` namespace to accept JWTs from the issuer `testing@secure. istio.io` with a URL to confirm the tokens at `https://raw.githubusercontent.com/ istio/istio/release-1.11/security/tools/jwt/samples/jwks.json`.

This URL contains the key used to validate the tokens:

```
{ "keys":[ {"e":"AQAB","kid":"DHFbpoIUqrY8t2zpA2qXfC
mr5VO5ZEr4RzHU_-envvQ","kty":"RSA","n":"xAE7eB6qugXy
CAG3yhh7pkDkT65pHymX-P7KfIupjf59vsdo91bSP9C8H07pSAGQ-
O1MV_xFj9VswgsCg4R6otmg5PV2He95lZdHtOcU5DXIg_
pbhLdKXbi66GlVeK6ABZOUW3WYtnNHD-91gVuoeJT_DwtGGcp4ignkgXfkiEm4sw-4sfb4q
dt5oLbyVpmW6x9cfa7vs2WTfURiCrBoUqgBo_-4WTiULmmHSGZHOjzwa8WtrtOQGsAFjIbn
o85jp6MnGGGZPYZbDAa_b3y5u-YpW7ypZrvD8BgtKVjgtQgZhLAGezMt0ua3DRrWnKqTZ0
BJ_EyxOGuHJrLsn00fnMQ"}]}
```

When a token is presented, it will be verified that it came from the issuer defined in the `jwtRules` section of the `RequestAuthenctication` object.

Service entries

The next object is the `ServiceEntry` object, which allows you to create entries in the service mesh to allow auto-discovered mesh services to communicate with the manually entered services:

```
apiVersion: networking.istio.io/v1alpha3
kind: ServiceEntry
```

```
metadata:
  name: api-server
  namespace: sales
spec:
  hosts:
  - api.foowidgets.com
  ports:
  - number: 80
    name: http
    protocol: HTTP
```

This manifest will create an entry that logically adds an external service to the service mesh, so it appears to be in the mesh.

Sidecars

First, we know this can be confusing – this object is not the sidecar itself, it is an object that allows you to define what items your sidecar considers to be "in the mesh." Depending on the size of your cluster, you may have thousands of services in the mesh and if you do not create a sidecar object, your Envoy sidecar will assume that your service needs to communicate with every other service.

Typically, you may only need your namespace to communicate with services in the same namespace, or a small number of other namespaces. Since tracking every service in the mesh requires resources, it's considered good practice to create a sidecar object to reduce the required memory in each Envoy sidecar.

To create a sidecar object that limits the services in your Envoy proxy, you would deploy the manifest shown below:

```
apiVersion: networking.istio.io/v1beta1
kind: Sidecar
metadata:
  name: sales-sidecar
  namespace: sales
spec:
  egress:
  - hosts:
    - "./*"
    - "istio-system/*"
```

The spec in this manifest contains a list of hosts for the mesh, the ./* references the namespace where the object was created, and all sidecars should contain the namespace where Istio was deployed, which would be istio-system, by default.

If we had three namespaces that needed to communicate across the mesh, we would simply need to add the additional namespaces to the hosts' entries:

```
apiVersion: networking.istio.io/v1beta1
kind: Sidecar
metadata:
  name: sales-sidecar
  namespace: sales
spec:
  egress:
  - hosts:
    - ./*
    - istio-system/*
    -   sales2
    -   sales3
```

Failing to limit the mesh objects may result in your Envoy sidecar CrashLooping due to resources. You may experience an **out of memory (OOM)** event, or simply CrashLoops that do not show any details of the root cause. If you experience these scenarios, deploying a sidecar object may resolve the issue.

Envoy filters

Envoy filters provide you with the ability to create custom configurations that are generated by Istio. Remember that Pilot (part of istiod) is responsible for sidecar management. When any configuration is sent to Istio, Pilot will convert the configuration for Envoy to utilize. Since you are "limited" by the options in the Istio custom resource, you may not have all of the potential configuration options that are required for a workload and that's where Envoy filters come in.

Filters are very powerful, and potentially dangerous, configuration objects. They allow you to customize values that you cannot customize from a standard Istio object, allowing you to add filters, listeners, fields, and more. This brings a quote used in Spider-Man from the late Stan Lee to mind, "With great power comes great responsibility." Envoy filters provide you with extended configuration options, but if a filter is misused, it could bring down the entire service mesh.

Envoy filters are complex and, for the purposes of this book, are not a topic that needs deep understanding to understand Istio in general. You can read more about Envoy filters on the Istio site at `https://istio.io/latest/docs/reference/config/networking/envoy-filter/`.

Deploying add-on components to provide observability

By now, you know how to deploy Istio and understand some of the most used objects, but you haven't seen one of the most useful features yet – observability. At the beginning of the chapter, we mentioned that observability was one of our favorite features provided by Istio, and in this chapter, we will explain how to deploy a popular Istio add-on called Kiali.

Installing Prometheus

Before we install Kiali, we need to deploy an open-source monitoring and alert component called Prometheus that was developed by SoundCloud to store our mesh metrics. Prometheus was developed in 2012 and in 2016 it was added to the **Cloud Native Computing Foundation (CNCF)**, becoming only the second project in the CNCF behind Kubernetes.

People who are newer to Prometheus and Kubernetes often misunderstand the features provided by Prometheus. Prometheus does not provide logging for your containers or infrastructure, that's where products like Elasticsearch and Kibana come in. Instead, Prometheus keeps track of your cluster metrics, which are used for performance tracking. Metrics include information like throughput, CPU usage, latency, and more. You can read more about Prometheus at their site, `https://prometheus.io/`.

To deploy Prometheus, we have included a custom Prometheus installation in the `chapter12` directory. You can deploy it using `kubectl apply`.

```
kubectl apply -f prometheus-deployment.yaml
```

Many Prometheus example deployments do not maintain state, so for our deployment we have added persistency, leveraging the provisioner built into KinD, using a persistent volume claim named `prom-pvc`.

Installing Jaeger

The next component we need to deploy is Jaegar, which is an open-source offering that provides tracing between services in Istio. Tracing may be a new term to some readers and, at a high level, traces are a representation of the execution path to a service. These allow us to view the actual path of the communication between services, providing an easy-to-understand view that provides metrics about performance and latency, allowing you to resolve issues quicker.

To deploy Jaeger, we have included a manifest in the `chapter12` directory called `jaeger-deployment.yaml`. You can deploy it using `kubectl apply`.

```
kubectl apply -f jaeger-deployment.yaml
```

Similar to the Prometheus installation, most deployments you find on the internet do not maintain persistency. We have added a persistent volume to our deployment called `jaeger-pvc` that is allocated using the KinD auto provisioner.

With Prometheus and Jaeger deployed, we can move on to the next section, which will cover the main topic for observability, Kiali.

Installing Kiali

Kiali provides a powerful management console for our service mesh. It provides graphical views of our services, pods, traffic security, and more. Since it's a very useful tool for both developers and operators, the remainder of this chapter will focus on deploying and using Kiali.

There are a few options to deploy Kiali, but we will use the most common installation method, using the Helm chart.

```
helm install --namespace istio-system --set auth.strategy="anonymous"
--repo https://kiali.org/helm-charts kiali-server kiali-server
```

This will only deploy Kiali itself, it does not expose it for external access. We have created an Ingress manifest that will create an Ingress rule using the `nip.io` format we have used throughout the book. The manifest is located in the `chapter12/kiali` directory, called `create-kiali-istio-objs.sh`. Change your directory to `chapter12/kiali` to execute the script, which will create the VirtualService and Gateway objects for Kiali, using the name `kiali.w.x.y.z.nip.io`.

Once the Ingress has been created, the script will display the URL to access the Kiali dashboard. For this example, the Docker host has the IP address `10.2.1.165`.

The Kiali ingress rule has been created. You can open the UI using `http://kiali.10.2.1.165.nip.io/`.

This deploys an anonymous access dashboard, however, Kiali can accept other authentication mechanisms to secure the dashboard. In the next chapter, we will modify the Kiali deployment to accept JWTs, using OpenUnison as the provider.

Deploying an application into the service mesh

We could define the components and objects of Istio all day, but if you are like us, examples and use-cases are often more beneficial to understanding advanced concepts like the features provided by Istio. In this section, we will explain many of the custom resources in detail, providing examples that you can deploy in your KinD cluster.

Deploying your first application into the mesh

Finally! We have Istio and the add-on components installed and we can move on to installing a real application in the service mesh to verify everything is working.

For this section, we will deploy an example application from Google called the Boutique app. In the next chapter, we will deploy a different application and explain all of the details and communication between the services, but the Boutique app is a great application to test out the mesh before we get into that level of information.

To deploy Google's Boutique app, execute the following steps:

1. Create a new namespace called `demo` and enable Istio by labeling the namespace

   ```
   kubectl create ns demo
   kubectl label ns demo istio-injection=enabled
   ```

2. Change your working directory to the `chapter12/example-app` directory

3. Deploy the Istio components for the Boutique app using the `istio-manifest.yaml` in the `example-app` directory

   ```
   kubectl create -f ./istio-manifests.yaml -n demo
   ```

4. Next, we will deploy the Boutique application and required services

   ```
   kubectl create -f ./kubernetes-manifests.yaml -n demo
   ```

5. Finally, to create the Gateway and VirtualService that will be used to access the Boutique application, execute the `create-gw-vs.sh` script

   ```
   ./create-gw-vs.sh
   ```

Once you execute each step, you will have a working demo application in the demo namespace. We will use this application to demonstrate the observability features of Istio and Kiali.

Using Kiali to observe mesh workloads

Kiali provides observability in your service mesh. It provides a number of advantages to you and your developers, including a visual map of the traffic flow between objects, verifying mTLS between the services, logs, and detailed metrics.

The Kiali overview screen

If you navigate to the homepage of Kiali, by using the URL provided when you executed the `create-ingress` script, this will open the Kiali overview page where you will see a list of namespaces in the cluster.

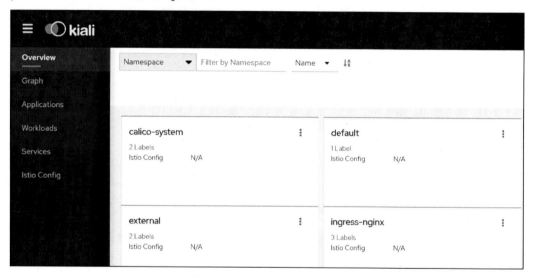

Figure 12.3: The Kiali homepage

Kiali will show all namespaces in the cluster, even if they do not have Istio enabled. In our current deployment, it will show all namespaces, regardless of any RBAC that has been implemented since its running without any authentication. As mentioned in the *Installing Kiali* section, we will secure Kiali with JWTs in the next chapter.

Using the Graph view

The first part of the dashboard that we will visit is the Graph view, which provides a graphical view of our application. Initially, it may look like a simple static graphical representation of the objects that make up the workload, but this is simply the default view when you open the Graph view; it isn't limited to a simple static view, as you will see in this section.

Since we deployed the example application into the demo namespace, click the three dots in the demo namespace tile and then select **Graph**:

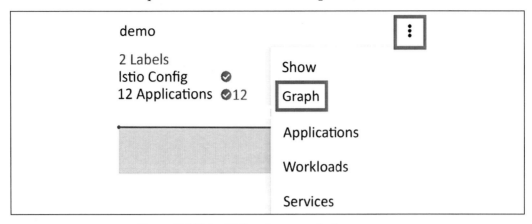

Figure 12.4: Using Kiali to show a graph of a namespace

This will take you to a new dashboard view that shows the demo application objects:

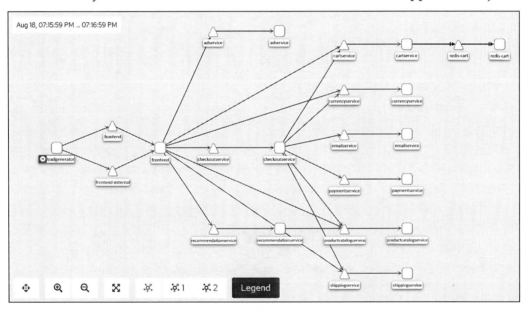

Figure 12.5: Kiali graph example

There are a lot of objects in the graph, and if you are new to Kiali, you may be wondering what each of the icons represents. Kiali provides a legend to help you identify what role each icon plays.

If you click on the graph, you will see the legend – an abbreviated legend list is shown below:

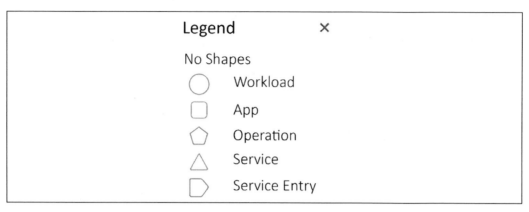

Figure 12.6: Kiali graph legend example

By default, this view only shows the paths between the application objects in a static view. However, you are not limited only to the static view – this is where Kiali starts to shine. We can actually enable a live traffic view, enabling us to watch the traffic flow for all requests.

To enable this option, click the **Display** option that is just above the Graph view, and in the list of options, enable traffic animation by checking the box, as shown in *Figure 12.7: Enabling traffic animation*.

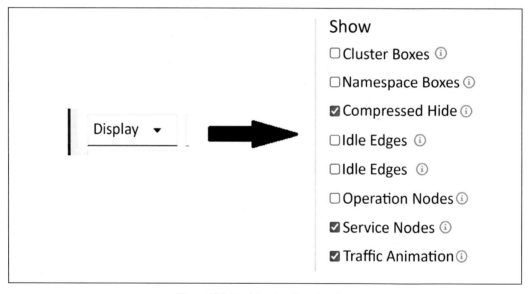

Figure 12.7: Enabling traffic animation

It's difficult to display in a static image, but once you have enabled the traffic animation option, you will see the flow of all requests in real time.

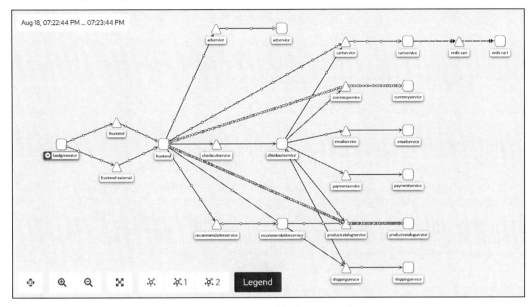

Figure 12.8: Kiali traffic flow example

You are not limited to only traffic flow animations; you can use the **Display** option to enable a number of other options in the **Graph** view, including items like response time, throughput, traffic rate, and security.

In *Figure 12.9: Kiali graph display options*, we have enabled throughput, traffic distribution, traffic rate, and security:

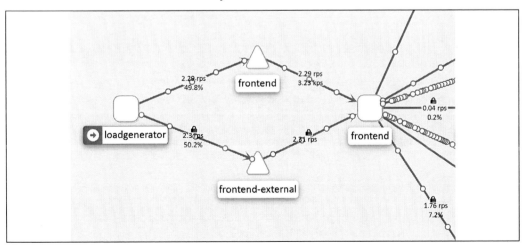

Figure 12.9: Kiali graph display options

As you can see in the image, the lines between objects now include additional information, including:

- A lock, which confirms that the communication is encrypted via the sidecar and mTLS
- A percentage, which shows the traffic distribution
- RPS, which is the requests per second

As you can see, the Kiali graph view is a powerful tool for observing the end-to-end communication for your workload. This is just one of the additional benefits of using a service mesh. The observability that a mesh provides is an incredibly valuable tool for finding issues that would have been very difficult to uncover in the past.

We are not limited to only the Graph view; we also have three additional views that offer additional insight into the application. On the left-hand side of the Kiali dashboard, you will see the other three views, Applications, Workloads, and Services. You will also notice that there is one other option, Istio Config, which allows you to view the objects in the namespace that control the Istio features for the namespace.

Using the Application view

The Application view shows you the details for the workloads that have the same labeling, allowing you to break down the view into smaller sections.

Using the Boutique application view that we have opened in Kiali, click on the **Applications** link in the left-hand options. This will take you to the overview page for the applications broken down by labels.

Figure 12.10: Kiali application view

Each of the applications can provide additional information by clicking the name of the service. If we were to click the **adservice** application, Kiali would open a page providing an overview of what the adservice application interacts with. For each application, you can also look at the overview, traffic, inbound and outbound metrics, and traces.

The overview page presents you with a dedicated view of the objects that communicate with adservice. We saw a similar communications view in the graph view, but we also saw every other object – including objects that have nothing to do with adservice. As a refresher, reference *Figure 12.11: Viewing the communication in the Graph view*, which shows the three components that make up the communication for adservice.

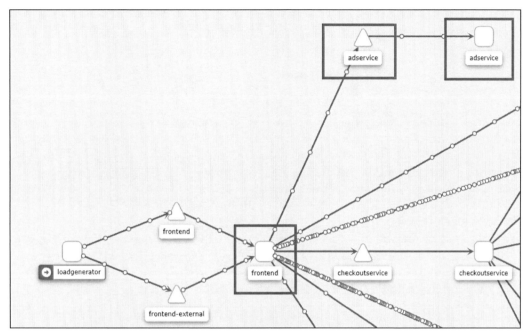

Figure 12.11: Viewing the communication in the Graph view

The Application view will streamline what we can see, making it easier to navigate the application.

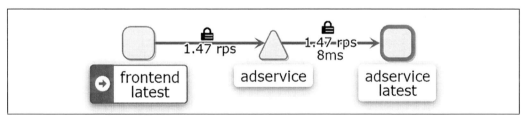

Figure 12.12: Simplified communication view using the Application view

As you can see, the Application view contains the components from the graph view. The communications path that involves adservice starts with the frontend pod, which targets the adservice service, which ultimately routes the traffic to the adservice pod.

We can see additional details in the application by clicking on one of the tabs at the top of the **Application** view. The first tab next to the overview is the **Traffic** tab, which provides you with a view of the traffic for the application.

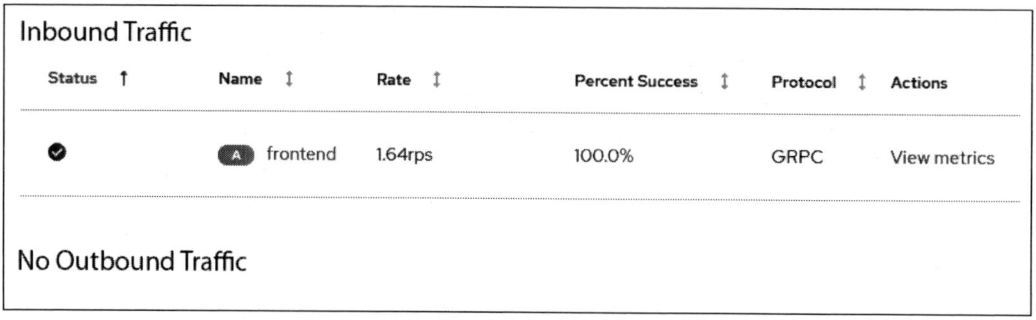

Inbound Traffic					
Status ↑	Name ↕	Rate ↕	Percent Success ↕	Protocol ↕	Actions
✓	(A) frontend	1.64rps	100.0%	GRPC	View metrics

No Outbound Traffic

Figure 12.13: Viewing application traffic

The Traffic tab will show inbound and outbound traffic to the application. In the adservice example from the Boutique store, we can see that that adservice has received inbound requests from the frontend. Below the inbound traffic, we can see the outbound traffic and, in our example, Kiali is telling us that there is no outbound traffic. As we can see in the overview in *Figure 12.12: Simplified communication view using the Application view*, the adservice pod does not have any object that it connects to, therefore, we would not have any traffic to view. To get additional details on the traffic, you can click on the **View Metrics** link under **Actions** – this action is the same as if you were to click the **Inbound Metrics** tab.

The **Inbound Metrics** tab will provide you with additional details about the incoming traffic. *Figure 12.14: Viewing inbound metrics* shows an abbreviated example for the adservice traffic.

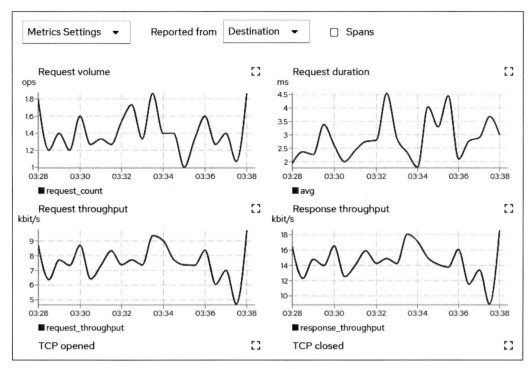

Figure 12.14: Viewing inbound metrics

The inbound metrics will display a number of different metrics including request volume, request duration, request and response size, request and response throughput, gRPC received and sent, TCP opened and closed, and TCP received and sent. This page will update in real time, allowing you to view the metrics as they are captured.

Finally, the last tab will allow you to look at the traces for the adservice application. This is why we deployed Jaeger in our cluster when we installed Istio. Tracing is a fairly complex topic and is outside the scope of this chapter. To learn more about tracing using Jaeger, head over to the Jaeger site at `https://www.jaegertracing.io/`.

Using the Workloads view

The next view we will discuss is the **Workloads** view, which breaks down the views to the workload type, like deployments. If you click on the **Workloads** link in Kiali, you will be taken to a breakdown of the Boutique workloads.

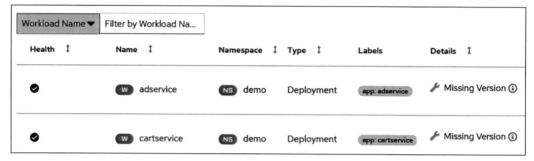

Figure 12.15: The Workloads view

You may notice that there is a warning under the **Details** column that tells us we are missing a version of the deployments. This is one of the features of this view. It will offer details like a workload not being assigned a version, which is not an issue for standard functionality in the mesh, but it will limit the use of certain features, like routing and some telemetry. It's a best practice to always version your application, but for the example, Boutique from Google, they do not include a version in the deployments.

The **Workloads** view offers some of the same details as the **Applications** view, including traffic, inbound metrics, outbound metrics, and tracing – however, in addition to these details, we can now view the logs and details about Envoy.

If you click on the **Logs** tab, you will see the logs for the adservice container.

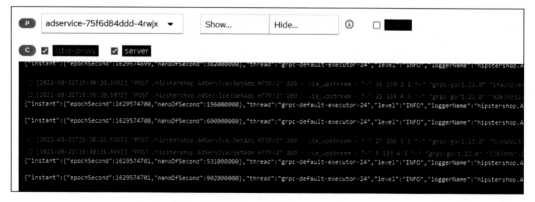

Figure 12.16: Viewing the container logs

This is a real-time view of the logs that are being generated by the adservice container. In this view, you can create a filter to show or hide certain keywords, scroll back to previous events, change the default buffer size from 100 lines, copy the logs to your clipboard, or enter a fullscreen log view. Many users find this tab very useful since it doesn't require them to use kubectl to look at the logs; they can simply open up Kiali in a browser and quickly view the logs in the GUI.

The last tab we will discuss is the **Envoy** tab, which provides additional details about the Envoy sidecar. The details in this tab are extensive – it contains all of the mesh objects that you have included in the namespace (recall that we created a sidecar object to limit the objects to only the namespace and the istio-system namespace), all of the listeners, routes, the bootstrap configuration, config, and metrics.

By this point in the chapter, you can probably see how Istio requires its own book to cover all of the base components. All of the tabs in the **Envoy** tab provide a wealth of information, but it gets very detailed and we can't fit them all in this chapter, so for the purposes of this chapter, we will only discuss the **Metrics** tab.

Clicking on the **Metrics** tab, you will see metrics pertaining to the uptime of Envoy, the allocated memory, heap size, active upstream connections, upstream total requests, downstream active connections, and downstream HTTP requests.

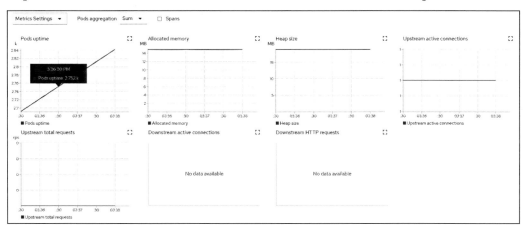

Figure 12.17: Envoy metrics

Like most metrics, these will be beneficial if you experience issues with the Envoy proxy container. The uptime will let you know how long the pod has been running, the allocated memory tells you how much memory has been allocated to the pod, which may help to identify why an OOM condition occurred, and active connections will identify if the service has issues if the connection count is lower than expected, or at zero.

Using the Services view

Finally, we will discuss the last view for the application, the Services view. Just as the name implies, this will provide a view of the services that are part of the workload. You can open the Services view by clicking on the **Services** option in Kiali.

Figure 12.18: The Services view

Similar to the other views, this will provide the names of the services and the health of each of the services. If you click on any individual service, you will be taken to the details of the service. If you were to click **adservice**, you would be taken to the overview for the service.

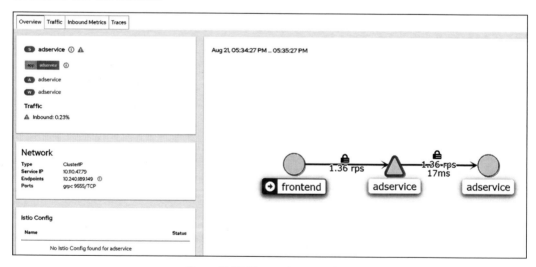

Figure 12.19: The services overview

The **Overview** page should have some objects familiar to you. Just like the other views, it provides a view of just the objects that communicate with adservice, and it has tabs for traffic, inbound metrics, and traces – however, in addition to these, it also shows the network information for the service. In our example, the service has been configured to use a ClusterIP type, the service IP assigned is `10.110.47.79`, it has an endpoint of `10.240.189.149`, and it has the gRPC TCP port exposed on port `9555`.

This is information you could retrieve using kubectl, but for many people, it's quicker to grab the details from the Kiali dashboard.

The Istio config view

The last view we have is not related to the workload in particular, instead, it's a view for the Istio config for the namespace. This view will contain the Istio objects you have created. In our example, we have three objects, the gateway, the virtual service, and the sidecar.

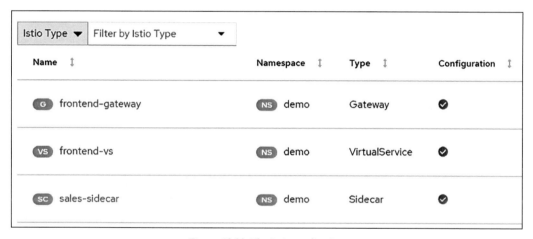

Figure 12.20: The Istio config view

You can view the YAML for each object by clicking the name. This allows you to directly edit the object in the Kiali dashboard. Any changes that are saved will edit the object in the cluster, so be careful if you are using this method to modify the object.

This view offers one addition that the other views do not – the ability to create a new Istio object using a wizard. To create a new object, click the **Actions** dropdown in the upper right-hand corner of the Istio config view. This will bring up a list of objects that you can create, as shown in *Figure 12.21: Istio object creation wizard.*

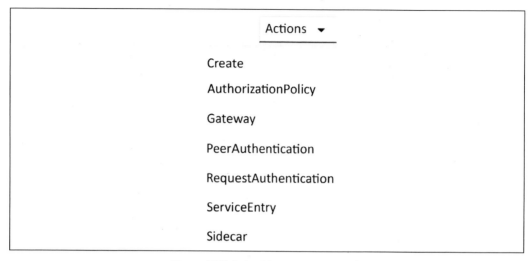

Figure 12.21: Istio object creation wizard

As you can see in the figure, Kiali provides a wizard to create 6 Istio objects including AuthorizationPolicies, Gateways, PeerAuthentication, RequestAuthentication, ServiceEntries, and Sidecars.

Each option has a wizard to guide you through the specific requirements for that object. For example, we could create a Sidecar using the wizard as shown in *Figure 12.22: Using the Istio object wizard.*

Create Sidecar

Name*	test-sidecar
Workload Selector	
Egress	Egress Host
	istio-system/*
	./*

Create   Cancel

Figure 12.22: Using the Istio object wizard

Once all fields have been entered correctly, you can click **Create** and it will create the new object in the cluster.

The wizards are a good tool for people who are new to Istio, but be careful not to rely on them too much. You should always understand how to create a manifest for all of your objects. Creating objects using wizards like these can lead to problems down the road without the knowledge of how the object works or is created.

With that last view, we have completed the Kiali section and the chapter.

Summary

In this chapter, we introduced you to the service mesh world, using the popular open-source project Istio. In the first section of the chapter, we explained some of the advantages of using a service mesh, which included security and observability for mesh services.

The second section of the chapter detailed the installation of Istio and the different installation profiles that are available. We deployed Istio into our KinD clusters and we also removed NGNIX to free up ports 80 and 443 to be used by Istio's ingress gateway. This section also included the objects that are added to a cluster once you deploy Istio. We covered the most common objects using example manifests that reinforce how to use each object in your own deployments.

To close out the chapter, we detailed how to install Kiali, Prometheus, and Jaeger to provide powerful observability in our service mesh. We also explained how to use Kiali to look into an application in the mesh to view the application metrics and logs.

In the next chapter, we will deploy a new application and bind it to the service mesh, building on many of the concepts that were presented in this chapter.

Questions

1. What Istio object(s) is used to route traffic between multiple versions of an application?

    a. Ingress rule

    b. VirtualService

    c. DestinationRule

    d. You can't route to multiple versions, only a single instance

    Answer: **b and c**

2. What tool(s) are required to provide observability in the service mesh?

    a. Prometheus

    b. Jaeger

    c. Kiali

    d. Kubernetes dashboard

    Answer: **a and c**

3. True or false: Istio features require developers to change their code to leverage features like mutual TLS and authorization.

    a. True

    b. False

    Answer: **False**

4. Istio made the control plane easier to deploy and configure by merging multiple components into a single executable called:

    a. Istio

    b. IstioC

    c. istiod

    d. Pilot

    Answer: **c. istiod**

Join our book's Discord space

Join the book's Discord workspace for a monthly *Ask me Anything* session with the authors: `https://packt.link/K8EntGuide`

13

Building and Deploying Applications on Istio

In the previous chapter, we deployed Istio and Kiali into our cluster. We also deployed an example application to see how the pieces fit together. In this chapter, we're going to look at what it takes to build applications that will run on Istio. We'll start by examining the differences between microservices and monolithic applications. We'll start by deploying a monolithic application on Istio, and then transition to building microservices that will run on Istio. This chapter will cover:

- Technical requirements
- Comparing microservices and monoliths
- Deploying a monolith
- Building a microservice
- Do I need an API gateway?

Once you have completed this chapter, you'll have a practical understanding of the difference between a monolith and a microservice, along with the information you'll need to determine which one is best for you, and will also have deployed a secured microservice in Istio.

Technical requirements

To run the examples in this chapter, you'll need:

- A running cluster with Istio deployed as outlined in *Chapter 12, An Introduction to Istio*
- Scripts from this book's GitHub repository

You can access the code for this chapter by going to this book's GitHub repository: `https://github.com/PacktPublishing/Kubernetes---An-Enterprise-Guide-2E/tree/main/chapter13`.

Comparing microservices and monoliths

Before we dive too deeply into code, we should spend some time discussing the differences between microservices and monolithic architecture. The microservices versus monolithic architecture debate is as old as computing itself (and the theory is probably even older). Understanding how these two approaches relate to each other and your problem set will help you decide which one to use.

My history with microservices versus monolithic architecture

Before we get into the microservices versus monoliths discussion, I wanted to share my own history with this conversation. I doubt it's unique, but it does frame my outlook on the discussion and adds some context to the recommendations in this chapter.

My introduction to this discussion was when I was a computer science student in college and had started using Linux and open source. One of my favorite books, *Open Sources: Voices from the Open Source Revolution,* had an appendix on the debate between Andrew Tanenbaum and Linus Torvalds on microkernels versus monolithic kernels. Tanenbaum was the inventor of Minix, and a proponent of a minimalist kernel with most of the functionality in user space. Linux, instead, uses a monolithic kernel design where much more is done in the kernel. If you've ever run `modprobe` to load a driver, you're interacting with the kernel! The entire thread is available at `https://www.oreilly.com/openbook/opensources/book/appa.html`.

Linus' core argument was that a well-managed monolith was much easier to maintain than a microkernel.

Tanenbaum instead pointed to the idea that microkernels were easier to port and that most "modern" kernels were microkernels. Windows, at the time Windows NT, is probably the most prevalent microkernel today. As a software developer, I'm constantly trying to find the smallest unit I can build. The microkernel architecture really appealed to that aspect of my talents.

At the same time, I was starting my career in IT primarily as a Windows developer in the data management and analysis space. I spent most of my time in ASP, Visual Basic, and SQL Server. I tried to convince my bosses that we should move off of a monolithic application design to using **Microsoft Transaction Server** (**MTS**). MTS was my first exposure to what we would call today a distributed application. My bosses and mentors all pointed out that our costs, and so our customer's costs, would go through the roof if we injected the additional infrastructure for no benefit other than a cleaner code base. There was nothing we were working on that couldn't be accomplished with our tightly bound trio of ASP, Visual Basic, and SQL Server at a much lower cost.

I later moved from data management into identity management. I also switched from Microsoft to Java. One of my first projects was to deploy an identity management vendor's product that was built using a distributed architecture. At the time I thought it was great, until I started trying to debug issues and trace down problems across dozens of log files. I quickly started using another vendor's product that was built as a monolith. Deployments were slow, as they required a full recompile, but otherwise management was much easier and it scaled every bit as well. We found that a distributed architecture didn't help because identity management was done by such a centralized team that having a monolith didn't impact productivity or management. The benefits of distributing implementation just didn't outweigh the additional complexity.

Fast forward to founding Tremolo Security. This was in 2010, so it was before Kubernetes and Istio came along. At the time, virtual appliances were all the rage! We decided OpenUnison would take the monolithic approach because we wanted to make it easier to deploy and upgrade. In *Chapter 5, Integrating Authentication into Your Cluster*, we deployed OpenUnison with some Helm Charts to layer on different configurations. How much harder would it have been had there been an authentication service to install, a directory service, a just-in-time provisioning service, etc.? It made for a much simpler deployment having one system.

With all that said, it's not that I'm anti-microservice—I'm not! When used correctly it's an incredibly powerful architecture used by many of the world's largest companies. I've learned through the years that if it's not the right architecture for your system, it will considerably impact your ability to deliver. Now that I've filled you in on my own journey through architectures, let's take a deeper look at the differences between microservices and monoliths.

Comparing architectures in an application

First, let's talk about what these two architecture approaches each do in a common example application, a storefront.

Monolithic application design

Let's say you have an online store. Your store will likely need a product lookup service, a shopping cart, a payment system, and a shipping system. This is a vast oversimplification of a storefront application, but the point of the discussion is how to break up development and not how to build a storefront. There are two ways you could approach building this application. The first is you could build a monolithic application where all the code for each service is stored and managed in the same tree. Your application infrastructure would probably look something like this:

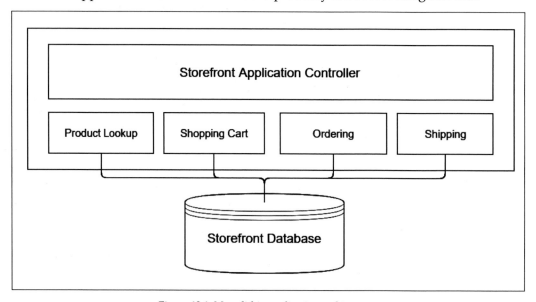

Figure 13.1: Monolithic application architecture

In our application, we have a single system with multiple modules. Depending on your programming language of choice these could be classes, structs, or other forms of code module. A central application manages the user's interaction with this code. This would likely be a web frontend with the modules being server-side code written up as web services or a post/response-style app.

Yes, web services can be used in a monolith! These modules likely need to store data, usually in some kind of a database. Whether it's a relational database or a document database isn't really important.

The biggest advantage to this monolithic architecture is it's relatively simple to manage and have the systems interact with each other. If the user wants to do a product search, the storefront will likely just execute some code like the following:

```
list_of_products = products.search(search_criteria);
display(list_of_products);
```

The application code only needs to know the interface of the services it's going to call. There's no need to "authenticate" that call from the application controller to the product directory module. There's no concern with creating rate-limiting systems or trying to work out which version of the service to use. Everything is tightly bound. If you make an update to any system, you know pretty quickly if you broke an interface since you're likely using a development tool that will tell you when module interfaces break. Finally, deployment is usually pretty simple. You upload your code to a deployment service (or create a container…this is a Kubernetes book!).

What happens if you need to have one developer update your ordering system while another developer is updating your payment system? They each have their own copies of the code that need to be merged. After merging, the changes from both branches need to be reconciled before deployment. This may be fine for a small system, but as your storefront grows this can become cumbersome to the point of being unmanageable.

Another potential issue is, what if there's a better language or system to build one of these services in than the overall application? I've been on multiple projects over the years where Java was a great choice for certain components, but C# had better APIs for others. Maybe one service team was built around Python and another on Ruby. Standardization is all well and good, but you wouldn't use the butt end of a screwdriver to drive in a nail for the sake of standardization, would you?

 This argument doesn't pertain to frontend versus backend. An application with a JavaScript frontend and a Golang backend can still be a monolithic application. Both the Kubernetes Dashboard and Kiali are examples of monolithic applications built on service APIs across different languages. Both have HTML and JavaScript frontends while their backend APIs are written in Golang.

Microservices design

What if we broke these modules up into services? Instead of having one single source tree, we would break our application up into individual services like the following:

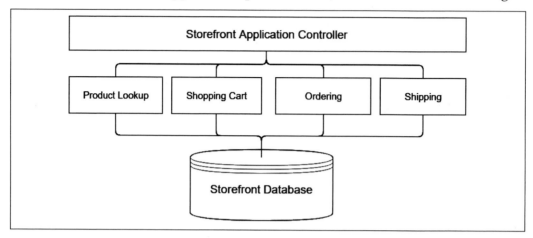

Figure 13.2: Simple microservices architecture

This doesn't look that much more complex. Instead of a big box there's a bunch of lines. Let's zoom in on the call from our frontend to our product lookup service:

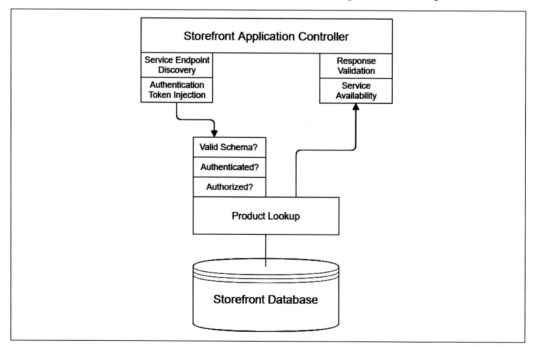

Figure 13.3: Service call architecture

It's no longer a simple function or method call. Now our storefront controller needs to determine where to send the service call to, and this will likely change in each environment. It also needs to inject some kind of authentication token, since you wouldn't want just anyone calling your services. Since the remote service no longer has a local code representation, you'll either need to build the call manually or use a schema language to describe your product listing service and combine it with a client binding. Once the call is made, the service needs to validate the call's schema and apply security rules for authentication and authorization. Once the response is packaged and sent back to our storefront controller, the controller needs to validate the schema of the response. If there's a failure, it needs to decide if it's going to retry or not.

Combine all this additional complexity with version management. Which version of the product lookup service should our storefront use? Are other services tightly coupled together? There are several benefits to the microservices approach, as we discussed earlier, in terms of version and deployment management. These advantages come with the cost of additional complexity.

Choosing between monoliths and microservices

Which of these two approaches is right for you? That really depends. What does your team look like? What are your management needs? Do you need the flexibility that comes from microservices or will a monolith's simpler design make for an easier-to-manage system?

Also, will your services need to be called by other systems? Look at the cluster we built in the last chapter. Kiali has its own services, but they're not likely to be used by other applications. Jaeger and Prometheus however do have services that are used by Kiali, even if those systems have their own frontends too. In addition to these services, Kiali uses the Kubernetes API. All these components are deployed separately and are managed separately. They need to be upgraded on their own, monitored, and so on. This can be a management headache because each system is independently managed and maintained. That said, it wouldn't make any sense for the Kiali team to re-implement Prometheus and Jaeger in their own project. It also wouldn't make sense to just import the entire source tree for these projects and be forced to keep them up to date.

Using Istio to help manage microservices

We've spent quite a bit of time talking about microservices and monoliths without talking about Istio. Earlier in this chapter, *Figure 13.3* pointed out decisions that were needed by our microservice before we can get to calling our code.

These should look familiar because we covered objects from Istio that service most of these needs in the last chapter! Istio can remove our need to write code to authenticate and authorize clients, discover where services are running, and manage traffic routing. Throughout the rest of this chapter, we're going to walk through building a small application off of a microservice using Istio to leverage these common services without having to build them into our code.

Deploying a monolith

This chapter is about microservices, so why are we starting with deploying monoliths in Istio? The first answer is, because we can! There's no reason to not get the benefits of Istio's built-in capabilities when working with monoliths in your cluster. Even though it's not a "microservice" it's still good to be able to trace through application requests, manage deployments, and so on. The second answer is, because we need to. Our microservice will need to know which user in our enterprise is calling it. To do that, Istio will need a JWT to validate. We'll use our OpenUnison to generate JWTs first so we can call our service manually and then so we can authenticate users from a frontend and allow that frontend to call our service securely.

Assuming you started with a fresh cluster, we're going to deploy OpenUnison the same way we did in *Chapter 5, Integration Authentication into Your Cluster*, but this time we have a script that does everything for you. Go into the `chapter13` directory and run `deploy_openunison_istio.sh`:

```
cd chapter13
./deploy_openunison_istio.sh
```

This is going to take a while to run. This script does a few things:

1. Deploys all of the OpenUnison components (including our testing "Active Directory") for impersonation so we don't need to worry about updating the API server for SSO to work.

2. Labels the `openunison` namespace with `istio-injection: enabled`. This tells Istio to enable sidecar injection for all pods. You can do this manually by running `kubectl label ns openunison istio-injection=enabled`.

3. Creates all of our Istio objects for us (we'll go into the details of these next).

4. Copies the `ou-tls-certificate` Secret from the `openunison` namespace to the `istio-system` namespace. Again, we'll dive into the details as to why in the next section.

Once the script is run, we're able to now log in to our monolith! Just like in *Chapter 5, Integrating Authentication into Your Cluster*, go to `https://k8sou.XX-XX-XX-XX.nip.io/` to log in, where XX-XX-XX-XX is your host's IP address.

For instance, my host runs on **192.168.2.114** so my URL is `https://k8sou.192-168-2-114.nip.io/`. Again, as in *Chapter 5*, the username is `mmosley` and the password is `start123`.

Now that our monolith is deployed, let's walk through the Istio-specific configuration as it relates to our deployment.

Exposing our monolith outside our cluster

Now that OpenUnison is running, let's look at the objects that expose it to our network. There are two main objects that do this work: `Gateway` and `VirtualService`. How these objects are configured was described in *Chapter 12*, *An Introduction to Istio*. Now we'll look at running instances to show how they grant access. First, let's look at the important parts of our Gateways. There are two. The first one, `openunison-gateway-orchestra`, handles access to the OpenUnison portal and the Kubernetes Dashboard:

```
apiVersion: networking.istio.io/v1beta1
kind: Gateway
metadata:
spec:
  selector:
    istio: ingressgateway
  servers:
  - hosts:
    - k8sou.192-168-2-114.nip.io
    - k8sdb.192-168-2-114.nip.io
    port:
      name: http
      number: 80
      protocol: HTTP
    tls:
      httpsRedirect: true
  - hosts:
    - k8sou.192-168-2-114.nip.io
    - k8sdb.192-168-2-114.nip.io
    port:
      name: https-443
      number: 443
      protocol: HTTPS
    tls:
      credentialName: ou-tls-certificate
      mode: SIMPLE
```

The selector tells Istio which ingress-ingressgateway pod to work with. The default gateway deployed to istio-system has the label istio: ingressgateway, which will match this one. You could run multiple gateways, using this section to determine which one you want to expose your service to. This is useful if you have multiple networks with different traffic or you want to separate traffic between applications on a cluster.

The first entry in the servers list tells Istio that if a request comes on HTTP to port 80 for either of our hosts, then we want Istio to send a redirect to the HTTPS port. This is a good security practice so, folks, don't try to bypass HTTPS. The second entry in servers tells Istio to accept HTTPS connections on port 443 using the certificate in the Secret named ou-tls-certificate. This Secret must be a TLS Secret and must be in the same namespace as the pod running the ingress gateway. For our cluster, this means that the ou-tls-certificate **MUST** be in the istio-system namespace. That's why our deployment script copied the secret for us. This is different from using an Ingress object with NGINX, where you keep the TLS Secret in the same namespace as your Ingress object.

> If you don't include your Secret in the correct namespace, it can be difficult to debug. The first thing you'll notice is that when you try to connect to your host, your browser will report that the connection has been reset. This is because Istio doesn't have a certificate to serve. Kiali won't tell you there's a configuration issue, but looking at the istiod pod in istio-system's logs, you'll find failed to fetch key and certificate for kubernetes:// secret-name where secret-name is the name of your Secret. Once you copy your Secret into the correct namespace, your app will start working on HTTPS.

The second Gateway, openunison-api-gateway-orchestra, is used to expose OpenUnison directly via HTTPS for the API server host. This bypasses most of Istio's built-in functionality so it's not something we'll want to do unless needed. The important difference in this Gateway versus our other Gateway is how we configure TLS:

```
- hosts:
  - k8sapi.192-168-2-114.nip.io
  port:
    name: https-443
    number: 443
    protocol: HTTPS
  tls:
    mode: PASSTHROUGH
```

We use PASSTHROUGH as the mode instead of SIMPLE. This tells Istio to not bother trying to decrypt the HTTPS request and instead send it downstream. We have to do this for the Kubernetes API calls because Envoy doesn't support the SPDY protocol used by kubectl for exec, cp, and port-forward so we need to bypass it. This of course means that we lose much of Istio's capabilities so it's not something we want to do if we can avoid it.

While the Gateway objects tell Istio how to listen for connections, the VirtualService objects tell Istio where to send the traffic to. Just like with the Gateway objects, there are two VirtualService objects. The first object handles traffic for both the OpenUnison portal and the Kubernetes Dashboard. Here are the important parts:

```
spec:
  gateways:
  - openunison-gateway-orchestra
  hosts:
  - k8sou.192-168-2-114.nip.io
  - k8sdb.192-168-2-114.nip.io
  http:
  - match:
    - uri:
        prefix: /
    route:
    - destination:
        host: openunison-orchestra
        port:
          number: 80
```

The gateways section tells Istio which Gateway objects to link this to. You could in theory have multiple Gateways as sources for traffic. The hosts section tells Istio which hostnames to apply this configuration to, with the match section telling Istio what conditions to match requests on. This section can provide quite a bit of power for routing microservices, but for monoliths just / is usually good enough.

Finally, the route section tells Istio where to send the traffic. destination.host is the name of the Service you want to send the traffic to. We're sending all traffic to port 80, sort of.

The NGINX Ingress version of this configuration sent all traffic to OpenUnison's HTTPS port (8443). This meant that all data was encrypted over the wire from the user's browser all the way to the OpenUnison pod. We're not doing that here because we're going to rely on mTLS from Istio's sidecar.

Even though we're sending traffic to port 80 using HTTP, the traffic will be encrypted from when it leaves the ingressgateway pod until it arrives at the sidecar on our OpenUnison pod that is intercepting all of OpenUnison's inbound network connections. There's no need to configure TLS explicitly!

Now that we're routing traffic from our network to OpenUnison, let's tackle a common requirement of monolithic applications: sticky sessions.

Configuring sticky sessions

Most monolithic applications require sticky sessions. Enabling sticky sessions means that every request in a session is sent to the same pod. This is generally not needed in microservices because each API call is distinct. Web applications that users interact with generally need to manage state, usually via cookies. Those cookies don't generally store all of the session's state though because the cookies would get too big and would likely have sensitive information. Instead, most web applications use a cookie that points to a session that's saved on the server, usually in memory. While there are ways to make sure this session is available to any instance of the application in a highly available way, it's not very common to do so. These systems are expensive to maintain and are generally not worth the work.

OpenUnison is no different than most other web applications and needs to make sure that sessions are sticky to the pod they originated from. To tell Istio how we want sessions to be managed, we use DestinationRule. DestinationRule objects tell Istio what to do about traffic routed to a host by a VirtualService. Here's the important parts of ours:

```
spec:
  host: openunison-orchestra
  trafficPolicy:
    loadBalancer:
      consistentHash:
        httpCookie:
          name: openunison-orchestra
          path: /
          ttl: 0s
    tls:
      mode: ISTIO_MUTUAL
```

The host in the rule refers to the target (Service) of the traffic, not the hostname in the original URL. trafficPolicy.loadBalancer.consistentHash tells Istio how we want to manage stickiness. Most monolithic applications will want to use cookies. ttl is set to 0s so the cookie is considered a "session cookie." This means that when the browser is closed the cookie disappears from its cookie jar.

You should avoid cookies with specific times to live. These cookies are persisted by the browser and can be treated as a security risk by your enterprise.

With OpenUnison up and running and understanding how Istio is integrated, let's take a look at what Kiali will tell us about our monolith.

Integrating Kiali and OpenUnison

First, let's integrate OpenUnison and Kiali. Kiali, like any other cluster management system, should be configured to require access. Kiali, just like the Kubernetes Dashboard, can integrate with Impersonation so that Kiali will interact with the API server using the user's own permissions. Doing this is pretty straight forward. We created a script in the `chapter13` folder called `integrate-kiali-openunison.sh` that:

1. Deletes the old `Gateway` and `VirtualService` for Kiali

2. Updates the Kiali Helm Chart to use `header` for `auth.strategy` and restarts Kiali to pick up the changes

3. Deploys the openunison-kiali Helm Chart that configures OpenUnison to integrate with Kiali and adds a "badge" to the main screen of our portal

The integration works the same way as the dashboard, but if you're interested in the details you can read about them at `https://openunison.github.io/applications/kiali/`.

With the integration completed, let's see what Kiali can tell us about our monolith. First, log in to OpenUnison. You'll see a new badge on the portal screen:

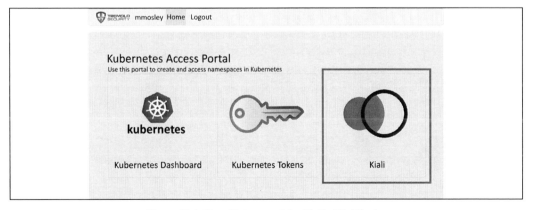

Figure 13.4: OpenUnison portal with the Kiali badge

Next, click on the **Kiali** badge to open Kiali, then click on **Graphs**, and choose the **openunison** namespace. You'll see a graph similar to:

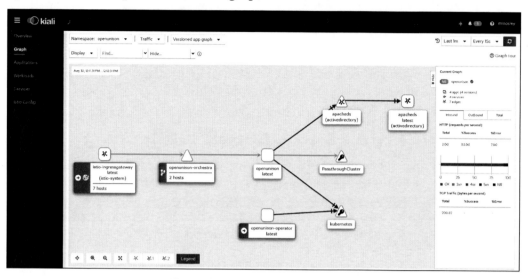

Figure 13.5: OpenUnison graph in Kiali

You can now view the connections between OpenUnison, apacheds, and other containers the same way you would with a microservice! Speaking of which, now that we've learned how to integrate a monolith into Istio, let's build a microservice and learn how it integrates with Istio.

Building a microservice

We spent quite a bit of time talking about monoliths. First, we discussed which is the best approach for you, then we spent some time showing how to deploy a monolith into Istio to get many of the benefits from it that microservices do. Now, let's dive into building and deploying a microservice. Our microservice will be pretty simple. The goal is to show how a microservice is built and integrated into an application, rather than how to build a full-fledged application based on microservices. Our book is focused on enterprise so we're going to focus on a service that:

1. Requires authentication from a specific user
2. Requires authorization for a specific user based on a group membership or attribute
3. Does something very **important**
4. Generates some log data about what happened

This is common in enterprise applications and the services they're built on. Most enterprises need to be able to associate actions, or decisions, to a particular person in that organization. If an order is placed, who placed it? If a case is closed, who closed it? If a check is cut, who cut it? There are of course many instances where a user isn't responsible for an action. Sometimes it's another service that is automated. A batch service that pulls in data to create a warehouse isn't associated with a particular person. This is an **interactive** service, meaning that an end user is expected to interact with it, so we're going to assume the user is a person in the enterprise.

Once you know who is going to use the service, you'll then need to know if the user is authorized to do so. In the previous paragraph we identified that you need to know "who cut the check?" Another important question is, "are they allowed to cut the check?" You really don't want just anybody in your organization sending out checks, do you? Identifying who is authorized to perform an action can be the subject of multiple books, so to keep things simple we'll make our authorization decisions based on group membership, at least at a high level.

Having identified the user and authorized them, the next step is to do something **important**. It's an enterprise, filled with important things that need doing! Since writing a check is something we can all relate to and represents many of the challenges enterprise services face, we're going to stick with this as our example. We're going to write a check service that will let us send out checks.

Finally, having done something **important**, we need to make a record of it. We need to track who called our service, and once the service does the important parts, we need to make sure we record it somewhere. This can be recorded in a database, another service, or even sent to standard-out so it can be collected by a log aggregator.

Having identified all the things our service will do, the next step is to identify which part of our infrastructure will be responsible for each decision and action. For our service:

Action	Component	Description
User Authentication	OpenUnison	Our OpenUnison instance will authenticate users to our "Active Directory"
Service Routing	Istio	How we will expose our service to the world
Service Authentication	Istio	The `RequestAuthentication` object will describe how to validate the user for our service
Service Coarse Grained Authorization	Istio	`AuthorizationPolicy` will make sure users are members of a specific group to call our service

Fine-Grained Authorization, or Entitlements	Service	Our service will determine which payees you're able to write checks for
Writing a check	Service	The point of writing this service!
Log who wrote the check and to whom it was sent	Service	Write this data to standard-out
Log aggregation	Kubernetes	Maybe Elastic?

Table 13.1: Service responsibilities

We'll build each of these components, layer by layer in the following sections. Before we get into the service itself, we need to say hello to the world.

Deploying Hello World

Our first service will be a simple Hello World service that will serve as the starting point for our check-writing service. Our service is built on Python using Flask. We're using this because it's pretty simple to use and deploy. Go to `chapter13/hello-world` and run the `deploy_helloworld.sh` script. This will create our `Namespace`, `Deployment`, `Service`, and `Istio` objects. Look at the code in the `service-source ConfigMap`. This is the main body of our code and the framework on which we will build our check service. The code its self doesn't do much:

```
@app.route('/')
def hello():
    retVal = {
        "msg":"hello world!",
        "host":"%s" % socket.gethostname()

    }
    return json.dumps(retVal)
```

This code accepts all requests to / and runs our function called `hello()`, which sends a simple response. We're embedding our code as a `ConfigMap` for the sake of simplicity.

If you've read all the other chapters up to this point, you'll notice that we're violating some cardinal rules with this container from a security standpoint. It's a Docker Hub container running as root. That's OK for now. We didn't want to get bogged down in build processes for this chapter. In *Chapter 14, Provisioning a Platform*, we'll walk through using Tekton to build out a more secure version of the container for this service.

Once our service is deployed, we can test it out by using `curl`:

```
curl http://service.192-168-2-114.nip.io/
{"msg": "hello world!", "host": "run-service-785775bf98-fln49"}%
```

This code isn't terribly exciting, but next we'll add some security to our service.

Integrating authentication into our service

In *Chapter 12, An Introduction to Istio*, we introduced the `RequestAuthentication` object. Now we will use this object to enforce authentication. We want to make sure that in order to access our service, you must have a valid JWT. In the previous example, we just called our service directly. Now we want to only get a response if a valid JWT is embedded in the request. We need to make sure to pair our `RequestAuthentication` with an `AuthorizationPolicy` that forces Istio to require a JWT, otherwise Istio will only reject JWTs that don't conform to our `RequestAuthenction` but will allow requests that have no JWT at all.

Even before we configure our objects, we need to get a JWT from somewhere. We're going to use OpenUnison. To work with our API, let's deploy the pipeline token generation chart we deployed in *Chapter 5, Integrating Authentication into Your Cluster*. Go to the `chapter5` directory and run the Helm Chart:

```
$ helm install orchestra-token-api token-login -n openunison -f /tmp/
openunison-values.yaml
NAME: orchestra-token-api
LAST DEPLOYED: Tue Aug 31 19:41:30 2021
NAMESPACE: openunison
STATUS: deployed
REVISION: 1
TEST SUITE: None
```

This will give us a way to easily generate a JWT from our internal "Active Directory". Next, we'll deploy the actual policy objects. Go into the `chapter13/authentication` directory and run `deploy-auth.sh`. It will look like:

```
./deploy-auth.sh
getting oidc config
getting jwks
requestauthentication.security.istio.io/hello-world-auth created
authorizationpolicy.security.istio.io/simple-hellow-world created
```

There are two objects that are created. The first is the `RequestAuthentication` object and then a simple `AuthorizationPolicy`. First, we will walk through `RequestAuthentication`:

```
apiVersion: security.istio.io/v1beta1
kind: RequestAuthentication
metadata:
  creationTimestamp: "2021-08-31T19:45:30Z"
  generation: 1
  name: hello-world-auth
  namespace: istio-hello-world
spec:
  jwtRules:
  - audiences:
    - kubernetes
    issuer: https://k8sou.192-168-2-119.nip.io/auth/idp/k8sIdp
    jwks: '{"keys...'
    outputPayloadToHeader: User-Info
  selector:
    matchLabels:
      app: run-service
```

This object first specifies how the JWT needs to be formatted in order to be accepted. We're cheating here a bit by just leveraging our Kubernetes JWT. Let's compare this object to our JWT:

```
{
  "iss": "https://k8sou.192-168-2-119.nip.io/auth/idp/k8sIdp",
  "aud": "kubernetes",
  "exp": 1630421193,
  "jti": "JGnXlj0I5obI3Vcmb1MCXA",
  "iat": 1630421133,
  "nbf": 1630421013,
  "sub": "mmosley",
  "name": " Mosley",
  "groups": [
    "cn=group2,ou=Groups,DC=domain,DC=com",
    "cn=k8s-cluster-admins,ou=Groups,DC=domain,DC=com"
  ],
  "preferred_username": "mmosley",
  "email": "mmosley@tremolo.dev"
}
```

The `aud` claim in our JWT lines up with the audiences in our `RequestAuthentication`. The `iss` claim lines up with `issuer` in our `RequestAuthentication`. If either of these claims don't match, then Istio will return a 401 HTTP error code to tell you the request is unauthorized.

We also specify `outputPayloadToHeader: User-Info` to tell Istio to pass the user info to the downstream service as a base64-encoded JSON header with the name `User-Info`. This header can be used by our service to identify who called it. We'll get into the details of this when we get into entitlement authorization.

Additionally, the `jwks` section specifies the RSA public keys used to verify the JWT. This can be obtained by first going to the `issuer`'s OIDC discovery URL and getting the URL from the `jwks` claim.

> We didn't use the `jwksUri` configuration option to point to our certificate URL directly because Istio would not be able to validate our self-signed certificate. The demo Istio deployment we're using would require patching the `istiod` `Deployment` to mount a certificate from a `ConfigMap`, which we didn't want to do in this book. It is however the best way to integrate with an identity provider so if and when keys rotate, you don't need to make any updates.

It's important to note that the `RequestAuthentication` object will tell Istio what form the JWT needs to take, but not what data about the user needs to be present. We'll cover that next in authorization.

Speaking of authorization, we want to make sure to enforce that the requirement for a JWT, so we created this very simple `AuthorizationPolicy`:

```
apiVersion: security.istio.io/v1beta1
kind: AuthorizationPolicy
metadata:
  name: simple-hellow-world
  namespace: istio-hello-world
spec:
  action: ALLOW
  rules:
  - from:
    - source:
        requestPrincipals:
        - '*'
  selector:
    matchLabels:
      app: run-service
```

The from section says that there must be a `requestPrincipal`. This is telling Istio there must be a user (and in this case, anonymous is not a user). `requestPrincipal` comes from JWTs and represents users. There is also a `principal` configuration, but this represents the service calling our URL, which in this case would be `ingressgateway`. This tells Istio a user must be authenticated via a JWT.

With our policy in place, we can now test it. First, with no user:

```
curl -v http://service.192-168-2-119.nip.io/
*    Trying 192.168.2.119:80...
* TCP_NODELAY set
* Connected to service.192-168-2-119.nip.io (192.168.2.119) port 80
(#0)
> GET / HTTP/1.1
> Host: service.192-168-2-119.nip.io
> User-Agent: curl/7.68.0
> Accept: */*
>
* Mark bundle as not supporting multiuse
< HTTP/1.1 403 Forbidden
< content-length: 19
< content-type: text/plain
< date: Tue, 31 Aug 2021 20:23:14 GMT
< server: istio-envoy
< x-envoy-upstream-service-time: 2
<
* Connection #0 to host service.192-168-2-119.nip.io left intact
```

We see that the request was denied with a 403 HTTP code. We received 403 because Istio was expecting a JWT but there wasn't one. Next, let's generate a valid token the same way we did in *Chapter 5, Integrating Authentication into Your Cluster*:

```
curl -H "Authorization: Bearer $(curl --insecure -u 'mmosley:start123'
https://k8sou.192-168-2-119.nip.io/k8s-api-token/token/user 2>/dev/
null| jq -r '.token.id_token')" http://service.192-168-2-119.nip.io/
{"msg": "hello world!", "host": "run-service-785775bf98-6bbwt"}
```

Now a success! Our hello world service now requires proper authentication. Next, we'll update our authorization to require a specific group from Active Directory.

Authorizing access to our service

So far, we've built a service and made sure users must have a valid JWT from our identity provider before you can access it.

Now we want to apply what's often referred to as "coarse-grained" authorization. This is application-, or service-, level access. It says "You are generally able to use this service," but it doesn't say you're able to perform the action you wish to take. For our check-writing service, you may be authorized to write a check but there's likely more controls that limit who you can write a check for. If you're responsible for the **Enterprise Resource Planning (ERP)** system in your enterprise you probably shouldn't be able to write checks for the facilities vendors. We'll get into how your service can manage these business-level decisions in the next section, but for now we'll focus on the service-level authorization.

It turns out we have everything we need. Earlier we looked at our `mmosley` user's JWT, which had multiple claims. One such claim was the `groups` claim. We used this claim in *Chapter 5, Integrating Authentication into Your Cluster* and *Chapter 6, RBAC Policies and Auditing,* to manage access to our cluster. In a similar fashion we'll manage who can access our service based on our membership of a particular group. First, we'll delete our existing policy:

```
kubectl delete authorizationpolicy simple-hellow-world -n istio-hello-
world
authorizationpolicy.security.istio.io "simple-hellow-world" deleted
```

With the policy disabled, you can now access your service without any JWT. Next, we'll create a policy that requires you to be a member of the group `cn=group2,ou=Gro ups,DC=domain,DC=com` in our "Active Directory."

Deploy the below policy (in `chapter13/coursed-grained-authorization/coursed-grained-az.yaml`):

```
---
apiVersion: security.istio.io/v1beta1
kind: AuthorizationPolicy
metadata:
  name: service-level-az
  namespace: istio-hello-world
spec:
  action: ALLOW
  selector:
    matchLabels:
      app: run-service
  rules:
  - when:
    - key: request.auth.claims[groups]
      values: ["cn=group2,ou=Groups,DC=domain,DC=com"]
```

This policy tells Istio that only users with a claim called `groups` that has the value `cn =group2,ou=Groups,DC=domain,DC=com` are able to access this service. With this policy deployed you'll notice you can still access the service as `mmosley`, and trying to access the service anonymously still fails. Next, try accessing the service as `jjackson`, with the same password:

```
curl -H "Authorization: Bearer $(curl --insecure -u 'jjackson:start123'
https://k8sou.192-168-2-119.nip.io/k8s-api-token/token/user 2>/dev/
null| jq -r '.token.id_token')" http://service.192-168-2-119.nip.io/
RBAC: access denied
```

We're not able to access this service as `jjackson`. If we look at `jjackson`'s `id_token`, we'll see why:

```
{
   "iss": "https://k8sou.192-168-2-119.nip.io/auth/idp/k8sIdp",
   "aud": "kubernetes",
   "exp": 1630455027,
   "jti": "Ae4Nv22HHYCnUNJx780l0A",
   "iat": 1630454967,
   "nbf": 1630454847,
   "sub": "jjackson",
   "name": " Jackson",
   "groups": "cn=k8s-create-ns,ou=Groups,DC=domain,DC=com",
   "preferred_username": "jjackson",
   "email": "jjackson@tremolo.dev"
}
```

Looking at the claims, `jjackson` isn't a member of the group `cn=group2,ou=Groups,DC =domain,DC=com`.

Now that we're able to tell Istio how to limit access to our service to valid users, the next step is to tell our service who the user is. We'll then use this information to look up authorization data, log actions, and act on the user's behalf.

Telling your service who's using it

When writing a service that does anything involving a user, the first thing you need to determine is, "Who is trying to use my service?" So far, we have told Istio how to determine who the user is, but how do we propagate that information down to our service? Our `RequestAuthentication` included the configuration option `outputPayloadToHeader: User-Info`, which injects the claims from our user's authentication token as base64-encoded JSON into the HTTP request's headers. This information can be pulled from that header and used by your service to look up additional authorization data.

We can view this header with a service we built, called /headers. This service will just give us back all the headers that are passed to our service. Let's take a look:

```
curl  -H "Authorization: Bearer $(curl --insecure -u 'mmosley:start123'
https://k8sou.192-168-2-119.nip.io/k8s-api-token/token/user 2>/dev/
null| jq -r '.token.id_token')" http://service.192-168-2-119.nip.io/
headers 2>/dev/null | jq -r '.headers'
Host: service.192-168-2-119.nip.io
User-Agent: curl/7.75.0
Accept: */*
X-Forwarded-For: 192.168.2.112
X-Forwarded-Proto: http
X-Request-Id: 6397d068-537e-94b7-bf6b-a7c649db5b3d
X-Envoy-Attempt-Count: 1
X-Envoy-Internal: true
X-Forwarded-Client-Cert: By=spiffe://cluster.local/ns/istio-hello-
world/sa/default;Hash=1a58a7d0abf62d32811c084a84f0a0f42b28616ffde7b6b84
0c595149d99b2eb;Subject="";URI=spiffe://cluster.local/ns/istio-system/
sa/istio-ingressgateway-service-account
User-Info: eyJpc3MiOiJodHRwczovL2s4c291LjE5Mi0xNjgtMi0xMTkubmlwLmlvL2F1
dGgvaWRwL2
s4c0lkcCIsImF1ZCI6Imt1YmVybmV0ZXMiLCJleHAiOjE2MzA1MTY4MjQsImp0aSI6InY0e
kpCNzdfRktpOXJoQU5jWDVwS1EiLCJpYXQiOjE2MzA1MTY3NjQsIm5iZiI6MTYzMDUxNj
Y0NCwic3ViIjoibW1vc2xleSIsIm5hbWUiOiIgTW9zbGV5IiwiZ3JvdXBzIjpbImNuPWdy
b3VwMixvdT1Hcm91cHMsREM9ZG9tYWluLERDPWNvbSIsImNuPWs4cy1jbHVzdGVyLWFkbW
lucyxvdT1Hcm91cHMsREM9ZG9tYWluLERDPWNvbSJdLCJwcmVmZXJyZWRfdXNlcm5hbWUi
OiJtbW9zbGV5IiwiZW1haWwiOiJtbW9zbGV5QHRyZW1vbG8uaW8ifQ==
X-B3-Traceid: 28fb185aa113ad089cfac2d6884ce9ac
X-B3-Spanid: d40f1784a6685886
X-B3-Parentspanid: 9cfac2d6884ce9ac
X-B3-Sampled: 1
```

There are several headers here. The one we care about is User-Info. This is the name of the header we specified in our RequestAuthentication object. If we decode from base64, we'll get some JSON:

```
{
  "iss": "https://k8sou.192-168-2-119.nip.io/auth/idp/k8sIdp",
  "aud": "kubernetes",
  "exp": 1630508679,
  "jti": "5VoEAAgv1rkpf1vOJ9uo-g",
```

```
"iat": 1630508619,
"nbf": 1630508499,
"sub": "mmosley",
"name": " Mosley",
"groups": [
  "cn=group2,ou=Groups,DC=domain,DC=com",
  "cn=k8s-cluster-admins,ou=Groups,DC=domain,DC=com"
],
"preferred_username": "mmosley",
"email": "mmosley@tremolo.dev"
}
```

We have all the same claims as if we had decoded the token ourselves. What we don't have is the JWT. This is important from a security standpoint. Our service can't leak a token it doesn't possess.

Now that we know how to determine who the user is, let's integrate that into a simple who-am-i service that just tells us who the user is. First, let's look at our code:

```
@app.route('/who-am-i')
    def who_am_i():
        user_info = request.headers["User-Info"]
        user_info_json = base64.b64decode(user_info).decode("utf8")
        user_info_obj = json.loads(user_info_json)
        ret_val = {
          "name": user_info_obj["sub"],
            "groups": user_info_obj["groups"]
        }

        return json.dumps(ret_val)
```

This is pretty basic. We're getting the header from our request. Next, we're decoding it from base64 and finally we get the JSON and add it to a return. If this were a more complex service, this is where we might query a database to determine what entitlements our user has.

In addition to not requiring that our code knows how to verify the JWT, this also makes it easier for us to develop our code in isolation from Istio. Open a shell into your run-service pod and try accessing this service directly with any user:

```
kubectl exec -ti run-service-785775bf98-g86gl -n istio-hello-world –
bash
# export USERINFO=$(echo -n '{"sub":"marc","groups":["group1","gro
up2"]}' | base64 -w 0)
```

```
# curl -H "User-Info: $USERINFO" http://localhost:8080/who-am-i
{"name": "marc", "groups": ["group1", "group2"]}
```

We were able to call our service without having to know anything about Istio, JWTs, or cryptography! Everything was offloaded to Istio so we could focus on our service. While this does make for easier development, what are the impacts on security if there's a way to inject any information we want into our service?

Let's try this directly from a namespace that doesn't have the Istio sidecar:

```
$ kubectl run -i --tty curl --image=alpine --rm=true – sh
/ # apk update add curl
/ # curl -H "User-Info $(echo -n '{"sub":"marc","groups":["group1","gr
oup2"]}' | base64 -w 0)" http://run-service.istio-hello-world.svc/who-
am-i
RBAC: access denied
```

Our `RequestAuthentication` and `AuthorizationPolicy` stop the request. While we're not running the sidecar, our service is, and redirects all traffic to Istio where our policies will be enforced. What about if we try to inject our own `User-Info` header from a valid request?

```
export USERINFO=$(echo -n '{"sub":"marc","groups":["group1","group2"]}'
| base64 -w 0)

curl  -H "Authorization: Bearer $(curl --insecure -u 'mmosley:start123'
https://k8sou.192-168-2-119.nip.io/k8s-api-token/token/user 2>/dev/
null| jq -r '.token.id_token')" -H "User-Info: $USERINFO" http://
service.192-168-2-119.nip.io/who-am-i
{"name": "mmosley", "groups": ["cn=group2,ou=Groups,DC=domain,DC=com",
"cn=k8s-cluster-admins,ou=Groups,DC=domain,DC=com"]}
```

Once again, our attempt to override who the user is outside of a valid JWT has been foiled by Istio. We've shown how Istio injects the user's identity into our service, now we need to know how to authorize a user's entitlements.

Authorizing user entitlements

So far, we've managed to add quite a bit of functionality to our service without having to write any code. We added token-based authentication and coarse-grained authorization. We know who the user is and have determined that at the service level, they are authorized to call our service. Next, we need to decide if the user is allowed to do the specific action they're trying to do. This is often called fine-grained authorization or entitlements. In this section, we'll walk through multiple approaches you can take, and discuss how you should choose an approach.

Authorizing in service

Unlike coarse-grained authorizations and authentication, entitlements are generally not managed at the service mesh layer. That's not to say it's impossible. We'll talk about ways you can do this in the service mesh but in general, it's not the best approach. Authorizations are generally tied to business data that's usually locked up in a database. Sometimes that database is a generic relational database like MySQL or SQL Server, but it could really be anything. Since the data used to make the authorization decision is often owned by the service owner, not the cluster owner, it's generally easier and more secure to make entitlement decisions directly in our code.

Earlier, we discussed in our check-writing service that we don't want someone responsible for the ERP to cut checks to the facilities vendor. Where is the data that determines that? Well, it's probably in your enterprise's ERP system. Depending on how big you are, this could be a home-grown application all the way up to SAP or Oracle. Let's say you wanted Istio to make the authorization decision for our check-writing service. How would it get that data? Do you think the people responsible for the ERP want you, as a cluster owner, talking to their database directly? Do you, as a cluster owner, want that responsibility? What happens when something goes wrong with the ERP and someone points the finger at you for the problem? Do you have the resources to prove that you, and your team, were not responsible?

It turns out the silos in enterprises that benefit from the management aspects of microservice design also work against centralized authorization. In our example of determining who can write the check for a specific vendor, it's probably just easiest to make this decision inside our service. This way, if there's a problem it's not the Kubernetes team's responsibility to determine the issue and the people who are responsible are in control of their own destiny.

That's not to say there isn't an advantage to a more centralized approach to authorization. Having teams implement their own authorization code will lead to different standards being used and different approaches. Without careful controls, it can lead to a compliance nightmare. Let's look at how Istio could provide a more robust framework for authorization.

Using OPA with Istio

Using the Envoy filters feature discussed in *Chapter 12, An Introduction to Istio,* you can integrate the **Open Policy Agent (OPA)** into your service mesh to make authorization decisions. We discussed OPA in *Chapter 8, Extending Security Using Open Policy Agent.* There are a few key points about OPA we need to review:

- OPA does not (typically) reach out to external data stores to make authorization decisions. Much of the benefit of OPA requires that it uses its own internal database.

- OPA's database is not persistent. When an OPA instance dies, it must be repopulated with data.

- OPA's databases are not clustered. If you have multiple OPA instances, each database must be updated independently.

To use OPA to validate whether our user can write a check for a specific vendor, OPA would either need to be able to pull that data directly from the JWT or have the ERP data replicated into its own database. The former is unlikely to happen for multiple reasons. First, the issues with your cluster talking to your ERP will still exist when your identity provider tries to talk to your ERP. Second, the team that runs your identity provider would need to know to include the correct data, which is a difficult ask and is unlikely to be something they're interested in doing. Finally, there could be numerous folks from security to the ERP team who are not comfortable with this data being stored in a token that gets passed around. The latter, syncing data into OPA, is more likely to be successful.

There are two ways you could sync your authorization data from your ERP into your OPA databases. The first, is you could push the data. A "bot" could push updates to each OPA instance. This way, the ERP owner is responsible for pushing the data with your cluster just being a consumer. There's no simple way to do this though and security would be a concern to make sure someone doesn't push in false data. The alternative is to write a pull "bot" that runs as a sidecar to your OPA pods. This is how GateKeeper works. The advantage here is that you have the responsibility of keeping your data synced without having to build a security framework for pushing data.

In either scenario, you'll need to understand whether there are any compliance issues with the data you are storing. Now that you have the data, what's the impact of losing it in a breach? Is that a responsibility you want?

Centralized authorization services have been discussed for entitlements long before Kubernetes or even RESTful APIs existed. They even predate SOAP and XML! For enterprise applications, it's never really worked because of the additional costs in data management, ownership, and bridging silos. If you own all of the data, this is a great approach. When one of the main goals of microservices is to allow silos to better manage their own development, forcing a centralized entitlements engine is not likely to succeed.

Having determined how to integrate entitlements into our services, the next question we need to answer is, how do we call other services?

Calling other services

We've written services that do simple things, but what about when your service needs to talk to another service? Just like with almost every other set of choices in your cluster rollout, you have multiple options for authenticating to other services. Which choice you make will depend on your needs. We'll first cover the OAuth2 standard way of getting new tokens for service calls and how Istio works with it. We'll then cover some alternatives that should be considered anti-patterns but that you may choose to use anyway.

Using OAuth2 Token Exchange

Your service knows who your user is, but needs to call another service. How do you identify yourself to the second service? The OAuth2 specification, which OpenID Connect is built on, has RFC 8693 – OAuth2 Token Exchange for this purpose. The basic idea is that your service will get a fresh token from your identity provider for the service call based on the existing user. By getting a fresh token for your own call to a remote service, you're making it easier to lock down where tokens can be used and who can use them, and allowing yourself to more easily track a call's authentication and authorization flow. The following diagram gives a high-level overview.

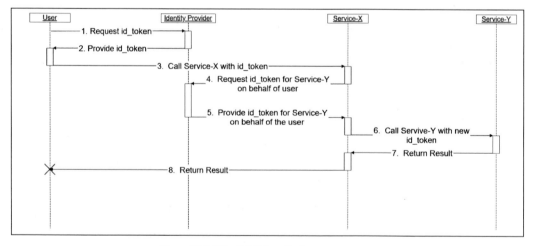

Figure 13.6: OAuth2 Token Exchange sequence

There are some details we'll walk through that depend on your use case:

1. The user requests an `id_token` from the identity provider. How the user gets their token doesn't really matter for this part of the sequence. We'll use a utility in OpenUnison for our lab.

2. Assuming you're authenticated and authorized, your identity provider will give you an `id_token` with an `aud` claim that will be accepted by Service-X.

3. The user uses the `id_token` as a bearer token for calling Service-X. It goes without saying that Istio will validate this token.

4. Service-X requests a token for Service-Y from the identity provider on behalf of the user. There are two potential methods to do this. One is impersonation, the other is delegation. We'll cover both in detail later in this section. You'll send your identity provider your original `id_token` and something to identify the service to the identity provider.

5. Assuming Service-X is authorized, the identity provider sends a new `id_token` to Service-X with the original user's attributes and an `aud` scoped to Service-Y.

6. Service-X uses the new `id_token` as the `Authorization` header when calling Service-Y. Again, Istio is validating the `id_token`.

Steps 7 and 8 in the previous diagram aren't really important here.

If you think this seems like quite a bit of work to make a service call, you're right. There are several authorization steps going on here:

1. The identity provider is authorizing that the user can generate a token scoped to Service-X

2. Istio is validating the token and that it's properly scoped to Service-X

3. The identity provider is authorizing that Service-X can get a token for Service-Y and that it's able to do so for our user

4. Istio is validating that the token used by Service-X for Service-Y is properly scoped

These authorization points provide a chance for an improper token to be stopped, allowing you to create very short-lived tokens that are harder to abuse and are more narrowly scoped. For instance, if the token used to call Service-X were leaked, it couldn't be used to call Service-Y on its own. You'd still need Service-X's own token before you could get a token for Service-Y. That's an additional step an attacker would need to take in order to get control of Service-Y. It also means breaching more than one service, providing multiple layers of security. This lines up with our discussion of defense in depth from *Chapter 8, Extending Security Using Open Policy Agent*. With a high-level understanding of how OAuth2 Token Exchange works, the next question we need to answer is how will your services authenticate themselves to your identity provider?

Authenticating your service

In order for the token exchange to work, your identity provider needs to know who the original user is and which service wants to exchange the token on behalf of the user. In the check-writing service example we've been discussing, you wouldn't want the service that provides today's lunch menu to be able to generate a token for issuing a check! You accomplish this by making sure your identity provider knows the difference between your check-writing services and your lunch menu service by authenticating each service individually.

There are three ways a service running in Kubernetes can authenticate itself to the identity provider:

1. Use the Pod's `ServiceAccount` token
2. Use Istio's mTLS capabilities
3. Use a pre-shared "client secret"

Throughout the rest of this section, we're going to focus on option #1, using the Pod's built-in `ServiceAccount` token. This token is provided by default for each running Pod. This token can be validated by either submitting it to the API server's `TokenReview` service or by treating it as a JWT and validating it against the public key published by the API server.

In our examples, we're going to use the `TokenReview` API to test the passed-in `ServiceAccount` token against the API server. This is the most backward-compatible approach and supports any kind of token integrated into your cluster. For instance, if you're deployed in a managed cloud with its own IAM system that mounts tokens, you could use that as well. This could generate a considerable amount of load on your API server, since every time a token needs to be validated it gets sent to the API server.

The `TokenRequest` API discussed in *Chapter 5, Integrating Authentication into Your Cluster*, can be used to cut down on this additional load. Instead of using the `TokenReview` API we can call the API server's issuer endpoint to get the appropriate token verification public key and use that key to validate the token's JWT. While this is convenient and scales better, it does have some drawbacks:

1. Starting in 1.21, `ServiceAccount` tokens are mounted using the `TokenRequest` API, but with lifespans of a year or more. You can manually change this to be as short as 10 minutes.

2. Validating the JWT directly against a public key won't tell you if the Pod is still running. The `TokenReview` API will fail if a `ServiceAcount` token is associated with a deleted `Pod`, adding an additional layer of security.

We're not going to use Istio's mTLS capabilities because it's not as flexible as tokens. It's primarily meant for intra-cluster communications, so if our identity provider were outside of the cluster, it would be much harder to use. Also, since mTLS requires a point-to-point connection, any TLS termination points would break its use. Since it's rare for an enterprise system to host its own certificate, even outside of Kubernetes, it would be very difficult to implement mTLS between your cluster's services and your identity provider.

Finally, we're not going to use a shared secret between our services and our identity provider because we don't need to. Shared secrets are only needed when you have no other way to give a workload an identity. Since Kubernetes gives every Pod its own identity, there's no need to use a client secret to identify our service.

Now that we know how our services will identify themselves to our identity provider, let's walk through an example of using OAuth2 Token Exchange to securely call one service from another.

Deploying and running the check-writing service

Having walked through much of the theory of using a token exchange to securely call services, let's deploy an example check-writing service. When we call this service, it will call two other services. The first service, `check-funds`, will use the impersonation profile of OAuth2 Token Exchange while the second service, `pull-funds`, will use delegation. We'll walk through each of these individually. First, use Helm to deploy an identity provider. Go into the `chapter13` directory and run:

```
helm install openunison-service-auth openunison-service-auth -n
openunison
NAME: openunison-service-auth
LAST DEPLOYED: Mon Sep 13 01:08:09 2021
NAMESPACE: openunison
STATUS: deployed
REVISION: 1
TEST SUITE: None
```

We're not going to go into the details of OpenUnison's configuration. Suffice to say this will set up an identity provider for our services and a way to get an initial token. Next, deploy the `write-checks` service:

```
cd write-checks/
./deploy_write_checks.sh
getting oidc config
getting jwks
namespace/write-checks created
```

```
configmap/service-source created
deployment.apps/write-checks created
service/write-checks created
gateway.networking.istio.io/service-gateway created
virtualservice.networking.istio.io/service-vs created
requestauthentication.security.istio.io/write-checks-auth created
authorizationpolicy.security.istio.io/service-level-az created
```

This should look pretty familiar after the first set of examples in this chapter. We deployed our service as Python in a `ConfigMap` and the same Istio objects we created in the previous service. The only major difference is in our `RequestAuthentication` object:

```
apiVersion: security.istio.io/v1beta1
kind: RequestAuthentication
metadata:
  name: write-checks-auth
  namespace: write-checks
spec:
  jwtRules:
  - audiences:
    - users
    - checkfunds
    - pullfunds
    forwardOriginalToken: true
    issuer: https://k8sou.192-168-2-119.nip.io/auth/idp/service-idp
    jwks: '{"keys"...
    outputPayloadToHeader: User-Info
  selector:
    matchLabels:
      app: write-checks
```

There's an additional setting, `forwardOriginalToken`, that tells Istio to send the service the original JWT used to authenticate the call. We'll need this token in order to prove to the identity provider we should even attempt to perform a token exchange. You can't ask for a new token if you can't provide the original. This keeps someone with access to your service's Pod from requesting a token on your behalf with just the service's `ServiceAccount`.

Earlier in the chapter we said we couldn't leak a token we didn't have, so we shouldn't have access to the original token. This would be true if we didn't need it to get a token for another service. Following the concept of least privilege, we shouldn't forward the token if we don't need to. In this case, we need it for a token exchange so it's worth the increased risk to have more secure service-to-service calls.

With our example check-writing service deployed, let's run it and work backward. Just like with our earlier examples, we'll use `curl` to get the token and call our service. In `chapter13/write-checks`, run `call_service.sh`:

```
./call_service.sh
{
  "msg": "hello world!",
  "host": "write-checks-84cdbfff74-tgmzh",
  "user_jwt": "...",
  "pod_jwt": "...",
  "impersonated_jwt": "...",
  "call_funds_status_code": 200,
  "call_funds_text": "{\"funds_available\": true, \"user\":
\"mmosley\"}",
  "actor_token": "...",
  "delegation_token": "...",
  "pull_funds_text": "{\"funds_pulled\": true, \"user\": \"mmosley\",
\"actor\": \"system:serviceaccount:write-checks:default\"}"
}
```

The output you see is the result of the calls to `/write-check`, which then calls `/check-funds` and `/pull-funds`. Let's walk through each call, the tokens that are generated, and the code that generates them.

Using Impersonation

We're not talking about the same Impersonation you used in *Chapter 5, Integrating Authentication into Your Cluster*. It's a similar concept, but this is specific to token exchange. When `/write-check` needs to get a token to call `/check-funds`, it asks OpenUnison for a token on behalf of our user, `mmosley`. The important aspect of Impersonation is that there's no reference to the requesting client in the generated token. The `/check-funds` service has no knowledge that the token it's received wasn't retrieved by the user themselves. Working backward, the `impersonated_jwt` in the response to our service call is what `/write-check` used to call `/check-funds`. Here's the payload after dropping the result into `jwt.io`:

```
{
  "iss": "https://k8sou.192-168-2-119.nip.io/auth/idp/service-idp",
  "aud": "checkfunds",
  "exp": 1631497059,
  "jti": "C8Qh8iY9FJdFzEO3pLRQzw",
  "iat": 1631496999,
  "nbf": 1631496879,
  "nonce": "bec42c16-5570-4bd8-9038-be30fd216016",
```

```
  "sub": "mmosley",
  "name": " Mosley",
  "groups": [
    "cn=group2,ou=Groups,DC=domain,DC=com",
    "cn=k8s-cluster-admins,ou=Groups,DC=domain,DC=com"
  ],
  "preferred_username": "mmosley",
  "email": "mmosley@tremolo.dev",
  "amr": [
    "pwd"
  ]
}
```

The two important fields here are `sub` and `aud`. The `sub` field tells `/check-funds` who the user is and the `aud` field tells Istio which services can consume this token. Compare this to the payload from the original token in the `user_jwt` response:

```
{
  "iss": "https://k8sou.192-168-2-119.nip.io/auth/idp/service-idp",
  "aud": "users",
  "exp": 1631497059,
  "jti": "C8Qh8iY9FJdFzEO3pLRQzw",
  "iat": 1631496999,
  "nbf": 1631496879,
  "sub": "mmosley",
  "name": " Mosley",
  "groups": [
    "cn=group2,ou=Groups,DC=domain,DC=com",
    "cn=k8s-cluster-admins,ou=Groups,DC=domain,DC=com"
  ],
  "preferred_username": "mmosley",
  "email": "mmosley@tremolo.dev",
  "amr": [
    "pwd"
  ]
}
```

The original `sub` is the same, but the `aud` is different. The original `aud` is for users while the impersonated `aud` is for `checkfunds`. This is what differentiates the impersonated token from the original one. While our Istio deployment is configured to accept both audiences for the same service, that's not a guarantee in most production clusters. When we call `/check-funds`, you'll see that in the output we echo the user of our token, `mmosley`.

Now that we've seen the end product, let's see how we get it. First, we get the original JWT that was used to call /write-check:

```
# let's first get the original JWT. We'll
# use this as an input for impersonation

az_header = request.headers["Authorization"]
user_jwt = az_header[7:]
```

Once we have the original JWT, we need the Pod's ServiceAccount token:

```
# next, get the pod's ServiceAccount token
# so we can identify the pod to the IdP for
# an impersonation token

pod_jwt = Path('/var/run/secrets/kubernetes.io/serviceaccount/token').
read_text()
```

We now have everything we need to get an impersonation token. We'll create a POST body and an Authorization header to authenticate us to OpenUnison to get our token:

```
# with the subject (user) jwt and the pod
# jwt we can now request an impersonated
# token for our user from openunison

impersonation_request = {
    "grant_type":"urn:ietf:params:oauth:grant-type:token-exchange",
    "audience":"checkfunds",
    "subject_token":user_jwt,
    "subject_token_type":"urn:ietf:params:oauth:token-type:id_token",
    "client_id":"sts-impersonation"
}

impersonation_headers = {
    "Authorization": "Bearer %s" % pod_jwt
}
```

The first data structure we created is the body of an HTTP POST that will tell OpenUnison to generate an impersonation token for the clientfunds aud using our existing user (user_jwt). OpenUnison will authenticate our service by verifying the JWT sent in the Authorization header as a Bearer token using the TokenReview API. OpenUnison will then apply its internal policy to verify that our service is able to generate a token for mmosley for the clientfunds audience and then generate an access_token, id_token, and refresh_token.

We'll use the `id_token` to call `/check-funds`:

```
resp = requests.post("https://k8sou.IPADDR.nip.io/auth/idp/service-idp/
token",verify=False,data=impersonation_request,headers=impersonation_
headers)

response_payload = json.loads(resp.text)

impersonated_id_token = response_payload["id_token"]

# with the impersonated user's id_token, call another
# service as that user

call_funds_headers = {
    "Authorization": "Bearer %s" % impersonated_id_token
}

resp = requests.get("http://write-checks.IPADDR.nip.io/check-
funds",verify=False,headers=call_funds_headers)
```

Since the final JWT makes no mention of the impersonation, how do we track a request back to our service? Hopefully, you're piping your logs into a centralized logging system. If we look at the `jti` claim of our impersonation token we can find the impersonation call in the OpenUnison logs:

```
INFO  AccessLog - [AzSuccess] - service-idp - https://
k8sou.192-168-2-119.nip.io/auth/idp/service-idp/token - username=system
:serviceaccount:write-checks:default,ou=oauth2,o=Tremolo - client 'sts-
impersonation' impersonating 'mmosley', jti : 'C8Qh8iY9FJdFzEO3pLRQzw'
```

So, we at least have a way of tying them together. We can see our Pod's service account was authorized to create the impersonation token for `mmosley`.

Having worked through an example of impersonation, next let's cover token delegation.

Using delegation

In the last example we used impersonation to generate a new token on behalf of our user, but our downstream service had no knowledge the impersonation happened. Delegation is different in that the token carries information about both the original user and the service, or actor, that requested it. This means that the service being called knows both the originator of the call and the service that is making the call. We can see this in the `pull_funds_text` value from the response of our `call_service.sh` run. It contains both our original user, `mmosley`, and the `ServiceAccount` for the service that made the call, `system:serviceaccount:write-checks:default`. Just as with impersonation, let's look at the generated token:

```
{
  "iss": "https://k8sou.192-168-2-119.nip.io/auth/idp/service-idp",
  "aud": "pullfunds",
  "exp": 1631497059,
  "jti": "xkaQhMgKgRvGBqAsOWD1XA",
  "iat": 1631496999,
  "nbf": 1631496879,
  "nonce": "272f1900-f9d9-4161-a31c-6c6dde80fcb9",
  "sub": "mmosley",
  "amr": [
    "pwd"
  ],
  "name": " Mosley",
  "groups": [
    "cn=group2,ou=Groups,DC=domain,DC=com",
    "cn=k8s-cluster-admins,ou=Groups,DC=domain,DC=com"
  ],
  "preferred_username": "mmosley",
  "email": "mmosley@tremolo.dev",
  "act": {
    "sub": "system:serviceaccount:write-checks:default",
    "amr": [
      "k8s-sa"
    ],
    .
    .
    .
  }
}
```

In addition to the claims that identify the user as mmosley, there's an act claim
that identifies the ServiceAccount that's used by /write-checks. Our service can
make additional authorization decisions based on this claim or simply log it to
note that the token it received was delegated to a different service. In order to
generate this token, we start out by getting the original subject's JWT and the Pod's
ServiceAccount token. Instead of calling OpenUnison for a delegated token, first our
client has to get an actor token by using the client_credentials grant. This will get
us the token that will eventually go into the act claim:

```
client_credentials_grant_request = {
  "grant_type": "client_credentials",
  "client_id" : "sts-delegation"
}
```

```
delegation_headers = {
  "Authorization": "Bearer %s" % pod_jwt
}

resp = requests.post("https://k8sou.IPADDR.nip.io/auth/idp/
service-idp/token",verify=False,data=client_credentials_grant_
request,headers=delegation_headers)

response_payload = json.loads(resp.text)
actor_token = response_payload["id_token"]
```

We authenticate to OpenUnison using our Pod's native identity. OpenUnison returns an `access_token` and an `id_token`, but we only need the `id_token`. With our actor token in hand, we can now get our delegation token:

```
delegation_request = {
  "grant_type":"urn:ietf:params:oauth:grant-type:token-exchange",
  "audience":"pullfunds",
  "subject_token":user_jwt,
  "subject_token_type":"urn:ietf:params:oauth:token-type:id_token",
  "client_id":"sts-delegation",
  "actor_token": actor_token,
  "actor_token_type": "urn:ietf:params:oauth:token-type:id_token"
}

resp = requests.post("https://k8sou.IPADDR.nip.io/auth/idp/service-idp/
token",verify=False,data=delegation_request)

response_payload = json.loads(resp.text)

delegation_token = response_payload["id_token"]
```

Similarly to impersonation, in this call we send the original user's token (`user_jwt`), but also the `actor_token` we just received from OpenUnison. We also don't send an Authorization header. The `actor_token` authenticates us already. Finally, we're able to use our returned token to call `/pull-funds`.

Now that we've looked at the most correct way to call services, using both impersonation and delegation, let's take a look at some anti-patterns and why you shouldn't use them.

Passing tokens between services

Where in the previous section we used an identity provider to generate either impersonation or delegation tokens, this method skips that and just passes the original token from service to service. This is a simple approach that's easy to implement. It also creates a larger blast radius. If the token gets leaked, and given that it's now being passed to multiple services, the likelihood of it leaking goes up quite a bit, you've now not just exposed one service. You've exposed all the services that trust that token.

While using OAuth2 Token Exchange does require more work, it will limit your blast radius should a token be leaked. Next, we'll look at how you may simply tell a downstream service who's calling it.

Using simple impersonation

Where the previous examples of service-to-service calls rely on a third party to generate a token for a user, direct impersonation is where your service's code uses a service account (in the generic sense, not the Kubernetes version) to call the second service and just tells the service who the user is as an input to the call. For instance, instead of calling OpenUnison to get a new token, `/write-check` could have just used the Pod's `ServiceAccount` token to call `/check-funds` with a parameter containing the user's ID. Something like this would work as follows:

```
call_headers = {
  "Authorization": "Bearer %s" % pod_jwt
}

resp = requests.post("https://write-checks.IPADDR.nip.io/check-funds
?user=mmosley",verify=False,data=impersonation_request,headers=call_
headers)
```

This is, again, very simple. You can tell Istio to authenticate a Kubernetes `ServiceAccount`. This takes two lines of code to do something that took fifteen to twenty using a token service. Just like with passing tokens between services, this approach leaves you exposed in multiple ways. First, if anyone gets the `ServiceAccount` used by our service, they can impersonate anyone they want without checks. Using the token service ensures that a compromised service account doesn't lead to it being used to impersonate anyone.

You might find this method very similar to the impersonation we used in *Chapter 5, Integrating Authentication into Your Cluster*. You're correct. While this uses the same mechanism, a `ServiceAccount` and some parameters to specify who the user is, the type of impersonation Kubernetes uses for the API server is often referred to as a *protocol transition*.

This is used when you are moving from one protocol (OpenID Connect) to another (a Kubernetes service account). As we discussed in *Chapter 5*, there are several controls you can put in place with Kubernetes impersonation including using `NetworkPolicies`, `RBAC`, and `TokenRequest` API. It's also a much more isolated use case than a generic service.

We've walked through multiple ways for services to call and authenticate each other. While it may not be the simplest way to secure access between services, it will limit the impact of a leaked token. Now that we know how our services will talk to each other, the last topic we need to cover is the relationship between Istio and API gateways.

Do I need an API gateway?

If you're using Istio, do you still need an API gateway? In the past, Istio has been primarily concerned with routing traffic for services. It got traffic into the cluster and figured out where to route it to. API gateways have more typically been focused on application-level functionality such as authentication, authorization, input validation, and logging.

For example, earlier in this chapter we identified schema input validation as a process that needs to be repeated for each call and shouldn't need to be done manually. This is important to protect against attacks that can leverage unexpected input and also makes for a better developer experience to provide feedback to developers sooner in the integration process. This is a common function for API gateways, but is not available in Istio.

Another example of a function that is not built into Istio, but is common for API gateways, is logging authentication and authorization decisions and information. Throughout this chapter, we have leveraged Istio's built-in authentication and authorization to validate service access, but Istio makes no record of that decision other than that a decision was made. It doesn't record who accessed a particular URL, only where it was accessed from. Logging who accessed a service, from an identity standpoint, is left to each individual service. This is a common function for API gateways.

Finally, API gateways are able to handle more complex transformations. Gateways will typically provide functionality for mapping inputs, outputs, or even integrating with legacy systems.

These functions could all be integrated into Istio, either directly or via Envoy filters. We saw an example of this when we looked at using OPA to make more complex authorization decisions than what the `AuthorizationPolicy` object provides. Over the last few releases, though, Istio has moved more into the realm of traditional API gateways, and API gateways have begun taking on more service mesh capabilities.

I suspect there will be considerable overlap between these systems in the coming years, but as of today, Istio isn't yet capable of fulfilling all the functions of an API gateway.

We've had quite the journey building out the services for our Istio service mesh. You should now have the tools you need to begin building services in your own cluster.

Summary

In this chapter, we learned how both monoliths and microservices run in Istio. We explored why and when to use each approach. We deployed a monolith, taking care to ensure our monolith's session management worked. We then moved into deploying microservices, authenticating requests, authorizing requests, and finally how services can securely communicate. To wrap things up, we discussed whether an API gateway is still necessary when using Istio.

Istio can be complex, but when used properly it can provide considerable power. What we didn't cover in this chapter is how to build containers and manage the deployment of our services. We're going to tackle that next in *Chapter 14, Provisioning a Platform*.

Questions

1. True or false: Istio is an API Gateway.

   a. True

   b. False

   Answer: b. False – Istio is a service mesh, and while it has many functions of a gateway, it doesn't have all of them (such as schema checking).

2. Should I always build applications as microservices?

   a. Obviously, this is the way.

   b. Only if a microservices architecture aligns with your organization's structure and needs.

   c. No, microservices are more trouble than they're worth.

   d. What's a microservice?

   Answer: b – Microservices are great when you have a team that is able to make use of the granularity they provide.

3. What is a monolith?

   a. A large object that appears to be made from a single piece by an unknown maker

   b. An application that is self-contained

    c.   A system that won't run on Kubernetes

    d.   A product from a new start-up

Answer: b – A monolith is a self-contained application that can run quite well on Kubernetes.

4.   How should you authorize access to your services in Istio?

    a.   You can write a rule that limits access in Istio by a claim in the token.

    b.   You can integrate OPA with Istio for more complex authorization decisions.

    c.   You can embed complex authorization decisions in your code.

    d.   All of the above.

Answer: d – These are all valid strategies from a technical standpoint. Each situation is different, so look at each one to determine which one is best for you!

5.   True or false: Calling services on behalf of a user without token exchange is a secure approach.

    a.   True

    b.   False

Answer: b – False: Without using token exchange to get a new token for when the user the next service, you leave yourself open to various attacks because you can't limit calls or track them.

6.   True or false: Istio supports sticky sessions.

    a.   True

    b.   False

Answer: a. True – It's not a default, but it is supported.

Join our book's Discord space

Join the book's Discord workspace for a monthly *Ask me Anything* session with the authors: `https://packt.link/K8EntGuide`

14

Provisioning a Platform

Every chapter in this book, up until this point, has focused on the infrastructure of your cluster. We have explored how to deploy Kubernetes, how to secure it, and how to monitor it. What we haven't talked about is how to deploy applications.

In this, our final chapter, we're going to work on building an application deployment platform using what we've learned about Kubernetes. We're going to build our platform based on some common enterprise requirements. Where we can't directly implement a requirement, because building a platform on Kubernetes can fill its own book, we'll call it out and provide some insights.

In this chapter, we will cover the following topics:

- Designing a pipeline
- Preparing our cluster
- Deploying GitLab
- Deploying Tekton
- Deploying ArgoCD
- Automating project onboarding using OpenUnison

You'll have a good starting point for building out you own GitOps platform on Kubernetes by the end of this chapter. It's not designed for production use, but should get you well on your way.

Technical requirements

To perform the exercises in this chapter, you will need a clean KinD cluster with a minimum of 16 GB of memory, 75 GB storage, and 4 CPUs. The system we will build is minimalist but still requires considerable horsepower to run.

You can access the code for this chapter at the following GitHub repository: `https://github.com/PacktPublishing/Kubernetes---An-Enterprise-Guide-2E/tree/main/chapter14`.

Designing a pipeline

The term "pipeline" is used extensively in the Kubernetes and DevOps world. Very simply, a pipeline is a process, usually automated, that takes code and gets it running. This usually involves the following:

Figure 14.1: A simple pipeline

Let's quickly run through the steps involved in this process:

1. Storing the source code in a central repository, usually Git

2. When code is committed, building it and generating artifacts, usually a container

3. Telling the platform – in this case, Kubernetes – to roll out the new containers and shut down the old ones

This is about as basic as a pipeline can get and isn't of much use in most deployments. In addition to building our code and deploying it, we want to make sure we scan containers for known vulnerabilities. We may also want to run our containers through some automated testing before going into production. In enterprise deployments, there's often a compliance requirement where someone takes responsibility for the move to production as well. Taking this into account, the pipeline starts to become more complex.

Figure 14.2: Pipeline with common enterprise requirements

The pipeline has added some extra steps, but it's still linear with one starting point, a commit. This is also very simplistic and unrealistic. The base containers and libraries your applications are built on are constantly being updated as new **Common Vulnerabilities and Exposures (CVEs)**, a common way to catalog and identify security vulnerabilities, are discovered and patched. In addition to having developers that are updating application code for new requirements, you will want to have a system in place that scans both the code and the base containers for available updates. These scanners watch your base containers and can do something to trigger a build once a new base container is ready. While the scanners could call an API to trigger a pipeline, your pipeline is already waiting on your Git repository to do something, so it would be better to simply add a commit or a pull request to your Git repository to trigger the pipeline.

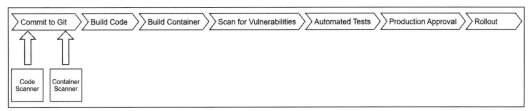

Figure 14.3: Pipeline with scanners integrated

This means your application code is tracked and your operational updates are tracked in Git. Git is now the source of truth for not only what your application code is but also operation updates. When it's time to go through your audits, you have a ready-made change log! If your policies require you to enter changes into a change management system, simply export the changes from Git.

So far, we have focused on our application code and just put **Rollout** at the end of our pipeline. The final rollout step usually means patching a `Deployment` or `StatefulSet` with our newly built container, letting Kubernetes do the work of spinning up new `Pods` and scaling down the old ones. This could be done with a simple API call, but how are we tracking and auditing that change? What's the source of truth?

Our application in Kubernetes is defined as a series of objects stored in `etcd` that are generally represented as code using YAML files. Why not store those files in a Git repository too? This gives us the same benefits as storing our application code in Git. We have a single source of truth for both the application source and the operations of our application! Now, our pipeline involves some more steps.

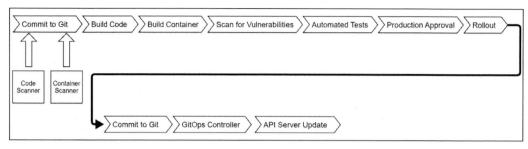

Figure 14.4: GitOps pipeline

In this diagram, our rollout updates a Git repository with our application's Kubernetes YAML. A controller inside our cluster watches for updates to Git and when it sees them, gets the cluster in sync with what's in Git. It can also detect drift in our cluster and bring it back to alignment with our source of truth.

This focus on Git is called **GitOps**. The idea is that all of the work of an application is done via code, not directly via APIs. How strict you are with this idea can dictate what your platform looks like. Next, we'll explore how opinions can shape your platform.

Opinionated platforms

Kelsey Hightower, a developer advocate for Google and leader in the Kubernetes world, once said: "Kubernetes is a platform for building platforms. It's a better place to start; not the endgame." When you look at the landscape of vendors and projects building Kubernetes-based products, they all have their own opinions of how systems should be built. As an example, Red Hat's **OpenShift Container Platform (OCP)** wants to be a one-stop shop for multi-tenant enterprise deployment. It builds in a great deal of the pipeline we discussed. You define a pipeline that is triggered by a commit, which builds a container and pushes it into its own internal registry that then triggers a rollout of the new container. Namespaces are the boundaries of tenants. Canonical is a minimalist distribution that doesn't include any pipeline components. Managed vendors such as Amazon, Azure, and Google provide the building blocks of a cluster and the hosted build tools of a pipeline, but leave it to you to build out your platform.

There is no correct answer as to which platform to use. Each is opinionated and the right one for your deployment will depend on your own requirements. Depending on the size of your enterprise, it wouldn't be surprising to see more than one platform deployed!

Having looked at the idea of opinionated platforms, let's explore the security impacts of building a pipeline.

Securing your pipeline

Depending on your starting point, this can get complex quickly. How much of your pipeline is one integrated system, or could it be described using a colorful American colloquialism involving duct tape? Even in platforms where all the components are there, tying them together can often mean building a complex system. Most of the systems that are part of your pipeline will have a visual component. Usually, the visual component is a dashboard. Users and developers may need access to that dashboard. You don't want to maintain separate accounts for all those systems, do you? You'll want to have one login point and portal for all the components of your pipeline.

After determining how to authenticate the users who use these systems, the next question is how to automate the rollout. Each component of your pipeline requires configuration. It can be as simple as an object that gets created via an API call or as complex as tying together a Git repo and build process with SSH keys to automate security. In such a complex environment, manually creating pipeline infrastructure will lead to security gaps. It will also lead to impossible-to-manage systems. Automating the process and providing consistency will help you both secure your infrastructure and keep it maintainable.

Finally, it's important to understand the implications of GitOps on our cluster from a security standpoint. We discussed authenticating administrators and developers to use the Kubernetes API and authorizing access to different APIs in *Chapter 5, Integrating Authentication into Your Cluster*, and *Chapter 6, RBAC Policies and Auditing*. What is the impact if someone can check in a `RoleBinding` that assigns them the `admin ClusterRole` for a namespace and a GitOps controller automatically pushes it through to the cluster? As you design your platform, consider how developers and administrators will want to interact with it. It's tempting to say "Let everyone interact with their application's Git registry," but that means putting the burden on you as the cluster owner for many requests. As we discussed in *Chapter 6, RBAC Policies and Auditing*, this could make your team the bottleneck in an enterprise. Understanding your customers, in this case, is important in knowing how they want to interact with their operations even if it's not how you intended.

Having touched on some of the security aspects of GitOps and a pipeline, let's explore the requirements for a typical pipeline and how we will build it.

Building our platform's requirements

Kubernetes deployments, especially in enterprise settings, will often have the following basic requirements:

- **Development and test environments**: At least two clusters to test the impacts of changes on the cluster level on applications

- **Developer sandbox**: A place where developers can build containers and test them without worrying about impacts on shared namespaces

- **Source control and issue tracking**: A place to store code and track open tasks

In addition to these basic requirements, enterprises will often have additional requirements, such as regular access reviews, limiting access based on policy, and workflows that assign responsibility for actions that could impact a shared environment. Finally, you'll want to make sure that policies are in place to protect nodes.

For our platform, we want to encompass as many of these requirements as possible. To better automate deployments onto our platform, we're going to define each application as having the following:

- **A development namespace**: Developers are administrators

- **A production namespace**: Developers are viewers

- **A source control project**: Developers can fork

- **A build process**: Triggered by updates to Git

- **A deploy process**: Triggered by updates to Git

In addition, we want our developers to have their own sandbox so that each user will get their own namespace for development.

 In a real deployment, you will want to separate your development and production environments into separate clusters. This makes it much easier to test cluster-wide operations, such as upgrades, without impacting running applications. We're doing everything in one cluster to make it easier for you to set up on your own.

To provide access to each application, we will define three roles:

- **Owners**: Users that are application owners can approve access for other roles inside their application. This role is assigned to the application requestor and can be assigned by application owners. Owners are also responsible for pushing changes into development and production.

- **Developers**: These are users that will have access to an application's source control and can administer the application's development namespace. They can view objects in the production namespace but can't edit anything. This role can be requested by any user and is approved by an application owner.

- **Operations**: These users have the capabilities as developers, but can also make changes to the production namespace as needed. This role can be requested by any user and is approved by the application owner.

We will also create some environment-wide roles:

- **System approvers**: Users with this role can approve access to any system-wide roles.

- **Cluster administrators**: This role is specifically for managing our cluster and the applications that comprise our pipeline. It can be requested by anyone and must be approved by a member of the system approvers role.

- **Developers**: Anyone who logs in gets their own namespace for development. These namespaces cannot be requested for access by other users. These namespaces are not directly connected to any CI/CD infrastructure or Git repositories.

Even with our very simple platform, we have six roles that need to be mapped to the applications that make up our pipeline. Each application has its own authentication and authorization processes that these roles will need to be mapped to. This is just one example of why automation is so important to the security of your clusters. Provisioning this access manually based on email requests can become unmanageable quickly.

The workflow that developers are expected to go through with an application will line up with the GitOps flow we designed previously:

- Application owners will request that an application be created. Once approved, a Git repository will be created for application code, pipeline build manifests, and Kubernetes manifests. Development and production namespaces will be created as well with the appropriate `RoleBinding` objects. Groups will be created that reflect the roles for each application, with approval for access to those groups delegated to the application owner.

- Developers and operations staff are granted access to the application by either requesting it or having it provided directly by an application owner. Once granted access, updates are expected in both the developer's sandbox and the development namespace. Updates are made in a user's fork for the Git repository, with pull requests used to merge code into the main repositories that drive automation.

- All builds are controlled via "scripts" in the application's source control.

- All artifacts are published to a centralized container registry.

- All production updates must be approved by application owners.

This basic workflow doesn't include typical components of a workflow, such as code and container scans, periodic access recertifications, or requirements for privileged access. The topic of this chapter can easily be a complete book on its own. The goal isn't to build a complete enterprise platform but to give you a starting point for building and designing your own system.

Choosing our technology stack

In the previous parts of this section, we talked about pipelines in a generic way. Now, let's get into the specifics of what technology is needed in our pipeline. We identified earlier that every application has application source code and Kubernetes manifest definitions. It also has to build containers. There needs to be a way to watch for changes to Git and update our cluster. Finally, we need an automation platform so that all these components work together.

Based on our requirements for our platform, we want technology that has the following features:

- **Open source**: We don't want you to buy anything just for this book!

- **API-driven**: We need to be able to provide components and access in an automated way

- **Has a visual component that supports external authentication**: This book focuses on enterprise, and everyone in the enterprise loves their GUIs, just not having different credentials for each application

- **Supported on Kubernetes**: This is a book on Kubernetes

To meet these requirements, we're going to deploy the following components to our cluster:

- **Git Registry – GitLab**: GitLab is a powerful system that provides a great UI and experience for working with Git that supports external authentication (that is, **Single Sign-On (SSO)**). It has integrated issue management and an extensive API. It also has a Helm chart that we have tailored for the book to run a minimal install.

- **Automated Builds – Tekton**: Originally the build portion of the Knative project for Kubernetes function-as-a-service deployments, Tekton was spun off into its own project to provide build services for generic applications. It runs in Kubernetes with all interactions being via the Kubernetes API. We're also going to deploy the dashboard since it supports SSO in a similar way to the Kubernetes dashboard.

- **Container Registry – simple Docker registry**: There are many very capable open source registries. Since this deployment will get complex quickly, we decided just to use the registry provided by Docker. There won't be any security on it, so don't use it in production!

- **GitOps – ArgoCD**: ArgoCD is a project from Intuit to build a feature-rich GitOps platform. It's Kubernetes native, has its own API, and stores its objects as Kubernetes custom resources, making it easier to automate. Its UI and CLI tools both integrate with SSO using OpenID Connect.

- **Access, authentication, and automation – OpenUnison**: We'll continue to use OpenUnison for authentication into our cluster. We're also going to integrate the UI components of our technology stack as well to provide a single portal for our platform. Finally, we'll use OpenUnison's workflows to manage access to each system based on our role structure and provision the objects needed for everything to work together. Access will be provided via OpenUnison's self-service portal.

- **Node Policy Enforcement – GateKeeper:** The GateKeeper deployment from *Chapter 9, Node Security with GateKeeper*, will enforce the fact that each namespace has a minimum set of policies.

Reading through this technology stack, you might ask "Why didn't you choose *XYZ?*" The Kubernetes ecosystem is diverse with no shortage of great projects and products for your cluster. This is by no means a definitive stack, nor is it even a "recommended" stack. It's a collection of applications that meets our requirements and lets us focus on the processes being implemented, rather than learning a specific technology.

You might also find that there's quite a bit of overlap between even the tools in this stack. For instance, GitLab has GitOps capabilities and its own build system, but we chose not to use them for this chapter. We did that so that you can see how to tie different systems together to build a platform. Your platform may use GitHub's SaaS solution for source control, but run builds internally and combine with Amazon's container registry. We wanted you to see how these systems can be connected to build a platform instead of focusing on specific tools.

This section was a very deep exploration of the theory behind pipeline design and looking at common requirements for building a Kubernetes-based platform. We identified technology components that can implement those requirements and why we chose them. With this knowledge in hand, it's time to build!

Preparing our cluster

Before we begin deploying our technology stack, we need to do a couple of things. I recommend starting with a fresh cluster. If you're using the KinD cluster from this book, start with a new cluster. We're deploying several components that need to be integrated and it will be simpler and easier to start fresh rather than potentially struggling with previous configurations. Before we start deploying the applications that will make up our stack, we're going to deploy JetStack's cert-manager to automate certificate issuing, a simple container registry, and OpenUnison for authentication and automation.

Before creating your cluster, let's generate a root certificate for our **certificate authority (CA)** and make sure our host trusts it. This is important so that we can push a sample container without worrying about trust issues:

1. Create a self-signed certificate that we'll use as our CA. The `chapter14/shell` directory of the Git repository for this book contains a script called `makeca.sh` that will generate this certificate for you:

    ```
    $ cd chapter14/shell/
    $ sh ./makeca.sh
    Generating RSA private key, 2048 bit long modulus (2 primes)
    ...............................................................
    ...............................................................
    ................+++++
    ........................+++++
    e is 65537 (0x010001)
    ```

2. Trust the CA certificate on your local VM where you're deploying KinD. Assuming you're using Ubuntu 20.04:

    ```
    $ cd chapter14/shell/ssl/
    $ sudo cp tls.crt /usr/local/share/ca-certificates/internal-ca.
    crt
    $ sudo update-ca-certificates
    $ sudo reboot
    ```

Once your VM is back, deploy a fresh cluster by running `chapter2/create-cluster.sh`.

Once done, wait for the pods to finish running before moving on to deploying `cert-manager`.

Deploying cert-manager

JetStack, a Kubernetes-focused consulting company, created a project called `cert-manager` to make it easier to automate the creation and renewal of certificates. This project works by letting you define issuers using Kubernetes custom resources and then using annotations on `Ingress` objects to generate certificates using those issuers. The end result is a cluster running with properly managed and rotated certificates without generating a single **certificate signing request (CSR)** or worrying about expiration!

The `cert-manager` project is most often mentioned with *Let's Encrypt* (`https://letsencrypt.org/`) to automate the publishing of certificates that have been signed by a commercially recognized certificate authority for free (as in beer). This is possible because *Let's Encrypt* automates the process. The certificates are only good for 90 days and the entire process is API-driven. In order to drive this automation, you must have some way of letting *Let's Encrypt* verify ownership of the domain you are trying to get a certificate for. Throughout this book, we have used `nip.io` to simulate a DNS. If you have a DNS service that you can use and is supported by `cert-manager`, such as Amazon's Route 53, then this is a great solution.

Since we're using `nip.io`, we will deploy `cert-manager` with a self-signed certificate authority. This gives us the benefit of having a certificate authority that can quickly generate certificates without having to worry about domain validation. We will then instruct our workstation to trust this certificate as well as the applications we deploy so that everything is secured using properly built certificates.

 Using a self-signed certificate authority is a common practice for most enterprises for internal deployments. This avoids having to deal with potential validation issues where a commercially signed certificate won't provide much value. Most enterprises can distribute an internal certificate authority's certificates via their Active Directory infrastructure. Chances are your enterprise has a way to request either an internal certificate or a wildcard that could be used too.

The steps to deploy `cert-manager` are as follows:

1. From your cluster, deploy the `cert-manager` manifests:

```
$ kubectl apply -f https://github.com/jetstack/cert-manager/
releases/download/v1.5.3/cert-manager.yaml
```

2. There is now an SSL directory with a certificate and a key. The next step is to create a secret from these files that will become our certificate authority:

```
$ cd chapter14/shell/ssl/
$ kubectl create secret tls ca-key-pair --key=./tls.key
--cert=./tls.crt -n cert-manager
secret/ca-key-pair created
```

3. Next, create the `ClusterIssuer` object so that all of our `Ingress` objects can have properly minted certificates:

```
$ cd ../../yaml/
$ kubectl create -f ./certmanager-ca.yaml
clusterissuer.cert-manager.io/ca-issuer created
```

4. With `ClusterIssuer` created, any `Ingress` object with the `cert-manager.io/cluster-issuer: "ca-issuer"` annotation will have a certificate signed by our authority created for them. One of the components we will be using for this is our container registry. Kubernetes uses Docker's underlying mechanisms for pulling containers, and KinD will not pull images from registries running without TLS or using an untrusted certificate. To get around this issue, we need to import our certificate into both our worker and nodes:

```
$ cd ~/
$ kubectl get secret ca-key-pair -n cert-manager -o json | jq -r
'.data["tls.crt"]' | base64 -d > internal-ca.crt
$ docker cp internal-ca.crt cluster01-worker:/usr/local/share/
ca-certificates/internal-ca.crt
$ docker exec -ti cluster01-worker update-ca-certificates
Updating certificates in /etc/ssl/certs...
1 added, 0 removed; done.
Running hooks in /etc/ca-certificates/update.d...
done.
$ docker restart cluster01-worker
```

At this point, wait for `cluster01-worker` to finish restarting. Also, wait for all the pods in the cluster to come back:

```
$ docker cp internal-ca.crt cluster01-control-plane:/usr/local/
share/ca-certificates/internal-ca.crt
$ docker exec -ti cluster01-control-plane update-ca-certificates
```

```
Updating certificates in /etc/ssl/certs...
1 added, 0 removed; done.
Running hooks in /etc/ca-certificates/update.d...
done.
$ docker restart cluster01-control-plane
```

The first command extracts the certificate from the secret we created to host the certificate. The next set of commands copies the certificate to each container, instructs the container to trust it, and finally, restarts the container. Once your containers are restarted, wait for all the Pods to come back; it could take a few minutes.

 Now would be a good time to download `internal-ca.crt`; install it onto your local workstation and potentially into your browser of choice. Different operating systems and browsers do this differently, so check the appropriate documentation on how to do this. Trusting this certificate will make things much easier when interacting with applications, pushing containers, and using command-line tools.

With `cert-manager` ready to issue certificates and both your cluster and your workstation trusting those certificates, the next step is to deploy a container registry.

Deploying the Docker container registry

Docker, Inc. provides a simple registry. There is no security on this registry, so it is most certainly not a good option for production use. The `chapter14/docker-registry/docker-registry.yaml` file will deploy the registry for us and create an `Ingress` object. The `chapter14/docker-registry/deploy-docker-registry.sh` script will deploy the registry for you:

```
$ ./deploy-docker-registry.sh
namespace/docker-registry created
k8spsphostfilesystem.constraints.gatekeeper.sh/docker-registry-host-
filesystem unchanged
statefulset.apps/docker-registry created
service/docker-registry created
ingress.networking.k8s.io/docker-registry created
```

Once the registry is running, you can try accessing it from your browser:

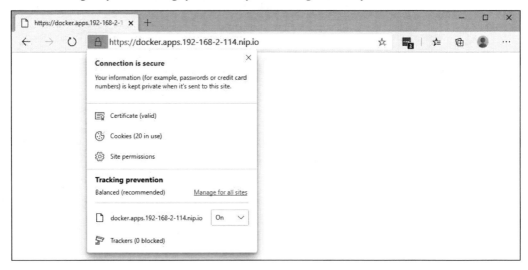

Figure 14.5: Accessing the container registry in a browser

You won't see much since the registry has no web UI, but you also shouldn't get a certificate error. That's because we deployed `cert-manager` and are issuing signed certificates! With our registry running, we'll deploy OpenUnison and GateKeeper.

Deploying OpenUnison and GateKeeper

In *Chapter 5, Integrating Authentication into Your Cluster*, we introduced OpenUnison to authenticate access to our KinD deployment. OpenUnison comes in two flavors. The first, which we have had deployed in earlier chapters' examples, is a login portal that lets us authenticate using a central source and pass group information to our RBAC policies. The second, which we'll deploy in this chapter, is a **Namespace as a Service (NaaS)** portal that we'll use as the basis for integrating the systems that will manage our pipeline. This portal will also give us a central UI for requesting projects to be created and managing access to our project's systems.

We defined the fact that each project we deploy will have three "roles" that will span several systems. Will your enterprise let you create and manage groups for every project we create? Some might, but Active Directory is a critical component in most enterprises, and write access can be difficult to get. It's unlikely that the people who run your Active Directory are the same people who you report to when managing your cluster, complicating your ability to get an area of Active Directory that you have administrative rights in. The OpenUnison NaaS portal lets you manage access with local groups that can be easily queried, just like with Active Directory, but you have the control to manage them.

To facilitate OpenUnison's automation capabilities, we need to deploy a database to store persistent data and an SMTP server to notify users when they have open requests or when requests have been completed. For the database, we'll deploy the open source MariaDB. For a **Simple Mail Transfer Protocol (SMTP)** (email) server, most enterprises have very strict rules about sending emails. We don't want to have to worry about getting email set up for notifications, so we'll run a "black hole" email service that just disregards all SMTP requests.

Don't worry about having to go back through previous chapters to get OpenUnison and GateKeeper up and running. We created two scripts to build everything out for you:

```
$ .
$ ./deploy_gatekeeper.sh
 .
 .
 .
$ cd ../openunison
$ ./deploy_openunison_imp.sh
 .
 .
 .
OpenUnison is deployed!
```

It will take a few minutes, but once done, your environment will be ready for the next step. We'll be using OpenUnison for SSO with GitLab and ArgoCD so we want to have it ready to go. We'll come back to OpenUnison later in the chapter as we deploy the integration of our platform components. With your cluster prepared, the next step is to deploy the components for our pipeline.

Deploying GitLab

When building a GitOps pipeline, one of the most important components is a Git repository. GitLab has many components besides just Git, including a UI for navigating code, a web-based **integrated development environment (IDE)** for editing code, and a robust identity implementation to manage access to projects in a multi-tenant environment. This makes it a great solution for our platform since we can map our "roles" to GitLab groups.

In this section, we're going to deploy GitLab into our cluster and create two simple repositories that we'll use later when we deploy Tekton and ArgoCD. We'll focus on the automation steps when we revisit OpenUnison to automate our pipeline deployments.

GitLab deploys with a Helm chart. For this book, we built a custom `values` file to run a minimal install. While GitLab comes with features that are similar to ArgoCD and Tekton, we won't be using them. We also didn't want to worry about high availability. Let's begin:

1. Create a new namespace called `gitlab`:

```
$ kubectl create ns gitlab
namespace/gitlab created
```

2. We need to add our certificate authority as a secret for GitLab to trust talking to OpenUnison and the webhooks we will eventually create for Tekton:

```
$ mkdir /tmp/gitlab-secret
$ kubectl get secret ca-key-pair \
  -n cert-manager -o json | jq -r '.data["tls.crt"]' \
  | base64 -d > /tmp/gitlab-secret/tls.crt
$ kubectl create secret generic \
  internal-ca --from-file=/tmp/gitlab-secret/ -n gitlab
```

3. Deploy a `Secret` for GitLab that configures its OpenID Connect provider to use OpenUnison for authentication:

```
$ cd chapter14/gitlab/sso-secret
$ ./deploy-gitlab-secret.sh
secret/gitlab-oidc created
```

4. This `Secret` needs to be created before deploying the Helm chart because, just as with OpenUnison, you shouldn't keep secrets in your charts, even if they're encrypted. Here's what the base64-decoded data from the secret will look like once created:

```
name: openid_connect
label: OpenUnison
args:
  name: openid_connect
  scope:
    - openid
    - profile
  response_type: code
  issuer: https://k8sou.apps.192-168-2-114.nip.io/auth/idp/
k8sIdp
  discovery: true
  client_auth_method: query
  uid_field: sub
  send_scope_to_token_endpoint: false
```

```
client_options:
    identifier: gitlab
    secret: secret
    redirect_uri: https://gitlab.apps.192-168-2-114.nip.io/
users/auth/openid_connect/callback
```

 We're using a client secret of **secret**. This should not be done for a production cluster. If you're deploying GitLab into production using our templates as a starting point, make sure to change this.

5. If your cluster is running on a single VM, now would be a good time to create a snapshot. If something goes wrong during the GitLab deployment, it's easier to revert back to a snapshot since the Helm chart doesn't do a great job of cleaning up after itself on a delete.

6. Add the chart to your local repository and deploy GitLab:

```
$ cd chapter14/gitlab/helm
$ ./gen-helm-values.sh
$ helm repo add gitlab https://charts.gitlab.io
    "gitlab" has been added to your repositories
$ helm repo update
$ helm install gitlab gitlab/gitlab -n gitlab -f /tmp/gitlab-
values.yaml
NAME: gitlab
LAST DEPLOYED: Mon Sep 27 14:00:44 2021
NAMESPACE: gitlab
STATUS: deployed
REVISION: 1
```

7. It will take a few minutes to run. Even once the Helm chart has been installed, it can take 15–20 minutes for all the Pods to finish deploying.

8. We next need to update our GitLab shell to accept SSH connections on port 2222. This way, we can commit code without having to worry about blocking SSH access to your KinD server. Run the following to patch the `Deployment`:

```
kubectl patch deployments gitlab-gitlab-shell -n gitlab -p '{"sp
ec":{"template":{"spec":{"containers":[{"name":"gitlab-shell","p
orts":[{"containerPort":2222,"protocol":"TCP","name":"ssh","host
Port":2222}]}]}}}}'
```

9. Once the Pod relaunches, you'll be able to SSH to your GitLab hostname on port 2222.

10. To get your root password to log in to GitLab, get it from the secret that was generated:

```
$ kubectl get secret gitlab-gitlab-initial-root-password -o json
-n gitlab | jq -r '.data.password' | base64 -d
10xtSWXfbvH5umAbCk9NoN0wAeYsUo9jRVbXrfLn KbzBoPLrCGZ6kYRe8wdREcDl
```

You now can log in to your GitLab instance by going to `https://gitlab.apps.x-x-x-x.nip.io`, where `x-x-x-x` is the IP of your server. Since my server is running on `192.168.2.119`, my GitLab instance is running on `https://gitlab.apps.192-168-2-119.nip.io/`.

Creating example projects

To explore Tekton and ArgoCD, we will create two projects. One will be for storing a simple Python web service, while the other will store the manifests for running the service. Let's deploy these projects:

1. You'll need to upload an SSH public key. To interact with GitLab's Git repositories, we're going to be centralizing authentication via OpenID Connect. GitLab won't have a password for authentication. To upload your SSH public key, click on your user icon in the upper right-hand corner, and then click on the **SSH Keys** menu on the left-hand task bar. Here you can paste your SSH public key.

2. Create a project and call it `hello-python`. Keep the visibility **private**.

3. Clone the project using SSH. Because we're running on port `2222`, we need to change the URL provided by GitLab to be a proper SSH URL. For instance, my GitLab instance gives me the URL `git@gitlab.apps.192-168-2-114.nip.io:root/hello-python.git`. This needs to be changed to `ssh://git@gitlab.apps.192-168-2-114.nip.io:2222/root/hello-python.git`.

4. Once cloned, copy the contents of `chapter14/python-hello` into your repository and push to GitLab:

```
$ cd chapter14/example-apps/python-hello
$ git archive --format=tar HEAD > /path/to/hello-python/data.tar
$ cd /path/to/hello-python
$ tar -xvf data.tar
README.md
source/
source/Dockerfile
source/helloworld.py
source/requirements.txt
```

```
$ rm data.tar
$ git add *
$ git commit -m 'initial commit'
$ git push
```

5. In GitLab, create another project called `hello-python-operations` with visibility set to **private**. Clone this project, copy the contents of `chapter14/example-apps/python-hello-operations` into the repository, and then push it.

Now that GitLab is deployed with some example code, we are able to move on to the next step – building an actual pipeline!

Deploying Tekton

Tekton is the pipeline system we're using for our platform. Originally part of the Knative project for building function-as-a-service on Kubernetes, Tekton has broken out into its own project. The biggest difference between Tekton and other pipeline technologies you may have run is that Tekton is Kubernetes-native. Everything from its execution system, definition, and webhooks for automation are able to run on just about any Kubernetes distribution you can find. For example, we'll be running it in KinD and Red Hat has moved to Tekton as the main pipeline technology used for OpenShift, starting with 4.1.

The process of deploying Tekton is pretty straightforward. Tekton is a series of operators that look for the creation of custom resources that define a build pipeline. The deployment itself only takes a couple of `kubectl` commands:

```
$ kubectl create ns tekton-pipelines
$ kubectl create -f chapter14/yaml/tekton-pipelines-policy.yaml
$ kubectl apply -f https://storage.googleapis.com/tekton-releases/
pipeline/latest/release.yaml
$ kubectl apply -f https://storage.googleapis.com/tekton-releases/
triggers/latest/release.yaml
$ kubectl apply --filename https://storage.googleapis.com/tekton-
releases/triggers/latest/interceptors.yaml
```

The first command deploys the base system needed to run Tekton pipelines. The second command deploys the components needed to build webhooks so that pipelines can be launched as soon as code is pushed. Once both commands are done and the Pods in the `tekton-pipelines` namespace are running, you're ready to start building a pipeline! We'll use our Python Hello World web service as an example.

Building Hello World

Our Hello World application is really straightforward. It's a simple service that echoes back the obligatory "hello" and the host the service is running on just so we feel like our service is doing something interesting. Since the service is written in Python, we don't need to "build" a binary, but we do want to build a container. Once the container is built, we want to update the Git repository for our running namespace and let our GitOps system reconcile the change to redeploy our application. The steps for our build will be as follows:

1. Check out our latest code
2. Create a tag based on a timestamp
3. Build our image
4. Push to our registry
5. Patch a Deployment YAML file in the `operations` namespace

We'll build our pipeline one object at a time. The first set of tasks is to create an SSH key that Tekton will use to pull our source code:

1. Create an SSH key pair that we'll use for our pipeline to check out our code. When prompted for a passphrase, just hit *Enter* to skip adding a passphrase:

   ```
   $ ssh-keygen -t rsa -m PEM -f ./gitlab-hello-python
   ```

2. Log in to GitLab and navigate to the `hello-python` project we created. Click on **Settings | Repository | Deploy Keys**, and click **Expand**. Use `tekton` as the title and paste the contents of the `github-hello-python.pub` file you just created into the **Key** section. Keep **Write access allowed** *unchecked* and click **Add Key**.

3. Next, create the `build-python-hello` namespace and the following secret. Replace the `ssh-privatekey` attribute with the Base64-encoded content of the `gitlab-hello-python` file we created in *step 1*. The annotation is what tells Tekton which server to use this key with. The server name is the `Service` in the GitLab namespace:

   ```
   apiVersion: v1
   data:
     ssh-privatekey: ...
   kind: Secret
   metadata:
     annotations:
       tekton.dev/git-0: gitlab-gitlab-shell.gitlab.svc.cluster.
   local
   ```

```
    name: git-pull
    namespace: build-python-hello
  type: kubernetes.io/ssh-auth
```

4. Create an SSH key pair that we'll use for our pipeline to push to the `operations` repository. When prompted for a passphrase, just hit *Enter* to skip adding a passphrase:

```
$ ssh-keygen -t rsa -m PEM -f ./gitlab-hello-python-operations
```

5. Log in to GitLab and navigate to the `hello-python-operations` project we created. Click on **Settings** | **Repository** | **Deploy Keys**, and click **Expand**. Use **tekton** as the title and paste the contents of the `github-hello-python-operations.pub` file you just created into the **Key** section. Make sure **Write access allowed** is *checked* and click **Add Key**.

6. Next, create the following secret. Replace the `ssh-privatekey` attribute with the Base64-encoded content of the `gitlab-hello-python-operations` file we created in *step 4*. The annotation is what tells Tekton which server to use this key with. The server name is the **Service** we created in *step 6* in the GitLab namespace:

```
apiVersion: v1
data:
  ssh-privatekey: ...
kind: Secret
metadata:
  name: git-write
  namespace: python-hello-build
type: kubernetes.io/ssh-auth
```

7. Create a service account for tasks to run, as with our secret:

```
$ kubectl create -f chapter14/example-apps/tekton/tekton-
serviceaccount.yaml
```

8. We need a container that contains both `git` and `kubectl`. We'll build `chapter14/example-apps/docker/PatchRepoDockerfile` and push it to our internal registry. Make sure to replace `192-168-2-114` with the hostname for your server's IP address:

```
$ docker build -f ./PatchRepoDockerfile -t \
    docker.apps.192-168-2-114.nip.io/gitcommit/gitcommit .
$ docker push \
    docker.apps.192-168-2-114.nip.io/gitcommit/gitcommit
```

The previous steps set up one key that Tekton will use to pull source code from our service's repository and another key that Tekton will use to update our deployment manifests with a new image tag. The operations repository will be watched by ArgoCD to make updates. Next, we will work on deploying a Tekton pipeline to build our application.

Tekton organizes a "pipeline" into several objects. The most basic unit is a Task, which launches a container to perform some measure of work. Tasks can be thought of like jobs; they run to completion but aren't long-running services. Tasks are collected into Pipelines, which define an environment and order of Task execution. Finally, a PipelineRun (or TaskRun) is used to initiate the execution of a Pipeline (or specific Task) and track its progress. There are more objects than is typical for most pipeline technologies, but this brings additional flexibility and scalability. By leveraging Kubernetes native APIs, it lets Kubernetes do the work of figuring out where to run, what security contexts to use, and so on. With a basic understanding of how Tekton pipelines are assembled, let's walk through a pipeline for building and deploying our example service.

Every Task object can take inputs and produce results that can be shared with other Task objects. Tekton can provide runs (whether it's TaskRun or PipelineRun) with a workspace where the state can be stored and retrieved from. Writing to workspaces allows us to share data between Task objects.

Before deploying our task and pipeline, let's step through the work done by each task. The first task generates an image tag and gets the SHA hash of the latest commit. The full source can be found in chapter14/example-apps/tekton/tekton-task1.yaml:

```
- name: create-image-tag
  image: docker.apps.192-168-2-114.nip.io/gitcommit/gitcommit
  script: |-
    #!/usr/bin/env bash
    export IMAGE_TAG=$(date +"%m%d%Y%H%M%S")
    echo -n "$(resources.outputs.result-image.url):$IMAGE_TAG" > /
tekton/results/image-url
    echo "'$(cat /tekton/results/image-url)'"
    cd $(resources.inputs.git-resource.path)
    RESULT_SHA="$(git rev-parse HEAD | tr -d '\n')"
    echo "Last commit : $RESULT_SHA"
    echo -n "$RESULT_SHA" > /tekton/results/commit-tag
```

Each step in a task is a container. In this case, we're using the container we built previously that has kubectl and git in it.

We don't need `kubectl` for this task, but we do need `git`. The first block of code generates an image name from the `result-image` URL and a timestamp. We could use the latest commit, but I like having a timestamp so that I can quickly tell how old a container is. We save the full image URL to `/text/results/image-url`, which corresponds to a `result` we defined in our task called `image-url`. A `result` on a `Task` tells Tekton that there should be data stored with this name in the workspace so it can be referenced by our pipeline or other tasks by referencing `$(tasks.generate-image-tag.results.image-url)`, where `generate-image-tag` is the name of our `Task`, and `image-url` is the name of our `result`.

Our next task, in `chapter14/example-apps/tekton/tekton-task2.yaml`, generates a container from our application's source using Google's Kaniko project (`https://github.com/GoogleContainerTools/kaniko`). Kaniko lets you generate a container without needing access to a Docker daemon. This is great because you don't need a privileged container to build your image:

```
steps:
- args:
  - --dockerfile=$(params.pathToDockerFile)
  - --destination=$(params.imageURL)
  - --context=$(params.pathToContext)
  - --verbosity=debug
  - --skip-tls-verify
  command:
  - /kaniko/executor
  env:
  - name: DOCKER_CONFIG
    value: /tekton/home/.docker/
  image: gcr.io/kaniko-project/executor:latest
  name: build-and-push
  resources: {}
```

The Kaniko container is what's called a "distro-less" container. It's not built with an underlying shell, nor does it have many of the command-line tools you may be used to. It's just a single binary. This means that any variable manipulation, such as generating a tag for the image, needs to be done before this step. Notice that the image being created doesn't reference the result we created in the first task. It instead references a parameter called `imageURL`. While we could have referenced the result directly, it would make it harder to test this task because it is now tightly bound to the first task. By using a parameter that is set by our pipeline, we can test this task on its own. Once run, this task will generate and push our container.

Our last task, in `chapter14/example-apps/tekton/tekton-task-3.yaml`, does the work to trigger ArgoCD to roll out a new container:

```
- image: docker.apps.192-168-2-114.nip.io/gitcommit/gitcommit
  name: patch-and-push
  resources: {}
  script: |-
    #!/bin/bash
    export GIT_URL="$(params.gitURL)"
    export GIT_HOST=$(sed 's/.*[@]\(.*\)[:].*/\1/' <<< "$GIT_URL")
    mkdir /usr/local/gituser/.ssh
    cp /pushsecret/ssh-privatekey /usr/local/gituser/.ssh/id_rsa
    chmod go-rwx /usr/local/gituser/.ssh/id_rsa
    ssh-keyscan -H $GIT_HOST > /usr/local/gituser/.ssh/known_hosts
    cd $(workspaces.output.path)
    git clone $(params.gitURL) .
    kubectl patch --local -f src/deployments/hello-python.yaml
-p '{"spec":{"template":{"spec":{"containers":[{"name":"python-
hello","image":"$(params.imageURL)"}]}}}}' -o yaml > /tmp/hello-python.
yaml
    cp /tmp/hello-python.yaml src/deployments/hello-python.yaml
    git add src/deployments/hello-python.yaml
    git commit -m 'commit $(params.sourceGitHash)'
    git push
```

The first block of code copies the SSH keys into our home directory, generates `known_hosts`, and clones our repository into a workspace we defined in the `Task`. We don't rely on Tekton to pull the code from our `operations` repository because Tekton assumes we won't be pushing code, so it disconnects the source code from our repository. If we try to run a commit, it will fail. Since the step is a container, we don't want to try to write to it, so we create a workspace with `emptyDir`, just like `emptyDir` in a `Pod` we might run. We could also define workspaces based on persistent volumes. This could come in handy to speed up builds where dependencies get downloaded.

We're copying the SSH key from `/pushsecret`, which is defined as a volume on the task. Our container runs as user `431`, but the SSH keys are mounted as root by Tekton. We don't want to run a privileged container just to copy the keys from a `Secret`, so instead, we mount it as if it were just a regular Pod.

Once we have our repository cloned, we patch our deployment with the latest image and finally, commit the change using the hash of the source commit in our application repository. Now we can track an image back to the commit that generated it! Just as with our second task, we don't reference the results of tasks directly to make it easier to test.

We pull these tasks together in a pipeline – specifically, `chapter14/example-apps/tekton/tekton-pipeline.yaml`. This YAML file is several pages long, but the key piece defines our tasks and links them together. You should never hardcode values into your pipeline. Take a look at our third task's definition in the pipeline:

```
- name: update-operations-git
    taskRef:
      name: patch-deployment
    params:
      - name: imageURL
        value: $(tasks.generate-image-tag.results.image-url)
      - name: gitURL
        value: $(params.gitPushUrl)
      - name: sourceGitHash
        value: $(tasks.generate-image-tag.results.commit-tag)
    workspaces:
    - name: output
      workspace: output
```

We reference parameters and task results, but nothing is hardcoded. This makes our `Pipeline` reusable. We also include the `runAfter` directive in our second and third tasks to make sure that our tasks are run in order. Otherwise, tasks will be run in parallel. Given each task has dependencies on the task before it, we don't want to run them at the same time. Next, let's deploy our pipeline and run it:

1. Add `chapter14/yaml/gitlab-shell-write.yaml` to your cluster; this is an endpoint so that Tekton can write to SSH using a separate key.

2. Run `chapter14/shell/exempt-python-build.sh` to disable GateKeeper in our build namespace. This is needed because Tekton's containers for checking out code run as root and do not work when running with a random user ID.

3. Add the `chapter14/example-apps/tekton/tekton-source-git.yaml` file to your cluster; this tells Tekton where to pull your application code from.

4. Edit `chapter14/example-apps/tekton/tekton-image-result.yaml`, replacing `192-168-2-114` with the hash representation of your server's IP address, and add it to your cluster.

5. Edit `chapter14/example-apps/tekton/tekton-task1.yaml`, replacing the image host with the host for your Docker registry, and add the file to your cluster.

6. Add `chapter14/example-apps/tekton/tekton-task2.yaml` to your cluster.

7. Edit `chapter14/example-apps/tekton/tekton-task3.yaml`, replacing the image host with the host for your Docker registry, and add the file to your cluster.

8. Add `chapter14/example-apps/tekton/tekton-pipeline.yaml` to your cluster.

9. Add `chapter14/example-apps/tekton/tekton-pipeline-run.yaml` to your cluster.

You can check on the progress of your pipeline using `kubectl`, or you can use Tekton's CLI tool called `tkn` (https://github.com/tektoncd/cli). Running `tkn pipelinerun describe build-hello-pipeline-run -n python-hello-build` will list out the progress of your build. You can rerun the build by recreating your run object, but that's not very efficient. Besides, what we really want is for our pipeline to run on a commit!

Building automatically

We don't want to manually run builds. We want builds to be automated. Tekton provides the trigger project to provide webhooks so that whenever GitLab receives a commit, it can tell Tekton to build a `PipelineRun` object for us. Setting up a trigger involves creating a Pod, with its own service account that can create `PipelineRun` objects, a Service for that Pod, and an `Ingress` object to host HTTPS access to the Pod. You also want to protect the webhook with a secret so that it isn't triggered inadvertently. Let's deploy these objects to our cluster:

1. Add `chapter14/example-apps/tekton/tekton-webhook-cr.yaml` to your cluster. This `ClusterRole` will be used by any namespace that wants to provision webhooks for builds.

2. Edit `chapter14/example-apps/tekton/tekton-webhook.yaml`. At the bottom of the file is an `Ingress` object. Change `192-168-2-119` to represent the IP of your cluster, with dashes instead of dots. Then, add the file to your cluster:

```
apiVersion: networking.k8s.io/v1
kind: Ingress
metadata:
  name: gitlab-webhook
  namespace: python-hello-build
  annotations:
    cert-manager.io/cluster-issuer: ca-issuer
spec:
  rules:
  - host: "python-hello-application.build.192-168-2-119.nip.io"
    http:
      paths:
      - backend:
          service:
            name: el-gitlab-listener
```

```
            port:
                number: 8080
            pathType: Prefix
            path: "/"
    tls:
    - hosts:
        - "python-hello-application.build.192-168-2-114.nip.io"
        secretName: ingresssecret
```

3. Log in to GitLab. Go to **Admin Area | Network**. Click on **Expand** next to **Outbound Requests**. Check the **Allow requests to the local network from web hooks and services** option and click **Save changes**.

4. Go to the `hello-python` project we created and click on **Settings | Webhooks**. For the URL, use your `Ingress` host with HTTPS – for instance, `https://python-hello-application.build.192-168-2-119.nip.io/`. For **Secret Token**, use `notagoodsecret`, and for **Push events**, set the branch name to `main`. Finally, click on **Add webhook**.

5. Once added, click on **Test**, choosing **Push Events**. If everything is configured correctly, a new `PipelineRun` object should have been created. You can run `tkn pipelinerun list -n python-hello-build` to see the list of runs; there should be a new one running. After a few minutes, you'll have a new container and a patched Deployment in the `python-hello-operations` project!

We covered quite a bit in this section to build our application and deploy it using GitOps. The good news is that everything is automated; a push will create a new instance of our application! The bad news is that we had to create over a dozen Kubernetes objects and manually make updates to our projects in GitLab. In the last section, we'll automate this process. First, let's deploy ArgoCD so that we can get our application running!

Deploying ArgoCD

So far, we have a way to get into our cluster, a way to store code, and a system for building our code and generating images. The last component of our platform is our GitOps controller. This is the piece that lets us commit manifests to our Git repository and make changes to our cluster. ArgoCD is a tool from Intuit that provides a great UI and is driven by a combination of custom resources and Kubernetes-native `ConfigMap` and `Secret` objects. It has a CLI tool, and both the web and CLI tools are integrated with OpenID Connect, so it will be easy to add SSO with OpenUnison.

Let's deploy ArgoCD and use it to launch our `hello-python` web service:

1. Deploy using the standard YAML from `https://argo-cd.readthedocs.io/en/stable/`:

```
$ kubectl create namespace argocd
$ kubectl apply -f chapter14/argocd/argocd-policy.yaml
$ kubectl apply -n argocd -f https://raw.githubusercontent.com/
argoproj/argo-cd/stable/manifests/install.yaml
```

2. Create the `Ingress` object for ArgoCD by running `chapter14/deploy-argocd-ingress.sh`. This script sets the IP in the hostname correctly and adds the ingress objects to the cluster.

3. Get the root password by running `kubectl get secret argocd-initial-admin-secret -n argocd -o json | jq -r '.data.password' | base64 -d`. Save this password.

4. We need to tell ArgoCD to run as a user and group 999 so our default mutation doesn't assign a user of 1000 and a group of 2000 to make sure SSH keys are read properly. Run the following patches:

```
$ kubectl patch deployment argocd-server -n argocd -p '{"spec":{
"template":{"spec":{"containers":[{"name":"argocd-server","secur
ityContext":{"runAsUser":999,"runAsGroup":999}}]}}}}'
$ kubectl patch deployment argocd-repo-server  -n argocd -p
'{"spec":{"template":{"spec":{"containers":[{"name":"argo
cd-repo-server","securityContext":{"runAsUser":999,"runAsGro
up":999}}]}}}}'
```

5. Edit the `argocd-server` Deployment in the `argocd` namespace. Add `--insecure` to the command:

```
spec:
  containers:
  - command:
    - argocd-server
    - --repo-server
    - argocd-repo-server:8081
    - --insecure
```

6. You can now log in to ArgoCD by going to the `Ingress` host you defined in *step 2*. You will need to download the ArgoCD CLI utility as well from `https://github.com/argoproj/argo-cd/releases/latest`. Once downloaded, log in by running `./argocd login grpc-argocd.apps.192-168-2-114.nip.io`, replacing `192-168-2-114` with the IP of your server, and with dashes instead of dots.

7. Create the `python-hello` namespace.

8. Add `chapter14/yaml/python-hello-policy.yaml` to your cluster so we can run our service under strict security policies. We don't need a privileged container so why run with one?

9. Before we can add our GitLab repository, we need to tell ArgoCD to trust our GitLab instance's SSH host. Since we will have ArgoCD talk directly to the GitLab shell service, we'll need to generate `known_host` for that Service. To make this easier, we included a script that will run `known_host` from outside the cluster but rewrite the content as if it were from inside the cluster. Run the `chapter14/shell/getSshKnownHosts.sh` script and pipe the output into the `argocd` command to import `known_host`. Remember to change the hostname to reflect your own cluster's IP address:

```
$ ./chapter14/argocd/getSshKnownHosts.sh gitlab.apps.192-168-2-
114.nip.io | argocd cert add-ssh --batch
Enter SSH known hosts entries, one per line. Press CTRL-D when
finished.
Successfully created 3 SSH known host entries
```

10. Next, we need to generate an SSH key to access the `python-hello-operations` repository:

```
$ ssh-keygen -t rsa -m PEM -f ./argocd-python-hello
```

11. In GitLab, add the public key to the `python-hello-operations` repository by going to the project and clicking on **Settings | Repository**. Next to **Deploy Keys**, click **Expand**. For **Title**, use `argocd`. Use the contents of `argocd-python-hello.pub` and click **Add key**. Then, add the key to ArgoCD using the CLI and replace the public GitLab host with the `gitlab-gitlab-shell` Service hostname:

```
$ argocd repo add git@gitlab-gitlab-shell.gitlab.svc.cluster.
local:root/hello-python-operations.git --ssh-private-key-path ./
argocd-python-hello
repository 'git@gitlab-gitlab-shell.gitlab.svc.cluster.
local:root/hello-python-operations.git' added
```

12. Our last step is to create an `Application` object. You can create it through the web UI or the CLI. You can also create it by creating an `Application` object in the `argocd` namespace, which is what we'll do. Create the following object in your cluster (`chapter14/example-apps/argocd/argocd-python-hello.yaml`):

```
apiVersion: argoproj.io/v1alpha1
kind: Application
metadata:
```

```
    name: python-hello
    namespace: argocd
spec:
  destination:
    namespace: python-hello
    server: https://kubernetes.default.svc
  project: default
  source:
    directory:
      jsonnet: {}
      recurse: true
    path: src
    repoURL: git@gitlab-gitlab-shell.gitlab.svc.cluster.
local:root/hello-python-operations.git
    targetRevision: HEAD
  syncPolicy:
    automated: {}
```

This is about as basic a configuration as is possible. We're working off simple manifests. ArgoCD can work from JSONnet and Helm too. After this application is created, look at the Pods in the `python-hello` namespace. You should have one running! Making updates to your code will result in updates to the namespace.

We now have a code base that can be deployed automatically with a commit. We spent two dozen pages, ran dozens of commands, and created more than 20 objects to get there. Instead of manually creating these objects, it would be best to automate the process. Now that we have the objects that need to be created, we can automate the onboarding. In the next section, we will take the manual process of building the links between GitLab, Tekton, and ArgoCD to line up with our business processes.

Automating project onboarding using OpenUnison

Earlier in this chapter, we deployed the OpenUnison NaaS portal. This portal lets users request new namespaces to be created and allows developers to request access to these namespaces via a self-service interface. The workflows built into this portal are very basic but create the namespace and appropriate `RoleBinding` objects. What we want to do is build a workflow that integrates our platform and creates all of the objects we created manually earlier in this chapter. The goal is that we're able to deploy a new application into our environment without having to run the `kubectl` command (or at least minimize its use).

This will require careful planning. Here's how our developer workflow will run:

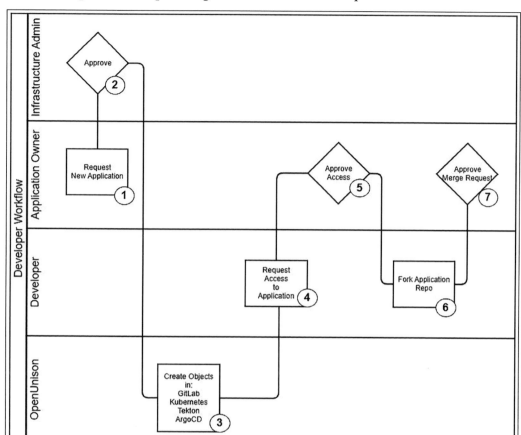

Figure 14.6: Platform developer workflow

Let's quickly run through the workflow that we see in the preceding figure:

1. An application owner will request an application be created.
2. The infrastructure admin approves the creation.
3. At this point, OpenUnison will deploy the objects we created manually. We'll detail those objects shortly.
4. Once created, a developer is able to request access to the application.
5. The application owner(s) approves access to the application.
6. Once approved, the developer will fork the application source base and do their work. They can launch the application in their developer workspace. They can also fork the build project to create a pipeline and the development environment operations project to create manifests for the application.

7. Once the work is done and tested locally, the developer will push the code into their own fork and then request a merge request.

8. The application owner will approve the request and merge the code from GitLab.

Once the code is merged, ArgoCD will synchronize the build and operations projects. The webhook in the application project will kick off a Tekton pipeline that will build our container and update the development operations project with the tag for the latest container. ArgoCD will synchronize the updated manifest into our application's development namespace. Once testing is completed, the application owner submits a merge request from the development operations workspace to the production operations workspace, triggering ArgoCD to launch into production.

Nowhere in this flow is there a step called "operations staff uses `kubectl` to create a namespace." This is a simple flow and won't totally avoid your operations staff from using `kubectl`, but it should be a good starting point. All this automation requires an extensive set of objects to be created:

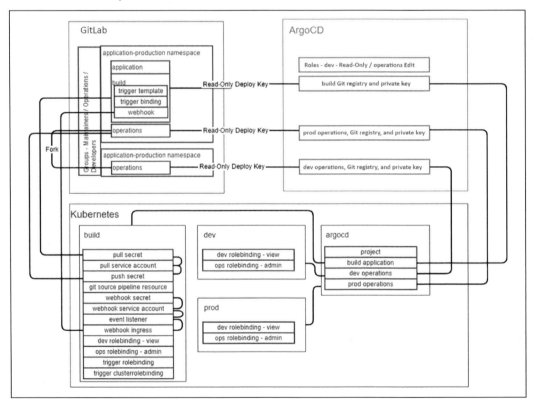

Figure 14.7: Application onboarding object map

The above diagram shows the objects that need to be created in our environment and the relationships between them. With so many moving parts, it's important to automate the process. Creating these objects manually is both time-consuming and error-prone. We'll work through that automation later in this chapter.

In GitLab, we create a project for our application code, operations, and build pipeline. We also fork the operations project as a development operations project. For each project, we generate deploy keys and register webhooks. We also create groups to match the roles we defined earlier in this chapter.

For Kubernetes, we create namespaces for the development and production environments. We also create a namespace for the Tekton pipeline. We add the keys as needed to `Secrets`. In the build namespace, we create all the scaffolding to support the webhook that will trigger automatic builds. That way, our developers only need to worry about creating their pipeline objects.

In our last application, ArgoCD, we will create an `AppProject` that hosts both our build and operations namespaces. We will also add the SSH keys we generated when creating our GitLab projects. Each project also gets an `Application` object in our `AppProject` that instructs ArgoCD how to synchronize from GitLab. Finally, we add RBAC rules to ArgoCD so that our developers can view their application synchronization status but owners and operations can make updates and changes.

Designing a GitOps strategy

We have outlined the steps we want for our developer workflow and how we'll build those objects. Before we get into talking about implementation, let's work through how ArgoCD, OpenUnison, and Kubernetes will interact with each other.

So far, we've deployed everything manually in our cluster by running `kubectl` commands off of manifests that we put in this book's Git repo. That's not really the ideal way to do this. What if you needed to rebuild your cluster? Instead of manually recreating everything, wouldn't it be better to just let ArgoCD deploy everything from Git? We're not going to do that for this chapter, but it's something you should aim for as you design your own GitOps-based cluster. The more you can keep in Git, the better.

That said, how will OpenUnison communicate with the API server when it performs all this automation for us? The "easiest" way for OpenUnison is to just call the API server.

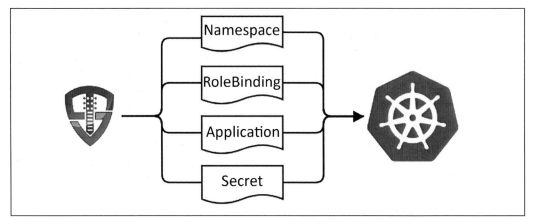

Figure 14.8: Writing objects directly to the API server

This will work. We'll get to our end goal of a developer workflow using GitOps, but what about our cluster management workflow? We want to get as many of the benefits from GitOps as cluster operators as our developers do! To that end, a better strategy would be to write our objects to a Git repository. That way, when OpenUnison creates these objects, they're tracked in Git, and if changes need to be made outside of OpenUnison, those changes are tracked too.

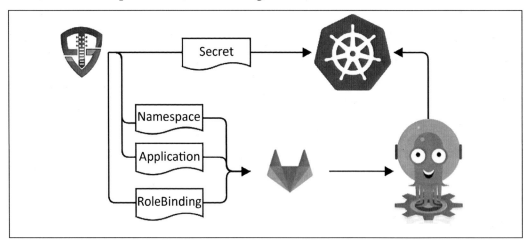

Figure 14.9: Writing objects to Git

When OpenUnison needs to create objects in Kubernetes, instead of writing them directly to the API server, it will write them into a management project in GitLab. ArgoCD will synchronize these manifests into the API server.

This is where we'll write any objects we don't want our users to have access to. This would include cluster-level objects, such as `Namespaces`, but also namespace objects we don't want our users to have write access to, such as `RoleBindings`. This way, we can separate operations object management from application object management.

Here's an important security question to answer: if ArgoCD is writing these objects for us, what's stopping a developer from checking in a `RoleBinding` or a `ResourceQuota` into their repo and letting ArgoCD synchronize it into the API server? At the time of publication, the only way to limit this is to tell ArgoCD which objects can be synchronized in the `AppProject` object. This isn't quite as useful as relying on RBAC, but should cover most use cases. For our deployments, we're going to allow just `Deployment`, `Service`, and `Ingress` objects. It wouldn't be unreasonable to add additional types for different use cases. Those updates can be made quite easily by updating an `AppProject` object in the management Git repo.

Finally, look at *Figure 14.9* and you'll notice that we're still writing `Secret` objects to the API server. Don't write your secret information to Git. It doesn't matter if the data is encrypted or not; either way, you're asking for trouble. Git is specifically designed to make it easier to share code in a decentralized way, whereas your secret data should be tracked carefully by a centralized repository. These are two opposing requirements.

As an example of how easy it is to lose track of sensitive data, let's say you have a repo with `Secrets` in it on your workstation. A simple `git archive HEAD` will remove all Git metadata and give you clean files that can no longer be tracked. How easy is it to accidentally push a repo to a public repository by accident? It's just too easy to lose track of the code base.

Another example of why Git is a bad place to store secret information is that Git doesn't have any built-in authentication. When you use SSH or HTTPS when accessing a Git repo, either GitHub or GitLab is authenticating you, but Git itself has no form of built-in authentication. If you have followed the exercises in this chapter, go look at your Git commits. Do they say "root" or do they have your name? Git just takes the data from your Git configuration. There's nothing that ties that data to you. Is that an audit trail that will work for you as regards your organization's secret data? Probably not.

Some projects attempt to fix this by encrypting sensitive data in the repo. That way, even if the repo were leaked, you would still need the keys to decrypt the data. Where's the `Secret` for the encryption being stored? Is it in use by developers? Is there special tooling that's required? There are several places where it could go wrong. It's better to not use Git at all for sensitive data, such as `Secrets`.

In a production environment, you want to externalize your Secrets though, just like your other manifests. There are multiple Secret management systems out there such as HashiCorp's Vault. These tools deserve their own chapter, or book, and are well outside the scope of this chapter, but you should certainly include them as part of your cluster management plan.

You don't need to build this out yourself! chapter14/naas-gitops is a Helm chart we'll deploy that has all this automation built-in. We also included chapter14/example-app/python-hello as our example application, chapter14/example-app/python-hello-operations for our manifests, and chapter14/example-app/python-hello-build as our pipeline. You'll need to tweak some of the objects in these three folders to match your environment, mostly updating the hostnames.

With our developer workflow designed and example projects ready to go, next, we'll update OpenUnison, GitLab, and ArgoCD to get all this automation to work!

Integrating GitLab

We configured GitLab for SSO when we first deployed the Helm chart. The gitlab-oidc Secret we deployed has all the information GitLab needs to access SSO from OpenUnison. The naas-gitops Helm chart will configure SSO with GitLab and add a badge to the front page, just like for tokens and the dashboard. First, we need to update our OpenUnison Secret to complete the integration:

1. Log in to GitLab as root. Go to your user's profile area and click on **Access Tokens**. For **Name**, use openunison. Leave **Expires** blank and check the API scope. Click **Create personal access token**. Copy and paste the token into a notepad or some other place. Once you leave this screen, you can't retrieve this token again.

2. Edit the orchestra-secrets-source Secret in the openunison namespace. Add two keys:

```
apiVersion: v1
data:
  K8S_DB_SECRET: aW0gYSBzZWNyZXQ=
  OU_JDBC_PASSWORD: c3RhcnR0MTIz
  SMTP_PASSWORD: ""
  unisonKeystorePassword: aW0gYSBzZWNyZXQ=
  gitlab: c2VjcmV0
  GITLAB_TOKEN: S7CCuqHfpw3a6GmAqEYg
kind: Secret
```

Remember to Base64-encode the values. The `gitlab` key matches the secret in our `oidc-provider` Secret. `GITLAB_TOKEN` is going to be used by OpenUnison to interact with GitLab to provision the projects and groups we defined in our onboarding workflow. With GitLab configured, next is the TektonCD dashboard.

Integrating the TektonCD dashboard

The TektonCD project has a great dashboard that makes it very easy to visualize pipelines and follow their execution. We didn't include it in the first edition of this book because there was no security integrated. Now, however, the TektonCD dashboard works with security and authentication the same way the Kubernetes dashboard does. Using a reverse proxy, we can provide either a user's `id_token` or impersonation headers. The `naas-gitops` chart has all of the OpenUnison-specific configuration, and there's nothing special we need to do to integrate the two. That said, let's deploy:

```
$ kubectl apply --filename https://storage.googleapis.com/tekton-
releases/dashboard/latest/tekton-dashboard-release.yaml
```

This will deploy the TektonCD dashboard to the `tekton-pipelines` namespace, so we don't need to worry about adding node policies. We do need to remove several RBAC bindings though. We want the dashboard to run without any privileges to make sure that if someone did circumvent OpenUnison, they couldn't abuse it:

```
kubectl delete clusterrole tekton-dashboard-backend
kubectl delete clusterrole tekton-dashboard-dashboard
kubectl delete clusterrole tekton-dashboard-pipelines
kubectl delete clusterrole tekton-dashboard-tenant
kubectl delete clusterrole tekton-dashboard-triggers
kubectl delete clusterrolebinding tekton-dashboard-backend
kubectl delete rolebinding tekton-dashboard-pipelines -n tekton-
pipelines
kubectl delete rolebinding tekton-dashboard-dashboard -n tekton-
pipelines
kubectl delete rolebinding tekton-dashboard-triggers -n tekton-
pipelines
kubectl delete clusterrolebinding tekton-dashboard-tenant
```

With the RBAC bindings deleted, next, we'll integrate ArgoCD.

Integrating ArgoCD

ArgoCD has built-in support for OpenID Connect. It wasn't configured for us in the deployment, though:

1. Edit `argocd-cm` ConfigMap in the `argocd` namespace, adding the `url` and `oidc.config` keys, as shown in the following code block. Make sure to update `192-168-2-140` to match your cluster's IP address. Mine is `192.168.2.114`, so I'll be using `192-168-2-114`:

   ```
   apiVersion: v1
   data:
     url: https://argocd.apps.192-168-2-140.nip.io
     oidc.config: |-
       name: OpenUnison
       issuer: https://k8sou.apps.192-168-2-140.nip.io/auth/idp/
   k8sIdp
       clientID: argocd
       requestedScopes: ["openid", "profile", "email", "groups"]
   ```

   > We don't specify a client secret with ArgoCD because it has both a CLI and a web component. Just like with the API server, it makes no sense to worry about a client secret that will need to reside on every single workstation that will be known to the user. It doesn't add any security in this case, so we will skip it.

2. While most of ArgoCD is controlled with Kubernetes custom resources, there are some ArgoCD-specific APIs. To work with these APIs, we need to create a service account. We'll need to create this account and generate a key for it:

   ```
   $ kubectl patch configmap argocd-cm -n argocd -p
   '{"data":{"accounts.openunison":"apiKey","accounts.openunison.
   enabled":"true"}}'
   $ argocd account generate-token --account openunison
   ```

3. Take the output of the `generate-token` command and add it as the `ARGOCD_TOKEN` key to `orchestra-secrets-source` Secret in the `openunison` namespace. Don't forget to Base64-encode it.

4. Finally, we want to create ArgoCD RBAC rules so that we can control who can access the web UI and the CLI. Edit `argocd-rbac-cm ConfigMap` and add the following keys. The first key will let our systems administrators and our API key do anything in ArgoCD. The second key maps all users that aren't mapped by `policy.csv` into a role into a non-existent role so that they won't have access to anything:

```
data:
  policy.csv: |-
    g, k8s-cluster-k8s-administrators,role:admin
    g, openunison,role:admin
  policy.default: role:none
```

With ArgoCD integrated, the final step involves deploying our custom chart!

Updating OpenUnison

OpenUnison is already deployed. We need to deploy our Helm chart, which includes the automation that reflects our workflow:

```
$ cd chapter14/naas-gitops
$  kubectl delete configmap myvd-book -n openunison
configmap "myvd-book" deleted
$ helm install orchestra-naas . -n openunison -f /tmp/openunison-
values.yaml
NAME: orchestra-naas
LAST DEPLOYED: Thu Oct  7 13:51:19 2021
NAMESPACE: openunison
STATUS: deployed
REVISION: 1
TEST SUITE: None
$ helm upgrade orchestra tremolo/orchestra -n openunison -f /tmp/
openunison-values.yaml
```

Once the `openunison-orchestra` Pod is running again, log in to OpenUnison by going to `https://k8sou.apps.192-168-2-119.nip.io/`, replacing "192-168-2-119" with your own IP address, but with dashes instead of dots.

Use the username `mmosley` and the password `start123`. You'll notice that we have several new badges besides tokens and the dashboard.

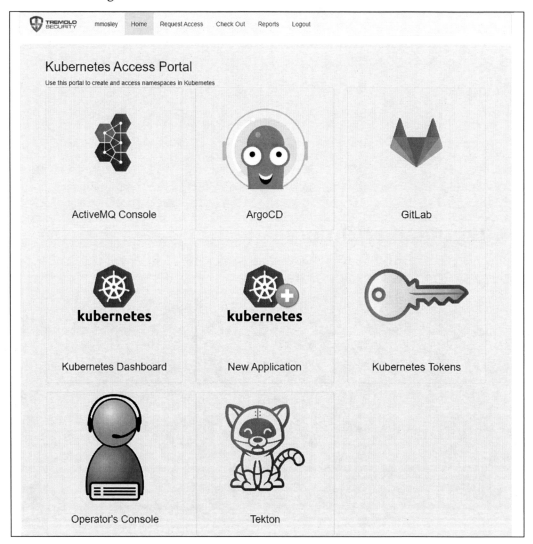

Figure 14.10: OpenUnison NaaS portal

Since we're the first person to log in, we automatically have admin access to the portal and cluster management access for the cluster. The ArgoCD and GitLab badges will lead you to those apps. Click on the **OpenID Connect** login button and you'll SSO into both. The Tekton badge gives you SSO access to Tekton's dashboard. This will be helpful in debugging pipelines. The **New Application** badge is where the magic happens. That's where you can create a new application that will generate all the linkages you need between GitLab, ArgoCD, Kubernetes, and Tekton.

Before we create a new application, we need to create our cluster management project in GitLab and set up ArgoCD to synchronize it to our cluster. We could do this manually, but that would be painful, so we have a workflow that will do it for you:

1. Click on the **Operator's Console** badge
2. Check **Last Name** and type `Mosley` in the box
3. Click **Search**
4. Check the box next to **Matt** and then click on **Initialization** in the new tree that appears below
5. In the **Reason** field, type `initialization`
6. Click **Submit Workflow**

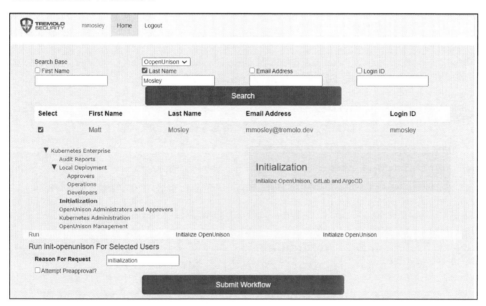

Figure 14.11: Initializing the cluster repo

If you watch the OpenUnison logs, you'll see quite a bit of action. This workflow:

1. Creates the **cluster-operations** project in GitLab
2. Creates the **cluster-operations** Application in ArgoCD
3. Creates a webhook on the **cluster-operations** project in GitLab to automatically trigger a synchronization event in ArgoCD when a push is merged into the main branch

With our technology stack in place, now it's time to roll out our first application.

Deploying an application

So far, we've explored the theory of building pipelines and workflows, and we have also deployed a technology stack that implements that theory. The last step is to walk through the process of deploying an application in our cluster. There will be three actors in this flow.

Username	Role	Notes
mmosley	System administrator	Has overall control of the cluster. Responsible for approving new applications.
jjackson	Application owner	Requests a new application. Is responsible for adding developers and merging pull requests.
app-dev	Application developer	Responsible for building code and manifests. Must work from forked versions of repos in GitLab.

Table 14.1: Users of the system

Through the remainder of this section, we'll walk through creating a new application and deploying it using our automated framework.

Creating the application in Kubernetes

As we move through this process, it will be helpful to have all three users able to log in. I generally use one browser with an incognito/private window for two users and a separate browser for the third. The password for all three users is start123.

Our first step is to log in to OpenUnison as jjackson. Upon logging in, you'll see that jjackson has a few less badges. That's because she's not an administrator. Once logged in, click on **New Application**. For **Application Name**, use **python-hello**, and for **Reason** use **demo**. Then, click **Submit Registration**.

Next, log in as mmosley. In the menu bar at the top of the screen, you'll see **Open Approvals** with a red **1** next to it. Click on **Open Approvals**.

Figure 14.12: Open Approvals

Next to the one open request, click **Review**. Scroll to the bottom and for **Justification**, put **demo** and click **Approve Request**. Then, click **Confirm Approval**. Now would be a good time to get a fresh cup of coffee. This will take a few minutes because multiple things are happening:

1. Projects in GitLab are being created to store your application code, pipelines, and manifests

2. Forks are being created for your manifests project

3. ArgoCD `AppProject` and `Applications` are being created

4. Namespaces are being created in your cluster for a development environment, build, and production

5. Tekton objects for building a pipeline are being created, with a webhook for triggers

6. Node security objects in dev and production namespaces are being created, so our applications will run without privilege

7. Webhooks are being created to link everything

8. Groups are being created in our database to manage access

We've built all the objects from the diagram in *Figure 14.7* without editing a single `yaml` file or running kubectl. Once done, you can log in to GitLab as `mmosley` and see that the cluster-operations project now has all of our cluster-level objects. Just as we described earlier in the chapter, all of our objects, except `Secrets`, are stored in Git.

With our scaffolding in place, the next step is to get our developers access so that they can start building.

Getting access to developers

Now that our development infrastructure is in place, the next step is to get our developer, **app-dev**, access.

Log in to OpenUnison with the username `app-dev` and the password `start123`. In the menu bar, click on **Request Access**.

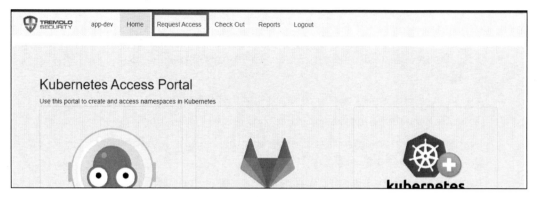

Figure 14.13: Request Access

Next, click on the triangle next to **Local Deployment** and then click on **Developers**. Click on **Add To Cart**.

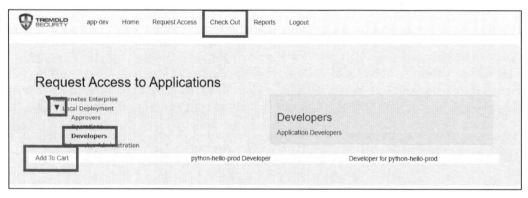

Figure 14.14: Adding developer access to the cart

Once you've added it to your cart, click on **Check Out** on the menu bar. On the right, where it says **Supply Reason**, type `for work` and click **Submit Request**.

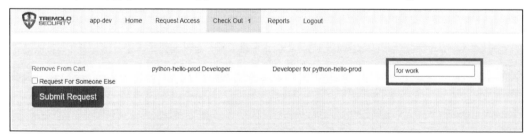

Figure 14.15: Adding developer access to the cart

At this point, log out and log back in as `jjackson`. On the upper menu bar, there will be an **Open Approvals** option with a red **1** next to it. Just as when we were initializing the system, click on **Open Approvals** and approve the request of **app-dev**.

This workflow is different from the new application workflow we ran to create `hello-python`. Where that workflow created objects across four systems, this workflow just adds our user to a group in OpenUnison's database. Every component's access is driven by these groups, so now, instead of having to hunt down `RoleBindings` and group memberships across four platforms, we can audit access at one point.

Log out and log back in as `app-dev`. Click on the GitLab badge and sign in with OpenUnison. You'll see four projects.

Figure 14.16: Developer projects

These projects will drive your application's development and deployment. Here are the descriptions for each project:

Name	Description
python-hello-application	Your application's source code.
python-hello-build	Your TektonCD pipeline definition. This code is synced by ArgoCD into the python-hello-build `Namespace` in your cluster.
dev/python-hello-operations	The manifests for your application, such as Deployment definitions. This is a fork of the production operations project and is synced to the python-hello-prod `Namespace` by ArgoCD.
production/python-hello-operations	The manifests for your application in production. Changes should be pull requests from the dev operations project. ArgoCD synchronizes this project to the python-hello-prod `Namespace`.

Table 14.2: Project descriptions

Notice that on each project, our user is a *developer*. This means that we can fork the repository and submit pull requests (or merge requests as they are called in GitLab), but we can't edit the contents of the project ourselves. The next step is to start checking out projects and checking in code.

Deploying dev manifests

The first thing we'll need to do is deploy our operational manifests into our "dev" environment. Inside GitLab, fork `python-hello-dev/python-hello-operations` into your personal namespace in GitLab. Make sure to fork from the python-hello-dev Namespace and NOT the python-hello-production Namespace.

Once forked, clone the project from your own namespace (**App Dev**). You'll need to attach an SSH key to your GitLab account. When you clone the project, you'll need to convert the URL provided by GitLab into an SSH URL. For instance, when I clone the repository, GitLab gives me `git@gitlab.apps.192-168-2-119.nip.io:app-dev/python-hello-operations.git`. However, when I clone the repository, I add `ssh://` to the front and `:2222` after the hostname so that Git can reach our GitLab SSH service:

```
$ git clone ssh://git@gitlab.apps.192-168-2-119.nip.io:2222/app-dev/
python-hello-operations.git
Cloning into 'python-hello-operations'...
The authenticity of host '[gitlab.apps.192.168.2.119.nip.io]:2222
([192.168.2.119]:2222)' can't be established.
ECDSA key fingerprint is SHA256:F8VKUrn0ugFoRrLSBc93JNdWsRv9Zwy9wF1L0ZP
qSf4.
Are you sure you want to continue connecting (yes/no/[fingerprint])?
Yes
Warning: Permanently added '[gitlab.apps.192.168.2.119.nip.
io]:2222,[192.168.2.119]:2222' (ECDSA) to the list of known hosts.
remote: Enumerating objects: 3, done.
remote: Counting objects: 100% (3/3), done.
remote: Compressing objects: 100% (2/2), done.
remote: Total 3 (delta 0), reused 3 (delta 0), pack-reused 0
Receiving objects: 100% (3/3), done.
```

With our repository cloned, the next step is to copy in our manifests. We have a script that makes this easier by updating IP addresses and hostnames:

```
$ cd chapter14/sample-repo/python-hello-operations
$ ./deployToGit.sh /path/to/python-hello-operations python-hello
[main 3ce8b5c] initial commit
```

```
  2 files changed, 37 insertions(+), 2 deletions(-)
  create mode 100644 src/deployments/hello-python.yaml
Enumerating objects: 8, done.
Counting objects: 100% (8/8), done.
Delta compression using up to 8 threads
Compressing objects: 100% (4/4), done.
Writing objects: 100% (6/6), 874 bytes | 874.00 KiB/s, done.
Total 6 (delta 0), reused 0 (delta 0)
To ssh://gitlab.apps.192-168-2-119.nip.io:2222/app-dev/python-hello-
operations.git 7f0fb7c..3ce8b5c  main -> main
```

Now, look in your forked project in GitLab and you will find a Deployment manifest that's ready to be synchronized into the development `Namespace` in our cluster. From inside your forked project, click on **Merge Requests** on the left-hand menu bar.

Figure 14.17: Merge requests menu

On the next screen, click on **New merge request**. This will bring up a screen to choose which branch you want to merge into dev. Choose **main** and then click **Compare branches and continue**.

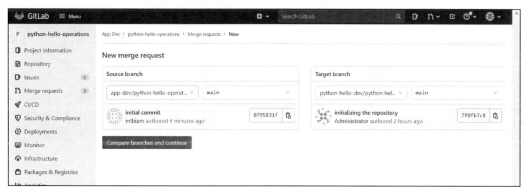

Figure 14.18: Merge requests

You can update the information in the merge request for additional data. Click on **Create merge request** at the bottom of the page.

After a moment, the request will be ready to merge, but the merge button will be grayed out. That's because our developer, **app-dev**, does not have those rights in GitLab. The next step is to log in as jjackson to approve the request. This would be a good time to log in to OpenUnison as jjackson in another browser or private/incognito browser window.

Once logged into GitLab as jjackson, navigate to the **python-hello-dev-python-hello-operations** project and click on **Merge requests** on the left-hand side, just as you did with the app-dev user. This time, you'll see the open merge request. Click on the request and click the merge button. You've now successfully merged the changes from app-dev into your application's dev environment.

Within 3 minutes, ArgoCD will pick up these changes and sync them into your python-hello-dev Namespace. Log in to ArgoCD as app-dev, and you'll see that the **python-hello-dev** application has synchronized, but it's in a broken state. That's because Kubernetes is trying to pull an image that doesn't yet exist.

Now that we've got our development manifests ready to go, the next step is to deploy our Tekton pipeline.

Deploying a Tekton pipeline

With our development manifests deployed, next we need to deploy a pipeline that will build a container and update our dev environment's manifests to point to that new container. We covered the manual steps on how to do this earlier in this chapter, so here we're going to focus on the process of deploying via GitOps. Log in to GitLab as app-dev and fork the python-hello-build project. There's only one of these! Just as before, clone the repository, remembering to use the SSH URL. Next, deploy our pipeline into the cloned repository:

```
$ cd chapter14/sample-repo/python-hello-build/
$ ./deployToGit.sh ~/demo-deploy/python-hello-build python-hello
 [main 0a6e833] initial commit
 6 files changed, 204 insertions(+), 2 deletions(-)
 create mode 100644 src/pipelineresources/tekton-image-result.yaml
 create mode 100644 src/pipelines/tekton-pipeline.yaml
 create mode 100644 src/tasks/tekton-task1.yaml
```

```
  create mode 100644 src/tasks/tekton-task2.yaml
  create mode 100644 src/tasks/tekton-task3.yaml
Enumerating objects: 18, done.
Counting objects: 100% (18/18), done.
Delta compression using up to 8 threads
Compressing objects: 100% (12/12), done.
Writing objects: 100% (13/13), 3.18 KiB | 3.18 MiB/s, done.
Total 13 (delta 1), reused 0 (delta 0)
To ssh://gitlab.apps.192-168-2-119.nip.io:2222/app-dev/python-hello-
build.git
   7120c3f..0a6e833  main -> main
```

Earlier in this chapter, we manually configured the objects needed to set up a webhook so that when developers merge their changes, the pipeline will kick off automatically. OpenUnison deployed all that boilerplate code for us, so we don't need to set it up on our own. If you look in the python-hello-build Namespace in our cluster, it already has a webhook running.

Just as with our manifests, create a merge request as **app-dev**, and merge it as **jjackson**. Taking a look at ArgoCD, you'll see that the python-hello-build Application has our new objects in it. With our pipeline deployed, the next step is to run our pipeline by checking in some code.

Running our pipeline

Everything is ready for us to build our code and deploy it into the development environment. First, as **app-dev**, fork the python-hello-application project and clone it. Once cloned, copy the application source into your repository:

```
$ cd chapter14/example-apps/python-hello
$ git archive --format=tar HEAD | tar xvf - -C /path/to/python-hello-
application/
$ cd /path/to/python-hello-application/
$ git add *
$ git commit -m 'initial commit'
$ git push
```

Just as with the other repositories, open a merge request as **app-dev**, and merge as **jjackson**. Then, go to your Tekton dashboard and pick **python-hello-build** from the namespace picker in the upper right-hand corner.

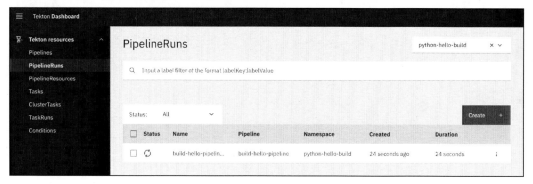

Figure 14.19: Tekton Dashboard

If everything went smoothly, you should now have a pipeline running to build a container and update our development environment. If we look in our dev operations project, we'll see that there's a new commit by Tekton that merged in a change to the image of our dev environment to match the image we just built. The commit has the hash of the commit to our application project, so we can tie them together. Lastly, go to ArgoCD and look at the python-hello-dev application. It's now synchronizing (or will within 3 minutes) our update to dev and rolling out our new image.

Taking a look at the deployed manifest, we will see that it has the default user and group ID configuration, drops all capabilities, and runs without privilege. That's because we deployed GateKeeper and automated the policies that keep our nodes safe from our Pods.

We now have a running Pod in dev, so it's time to promote to production.

Promoting to production

We've rolled out our application into development and done whatever testing we want to do. Now it's time to promote into production. Here is where the power of combining Git, Kubernetes, and automation really pays off. The move to production becomes the simplest part! Log in to GitLab as `jjackson` and navigate to the python-hello-dev/python-hello-operations project and create a merge request. This will merge our development environment into our production environment, which, in this case, means ArgoCD will update a `Deployment` to point to a new container. Once jjackson approves the merge, ArgoCD will get to work. Once synchronized, you're live!

We covered quite a bit of ground in this section. We deployed the application scaffolding into our environment, onboarded a developer, and rolled out our application with automated build pipelines. We used GitOps to manage everything and at no point did we use the `kubectl` command!

Summary

Coming into this chapter, we hadn't spent much time on deploying applications. We wanted to close things out with a brief introduction to application deployment and automation. We learned about pipelines, how they are built, and how they run on a Kubernetes cluster. We explored the process of building a platform by deploying GitLab for source control, built out a Tekton pipeline to work in a GitOps model, and used ArgoCD to make the GitOps model a reality. Finally, we automated the entire process with OpenUnison.

Using the information in this chapter should give you some direction as to how you want to build your own platform. Using the practical examples in this chapter will help you map the requirements of your organization to the technology needed to automate your infrastructure. The platform we built in this chapter is far from complete. It should give you a map for planning your own platform that matches your needs.

Finally, thank you! Thank you for joining us on this adventure of building out a Kubernetes cluster. We hope that you have as much fun reading this book and building out the examples as we did creating it!

Questions

1. True or false: A pipeline must be implemented to make Kubernetes work.

    a. True

    b. False

2. What are the minimum steps of a pipeline?

    a. Build, scan, test, and deploy

    b. Build and deploy

    c. Scan, test, deploy, and build

    d. None of the above

3. What is GitOps?

    a. Running GitLab on Kubernetes

    b. Using Git as an authoritative source for operations configuration

      c.   A silly marketing term

      d.   A product from a new start-up

4. What is the standard for writing pipelines?

      a.   All pipelines should be written in YAML.

      b.   There are no standards; every project and vendor has its own implementation.

      c.   JSON combined with Go.

      d.   Rust.

5. How do you deploy a new instance of a container in a GitOps model?

      a.   Use `kubectl` to update the `Deployment` or `StatefulSet` in the namespace.

      b.   Update the `Deployment` or `StatefulSet` manifest in Git, letting the GitOps controller update the objects in Kubernetes.

      c.   Submit a ticket that someone in operations needs to act on.

      d.   None of the above.

6. True or false: All objects in GitOps need to be stored in your Git repository.

      a.   True

      b.   False

7. True or false: You can automate processes any way you want.

      a.   True

      b.   False

Join our book's Discord space

Join the book's Discord workspace for a monthly *Ask me Anything* session with the authors: `https://packt.link/K8EntGuide`

Subscribe to our online digital library for full access to over 7,000 books and videos, as well as industry leading tools to help you plan your personal development and advance your career. For more information, please visit our website.

Why subscribe?

- Spend less time learning and more time coding with practical eBooks and Videos from over 4,000 industry professionals
- Improve your learning with Skill Plans built especially for you
- Get a free eBook or video every month
- Fully searchable for easy access to vital information
- Copy and paste, print, and bookmark content

At www.packt.com, you can also read a collection of free technical articles, sign up for a range of free newsletters, and receive exclusive discounts and offers on Packt books and eBooks.

Other Books
You May Enjoy

If you enjoyed this book, you may be interested in these other books by Packt:

Mastering Kubernetes, Third Edition

Gigi Sayfan

ISBN: 9781839211256

- Master the fundamentals of Kubernetes architecture and design

- Build and run stateful applications and complex microservices on Kubernetes

- Use tools like Kubectl, secrets, and Helm to manage resources and storage

- Master Kubernetes Networking with load balancing options like Ingress

- Achieve high-availability Kubernetes clusters

- Improve Kubernetes observability with tools like Prometheus, Grafana, and Jaeger

- Extend Kubernetes working with Kubernetes API, plugins, and webhooks

Microservices with Spring Boot and Spring Cloud, Second Edition

Magnus Larsson

ISBN: 9781801072977

- Build reactive microservices using Spring Boot

- Develop resilient and scalable microservices using Spring Cloud

- Use OAuth 2.1/OIDC and Spring Security to protect public APIs

- Implement Docker to bridge the gap between development, testing, and production

- Deploy and manage microservices with Kubernetes

- Apply Istio for improved security, observability, and traffic management

- Write and run automated microservice tests with JUnit, testcontainers, Gradle, and bash

Packt is searching for authors like you

If you're interested in becoming an author for Packt, please visit authors.packtpub.com and apply today. We have worked with thousands of developers and tech professionals, just like you, to help them share their insight with the global tech community. You can make a general application, apply for a specific hot topic that we are recruiting an author for, or submit your own idea.

Share your thoughts

Now you've finished *Kubernetes – An Enterprise Guide, Second Edition*, we'd love to hear your thoughts! Scan the QR code below to go straight to the Amazon review page for this book and share your feedback or leave a review on the site that you purchased it from.

https://packt.link/r/1803230037

Your review is important to us and the tech community and will help us make sure we're delivering excellent quality content.

Index

H

HAProxy traffic flow 59-61
Hello World
  deploying 456
Hello World application
  building 502-508
Helm
  chart values, customizing 152, 153
  reference link 140
  using, for K8GB installation 154, 155
Helm Values
  customizing 316-322
Helm Values file 315
Horizontal Pod Autoscalers (HPAs) 92, 93

I

identity federation 167
identity injection 248
id_token 170-172
Impersonation 194-196
  authentication, integrating with cloud-man-
      aged clusters 193
  cluster, configuring for 197, 198
  configuring, without OpenUnison 200
  security considerations 196, 197
  testing 198, 199
  using 473-476
impersonation RBAC policies 200
Ingress
  controller, installing 50, 51
  custom load balancer, adding 55
  resource 94, 95
insecure dashboard
  deploying 239-245
integrated development
      environment (IDE) 497
internal attack 245
Istio 397
  components 402
  concepts 402
  deployment methods 405, 406
  downloading 406
  features 399
  installing 405
  installing, with profile 407-409
  issues, identifying 400, 401

OPA, using with 466, 467
  security 401
  traffic management 400
  URL 398
  using, to manage microservices 447
  workload observability 399
Istio config view 437-439
Istiod 402
  reference link 402
Istiod pod
  breaking down 403
  Citadel 404
  Galley 403, 404
  Mixer 404
  Pilot 403
Istio-egressgateway 405
Istio-ingressgateway 404
Istio resources 409
  authorization policies 409, 410
  destination rules 417

J

Jaeger
  installing 423
  URL 433
JavaScript Object Notation (JSON) 75
JSON Web Tokens (JWTs) 165, 402

K

K8GB GIT repository
  reference link 151
K8GB load balancing options 152
  failover 151
  Helm chart values, customizing 152, 153
  manual 151
  Round Robin 151
  Weighted Round Robin 151
K8GB project 149
  application, adding with custom resources
      155, 156
  application, adding with Ingress annotations
      157
  CoreDNS servers, syncing 157-160
  deploying, to cluster 151
  features 150
  global load balancing, providing 157

Made in United States
North Haven, CT
31 May 2022

19674955R10315